A
HISTORY
OF MODERN
PSYCHOLOGY 3ed.

A HISTORY OF MODERN PSYCHOLOGY 3ed.

DUANE SCHULTZ

University of South Florida

ACADEMIC PRESS

New York/London/Toronto/Sydney/San Francisco
A Subsidiary of Harcourt Brace Jovanovich, Publishers

Cover Photo by Glen Heller

Academic Press, Inc.
111 Fifth Avenue,
New York, New York 10003

United Kingdom Edition published by
Academic Press, Inc. (London) Ltd.
24/28 Oval Road, London NW1 7DX

ISBN: 0-12-633060-3
Library of Congress Catalog Card Number: 80-616
Printed in the United States of America

To My Parents

CONTENTS

Contents

14
PSYCHOANALYSIS:
AFTER THE
FOUNDING 342

15
MORE RECENT
DEVELOPMENTS 367

PREFACE

This new edition retains the same overall format, scope, and focus as the earlier ones. Three premises continue to underlie and characterize its approach. First, our discussion of the history of psychology concentrates on the last century of development in the field. It does not attempt to cover earlier philosophical thought, except where such thought relates directly to the establishment of psychology as a separate discipline, as is the case with the British empiricists, for example. In short, the book is a history of modern psychology, not of psychology and all the work in philosophy that preceded it.

The second premise is defined by one of the most striking and consistent characteristics of the century-old history of modern psychology: the continuous development and decline of different systematic positions or schools of thought. A definite continuity of development can be seen from each of these schools of thought to the one that subsequently replaced it. This orderly and meaningful developmental pattern is, I believe, the most useful framework within which to understand the history of psychology.

Our discussion will demonstrate how each system grew out of or revolted against the existing order, and how each, in turn, inspired a new point of view that opposed and eventually replaced, or at least supplemented, the older system. Outstanding figures in the history of psychology are discussed within the context of the systematic position they helped to formulate, advance, or destroy.

Each systematic position is discussed in terms of three stages or levels of development: (1) historical antecedents or precursors, (2) formal founding and development, and (3) later influence. Contemporary influences on the various systems are discussed to demonstrate the continuity of development from the old to the new, i.e., how psychology as we know it today evolved from these earlier positions. The discussion of each school concludes with criticisms and contributions of the position, so that the student can see the weaknesses of each system as well as its importance in psychology's later development.

The third premise is concerned with the determining influence of the *Zeitgeist* on each school of thought. The development and decline of each systematic position are discussed in terms of the general intellectual and social climate of the era or region in which it occurred. Using this approach, the student is able to understand that changes in psychological thinking were influenced and augmented by broader changes in our attitudes toward ourselves and the world around us.

The style of writing and level of difficulty of this text are intended expressly for the undergraduate student's initial exposure to the history of the discipline. I want to tell the continuing story of psychology's development and progress, rather than to provide a catalogue of dates, names, theories, and events. I have tried to present the history of psychology here as I do in the classroom.

Having the opportunity to revise the book has been a stimulating, enjoyable, and rewarding task. Aside from the chance to correct errors, eliminate sexist language, and rephrase difficult concepts, a revision allows the time to incorporate the results of new scholarly work in the field and to reflect feedback from the instructors and students who have used the second edition. Changes range from the insertion of a clarifying word to the addition of new sections and the rewriting of chapters.

Chapter 1 has been substantially rewritten to incorporate the following material: the role of history in understanding the diversity and divisiveness of contemporary psychology; the similarity between the history of psychology and the case history of a patient, showing how both attempt to understand the present by examining the influences from the past; the similarity between the evolution of a discipline and the evolution of a living species, showing that both have to be responsive to the environment or context in which they function; and the relevance of Kuhn's work, showing that psychology is still in the preparadigmatic stage characterized by competing schools of thought.

Chapter 15 has also been rewritten to focus on more recent developments in the two major forces in contemporary psychology—behaviorism and psychoanalysis—and the evolution of the third force, humanistic psychology. Included are discussions of the cognitive revolution and the work of Bandura; the neo-Freudian theories of Allport, Murray, and Erikson; and the humanistic approaches of Maslow and Rogers. The impact of the "new" physics on the cognitive revolution and humanistic psychology are covered, and these developments are treated in historical perspective as outgrowths of earlier points of view.

Other changes for the third edition include new material on the influence of mechanism on Descartes's thinking; the impact of astronomy on the new psychology; the changes Titchener began to make in his system toward the end of his life; the influence of Darwin in broadening the methodology of psychology; the influence of mentalism and introspection by analogy on the work of the early animal psychologists; the work of Spencer and its importance for American psychology; behavior modification; the impact of field physics on Gestalt psychology; the historical antecedents of Freudian psychoanalysis; and the scientific credibility of psychoanalysis.

The four original source articles—by Titchener, Carr, Wertheimer, and Watson—have been retained. User reaction to these materials has been favorable. These statements by psychology's important figures seem to be of value to the student by presenting a position in the proponent's own words and illustrating what the psychology student of the day was reading.

An instructor's handbook for the history of psychology, prepared by Ludy T. Benjamin, Jr., includes reference sources, teaching activities, lists of audiovisual materials, and test questions.

I am grateful to the many instructors and students who have written to me over the years with valuable suggestions and comments. The book has also benefited from the rigorous and scholarly evaluation of Ludy Benjamin, Albert M. Prestrude, and Michael Wertheimer. At Academic Press, my editor, James D. Anker, has provided continuing encouragement and assistance. My greatest debt remains to my wife, Sydney Ellen, for her expert research, cogent criticisms, enthusiasm, and patient handling of the myriad details that miraculously turned a messy sheaf of handwritten pages into a finished book.

D. S.

The application of the experimental method to the problem of mind is the great outstanding event in the history of the study of the mind, an event to which no other is comparable.

E. G. Boring

1
THE STUDY OF THE HISTORY OF PSYCHOLOGY

INTRODUCTION

Of all the scholarly disciplines in existence today, psychology is probably the oldest. Interest in the topic can be traced to the earliest inquiring minds. We have been forever fascinated by our own behavior, and ruminations on human nature and conduct fill many philosophical and theological volumes. As early as the fourth and fifth centuries B.C. Plato, Aristotle, and other Greek scholars were grappling with many of the same problems that concern psychologists today—memory, learning, motivation, perception, dreaming, and irrational behavior. The same kinds of questions now being asked about human nature were asked centuries ago, which shows a vital continuity between the present and the past.

It would appear that since psychology began in antiquity, our study must also begin there, but there is another point to consider. Although psychology is one of the older disciplines, it is also one of the newer! This is an interesting paradox, one that was described succinctly by the psychologist Hermann Ebbinghaus, who wrote, "Psychology has a long past, but only a short history." The intellectual precursors of psychology are ancient indeed, but the modern tradition and form of psychology are little more than 100 years old. The centennial of the birth of modern psychology was celebrated in 1979.

The distinction between modern psychology and its antecedents has less to do with the kinds of questions asked about human nature than with the methods used to seek the answers. It is the approach taken, the techniques employed, that distinguish the older philosophy from modern psychology and denote the emergence of the latter as a separate discipline.

Until the last quarter of the nineteenth century philosophers attempted to study human nature through speculation, intuition, and generalization based on their own limited experience. A major transformation occurred when they began to apply the tools and methods of science to questions about human nature, methods that had already proved successful in the natural sciences. Only when researchers turned to carefully controlled observation and experimentation as the means for studying the human mind, did psychology begin to attain some degree of independence from its philosophical antecedents.

To break with philosophy, the new psychology needed to develop a more precise and objective way of dealing with its subject matter. Thus, much of the history of psychology after its separation from philosophy is an account of the continual refinement of its tools, techniques, and methods of study to achieve increased precision and objectivity in both its answers and its questions.

If we are to understand the complex issues that define and divide psychology today, the proper starting point for the history of the field is that time when it became a truly independent discipline, with unique methods of inquiry and theoretical rationales. We cannot deny that early scholars speculated on problems concerning the nature of the human species. Certainly they did. But their influence on the development of psychology as a separate and primarily experimental science is limited. Psychology is a product of the nineteenth and twentieth centuries, because only in the last 100 years or so have psychologists defined its subject matter and established its foundation, confirming its independence from philosophy. The early philosophers concerned themselves with problems that are still of general interest, but they approached these problems in a manner vastly different from that of today's psychologists. They were not psychologists by the contemporary definition of the term, and we will discuss their ideas only as they relate directly to the establishment of modern psychology.

Psychology became an experimental science at a time when European thought was imbued with positivism, empiricism, and materialism (see Chapter 2). While the nineteenth-century philosophers were clearing the way for an experimental attack on the functioning of the mind, another group of scholars was independently approaching some of the same problems from a different direction. Nineteenth-century physiologists were making great strides toward understanding the bodily mechanisms underlying mental processes. The methods of study of the physiologists differed markedly from those of the philosophers, but the eventual union of these disparate disciplines produced a field of study in which, at least in the formative years, an attempt was made to preserve the conflicting traditions and beliefs of both. Fortunately, the new psychology quickly succeeded in attaining an identity and stature of its own.

The idea that the methods of science could be applied to mental phenomena is inherited from both the philosophical ideas and the physiological techniques of the seventeenth to nineteenth centuries, an exciting era that becomes the starting point for our discussion of the history of modern psychology.

OVERVIEW OF THE DEVELOPMENT OF MODERN PSYCHOLOGY

The first sign of a distinct field of inquiry known as psychology was the adoption, in the last quarter of the nineteenth century, of the scientific method as the means for attempting to solve its problems. During that period there were several formal indications that psychology was beginning to flourish. In 1879[1] in Leipzig, Germany, Wilhelm Wundt established what is generally considered to be the first psychological laboratory in the world. Wundt also established the journal *Philosophische Studien,* in 1881, which is considered to be the first journal of psychology to contain experimental reports. In 1888 the University of Pennsylvania appointed James McKeen Cattell professor of psychology, the first professorship in psychology in the world. Before that time psychologists had received appointments in departments of philosophy. With Cattell's appointment, psychology received formal recognition in academic circles as an independent discipline. In 1887 G. Stanley Hall established the *American Journal of Psychology,* the first American psychology journal.

Between 1880 and 1895 dramatic and sweeping changes took place in psychology in the United States. During that time, 24 psychological laboratories and three psychology journals were established. In 1892 the first scientific organization of psychologists, the American Psychological Association, was founded.

In 1908 psychology was defined by William McDougall as the "science of behavior," apparently for the first time. Thus, by the early part of the twentieth century American psychology had succeeded in gaining its independence from philosophy, developing laboratories in which to apply the methods of science, establishing its own scientific organization, and giving itself a formal definition as a science—the science of behavior.

The new discipline had been launched and grew rapidly, particularly in the United States, which quickly assumed a position of dominance in the psychological world, a position it still holds. Today more than half the

---

[1] There is some dispute as to whether 1875 or 1879 was the founding year for the first experimental laboratory. Boring (1965) noted that Wundt was given space for experimental demonstrations in 1875, but it was not until 1879 that the space was used for independent research. R. I. Watson (1978) accorded the honor to 1875, while other sources (Chaplin & Krawiec, 1979; Flugel & West, 1964; Miller & Buckhout, 1973; Murphy & Kovach, 1972; Peters, 1965) agreed on 1879. In 1979 the American Psychological Association held the centennial celebration of the establishment of Wundt's laboratory. James McKeen Cattell (1928), who studied under Wundt, noted that the fiftieth anniversary of the founding of the laboratory was celebrated in Leipzig in 1926. Boring, Watson, and others noted that 1875 also saw William James equipping a small laboratory at Harvard. The significance of the event, however, is far more important than the precise date when it occurred.

world's psychologists are American, and a great many psychologists from other countries have received at least a portion of their training in the United States. A major share of the world's psychological literature is produced in this country.

There are several objective indicators of how vital and popular psychology has become. Consider the rate of increase in the membership of the American Psychological Association, the professional organization to which a majority of psychologists belong. The APA, established in 1892 with 26 charter members, had grown to include 1100 psychologists by 1930. By 1973 the membership stood at over 35,000 and in 1980 there were more than 50,000 members.

This population explosion of psychologists has been paralleled by an information explosion of research reports, theoretical and review articles, books, films, and other publications, making it increasingly difficult for psychologists to keep up with developments outside their areas of specialty. There are now more than 1000 journals that publish information of interest to psychologists.

Consider also the number of articles reviewed for the *Psychological Abstracts*, the reference journal that summarizes the world literature in psychology and related fields. In 1961 over 7000 articles were abstracted and in 1972 more than 24,000 articles appeared. In 1980 the number had increased to approximately 35,000. To keep abreast of all published works in psychology would require reading more than 75 books and journal articles every day.

Psychology has grown rapidly not only in terms of its practitioners, researchers, and scholars, and its published literature, but also in terms of its impact on our daily lives. Whatever your age, occupation, or leisure activities, your life is influenced in some way by the work of psychologists in advertising, architecture and design, criminal justice, education and training, industry, and the mental and physical health care fields. Few other disciplines have such a pervasive influence on the quality of life.

THE RELEVANCE OF
THE PAST FOR THE
PRESENT

This section might aptly be titled "Why study the history of psychology?" This is a legitimate question to ask when beginning any new course of study. How will your knowledge of and competence in psychology be enhanced by a study of the history of the field? The methods of present-day psychology certainly bear little formal resemblance to those used in the early psychological laboratories, and even less to the prescientific philosophical approaches. Indeed, the development of psychology has been so dynamic that the psychology of only 25 years ago seems remote. Will knowledge of the history of the field produce a better understanding of today's psychology? Considering the vast amount of material to be studied in psychology, is it worth the effort to learn what happened 50 or 100 years ago?

Obviously, I think the answer to the question is yes. One reason for studying the history of psychology relates to the amazing growth and influence of the field. Another reason relates to the divisiveness and fragmentation characteristic of psychology today. There is no single form, approach, or definition of modern psychology on which all psychologists would agree. There is an enormous amount of diversity in both professional specialization and subject matter (for example, psychologists may focus on conscious or unconscious forces, on overt behavior, or on physicochemical processes). In other words, there are many "psychologies" and they seem to have little in common save an interest in human nature or conduct and an approach that attempts to be scientific in one way or another.

The framework that binds these different forms and approaches of contemporary psychology is the historical development of the field—the evolution of the discipline of psychology over time. Only by exploring its origins can the diversity of modern psychology become clear; its history explains its present status.

The influence of the past in shaping the present is a belief and a technique invoked by many psychologists in their work. Clinical psychologists, for example, attempt to understand the current state and condition of their patients by exploring the past, by examining the forces that caused their patients to behave or think in certain ways. By taking case histories, psychologists reconstruct the evolution of the patients and, in the process, are often able to explain present behavior.

Psychologists of a different persuasion, the behaviorists, also agree on the influence of the past in shaping current behavior. They may believe, for example, that all human acts have been determined by previous conditioning and reinforcing experiences. Again, the present state is accounted for and understood in terms of the history.

So it is with the discipline of psychology. The study of the history of psychology is probably the only course in the psychology department curriculum that can help you to integrate the numerous areas and issues that compose modern psychology and to recognize the interrelationships among the various facts and theories. Students usually complete this course with a greater awareness of how all the different, and in some cases apparently unrelated, topics of psychology fit together. These topics are inextricably related through the pattern of their historical development.

The eminent historian of psychology E. G. Boring wrote that without a degree of historical sophistication in the field, the psychologist "sees the present in distorted perspective, he mistakes old facts and old views for new, and he remains unable to evaluate the significance of new movements and methods. In this matter I can hardly state my faith too strongly. A psychological sophistication that contains no component of historical orientation seems to me to be no sophistication at all" (1950b, p. ix).[2] Therefore, you might think of this course as a case history, and that is precisely what it is—an exploration of the early influences that made the "person" of psychology what it is today.

In general, psychologists recognize the value of studying the history of their field, as attested to by several factors. First, there is the obvious point that your psychology department offers the course you are now taking. Most psychology departments give such a course, and many require it for undergraduate and graduate degrees. Most other science departments do not offer courses in the history of their fields, but psychologists believe that the history of psychology is a useful addition to the curriculum.

At the professional level there are definite signs of a strong and vital interest in the history of psychology. In 1965 a multidisciplinary journal, the *Journal of the History of the Behavioral Sciences,* was begun under the editorship of a psychologist. Also in 1965 the Archives of the History of American Psychology was established at the University of Akron (Ohio) to serve the needs of scholars by collecting and preserving source materials in the history of psychology. The Division of the History of Psychology (Division 26) was formed within the American Psychological Association in 1966, and in 1969 the International Society for the History of the Behavioral and Social Sciences (the Cheiron Society) was established. Graduate work in the history of psychology is offered at several universities, and doctoral programs are available at the University of New Hampshire and at Carleton University (Ottawa, Ontario). The recent growth in the number of texts, monographs, biographies, journal articles, professional meetings, translated works, and sources for archival research all reflect the importance that psychologists attribute to the study of the history of psychology.

Why is psychology unique among the sciences in its expression of interest in its own background? It has been suggested that of all the sciences, psychology is unique in that it has attracted our attention and interest for centuries. From the beginnings of recorded time we have attempted to study and understand our own behavior and have reached many respectable insights and conclusions. A number of inaccuracies and myths about human nature have also survived from these early attempts. Because of our extreme complexity, many questions asked about human nature centuries ago are still asked, in one form or another. There is, then, a continuity of problems and questions (if not of methods) in psychology that is not found in the other sciences. Thus, there is a more tangible link with the past in psychology, a connection that many psychologists find interesting and useful to explore.

[2] This and all subsequent quotations credited to Boring, 1950b are from Edwin G. Boring, *A History of Experimental Psychology,* 2nd ed., © 1950. Reprinted by permission of Prentice-Hall, Inc., Englewood Cliffs, New Jersey.

6

The Study of the History of Psychology

Scientists must also be concerned with the history of their fields to avoid repeating the past. As we shall see, the history of science contains instances of supposedly new discoveries and insights that, as it turned out, had been anticipated years earlier, the "new" discovery being made in ignorance of the earlier work.

Knowledge of the past might help to predict the future. Boring took issue with this idea, noting that, "The past is not a crystal ball" (1963, p. 5) in which one may foresee the future. Esper (1964), however, argued that the past is the only basis on which one may intelligently plan for the future. Because one purpose of the study of the history of a science is to gain better understanding of the present, Esper asked what the functional significance of this understanding would be if not to provide some preparation for the future.

Rollo May (1967) suggested that only through the study of history can we see how cultural and social forces have molded the attitudes that have gone into shaping psychology as we know it today. Our methods, our theories, and, indeed, our selves are the products of forces and traditions evolving over time. If we were not aware of these forces, "we shall have cut ourselves off from our very roots. To cut off history is to sever our arterial link with humanity" (p.55).

Finally, Michael Wertheimer (1979) suggested that the study of history needs no defense. The fascination of the story is justification enough. The chapters that follow contain much in the way of human drama, revolutionary ideas and movements, and despair-filled defeats for individuals and their ideas.

It is hoped that by completing this course you will gain some appreciation of the substantial progress that has been made in knowledge and methodology in the comparatively short time since psychology became an independent discipline. There were false starts and mistakes, but there was a thread of continuity that shaped the nature of contemporary psychology and provides us with an understanding of its diversity.

THE EVOLUTION OF PSYCHOLOGY: CONCEPTIONS OF SCIENTIFIC HISTORY

Two approaches can be taken to explain how a science like psychology develops: the *personalistic* or "great man" theory and the *naturalistic* theory. The personalistic conception of scientific history focuses on the monumental achievements and contributions of certain individuals. According to this view, all progress and change are directly attributable to the will and force of unique persons who alone charted and changed the course of history. A Napoleon, a Hitler, or a Darwin were, so this theory goes, the prime movers and shapers of great events. The theory implies that the events would not have happened had it not been for the appearance of the great men and women. The theory says, in effect, "the person makes the times."

At first glance, it appears obvious that science is indeed the work of extremely creative and intelligent persons who determined its direction. We often define an era by the name of the person whose discoveries or theories marked the period; we talk about physics "after Einstein," psychology "after Watson," and so on. It is readily apparent, both in science and in the general culture, that individuals have produced dramatic, sometimes traumatic, changes that have altered the course of history. We have only to think of Freud to see the truth of that.

So the personalistic theory has merit, but is it sufficient to explain the development of science or of society? No. There have been too many instances when a scientist or philosopher has failed to change the times, when, so the expression goes, he or she has been "ahead of the times." The phrase seems to imply that the times may determine whether what the scholar is saying will be heeded or ignored, praised or forgotten, and the history of science is replete with instances of rejection of new discoveries or insights. Even the greatest minds (perhaps especially the greatest minds) have been constrained by what is called the *Zeitgeist*—the spirit or intellectual climate of the times. The acceptance and use of a discovery, therefore, may be limited by the dominant pattern of thought in a culture, region, or era. An idea that is too novel to gain acceptance in one period of civilization may be readily accepted a generation or a century later. Slow change seems to be the rule for scientific progress.

The notion that the person makes the times is thus not entirely correct. Perhaps, as the naturalistic theory of history would have it, "the times make the person," or at least make possible the acceptance of what he or she has to say. Unless the *Zeitgeist* is ready for the new idea, its proponent may not be heard or may be laughed at or even burned at the stake (this too depends on the *Zeitgeist*).

This suggests that, for example, if Darwin had died in his youth, a theory of evolution would still have been put forth in the middle of the nineteenth century. Someone else would have done it because the *Zeitgeist* was calling for a new way of looking at the origin of the human species.[3]

The inhibiting or delaying capacity of the *Zeitgeist* operates not only at the level of the general culture but also within science itself, and its effects are perhaps even more pronounced at this "local" level. There are, in the history of science, many instances of early discoveries that remained dormant for long periods before being recognized and accepted. The concept of conditioning of responses, for example, was first suggested by Robert Whytt in 1763, but no one was interested in the idea then. It was well over

---

[3] Someone else did do it (Chapter 6). His name was Alfred Russel Wallace, and he developed a theory of evolution that was amazingly similar to Darwin's.

100 years later, at a time when psychology was moving toward greater objectivity, that Ivan Pavlov expanded these early observations into the basis for a new system of psychology. Mendel's work on genetics was ignored for about 35 years (possibly because of its publication in an obscure journal) before making its impact. A discovery, then, must await its time.

Instances of simultaneous discovery also support the naturalistic theory of history. For example, there have been highly similar discoveries by individuals working far apart geographically and often in complete ignorance of one another's work. Postman (1962) noted that in 1900 three different investigators, working independently (indeed unknown to one another), rediscovered Mendel's work.

Existing theoretical positions in a field of science often exert a negative influence by standing in the way of progress. A theory may so dominate a discipline that investigation or even consideration of a new field of inquiry is inhibited. An accepted theory can also determine the way in which the phenomena or data pertaining to a problem are categorized, and this may prevent the scientist from looking at the data in a new way.

The *Zeitgeist* within science can also have this inhibiting effect on methods and techniques of investigation, on theoretical formulations, and on what is considered to be the proper subject matter for investigation. We shall describe in later chapters the early tendency of scientific psychology to focus on consciousness and subjective aspects of human nature. Even as the methods of study became more objective and precise, the focus of study continued for a long time to be subjective. Psychology had to wait until the second decade of the twentieth century before it finally lost its mind, and later lost consciousness altogether. A half century later, under the impact of a new *Zeitgeist*, psychology began to regain consciousness (Chapter 15). Thus, science is constantly reacting to the values of the changing *Zeitgeist*.

Perhaps this can best be understood in terms of an analogy with the evolution of a living species. Both a science and a living species change or evolve in response to the conditions and demands of the environment. What happens to a species over time? Very little, so long as its environment remains fairly constant. If the environment were to change, however, the species would have to adapt to the new conditions or face extinction.

Suppose that an ice age developed, or that a climate grew significantly warmer, or a swampy region dried out because of prolonged drought. The species that live in the affected areas must alter their form to survive. A hairless species must grow a covering of fur to cope with colder conditions. A short-legged species of bird must stretch its legs and evolve into a long-legged species if the ecology of the shallow waters in which it once found food changed and food was now available only in deeper waters.

Some species do not adapt successfully to environmental changes, and we know only their historical remains. Others do adapt and change their forms somewhat, while retaining their basic features; in such cases, the newer forms of the species remain recognizably linked with the older forms. Still other species are modified so radically that they become entirely new species, seemingly unrelated to their predecessors.

However mild or extreme the change, the point is that living species are altered in response to environmental demands. The more dramatic the environmental changes, the more radically the species must change.

A parallel can be drawn with the evolution of a science. It, too, exists in the context of an environment to which it must be continually responsive. The environment of a science is not so much physical as it is intellectual and social—in other words, the *Zeitgeist*. Like the physical environment, the *Zeitgeist* is subject to frequent change. The intellectual–social climate that characterizes one generation or century may be totally different by the next, as happened, for example, when the belief in God, dogma, and authority as the source of human knowledge was replaced by a belief in reason and science.

When such changes take place, the disciplines and value systems of a culture must adapt to the new environment. If they did not adapt and reflect the values of the new *Zeitgeist,* they would become extinct. A belief system centered on the worship of the sun does not have much chance of surviving when the *Zeitgeist* has changed to support the worship of a human figure such as Jesus.

This evolutionary process has marked the entire history of psychology. When the *Zeitgeist* favored speculation, meditation, and intuition as means to truth, psychology favored those means as well. When the climate of the times changed and dictated an observational–experimental approach to truth, the methods of psychology swung in that direction.

When one form of psychology found itself in two different social–intellectual environments, it became two species of psychology. This happened when structuralism, the first school of thought in psychology, emigrated to America, and what had been a uniquely German brand of psychology was modified to become a uniquely American variety. The structuralism that remained in Germany did not change.

This emphasis on the *Zeitgeist* does not negate the importance of the contributions of the great figures in the history of science, but it does put them in a different perspective. A Copernicus, in this view, does not singlehandedly change the course of history through the sheer force of genius. Of course such persons do affect the course of events, but they do so only because their path has already been cleared. We shall see that this is true of every major figure in the history of psychology.

The great scholars, as Boring (1963) has suggested, have become *eponyms,* that is, their names have been given to systematic positions or laws, and this process has fostered the belief that the discovery was the result of one person's sudden insight. In point of historical fact, the development of the "discovery" has usually been much more gradual. Eponymy may thus distort history by not taking proper account of the *Zeitgeist* and of earlier neglected contributions.

A history of a science such as psychology must, it seems, be eponymous, because it chooses representative individuals to exemplify the development of the science. What would the history of psychology be like if the names of all the leaders were left out? It would still exist, but the historian would be forced to find other labels with which to designate eras, schools of thought, theories, and the like. In addition, an eponymous account of the growth of psychology need not distort historical development. We must remember that the thinking of the important theorists and researchers, and the acceptance of their achievements, were strongly influenced by the spirit of the times in which they worked.

It should be clear by now that the history of psychology must be considered in terms of both personalistic and naturalistic theories of history. Yet the *Zeitgeist* seems to play the major role; no matter how great the contributions of the significant figures in history and in science, if their ideas had been too far out of phase with the climate of the times, their insights would have died in obscurity. Individual creative work is more a mirror, magnifying and elaborating the spirit of the times, than a beacon, though both shed light on the path ahead.

LANDMARKS OF DEVELOPMENT: SCHOOLS OF THOUGHT IN PSYCHOLOGY

We have noted that psychology evolved as a separate scientific discipline in the last quarter of the nineteenth century. In the initial years the direction of the new psychology was influenced profoundly by one man, Wilhelm Wundt, who had definite ideas about the form this new science—*his* new science—should take. He determined the subject matter, the method of research, the topics that researchers should study, and the goals of the new science. He was, of course, guided and influenced by the spirit of his times, and by the current thinking in philosophy and physiology. Nevertheless, it was Wundt in his role as agent of the times who drew together various lines of thought and, through the force of his personality and his intensive and exacting writing and research, fashioned the new psychology. He was a compelling agent of the inevitable and so, for a while, psychology was molded in his image.

In a very short time, however, the situation in psychology changed radically. Controversy arose among the growing number of psychologists. The spirit of the times was changing, as it always is, and new ideas were forming in other sciences and in the general culture. Reflecting these new currents of thought, some psychologists disagreed with Wundt's version of psychology and proposed their own views. As a result, by the turn of the century several systematic positions or schools of thought existed.

The term *school* refers to a group of psychologists who become associated ideologically, and sometimes geographically, with the leader of a movement. For the most part, the members of a school work on common problems and share a theoretical or systematic orientation.

The emergence of different schools of thought and their subsequent decline and replacement by still other schools is one of the more striking characteristics of the history of psychology. The phenomenon is not unique to psychology; all sciences experience a similar period of division early in their respective histories, when competing schools of thought fracture the field of study.

Kuhn (1970) argued that this stage of development in the life of a science—the time when it is still divided into schools of thought—is a *preparadigmatic* one. The more mature or advanced stage is reached when schools of thought no longer characterize the field, when the majority of the members of the discipline agree on theoretical and methodological rationales. Then a common paradigm defines the field and there are no longer competing factions.

In physics we can see paradigms at work. For example, the Galilean–Newtonian concept of mechanism was accepted and used by physicists for some 300 years. During that time virtually all work in physics was undertaken within the framework provided by mechanism. However, paradigms are not inviolate. They can and do change, once a majority of persons in a discipline agree on a new way of looking at or working with the subject matter of the field. This occurred in physics when the Galilean–Newtonian model was replaced by the Einsteinian model (Chapter 15). Kuhn refers to this replacement of one paradigm by another as a "scientific revolution."

Psychology has not yet reached the stage of paradigmatic science. For all of its 100-year history, "Psychology has been searching and sampling a variety of directions, trying different ways of talking about its subject matter, but no systematic view can be said to have become dominant for more than a couple of decades" (Mueller, 1979, p. 17). The field is specialized, divided into competing factions, each adhering to its own theoretical and methodological orientation. Each group approaches the study of human nature in a different way, using various techniques, and each faction has its followers, jargon, journals, and other characteristics of a school of thought. Schools of thought continue to typify not only the evolution of psychology, but also its present level of development.

Each of the early schools was a movement of protest—indeed, some were revolutions—against the prevailing systematic position of the day. Each pointed out what it saw as the shortcomings and failures of the older point of view and offered new definitions, concepts, and research strategies to correct the perceived weaknesses. When a new school of thought captured the attention of the scientific community, the rejection of a once honored position was the result. These intellectual conflicts between incompatible positions (the old and the new) were fought with feverish tenacity on both sides.

12

*The Study of the History of
Psychology*

Often the leaders of the older school were never wholly converted to the new school of thought. Usually older in years, these leaders were too deeply committed to their position, intellectually and emotionally, to change. Many of the younger, hence less committed, adherents became converts to the new position, leaving the others to cling to the old traditions, working in increasing isolation and loneliness.

> *What would happen to science if its great men did not eventually die, no one can guess. What does happen is that a new man takes up the work of an older man without the constraint of inertia from his past, that he thinks, works and writes more simply and directly, and that thus from the old he creates something new that gradually itself accumulates inertia. (Boring, 1950b, p. 399)*

The physicist Max Planck wrote more bluntly: "New scientific truth does not triumph by convincing its opponents and making them see the light, but rather because its opponents eventually die" (1949, p. 33).

Thus, different schools of thought developed over the course of the history of psychology, each one an effective protest against what had gone before. Each new school used its older opponent as a base from which to push and gain momentum. Each position proclaimed loudly what it was not and how it differed from the older theoretical system. As the new system developed and gained adherents and influence, it inspired opposition and the whole combative process began anew. What was once a pioneering, aggressive revolution became, with success, an established tradition, which then succumbed to the vigorous force of a youthful new movement.

Success destroys vigor. A movement feeds on opposition. When the opposition has been defeated, the passion and ardor of the once new movement die.

Although the dominance of at least some of these schools was only temporary, each played a vital role in the development of psychology. Their influence can be seen clearly in contemporary psychology, even though factions in the psychology of today bear little similarity to the earlier systems (because new doctrines again have replaced the old). Heidbreder (1933) compared the role of the schools of psychological thought to that of the scaffolding used in erecting a tall structure. Without the scaffolding from which to work, the building could not be erected. And yet, the scaffolding does not remain—it is torn down when it is no longer needed. In analogous fashion, the structure of today's psychology has been built within the general framework and guidelines established by the schools.

We cannot look on any of the schools as complete accounts of scientific fact; they are not finished products in any sense. Rather, they provide the tools, methods, and conceptual schemes that psychology has used to accumulate and organize a body of scientific fact. This does not imply that the psychology of today is in final form. New schools have replaced the old, but nothing guarantees their permanence in the evolutionary process of science building. The schools of psychology, therefore, are temporary but necessary stages in the development of psychology.

It is in terms of the historical development of these schools of thought that the exciting advance of psychology can best be understood. Individuals stand out as having made pioneering pronouncements and contributions, but their significance is most notable when considered in the context of the ideas that preceded theirs, on which they often built, and the work that followed theirs.

After taking a detailed look at the beginnings of experimental psychology (Chapters 2 and 3), we will consider each of the major psychological schools on three levels: *(1)* the prescientific development of the position, including the work of earlier scholars who developed their insights without the use of the experimental method; *(2)* the early attempts to attack particular problems using the methods of science; and *(3)* the formal establishment of each school and its contemporary derivatives.

A continuity of development emerges as we trace each school of thought to the one that subsequently replaced it. This orderly developmental pattern provides a useful framework within which to understand the history of psychology. We shall examine six schools of thought and describe their interrelationships, showing how each depended on at least one other school of thought or on work in other disciplines to help shape its nature.

Structuralism developed out of earlier work in philosophy and physiology. That initial school of thought led to three others—functionalism, behaviorism, and Gestalt psychology—which either evolved from or revolted against structuralism. On a roughly parallel course in time, though not in subject matter, methods, or aims, psychoanalysis evolved from work in philosophy on the nature of the unconscious and attempts in psychiatry to treat the mentally ill. Both psychoanalysis and behaviorism spawned a number of subschools. In more recent times—since the 1950s—humanistic psychology has developed in reaction to both behaviorism and psychoanalysis, while drawing on principles of Gestalt psychology. Thus, a pattern emerges in the cumulative building process that distinguishes the century of the history of psychology.

SUGGESTED READINGS

Boring, E. G. *Psychologist at large: An autobiography and selected essays.* New York: Basic Books, 1961.

Boring, E. G. *History, psychology, and science.* New York: Wiley, 1963.

Buss, A. R. The structure of psychological revolutions. *Journal of the History of the Behavioral Sciences,* 1978, *14,* 57–64.

Henle, M. Why study the history of psychology? *Annals of the New York Academy of Sciences,* 1976, *270,* 14–20.

Jaynes, J. Introduction: The study of the history of psychology. In M. Henle, J. Jaynes, & J. Sullivan (Eds.), *Historical conceptions of psychology.* New York: Springer, 1973. Pp. ix–xii.

Kuhn, T. S. *The structure of scientific revolutions* (2nd ed.). Chicago: University of Chicago Press, 1970.

Mueller, C. G. Some origins of psychology as science. *Annual Review of Psychology,* 1979, *30,* 9–29.

Palermo, D. S. Is a scientific revolution taking place in psychology? *Science Studies,* 1971, *1,* 135–155.

Raphelson, A. C. The unique role of the history of psychology in undergraduate education. *Teaching of Psychology,* 1979, *6,* 12–14.

Sarup, G. Historical antecedents of psychology: The recurrent issue of old wine in new bottles. *American Psychologist,* 1978, *33,* 478–485.

Warren, N. Is a scientific revolution taking place in psychology? Doubts and reservations. *Science Studies,* 1971, *1,* 407–413.

Watson, R. I. Psychology: A prescriptive science. *American Psychologist,* 1967, *22,* 435–443.

Watson, R. I. The history of psychology as a speciality: A personal view of its first 15 years. *Journal of the History of the Behavioral Sciences,* 1975, *11,* 5–14.

2

DIRECT PHILOSOPHICAL INFLUENCES ON PSYCHOLOGY

THE SPIRIT OF MECHANISM: THE UNIVERSE AS A MACHINE

In the royal gardens of Europe in the seventeenth century there appeared a whimsical form of amusement among the many marvels of a truly exciting age. Water, running through underground pipes, operated mechanical figures that performed a variety of movements, played musical instruments, and even produced wordlike sounds. Hidden pressure plates, activated when people unknowingly stepped on them, sent water flowing through the pipes to the machinery that moved the statues.

These amusements of the aristocracy reflected and reinforced the seventeenth-century fascination with the miracle of the machine. All manner of machines were invented, perfected, and improved for use in science, industry, and entertainment. Mechanical clocks with an accuracy never thought possible, as well as pumps, levers, pulleys, and cranes, were developed to serve human needs, and there seemed to be no limit to the kinds of machines that could be devised or the uses to which they could be put.

You may wonder what this has to do with the history of modern psychology. We refer, after all, to a time 200 years before the establishment of psychology as a science, focusing on technology and physics, disciplines seemingly far removed from the study of human nature.

The relationship, however, is direct and compelling, because those mechanical figures of the seventeenth century, and the guiding principle they embodied, dictated the direction and form the new psychology would take, and would follow for most of its existence.

We are dealing with the *Zeitgeist* of the seventeenth to nineteenth centuries, the intellectual soil that nourished the new psychology. The basic idea of the seventeenth century, the philosophy that would nurture the new psychology, was the spirit of *mechanism*—an image of the universe as the "great machine."

This idea originated in physics (or "natural philosophy," as it was then known) as a result of the work of Galileo and, later, Newton. The nature of all that existed in the universe was held to be nothing more than particles of matter in motion. Matter, according to Galileo, was composed of discrete corpuscles or atoms that affected each other by direct contact, as billiard balls do.[1]

If the universe consisted of atoms in motion, then every physical effect (the movement of each atom) would follow from a direct cause (the movement of the atom that struck it), and so should be subject to laws of measurement and calculation, and hence prediction. This game of billiards, the physical universe, was orderly, lawful, and predictable, like a clock or any other good machine. The physical universe was designed by God with absolute perfection (in the seventeenth century it was still possible for scientists to attribute cause and perfection to God), and once one knew the laws by which it worked, it was possible to know how it would behave in the future.

The methods and findings of science were growing apace with technology during this time and the two meshed very effectively. *Observation* and *experimentation* came to be the hallmarks of science, followed closely by *measurement*.

It began to appear that every function or phenomenon could be defined or described by a number, a characteristic vital to the study of the universe as a machine. Thermometers, barometers, slide rules, micrometers, pendulum clocks, and other measuring devices were developed and perfected in this age of the machine, and served to reinforce the notion that it was possible to measure all aspects of the mechanical universe.

What did the idea of mechanism and the methods of science imply, indeed dictate, for the study of human nature? Simply stated, it is this: If all the universe were like a machine—orderly, predictable, observable, measurable—could not human beings be considered in the same light?

Thus it was thought that humans were also mechanical and that the same experimental and quantitative methods that were so successful in exploring the secrets of the physical universe could be applied to the exploration of human nature. "Let us then conclude boldly," said the French philosopher La Mettrie, in 1748, "that man is a machine" (1748, pp. 148–149). This theme became a driving force of the *Zeitgeist*, not only in philosophy, but in all aspects of life, and drastically changed our image of ourselves.

And so there emerged during the seventeenth to nineteenth centuries the image of persons as machines and the method by which human nature could be investigated—the *scientific method*. We became machines, the

---

[1] Isaac Newton later improved on the Galilean version of mechanism by postulating that movement was communicated not by physical contact, but by attracting and repelling forces. This idea, though vastly important in physics, did not radically change the basic idea of mechanism and the way it was used in the new psychology.

modern world became dominated by the scientific outlook, and all aspects of life became subject to mechanical laws.

THE BEGINNINGS OF MODERN SCIENCE: RENE DESCARTES (1596–1650)

We noted that the seventeenth century saw far-ranging developments in science. Until that time philosophers had looked to the past for answers, to the works of Aristotle and other ancient scholars, and to the Bible. The ruling forces of inquiry were dogma and authority.

In the seventeenth century a new force—*empiricism,* or the observation of nature itself—became dominant. Knowledge handed down from the past became suspect, along with all philosophical and theological dogma. The golden age of the seventeenth century was illuminated by the discoveries and insights of many great men who successfully created or reflected the changing atmosphere in which scientific inquiry was flourishing. Although these people are of great importance in the history of science in general, for the most part their work is not *directly* related to the evolution of psychology.

One scholar, René Descartes, did contribute directly to the history of modern psychology. More than anyone else, he freed inquiry from the rigid theological and traditional dogmas that had dominated it for centuries. "Not since Aristotle had a philosopher constructed a new and influential system of thought that took into account the sum of knowledge, which in two thousand years had grown so significantly" (Herrnstein & Boring, 1965, p. 581). This great man, who symbolizes the transition from the Renaissance to the modern era of science, applied the idea of mechanism to the human body. Many believe that he inaugurated modern psychology.

The Life of Descartes

Descartes was born in March 1596 at La Haye in Touraine, France. His father was a councillor at the parliament of Brittany and from him Descartes inherited enough money to support his life of study and travel. Descartes, unlike others in similar circumstances, did not lead a life of dilettantism, a tendency apparently attributable to his genius, curiosity, and hunger for knowledge, his indifference to dogmatic authority, and his constant desire for evidence and proof.

From 1604 to 1612 he was a student at the Jesuit College at La Flèche, where he was educated in the humanities and mathematics and displayed considerable talent in philosophy, physics, and physiology, as well as in mathematics. Because Descartes's health was frail, the rector, Father Charlet, excused him from morning religious duties and allowed him to lie in bed,

Direct Philosophical Influences on Psychology

a habit he retained all his life. It was during these quiet mornings that he studied his lessons and did his most creative thinking.

After his formal education Descartes sampled the pleasures of Paris for a while and then, finding this life tiresome, went into seclusion to study mathematics. An illness during this time led to one of his major theories. In 1617 he became a gentleman volunteer in the army of Prince Maurice of Nassau (Holland), a strange act for one of such a contemplative nature.

He was, at various times in his life, very much a man of the world. He loved to dance and gamble, and he was a good gambler because of his mathematical talents. He was an adventurer and a swordsman who apparently partook of all the human vices and pleasures (Vrooman, 1970).

In addition to his theoretical work, Descartes was keenly interested in applying knowledge to practical concerns. For example, he once investigated different techniques that might keep his hair from turning gray. He also conducted some of the earliest experiments on the use of wheelchairs for the handicapped.

In November 1619, while serving in the army, Descartes had a series of dreams that would change his life radically. As he told it, he spent the day of November 10 alone in a stove-heated room, thinking about certain mathematical and scientific ideas. He fell asleep and in his dreams was, as he interpreted it, rebuked for his idleness and visited by the "spirit of truth," which took possession of his mind.

This profound experience persuaded him to devote his life to the proposition that mathematics could be applied to all the sciences and thus produce certainty of knowledge. He resolved to undertake no ties of marriage or friendship that might prevent him from pursuing these insights.

Although he returned to Paris in 1623 to pursue his favorite study of mathematics, Descartes found Parisian life too distracting and moved to Holland in 1628. His need for solitude and seclusion was so great during this period that he lived in 13 towns and 24 different houses over the next 20 years, keeping his address secret from all but his most intimate friends, with whom he corresponded voluminously. His only other apparent requirements were proximity to a Roman Catholic church and a university.

Most of Descartes's important works were written during these years in Holland, where freedom of thought was characteristic during the seventeenth century. However, he did encounter some religious persecution. At one time booksellers were forbidden to sell his works and he was brought before the magistrates to answer the charges of the theologians of Utrecht and Leyden that he was an atheist and a profligate, serious charges against a devout Catholic. White (1965) noted that Descartes "was condemned by Catholics and Protestants alike. Since Roger Bacon, perhaps, no great thinker had been so completely abased and thwarted by theological oppression" (p. 80).

Descartes's growing fame led Queen Christina of Sweden to invite him to instruct her in philosophy. Though reluctant to give up his freedom and solitude, he nonetheless had great respect for royal prerogative and went to Sweden on the warship sent to fetch him. The queen was not a very good student and she insisted on starting her lessons at 5 every morning in the poorly heated library during an unusually bitter winter. Descartes withstood the early rising and extreme cold for four months before succumbing to pneumonia on February 11, 1650.

The Contributions of Descartes

Descartes's most important work from the standpoint of the future development of psychology is his attempt to resolve the mind–body problem, an issue that had been controversial for centuries. Throughout the ages scholars had argued about how the mind, or purely mental qualities, could be distinguished from the body and all other physical qualities.

The basic and deceptively simple question is this: Are mind and body—the mental world and the material world—distinct essences or natures? Since the time of Plato most scholars had taken a *dualistic* position; that is, it was held that mind and body were of different natures. However, the acceptance of that position raises another question: What is the nature of the relationship between mind and body? Does one influence the other, or are they independent?

The theory held before Descartes was that there was essentially a one-way effect. Mind, it was said, could exert an enormous influence on the body, but the body had very little effect on the mind. Lowry (1971) has suggested that the mind and body were thought to be related to each other in the way a puppeteer and puppet are joined together. In this view, the mind is like the puppeteer, pulling the strings of the body.

Descartes accepted the dualistic position. In his view, mind and body were indeed different; however, he deviated from tradition in his definition of the nature of the relationship between the two.

It is true, Descartes said, that the mind influences the body. However, he argued, the body can exert a much greater influence than previously had been supposed. The relationship is one of mutual interaction; this idea, radical in the seventeenth century, had important implications.

After Descartes the mind (or soul or spirit) was no longer believed to be the master of the two entities, no longer the puppeteer functioning almost independently of the body. The body, the material side of humans, came to be viewed in a more central manner, and certain functions previously attributed to the mind were considered to be functions of the body.

For example, in the Middle Ages, the mind was held to be responsible not only for thought and reason, but also for reproduction, perception, and locomotion. Descartes argued that the mind had only one function—thought. All the other processes were functions of the body.

Descartes was the first to offer an approach to the mind–body problem

20

Among the contributions of French nativist philosopher René Descartes (1596–1650) to psychology were the doctrine of innate ideas and the theory of mind–body interaction. *(National Library of Medicine)*

that focused attention on a strictly physical–*psychological* duality. In so doing, he turned attention away from the study of the soul in the abstract to the study of the mind and the mental operations it performs. As a result, methods of inquiry changed from metaphysical analysis and deduction to induction and objective observation. Whereas one could only speculate on the existence of the soul, the mind and its operations could be *observed*.

Mind and body, then, are two separate entities. There is no qualitative similarity between the body or the physical world and the mind. Matter

The Beginnings of Modern Science:
René Descartes

and body are extended substances that operate by, and can be explained in terms of, mechanical principles. The soul or mind is unextended, free, and lacking in substance. But the most important point, the idea that was revolutionary, was that mind and body, though distinct, are capable of interacting within the human organism. The mind can influence the body and the body can influence the mind; this is the so-called theory of mind–body interaction.

Let us take a more detailed look at Descartes's conception of the body. Because the body is composed of physical matter, it must have those characteristics common to all matter—extension in space and capability of movement. If the body is matter, then the laws of physics and mechanics that account for movement and action in the physical world must also apply to the body.

The body, when considered apart from the mind (and it can be so considered because the two are separate entities), is like a machine whose operation can be adequately explained by the mechanical laws of the movement of objects in space. Following this line of reasoning, Descartes proceeded to account for physiological functioning in physical terms.

Descartes was strongly influenced by the mechanistic spirit of the age as reflected in those delightful mechanical figures mentioned earlier. While recovering from a nervous breakdown at the age of 18, he recuperated in a small village near Paris where the only amusement available to him was the recently completed Royal Gardens (Jaynes, 1970). He was fascinated by these mechanical marvels and spent hours walking on the pressure plates that caused the figures to move and dance and speak.

This experience helped to shape his view of the physical universe, in particular, his view of the human and animal body. He believed that the body operated exactly like a machine. Indeed, he recognized no difference between the hydraulically operated figures and the body, and he explained every aspect of physical functioning (digestion, circulation, sensation, motion, and so on) in mechanical terms.

When Descartes described the body, he referred to the figures he had seen in the Royal Gardens. He compared the body's nerves to the pipes through which the water passed, and the muscles and tendons to engines and springs. The movement of the models was not caused by voluntary action on their part, but by external objects; this involuntariness was reflected in Descartes's observation that movements of the body frequently occur without the individual's conscious intention. From this line of thought he arrived at the idea of the *undulatio reflexa*, a movement not supervised or determined by a will to move. Because of this notion, he is often called the author of the theory of reflex action. This idea of reflex action can also be seen as a precursor of modern stimulus–response psychology, in which an external object (a stimulus) brings about an involuntary response.

Support for his mechanical interpretation of the workings of the human body came from the exciting advances in physiology, of which Descartes was aware. In 1628 William Harvey had discovered the gross facts about the circulation of the blood, and much was being learned about the process of digestion. It was also known that the muscles of the body worked in opposing pairs, and that sensation and movement somehow depended on the nerves. Physiological research had made great strides in understanding the human body, though the information was far from complete. The nerves, for instance, were thought to be hollow tubes through which animal spirits flowed. The important point, however, is not the accuracy or comprehensiveness of seventeenth-century knowledge of human physiology, but rather that it was consonant with a mechanical, physical interpretation of the body.

Because animals did not possess souls, they were believed to be automata, machines that move themselves. Thus, the difference between humans and animals so important to the Christian religion was preserved. Also, animals were thought to be devoid of feelings. Descartes dissected animals—before anesthesia was available—and was "amused at their cries and yelps since these were nothing but the hydraulic hisses and vibrations of machines" (Jaynes, 1970, p. 224).

These views were part of an overall trend toward the notion that human behavior is predictable. The mechanical body will move and behave in expected ways so long as the inputs are known. Animals, being totally machinelike, belong entirely to the category of physical phenomena. Hence, animals have no immortality, are incapable of thought, and have no freedom of will. Descartes made some minor adjustments in his thinking about animals in later years, but he never altered his basic conviction that animal behavior can be explained mechanically.

The nonmaterial mind, according to Descartes, has the capacities of thought and consciousness, and, consequently, provides us with knowledge of the external world. It has none of the properties of matter. The most important characteristic of the mind is its capacity to think, and this sets it apart from the physical world of matter. This "thinking thing" is free, immaterial, and unextended, as noted.

Because the mind perceives and wills, it must somehow influence and be influenced by the body. Descartes recognized that when the mind "decides" to move from one point to another, for example, this decision is carried out by the body's nerves and muscles. Similarly, when the body is stimulated in some fashion, for example, by light or heat, the mind recognizes and interprets these sensory data and decides on the appropriate response.

Thus, Descartes was led to formulate a theory about the interaction of these different entities. First, he needed to find a point of interaction where the mind and the body engaged in their mutual influence. Several criteria were involved in the search for this place of interaction. Descartes conceived of the soul as unitary, which meant that it must interact with only one part of the body. He also believed that the point of interaction must be somewhere within the brain because research had demonstrated that sensations travel to the brain and movement originates within the brain. Clearly, then, the brain had to be the focal point for the mind's functions. The only structure of the brain that is single and unitary (that is, not divided and duplicated in both hemispheres) is the pineal body, or conarium, and Descartes considered this the logical choice for a point of interaction.

The manner in which this interaction between mind and body takes place was treated in mechanistic terms by Descartes. Movement of the animal spirits in the nerve tubes was thought to produce an impression on the conarium, and from this impression the mind produces a sensation. In other words, a quantity of motion (the flow of animal spirits) produces a purely mental quality (a sensation). The reverse also occurs, in that the mind can somehow make an impression on the conarium (in a manner never made clear), which, by inclining to one direction or another, influences the direction of the flow of the animal spirits to the muscles, resulting in a movement. Thus, a mental quality can influence motion, a property of the body.

It is important to remember that Descartes did not maintain that the soul is confined to or contained in the conarium. The conarium was designated as the point of interaction and nothing more. Descartes believed that the soul is united with all parts of the body; the entire body becomes the "seat of the soul."[2]

Because of its profound influence on the subsequent development of psychology, another of Descartes's formulations, the *doctrine of ideas*, deserves mention. Descartes believed that the mind gives rise to two kinds of ideas—*derived* and *innate*. Derived ideas are those produced by the direct application of an external stimulus, such as the sound of a bell or the sight of a tree. Thus, derived ideas are products of the experiences of the senses.

Of greater importance is the notion of innate ideas, which are not derived from sensory experiences. These ideas are not produced by objects in the external world impinging on the senses. The label *innate* describes their source—they develop out of the mind or consciousness alone. Their potential existence is independent of sense experience, though they may be realized or actualized in the presence of appropriate sense experiences. Some of these innate ideas, according to Descartes, are self, God, geometric axioms, perfection, and infinity.

The conception of innate ideas is discussed in later chapters. It eventually culminates in the nativistic theory of perception and the Gestalt school of psychology. We also will see its influence in the spirited opposition it inspired among the early British empiricists and associationists, and among the more modern empiricists such as Helmholtz and Wundt.

The work of Descartes served as an important catalyst for many trends that later became prominent in psychology. His most noteworthy systematic

[2] An interesting postscript to the death of a man who devoted so much of his life to the mind–body problem is that Descartes's body was buried in France, but for many years his skull remained in Sweden. The skull can now be seen in the Musee de L'Homme in Paris (Vrooman, 1970).

contributions are the mechanistic conception of the body, the theory of mind–body interaction, the localization of the mind's functions in the brain, and the doctrine of innate ideas.

With Descartes we see the doctrine of mechanism applied to the human body. So pervasive was the mechanistic philosophy, however, that it was only a matter of time before the human mind would also be reduced to nothing more than a machine. It is to that far-reaching event that we now turn.

BRITISH EMPIRICISM AND ASSOCIATIONISM

After Descartes, the development of modern science in general and of psychology in particular was rapid and prolific. By the middle of the nineteenth century the long period of prescientific psychology had come to an end. During this time European philosophical thought became infused with a new spirit—*positivism*. The term and the conception are the work of Auguste Comte, who was working on a systematic survey of all knowledge— an ambitious project indeed! To make the project more manageable, Comte decided to limit his work to facts that were beyond question; in other words, those facts determined through the methods of science. Positivism, then, refers to a system based exclusively on facts that are objectively observable and not debatable. Everything of a speculative or inferential nature is rejected as illusory.

Other ideas supportive of antimetaphysical positivism were extant in philosophy. The *materialists* believed that all things could be described in physical terms and understood in the light of the physical properties of matter and energy. They thought that consciousness, too, could be explained in the terms of physics and chemistry. In discussions of mental phenomena they tended to focus on their physical aspect—the anatomical and physiological structure of the brain.

A third group of philosophers, the *empiricists,* were also active, particularly in England. They were concerned with how the mind acquires knowledge, and argued that all knowledge is derived from sensory experience.

Our conception of ourselves and our world was rapidly changing. Positivism, empiricism, and materialism were to become the philosophical foundations of the new psychology. Discussions of psychological phenomena were beginning to be conducted within a framework of factual, observational, and quantitative evidence based on sensory experience. More emphasis was being placed on the physiological processes involved in mental functioning (Chapter 3).

Of the three new orientations, empiricism played the major role in shaping the early development of the new science of psychology. Empiricism provided the new psychology with both a method and a theory. The method of the empiricists was observation and, to some extent, experimentation. In contrast to the older rational and speculative methods of inquiry, the empirical method relied on objective observation. The theoretical aspect of empiricism related to the growth of the mind, to how the mind acquires knowledge. According to the empiricist view, the mind grows through the progressive accumulation of sensory experiences. This attitude is in opposition to the nativistic viewpoint exemplified by Descartes, which states that some ideas are innate at birth. We will now consider some of the major British empiricists—Locke, Berkeley, Hume, Hartley, and Mill.

John Locke (1632–1704)

Locke, the son of an attorney, studied at Westminster and Oxford, receiving his bachelor's degree in 1656 and his master's degree shortly thereafter. He remained at Oxford for several years, tutoring in Greek, rhetoric, and philosophy, and then took up the practice of medicine. He had also developed an interest in political matters and in 1667 went to London to become secretary to the Earl of Shaftesbury and, in time, the confidant and friend of this controversial statesman.

Shaftesbury's political stature and influence declined, and in 1681, after participating in a plot against Charles II, he fled to Holland. Although Locke was not involved in the plot, his relationship with Shaftesbury brought him under suspicion and he too fled to Holland. In 1689 he was able to return to England, where he took the post of commissioner of appeals and began to write on education, religion, and economics. He was particularly concerned with religious freedom and the right of men to govern themselves. Locke's writings brought him much fame and power and he was heralded throughout Europe as a champion of liberalism in government.

Locke's major work of importance to psychology is *An Essay Concerning Human Understanding*, which appeared in 1690 and was the culmination of some 20 years of study and thought. This classic, which had appeared in four editions by 1700 and had been published in French and Latin translations, marked the formal beginning of English empiricism.

Locke was concerned primarily with the question of how the mind acquires knowledge. In attacking this issue, he first denied the existence of Descartes's innate ideas, arguing that humans are not equipped at birth with any knowledge whatever. He admitted that certain ideas may seem to adults to be innate (such as the idea of God) because adults have been constantly taught the ideas since childhood and cannot remember any time when they were unaware of them. Thus, Locke explained the apparent innateness of ideas in terms of learning and habit.

How, then, does the mind acquire knowledge? To Locke, the answer, emphatically stated, was through experience. All knowledge is empirically derived. In a frequently cited passage from his *Essay*, Locke noted:

British empiricist John Locke (1632–1704) argued that at birth the mind is a blank slate that acquires knowledge only through sense experience. *(National Library of Medicine)*

Let us then suppose the mind to be, as we say, white paper, void of all characters, without any ideas:—How comes it to be furnished? Whence comes it by that vast store which the busy and boundless fancy of man has painted on it with an almost endless variety? Whence has it all the materials of reason and knowledge? To this I answer, in one word, from EXPERIENCE. In that all our knowledge is founded; and from that it ultimately derives itself. (Book II, Chapter 1)[3]

[3] Aristotle had a similar notion—that the mind at birth was a *tabula rasa,* a blank slate on which experience would write.

Locke recognized two different kinds of experiences, one deriving from *sensation* and the other from *reflection.* Some ideas arise from direct sensory input from physical objects in the environment. They are simple sense impressions. In addition to the operation of sensations on the mind, however, the operation of the mind itself—reflection—can give rise to ideas. It is important to remember that the mental function of reflection as a source of ideas also depends on sensory experience, because the ideas produced by reflection are based on those already experienced sensorially.

In the development of the individual, sensation appears first. It is a necessary precursor of reflection because there must be a reservoir of sense impressions for the mind to be able to reflect. In reflection, the individual remembers past sensory impressions and combines them in various ways to form abstractions and other higher-level ideas. All ideas, no matter how abstract and complex, arise from these two sources, but the ultimate source remains sense impressions or experience.

Locke also made the distinction between *simple* and *complex ideas.* Simple ideas can arise from both sources (sensation and reflection), are received passively by the mind, and are elemental or unanalyzable—they cannot be reduced to simpler ideas. As noted, the mind, through the process of reflection, can actively create new ideas through combinations of other ideas. These derived ideas are what Locke called complex ideas, and they are formed from simple ideas of both sensation and reflection. Complex ideas are compounded of simple ideas, and hence are capable of being analyzed or resolved into simple ideas.

This notion of a mental combination or compounding of ideas and their analysis marks the beginning of the "mental chemistry" that characterizes the notion of *association,* in which simple ideas may be linked to form complex ones. Association is an early name for what would come to be called learning. The decomposition of mental life into elements (simple ideas), and the compounding of these elements to form complex ideas, subsequently formed the core of the new scientific psychology.

In essence, Locke treated the mind as though it behaved in accordance with the laws of the physical universe. The basic particles, or corpuscles or atoms, of the mental world were the *simple ideas,* which were conceptually analogous to the material atoms in the Galilean–Newtonian mechanistic scheme.

As Lowry (1971) noted, "it is possible to see the whole of Locke's psychology as a kind of Newtonian cosmos in miniature" (p. 21). The basic elements of the mind—the simple ideas—are indivisible. They cannot be broken down into anything simpler and, like their counterparts in the material world, they can join in various ways to form more complex structures. This was a significant step in the direction of considering the mind, like the body, as a machine.

Another Lockean doctrine of considerable interest to psychology is the notion of *primary* and *secondary qualities* as they apply to simple ideas of

Direct Philosophical Influences on Psychology

sense. Primary qualities exist in the object whether we perceive them or not. For instance, the size and shape of a building are primary qualities, whereas the color of the building is not inherent in the object, but is dependent on the experiencing person. The secondary qualities, such as color, odor, sound, and taste, are not in the object, but exist in a person's perception of the object. The tickle of a feather is not in the feather itself but in our reaction to the feather. The pain inflicted by a knife is not in the knife itself but in our experience in relation to the knife.

A simple experiment will illustrate this doctrine. Take three containers of water—one cold, one lukewarm, one hot. Place one hand in cold water and the other in hot water, then place both hands in the pan of lukewarm water. One hand will perceive this water as warm and the other will perceive it as cool. The water, of course, is one temperature; it is not both warm and cool at the same time. Therefore, the qualities or experience of heat and cold must exist only in our perception and not in the object (the water).

These secondary qualities exist then, only in the act of perception. If one did not bite into a peach, the taste would not exist. The primary qualities, such as the shape of the peach, exist in it whether we perceive them or not.

This was not the first time a distinction between primary and secondary qualities had been suggested. Galileo had made essentially the same point: "I think that if ears, tongues, and noses were removed, shapes and numbers and motions [primary qualities] would remain, but not odors nor tastes nor sounds. The latter, I believe, are nothing more than names when separated from living beings" (Boas, 1961, p. 262).

The position is necessarily congruent with the spirit of mechanism. Indeed, Locke admitted as much when he noted that the distinction resulted from "a little excursion into natural philosophy."

The mechanical view of the universe held that matter in motion constituted the only objective reality. If matter were all that existed objectively, it would follow that perception of anything else—colors, odors, or tastes—would be subjective. Hence, the primary qualities are all that can exist independently of the perceiver.

In making this distinction, Locke recognized the subjectivity of much of our perception of the world, a view that increased the need to understand the mind and its world of conscious experience. The secondary qualities were introduced in an attempt to explain the fact that there is not always a precise correspondence between the physical world and our perception of it.

Once it was accepted that there was a distinction between primary and secondary qualities—some existing in reality and others existing only in perception—it was inevitable that someone would ask whether there was, after all, any difference between primary and secondary qualities. Perhaps all perception is in terms of secondary qualities, that is, subjective and dependent on the observer. The person who did ask (and answer) this question was George Berkeley.

George Berkeley
(1685–1753)

Berkeley was Locke's immediate successor in British empirical philosophy. Born and educated in Ireland, he was a deeply religious man and at the age of 24 was ordained a deacon in the Anglican Church. Shortly after he published two philosophical works that were to exert an influence on psychology: *An Essay towards a New Theory of Vision* (1709) and *A Treatise Concerning the Principles of Human Knowledge* (1710).

With these two books, his contribution to psychology ended. Thereafter he traveled extensively in Europe and returned to Ireland to hold a number of posts, including a teaching position at Trinity College. He became financially independent through a sizable gift of money from a woman who he apparently met only once at a dinner. He traveled in the United States, spent three years in Newport, Rhode Island, and gave his house and library to Yale University when he departed. The last years of his life were spent as Bishop of Cloyne in Ireland.

Berkeley's fame (or at least his name) lingers in the United States today. In the mid-nineteenth century a clergyman from Yale, the Reverend Henry Durant, established an academy in California. He named it Berkeley (Morgan, 1969) in honor of the good bishop, perhaps in recognition of Berkeley's poem *(On the Prospect of Planting Arts and Learning in America)*, which includes the line: "Westward the course of empire takes its way."

Berkeley agreed with Locke that all knowledge of the external world comes from experience, but he disagreed with Locke's distinction between primary and secondary qualities. Berkeley argued that there are no primary qualities at all. There are only what Locke called secondary qualities. To Berkeley, all knowledge was a function of the experiencing or perceiving person. The name given to his position some years later was *mentalism*, to denote Berkeley's emphasis on purely mental phenomena.

Berkeley argued that perception is the only reality of which we can be sure. We cannot know with certainty the nature of physical objects in the experiential world. All we can be sure of is how we perceive these objects. Because perception is within ourselves and thus subjective, it does not mirror the external world. To Berkeley, a physical object was nothing more than an accumulation of sensations experienced together, so that force of habit renders them associated in the human mind. The experiential world is the summation of our sensations.

There is, then, no material substance of which we can be certain, for if we take away the perception, the quality disappears. There can be no color, for instance, without the perception of color. Things exist only in being perceived.

Berkeley was not saying that real objects exist in the material world only when they are perceived. His thesis was that because all experience is within ourselves, relative to our own perception, we can never know with certainty the nature of real objects. We can know only our perception of them.

He recognized, however, that there was a certain degree of independence, consistency, and stability in the objects in the real world, and he had to find some way of accounting for this. He did so by invoking God. (He was, after all, a bishop.) God functioned as a kind of "permanent perceiver" of all the objects in the universe. A tree in an isolated forest could be said to exist and possess certain characteristics even if no one were there to perceive it, because God would always be perceiving it.

Berkeley used the theory of association to explain our knowledge of objects in the real world. This knowledge is essentially a construction or composition of simple ideas (the mental elements) held together by the mortar of association. Complex ideas are formed by the joining of simple ideas from various senses, as explained in this paragraph from Berkeley's *An Essay towards a New Theory of Vision*.

> *Sitting in my study I hear a coach drive along the street; I look through the casement and see it; I walk out and enter into it. Thus, common speech would incline one to think, I heard, saw, and touched the same thing, to wit, the coach. It is nevertheless certain the ideas intromitted by each sense are widely different, and distinct from each other; but, having been observed constantly to go together, they are spoken of as one and the same thing.*

Thus, the mind constructs complex ideas by fitting together the basic building blocks of the mind—the simple ideas. The mechanical analogy in the use of the words "construct" and "building blocks" is not coincidental.

Berkeley used the notion of association also to explain depth perception. In *An Essay towards a New Theory of Vision* he attacked the problem of how we perceive the third dimension of depth with a retina of only two dimensions. His answer was that we perceive the third dimension of depth as a result of experience, that is, through the recurring association of visual impressions with the sensations of touch and movement that occur in the ocular adjustments made when we look at objects at different distances, or in the bodily movements made in approaching or retreating from seen objects. In other words, the continuing sensory experiences of walking toward or reaching for objects, plus the sensations from the eye muscles, become associated to produce the perception of depth. For example, when an object is brought closer to the eyes, the pupils will turn inward, or converge. This convergence diminishes when the object is moved away. Thus, depth perception is not a simple sensory experience, but rather an association of ideas that must be learned.

Perhaps for the first time a purely psychological process was explained in terms of the association of sensations, and so Berkeley was continuing the growing associationist tradition in empiricism. His explanation fairly accurately anticipated the modern view of depth perception in that he discussed the important influences of the physiological cues of accommodation and convergence.

David Hume (1711–1776)

Hume, a philosopher and historian, studied law at the University of Edinburgh but did not graduate. He embarked on a career in business but found this not to his liking, so he lived on his small income during three years of self-study in philosophy in France. After returning to England, he published *A Treatise of Human Nature* (1739), his most important work for psychology. Other books followed, and he gained much fame as a writer while working as a tutor, companion, secretary, librarian, and judge–advocate in a military expedition. He was well received in Europe and held several posts in government.

Hume reemphasized Locke's notion of the compounding of simple ideas into complex ideas, developing and making more explicit the notion of association. He agreed with Berkeley on the nonexistence to the individual of the material world except when it is perceived, but took a further step. He abolished mind as a substance and said that it is a secondary quality like matter! The mind, too, is observable only through perception. Hume believed that mind is nothing more than the flow of ideas, sensations, memories, and the like.

Of greater importance to psychology, however, is the distinction he drew between two kinds of mental contents: *impressions* and *ideas.* Impressions are the basic elements of mental life and are akin to "sensation" and "perception" in today's terminology. Ideas are the mental experiences we have in the absence of any stimulating object; the modern equivalent is "image."

Hume did not define these two mental contents in physiological terms or in reference to any external stimulating object. He was careful not to assign any ultimate causes to impressions. These mental contents differ not in terms of their source or point of origin, but in terms of their relative strength or vivacity. Impressions are strong and vivid, whereas ideas are but weak copies of impressions.

Both of these mental contents may be simple or complex, and a simple idea resembles its simple impression. Complex ideas do not necessarily resemble any simple idea because complex ideas evolve from a combination of several simple ideas in some new pattern.

Complex ideas are compounded from simple ideas by association. Hume's laws of association are *resemblance* or similarity, and *contiguity* in time or place. The more similar and contiguous are two ideas, the more readily they will be associated.

Hume's work fits within the framework of the mechanistic spirit and continues the development of empiricism and associationism. He argued

Direct Philosophical Influences on Psychology

that just as astronomers had determined the laws and forces by which the heavenly bodies function, so it is possible to determine the laws of the mental universe. He believed that the laws of association of ideas were the mental counterpart of the law of gravity in the physical world, that is, a universal principle of the operation of the mind. Once again we see the notion that complex ideas are constructed mechanically by an amalgamation of simple ideas.

David Hartley
(1705–1757)

Hartley, the son of a minister, was preparing for a career in the church, but because of doctrinal difficulties, he turned to medicine instead. He led a quiet and uneventful life, practicing medicine and studying philosophy. In 1749 he published *Observations on Man, His Frame, His Duty, and His Expectations*, his most important work, often considered the first systematic discourse on associationism.

Hartley is important not so much for the originality of his work on associationism but for the great clarity and precision of his organization and systematization of previous work. The premises of associationism are certainly not new with Hartley, but he served the significant purpose of bringing together the earlier threads of thought. He is often acknowledged as the founder of associationism as a formal doctrine.

Hartley's fundamental law of association is *contiguity*, by which he attempted to explain memory, reasoning, emotion, and voluntary and involuntary action. Those ideas or sensations that occur together, either simultaneously or successively, become associated, so that an occurrence of one results in an occurrence of the other. Thus, repetition, in addition to contiguity, is necessary for the formation of associations.

Hartley agreed with Locke that all ideas and knowledge are derived from sensory experience; no associations are present at birth. As the child grows and accumulates a variety of sensory experiences, connections and trains of association of increasing complexity are established. In this way, higher systems of thought are developed by the time adulthood is reached. Thus, higher-order mental life may be analyzed or reduced to the elements or atoms from which it was formed through the mental compounding of associations. Hartley became the first to use the doctrine of association to explain all types of mental activity.

Like others before him, Hartley saw the world of the mind in mechanical terms. In one respect, however, he went beyond the aims of the earlier British empiricists and associationists. Not only did he explain the psychological processes in mechanical terms, but he also tried to explain the underlying physiological processes within the same sort of framework.

Newton had stated that impulses in the physical world are vibratory in

David Hartley (1705–1757) formalized the doctrine of associationism, which he used to explain all forms of mental activity.
(*National Library of Medicine*)

nature; Hartley used this principle to explain the operation of the brain and nervous system. Vibrations in the nerves (which he believed were solid, not hollow tubes as Descartes thought) transmit impulses from one part of the body to another. The vibrations in the nerves give rise to smaller vibrations in the brain, which Hartley considered to be the physiological

Direct Philosophical Influences on Psychology

counterparts of ideas. The importance of this notion for our purposes is not in the details of its operation, but in the fact that it was yet another attempt to use the principles of the mechanical universe as a model for understanding human nature.

James Mill (1773–1836)

James Mill was educated at Edinburgh and for a short time was a clergyman, but left the Church of Scotland to earn his livelihood as a writer. His writings were many and varied, and his most famous literary work is the *History of British India*, which took 11 years to write. His most important contribution to psychology is *Analysis of the Phenomena of the Human Mind*, which appeared in 1829.

Mill applied the notion of mechanism to the human mind with a directness and comprehensiveness not shown by his predecessors. His intention was to destroy the idea of subjective, psychical activities and to show that the mind was nothing more than a machine. Mill believed that others, in arguing that the mind was like a machine in its operations, had not gone far enough. The mind *was* a machine—it functioned in the same mechanical way as a clock functioned—set in operation by external physical forces and run by internal physical forces.

In Mill's view, the mind is totally passive; it is acted upon by external stimuli. The individual responds to these stimuli automatically and is incapable of acting spontaneously. Obviously, there is no freedom of the will. This point of view persists in the forms of psychology that have derived from the mechanistic spirit, notably contemporary behaviorism.

As the title of his major work suggests, Mill believed that the mind must be studied through its reduction or analysis into elementary components. This is, as we have seen, a strong tenet of the mechanistic spirit. To understand complex phenomena, be they in the mental or the physical world, it is necessary to break them down into the smallest parts. Mill wrote that "a distinct knowledge of the elements is indispensable to an accurate conception of that which is compounded of them" (1829, Vol. 1, p. 1).

He held that sensations and ideas are the only kinds of mental elements. Within the familiar empiricist–associationist tradition, all knowledge begins with sensations, from which are derived the higher-level complexes of ideas through the process of association. Association is a matter of contiguity or concurrence alone, and may be either synchronous or successive.

Mill believed that the mind has no creative function because association is a purely passive process. In other words, sensations that have occurred together in a certain order are mechanically reproduced as ideas, and these resulting ideas occur in the same order as their corresponding sensations. Association was treated in mechanistic terms, and the resulting ideas were merely the accumulation or sum of the individual elements.

CONTRIBUTIONS OF EMPIRICISM TO PSYCHOLOGY

With the development of empiricism, philosophy was turning away from its traditions of rationalism and dogmatism. It was still concerned with many of the same problems, but its method of attacking these problems had become empirical, atomistic, and mechanistic.

Consider again the emphases of empiricism: the primary role of the processes of sensation; the analysis of conscious experience into elements; the synthesis of elements to form more complex mental experiences through the mechanism of association; and the focus on conscious processes. The major role empiricism played in shaping the new scientific psychology will soon be evident, for we will see that the areas stressed by empiricism form the basic subject matter of psychology.

By the mid-nineteenth century, when psychology was on the verge of becoming a science, its philosophical anticipators had become empirical in both subject matter and method. Philosophy had done all it could; the theoretical rationale for a natural science of human nature had been established. What was needed to translate the theory into actuality was an experimental attack on the subject matter. And that was soon to develop under the influence of experimental physiology, which provided the kinds of experimentation that laid the foundation for the new psychology.

SUGGESTED READINGS

MIND–BODY PROBLEM

Feigl, H. Mind–body, *not* a pseudo problem. In S. Hood (Ed.) *Dimensions of mind.* New York: New York University Press, 1960. Pp. 24–36.

McDougall, W. *Body and mind.* New York: Macmillan, 1911. (Paperback edition, Boston: Beacon Press, 1961.)

Reeves, W. *Body and mind in Western thought.* Baltimore: Penguin, 1958.

Scher, J. M. (Ed.). *Theories of the mind.* New York: Free Press, 1962.

THE DEVELOPMENT OF SCIENCE

Butterfield, H. *The origins of modern science: 1300–1800.* New York: Macmillan, 1959.

Hall, A. R. *The scientific revolution: 1500–1800.* Boston: Beacon Press, 1956.

Sarton, G. *Six wings: Men of science in the Renaissance.* Bloomington: Indiana University Press, 1957.

Whitehead, A. N. *Science and the modern world.* New York: Macmillan, 1925.

THE MECHANISTIC PHILOSOPHY

Crombie, A. C. Early concepts of the senses and the mind. *Scientific American,* 1964, *210,* 108–116.

Hall, A. R. *From Galileo to Newton: 1630–1720.* London: Collins, 1963.

Jaynes, J. The problem of animate motion in the seventeenth century. *Journal of the History of Ideas,* 1970, *31,* 219–234.

Lowry, R. *The evolution of psychological theory: 1650 to the present.* Chicago: Aldine-Atherton, 1971. Chapters 1–4.

Matson, F. W. *The broken image.* New York: Braziller, 1964. Chapters 1–3.

Toulmin, S., & Goodfield, J. *The architecture of matter.* New York: Harper, 1962.

DESCARTES

Balz, A. G. A. *Descartes and the modern mind.* New Haven, Conn.: Yale University Press, 1952.

Fearing, F. René Descartes: A study in the history of the theories of reflex action. *Psychological Review,* 1929, *36,* 375–388.

Pirenne, M. H. Descartes and the body–mind problem in physiology. *British Journal of the Philosophy of Science,* 1950, *1,* 43–59.

Vrooman, J. *René Descartes: A biography.* New York: Putnam, 1970.

ASSOCIATIONISM AND THE
DEVELOPMENT OF
PSYCHOLOGY

Bricke, J. Hume's associationist psychology. *Journal of the History of the Behavioral Sciences,* 1974, *10,* 397–409.

Drever, J. The historical background for national trends in psychology: On non-existence of English Associationism. *Journal of the History of the Behavioral Sciences,* 1965, *1,* 123–130.

Miller, E. F. Hume's contribution to behavioral science. *Journal of the History of the Behavioral Sciences,* 1971, *7,* 154–168.

Misiak, H. *The philosophical roots of scientific psychology.* New York: Fordham University Press, 1961.

Oberg, B. B. David Hartley and the association of ideas. *Journal of the History of Ideas,* 1976, *37,* 441–454.

Rasmussen, E. T. Berkeley and modern psychology. *British Journal for the Philosophy of Science,* 1953, *4,* 2–12.

Warren, H. C. Mental association from Plato to Hume. *Psychological Review,* 1916, *23,* 208–230.

PHYSIOLOGICAL INFLUENCES ON PSYCHOLOGY

INTRODUCTION

It all started with a difference of five-tenths of a second in the observations made by two astronomers. The year was 1795. The royal astronomer of England, Nicholas Maskelyne, noticed that his assistant's observations of the time it took for a star to pass from one point to another were always slower than his own. Maskelyne admonished the man for making repeated mistakes and warned him to be more careful. The assistant tried, but the differences persisted. In time they increased, and five months later his observations were eight-tenths of a second slower than Maskelyne's. As a result the assistant was fired, and passed into that crowded place known as obscurity.

For the next 20 years the incident was ignored, until the phenomenon was investigated by F. W. Bessel, a German astronomer, who had long been interested in errors of measurement. He suspected that the mistakes made by Maskelyne's assistant were attributable to individual differences, over which one has no control. If this supposition were correct, Bessel reasoned, then such differences in observation would be found among all astronomers. He tested the hypothesis and found it to be correct: differences were common, even among the most experienced and famous of astronomers.

This finding was important because it pointed to two inexorable conclusions. First, it meant that astronomy would have to take into account the nature of the human observer because personal characteristics could influence the observations reported. Second, if the role of the human observer had to be considered in astronomy, then surely it would also have to be considered in every other science in which human observers were employed.

We described how philosophers such as Locke and Berkeley discussed the subjective nature of perception, arguing that there is not always, or even often, an exact correspondence between the nature of an object and an individual's perception of it. Here we have data from a hard science— astronomy—to demonstrate the same thing.

Scientists now had to focus on the role of the human observer and the nature of the process of observation to account fully for their results. It was this "methodological problem in astronomy that convinced the scientific community that their knowledge of the physical world would not be complete without an understanding of the mental processes through which the scientist was able to make his observations" (Kirsch, 1976, p. 120).

Science was forced to turn to the study of sensing and perceiving—psychological processes—through the study of the sense organs, those physiological mechanisms whereby we receive information about the world. And so the early physiologists began to investigate the process of sensation. Psychology was but a short and inevitable step away.

DEVELOPMENTS IN EARLY PHYSIOLOGY: AN OVERVIEW

The physiological research that directly stimulated and guided the new psychology was a product of the late nineteenth century. As with all endeavors, it had its antecedents, and it is instructive to consider briefly some of the earlier work in physiology.

Physiology became an experimentally oriented discipline during the 1830s, primarily under the influence of Johannes Müller (1801–1858), who strongly advocated the application of the experimental method to physiology. Müller wrote a *Handbook of Physiology*, which summarized the physiological research of the period and contained a large body of knowledge. The publication of revisions between 1833 and 1840, citing much new work, indicates how prolific research in experimental physiology had become. The need for such a book was reflected in the rapid translation into English of the first volume in 1838 and the second in 1842.

Müller is also of great importance to both physiology and psychology for his doctrine of the *specific energies of nerves*. The doctrine states that the arousal or stimulation of a given nerve always gives rise to a characteristic sensation because each sensory nerve has its own specific energy. This idea stimulated a great deal of research that sought to localize functions within the nervous system and to delimit sensory receptor mechanisms on the periphery of the organism.

Several early physiologists made substantial contributions to the study of brain functions. Their work is of importance to psychology because of their discoveries of specialized areas of the brain and the development of research methods that became widely used in later physiological psychology.

A pioneer in the investigation of *reflex behavior* was Marshall Hall (1790–1857), who observed that decapitated animals continued to move for some time when subjected to appropriate forms of stimulation. Hall concluded that various levels of behavior depend on different parts of the brain and nervous system. Specifically, he postulated that voluntary movement depends on the cerebrum, reflex movement on the spinal cord, involuntary movement on direct stimulation of the musculature, and respiratory movement on the medulla.

Pierre Flourens (1794–1867), in extending Hall's animal research, systematically destroyed various parts of the brain and spinal cord and observed the consequences. He concluded that the cerebrum controls the higher mental processes, parts of the midbrain control visual and auditory reflexes, the cerebellum controls coordination, and the medulla governs heartbeat, respiration, and other vital functions.

The findings of Hall and Flourens, though still generally valid, are for our purposes second in importance to their introduction of the method of *extirpation*. This technique essentially consists of investigating the function of a given part of the brain by removing or destroying it and observing the resulting changes in the animal's behavior.

In the middle of the nineteenth century two experimental approaches to the study of the brain were introduced. The *clinical method* was developed in 1861 by Paul Broca, who performed an autopsy on a man who had been unable to speak intelligibly for many years. The autopsy revealed a lesion in the third frontal convolution of the cerebral cortex. Broca labeled this section of the brain the speech center (since called, appropriately enough, Broca's area).

The clinical method has become a useful supplement to study by extirpation because it is somewhat difficult to secure human subjects who will agree to removal of part of the brain. As a sort of posthumous extirpation, the clinical method provides the opportunity of finding the damaged brain area assumed to be responsible for a behavioral condition that existed before the patient died.

The other experimental approach to brain study was *electrical stimulation*, introduced by G. Fritsch and E. Hitzig in 1870. As its name suggests, the method involves the exploration of the cerebral cortex with weak electric currents. Fritsch and Hitzig found that stimulating certain cortical areas resulted in motor responses. With the development of more sophisticated and precise electronic equipment, the method of electrical stimulation has become probably the single most productive technique for studying the functions of the brain.

Much was being learned, then, about the structure and functions of the human brain. Considerable research on the structure of the nervous system and the nature of neural activity was also conducted. As we have noted, there were two earlier theories about how nervous activity was transmitted in the body—the nerve tube theory embraced by Descartes, and Hartley's theory of vibrations.

Toward the end of the eighteenth century the Italian researcher Luigi Galvani had suggested that the nature of nerve impulses was electrical. Research in this area proceeded so rapidly and convincingly that before the middle of the nineteenth century this was accepted as fact. It was believed that the nervous system was essentially a conductor of electrical impulses and that the central nervous system functioned much like a switching station, shunting the impulses onto either sensory or motor nerve fibers.

Although this position was a great advance beyond the models of Descartes and Hartley, it was conceptually very similar, as Lowry (1971) points out. Both the newer and older points of view were reflexive in nature. Something from the external world (a stimulus) impinged on a sense organ and excited a nervous impulse that traveled to the appropriate place in the brain or central nervous system. There, in response to the impulse, a new impulse was generated and transmitted via the motor nerves to effect some response by the organism.

The anatomical structure of the nervous system was also being defined during the nineteenth century. It came to be understood that the nerve fibers were actually composed of separate structures—neurons—somehow joined together at synapses.

Such findings were congruent with a mechanistic and materialistic image of human beings. It was believed that the nervous system, like the mind, was composed of atomistic structures that, when combined, produced a more complex product.

The spirit of mechanism was just as dominant in the physiology of the nineteenth century as it was in the philosophy of that time. Nowhere was this more pronounced than in Germany. In the 1840s a group of scientists, many of them former students of Johannes Müller, formed the Berlin Physical Society. The scientists, all in their twenties, were committed to one overriding proposition: the belief that all phenomena, including those that pertained to living matter, could be accounted for in physical terms. What they hoped to do was to relate or connect physiology with physics. A physiology consonant with the spirit of mechanism was their goal.

In a dramatic gesture four of the young scientists (including Helmholtz, whom we will meet shortly) made a solemn oath—signing it in their own blood, according to legend—stating that the only forces active within the organism are the common physical–chemical ones. Materialism, mechanism, empiricism, experimentation, measurement—these forces formed the core of physiology by the mid-nineteenth century.

The developments in early physiology indicate the kinds of research techniques and discoveries that supported a scientific approach to the psychological investigation of the mind. We have suggested how the direction of research in physiology influenced the newly emerging psychology. The major point is that while philosophy was paving the way for an experimental attack on the mind, physiology was experimentally investigating the physiological mechanisms underlying mental phenomena. The next step was to apply the experimental method to the mind itself.

The British empiricists had argued that sensation is the only source of all our knowledge. The astronomer Bessel had demonstrated the importance of sensation and perception in science itself. Physiologists were defining the structure and function of the senses. It was time to experiment with and quantify this "doorway to the mind," the subjective, mentalistic experience of sensation. Techniques were available to investigate the body; now they were being developed to explore the mind. Experimental psychology was ready to begin.

THE BEGINNINGS OF EXPERIMENTAL PSYCHOLOGY

Four men are directly responsible for the initial applications of the experimental method to the subject matter of psychology: Hermann von Helmholtz, Ernst Weber, Gustav Theodor Fechner, Wilhelm Wundt. All four were German, well trained in physiology, and aware of the impressive developments in physiology and science in general in the middle of the nineteenth century.

Why Germany?

Scientific thought was developing in most of the countries of Western Europe in the nineteenth century, particularly in England, France, and Germany. No one country had a monopoly on the enthusiasm, conscientiousness, or optimism with which the tools of science were viewed and used. Why, then, did experimental psychology begin in Germany and not in France or England? Were there some unique characteristics that made German science a more fertile breeding ground for the new psychology?

Although generalizations may be suspect and exceptions to the rule frequently found, it can nonetheless be suggested that the times favored Germany as the point of origin for the new psychology. For a century German intellectual history had paved the way for an experimental science of psychology. Experimental physiology was firmly established and was recognized to a degree not yet achieved in France and England. There were very good reasons for this. The so-called German temperament was well suited to the careful and minute taxonomic description and classification needed for work in biology, zoology, and physiology. Whereas the deductive and mathematical approach to science was favored in France and England, Germany, with its emphasis on conscientious, thorough, and careful collection of observable facts, had adopted a classificatory or inductive approach.

Because biological and physiological science does not lend itself to grand generalizations from which facts can be deduced, biology was only slowly accepted into the scientific communities of France and England. Germany, however, with its interest and faith in description and categorization, welcomed biology to its family of sciences.

Further, the Germans construed science very broadly. Science in France and Britain was limited to physics and chemistry (which could be approached quantitatively), but science in Germany included a variety of areas—phonetics, philology, history, archeology, esthetics, logic, and the critical analysis of literature.

The French and British were skeptical about using science to study something as complex as the human mind. Not so the Germans, and they plunged ahead, unconstrained by prejudgments, using the tools of science to explore and measure the mind.

There was another, more prosaic, reason why the new psychology began in Germany—a matter of opportunity. As MacLeod (1975) reminds us, there were many more universities in Germany than in France or England. This meant that there were more positions for those interested in science. The chances of becoming a well-paid and respected professor were much higher in Germany, although it was difficult to attain such a position. The promising university scientist in Germany was required to produce research judged to be a major contribution by experts in the field, research that went beyond the usual doctoral dissertation. This meant that most of those admitted to a university career were of extremely high caliber. Once these scientists joined the university community, the pressure on them to produce something new, to make even greater contributions, was keen.

Thus, although the competition was intense and the pressure high, the rewards were more than worth the effort. Only the best succeeded in German science of the nineteenth century. The result was a series of advances in all the sciences, the new psychology included. It is no coincidence that the men who were directly responsible for the emergence of the new psychology were university professors.

Hermann von Helmholtz
(1821–1894)

Helmholtz, a prolific researcher in physics and physiology, was one of the greatest scientists of the nineteenth century. Psychology ranked third among his areas of scientific contribution, yet, together with the efforts of Fechner and Wundt, his work was instrumental in beginning the new psychology.

The Life of Helmholtz

Born in Potsdam, Germany, where his father taught in the *gymnasium*,[1] Helmholtz was initially tutored at home because of his delicate health. At the age of 17 he entered a Berlin medical institute where no tuition was charged to those who agreed to serve as surgeons in the army after graduation. Helmholtz served for seven years, during which time he continued his studies in mathematics and physics, published several articles, and presented a paper on the indestructibility of energy in which he

---

[1] In Europe, a high school–junior college preparatory for the university.

The work of the great physicist-physiologist Hermann von Helmholtz (1821–1894) on nerve conduction, color vision, and audition had a major influence on sensory psychology. *(Archives of the History of American Psychology)*

mathematically formulated the law of conservation of energy. After leaving the army, Helmholtz accepted a position as associate professor of physiology at Königsberg. For the next 30 years he held academic appointments in physiology at Bonn and Heidelberg, and in physics at Berlin.

The tremendously energetic Helmholtz published in several different areas. In the course of his work in physiological optics he invented the ophthalmoscope. His three-volume work *Physiological Optics* (1856–1866) was so influential and enduring that it was translated into English 60 years later. His research on acoustical problems resulted in the publication in 1863 of *On the Sensations of Tone*, which summarized his own research as well as the entire available literature. He also published on such diverse subjects as afterimages, color blindness, the Arabian–Persian musical scale, the form of the horopter (a curved surface in the visual field), human eye movements, the regulation of ice, geometrical axioms, and hay fever! In later years he contributed indirectly to the founding of wireless telegraphy and radio. In the fall of 1893, while returning from the Chicago World's Fair and visits to other parts of the United States, Helmholtz suffered a severe fall aboard ship. He never fully recovered his health and died 11 months later.

The Contributions of Helmholtz

Of interest to psychology are Helmholtz's investigations of the speed of the neural impulse, vision, and audition.

Before Helmholtz, it was thought that the speed of the neural impulse was instantaneous, or at least was too fast to be measured. Helmholtz provided the first empirical measurement of the rate of conduction by stimulating a motor nerve and the attached muscle from the leg of a frog (the nerve–muscle preparation), arranged so that the precise moment of stimulation, as well as the resulting movement, could be recorded. Working with different lengths of nerve, he recorded the delay between stimulation of the nerve near the muscle and the muscle's reaction, and then did the same for stimulation farther from the muscle. These measurements gave him the time taken for conduction. His results yielded the modest rate of 90 feet per second.

He also experimented on the reaction time for sensory nerves of human subjects, studying the complete circuit from stimulation of a sense organ to the resulting motor response. His findings showed such enormous differences between individuals and from one trial to the next with the same subject that he abandoned the research altogether.

Helmholtz's demonstrations that the speed of conduction was not instantaneous suggested that thought and movement follow one another at a measurable interval and do not occur simultaneously, as had previously been thought. Helmholtz, however, was interested only in the sheer speed of the nerve impulse and not in its psychological significance. Later, the psychological implications of his research were recognized by others, who went on to make reaction-time experiments a fruitful line of research in the new psychology. Helmholtz's research was one of the first demonstrations that it was possible to experiment on and measure a psychophysiological process.

Helmholtz's work on vision has had a profound influence. In addition to working on the external eye muscles and the mechanism by which the lenses are focused by the internal eye muscles, Helmholtz extended a theory of color vision originally published in 1802 by Thomas Young, which has since become known as the Young–Helmholtz theory of color vision. No less important is his work on audition, including perception of combination tones and individual tones, the nature of harmony and discord, and his resonance theory of hearing. The lasting influence of his theories of vision and hearing is attested to by their continued inclusion in modern textbooks of psychology.

Comment

Helmholtz was not a psychologist, nor were psychological problems his main interest, but he contributed a large and important body of knowledge to sensory psychology and helped to strengthen the newly developing experimental approach to the study of psychological problems. He considered psychology to be a separate discipline, allied to metaphysics. The psychology of the senses was an exception, as far as Helmholtz was concerned, because of its close association with physiology. He was not really involved (or concerned) with the establishment of psychology as an independent science, yet his influence was of such magnitude that he must be included among the direct contributors to the new science.

Ernst Weber (1795–1878)

Weber, the son of a theology professor, was born in Wittenberg, Germany. He received his doctorate at the University of Leipzig in 1815, and taught anatomy and physiology there from 1817 until his retirement in 1871. His primary research interest was the physiology of the sense organs, an area in which he made outstanding and lasting contributions.

Previous research on the sense organs had been confined almost exclusively to the higher senses of vision and audition. Weber's work consisted largely of exploring new fields, notably cutaneous and muscular sensations. He is particularly noteworthy for his brilliant application of the experimental methods of physiology to problems of a psychological nature. His experiments on the sense of touch mark a fundamental shift in the status of the subject matter of psychology. The ties with philosophy were, if not severed, at least severely weakened. Weber allied psychology with the natural sciences and helped to pave the way for the use of experimental investigation in the study of the mind.

The Two-Point Threshold

One of Weber's two major contributions to the new psychology involved his experimental determination of the accuracy of the two-point discrimination of the skin—the distance between two points that is necessary before

The experimental investigation of threshold perception by Ernst Weber (1795–1878) led to the formulation of the first quantitative law of psychology. *(National Library of Medicine)*

subjects report two distinct sensations. Without the use of vision, subjects are asked to report whether they feel one or two points touching the skin. When the two points of stimulation are close, subjects report a clear sensation of being touched at only one point. As the distance between the two sources of stimulation is increased, using an apparatus resembling a drawing compass, subjects report uncertainty as to whether they feel one or two sensations. Finally, a distance is reached where subjects report two distinct points of stimulation. Thus, a threshold is demonstrated at which the two points can be discriminated as such—the two-point threshold. Weber's research marks the first systematic, experimental demonstration of the concept of threshold, a concept widely used in the new psychology from its beginnings to the present day.

In additional research Weber demonstrated that this two-point threshold varies both in different parts of the body of the same subject, and from one subject to another for a given region of the body. Although his attempt to account for these findings by hypothesizing "sensory circles" (areas in which doubleness is not perceived) has diminished in importance, his experimental method remains of permanent significance.

The Just Noticeable
Difference

Weber's second and more significant contribution eventually led to the statement of the first truly quantitative law of psychology. He wanted to determine the smallest difference between weights—the just noticeable difference—that could be discriminated. To do so, he had subjects lift two weights, a standard and a comparison weight, and report whether one felt heavier than the other. Small differences between the weights resulted in judgments of sameness; large differences resulted in judgments of disparity between the weights. As the research progressed, Weber found that the just noticeable difference between two weights is a constant ratio, 1:40, of the standard weight. For example, a weight of 41 grams is reported as just noticeably different from a standard weight of 40 grams, an 82-gram weight just noticeably different from a standard weight of 80 grams.

Weber then undertook to investigate the contributions of muscular sensations in the discrimination of weights of differing magnitudes. He found that subjects could discriminate much more accurately when the weights to be judged were lifted by the subjects rather than simply placed in their hands. In lifting the weights, both tactile and muscular sensations are operative, whereas when the weight is placed in the hand, only tactile sensations are experienced. Because smaller differences in weight could be discriminated when the weights were lifted (a ratio of 1:40, as already noted) as compared to when the weights were placed in the hand (a ratio of 1:30 being necessary), Weber concluded that the internal muscle sense influenced discrimination.

From these experiments, Weber found that discrimination seemed to depend not on the absolute difference between two weights, but on the relative difference or the ratio of one to another. The just noticeable difference between two stimuli can then be stated as a fraction that is constant for a given sense modality. Weber conducted experiments involving

Physiological Influences on Psychology

visual discrimination and found that the fraction was smaller than it was with the muscle sense experiments. From this he suggested that there is a constant fraction for just noticeable differences for each of the senses.

Weber's experiments demonstrated that there is no direct one-to-one correspondence between the physical stimulus and the perception of it. However, like Helmholtz, Weber was concerned with physiological processes, so he did not appreciate the significance of his work for psychology. What his research revealed was a way of investigating the relationship between body and mind, between the stimulus and the resulting sensation. This was indeed a major breakthrough; all that was necessary was for someone to realize its significance.

Weber's research was experimental in the strictest sense of the term. Under well-controlled conditions, he systematically varied the stimuli and recorded the differential effects on the reported experience of the subject. His experiments stimulated a great deal of research and served to focus the attention of subsequent physiologists on the validity and importance of the experiment as a means of studying psychological phenomena. Weber's work on threshold measurement was to be of paramount importance to the new psychology, and his demonstration that sensations can be measured has influenced virtually every aspect of psychology to the present day.

Gustav Theodor Fechner
(1801–1887)

Fechner was a scholar whose remarkably diverse intellectual pursuits ranged over an active career of more than 70 years. Consider the scope of interests of this man, who was a physiologist for 7 years, a physicist for 15, an invalid for 12, a psychophysicist for 14, an experimental estheticist for 11, and a philosopher for about 40 years (Boring, 1950b). Of these endeavors, it is the work on psychophysics that brought him his greatest fame, even though he did not wish to be remembered by posterity as a psychophysicist. "The world, however, chose for him; it seized upon the psychophysical experiments, which Fechner meant merely as contributory to his philosophy, and made them into an experimental psychology" (Boring, 1950b, p. 276).

The Life of Fechner

Fechner was born in a small village in southeastern Germany where his father was the minister. He began medical studies at the University of Leipzig in 1817 at the age of 16, and remained at Leipzig for the rest of his life.

Even before he graduated from medical school, the humanistic side of Fechner showed signs of rebellion against the prevailing materialism of his scientific training. Under the pen name "Dr. Mises" he wrote satirical essays lampooning medicine and science, a practice that he continued over the next 25 years, suggesting the persistent conflict between these two sides of his personality—a love of science and the metaphysical. His first such essay, *Proof That the Moon Is Made of Iodine*,[2] attacked the then current medical fad of the use of iodine as a panacea. He was troubled by materialism and strove to establish his "day view," that the universe can be regarded from the point of view of consciousness, in opposition to what he called the "night view," which held that the universe, including consciousness, was inert matter.

After completing his medical studies, Fechner began a second career in physics and mathematics at Leipzig, during which time he translated French handbooks of physics and chemistry into German. By 1830 he had translated more than a dozen volumes, which served to gain him some recognition as a physicist. In 1824 he had begun lecturing in physics at Leipzig and conducting research of his own. By the late 1830s he had developed an interest in sensation and seriously injured his eyes by looking at the sun through colored glasses while studying afterimages.

In 1833, after many years of hard work, Fechner obtained the prestigious appointment of professor at Leipzig, whereupon he suffered a severe collapse that lasted for several years. He became extremely depressed, had difficulty sleeping, could not digest food (yet he felt no hunger and approached a state of starvation), and was unusually sensitive to light. He had to spend most of his time in a darkened room whose walls were painted black, listening while his mother read to him through a narrow opening in the door.

According to Ellenberger (1970), Fechner's illness was neurotic in nature, a suggestion that is supported by the bizarre way in which he was eventually cured. A friend dreamed that she had made him a meal of spiced raw ham soaked in Rhine wine and lemon juice. The next day she prepared the dish and brought it to Fechner, insisting that he eat it. He did, albeit reluctantly, and began to eat more and more of the meat every day, which caused him to feel somewhat better.

Then he had a dream in which the number 77 appeared. This convinced him that he would be completely cured in 77 days. And of course he was! He felt so well that his depression turned to euphoria and delusions of grandeur, and he claimed that God had chosen him to solve all the riddles in the world. Out of that delusional experience he developed the pleasure principle, a notion that was to influence Sigmund Freud many years later.

In 1844 Fechner was given a small pension from the university and thus was officially established as an invalid. Yet not one of the next 43 years of his life passed without a serious contribution from him, and his health remained excellent until his death at the age of 86.

---

[2] Several texts claim that this essay is entitled *Proof That* Man *Is Made of Iodine*. The original title in German is *Beweis dass der Mond aus Iodine bestehe*.

Physiological Influences on Psychology

The Contributions of
Fechner: Quantitative
Relationship Between Mind
and Body

The many hours Fechner spent in meditation and reflection deepened his religious awareness and concern with the problem of the soul. He turned to philosophy and began to direct the full force of his genius toward the question of the relationship between the mind and the body. He decided

By demonstrating that the amount of sensation depends on the amount of stimulation, Gustav Theodor Fechner (1801–1887) proved that the mental and material worlds could be related quantitatively. *(National Library of Medicine)*

that the two are identical; both are aspects of the same fundamental unity. They are related to each other as the inside of a circle is related to the outside. The apparent difference between the two, Fechner said, is merely the result of the way in which they are viewed. Fechner's fame, however, comes from his psychophysics, not his philosophy; his attempt to verify his philosophical views empirically is a milestone in the history of psychology.

On the morning of October 22, 1850—an important date in the history of psychology—Fechner had an insight that the law of the connection between mind and body can be found in a statement of quantitative relation between mental sensation and material stimulus. An increase in the intensity of a stimulus, he said, does not produce a one-to-one increase in the intensity of the sensation. Rather, a geometric series characterizes the stimulus, whereas an arithmetic series characterizes the sensation. For instance, adding the sound of one bell to that of an already ringing bell produces a greater increase in sensation than adding one bell to ten others already ringing. The effects of stimulus intensities are not absolute, but are relative to the amount of sensation already existing.

What this simple, yet brilliant, revelation pointed out was that the amount of sensation (the mental quality) depends on the amount of stimulation (the physical quality). To measure the change in sensation, one must measure the change in stimulation. Therefore, it is possible to relate the two worlds— mental and material—quantitatively. Fechner crossed the barrier between body and mind, or at least caused it to disappear, by relating one to the other empirically.

Although the concept was clear, how was it to be translated into actuality? One would have to measure precisely both intensities, the subjective and the objective, the mental sensation and the physical stimulus. To measure the physical intensity, the stimulus, is not difficult, but how does one measure sensation—the experience of consciousness that subjects report when they respond to a stimulus?

Fechner believed that there were two ways to measure sensations. First, he said, we can determine whether a stimulus is present or absent, sensed or not sensed. Then we can measure the stimulus intensity at which subjects report that sensation first occurs. What is being measured in this case is the *absolute threshold* of sensitivity, that point in stimulus intensity below which no sensation is reported, and above which subjects do experience a sensation.[3]

This measurement, though useful, is limited. It is possible to determine only one value of a sensation—its lowest level. To relate both intensities, we must be able to specify the full range of stimulus values and their resulting sensation values.

To accomplish this, Fechner proposed the use of the *differential threshold* of

---

[3] This is not the first use of the concept of threshold. Weber, as noted, used it, and earlier in the nineteenth century the German philosopher Herbart also discussed the idea (Chapter 13).

sensitivity—the least amount of change in a stimulus that will give rise to a change in sensation. For example, by how much must a weight be increased in heaviness before subjects will sense the change, before they will report a just noticeable difference in sensation?

To measure how heavy a particular weight appears to human subjects— how heavy it "feels"—we cannot use the physical measurement of the weight of the object. We can, however, use that physical measurement as a basis for measuring the psychological intensity of the sensation. First we measure by how much the weight must be decreased in intensity before subjects are barely able to discriminate the difference. Then the weight of the object is changed to this lower value and the size of the difference threshold measured again. Because both weight changes are just barely noticeable, Fechner assumed that they were subjectively equal. This process can be repeated until the object is barely felt by the subjects. If every decrement in weight is subjectively equal to every other decrement, the number of times the weight has to be decreased—that is, the number of just noticeable differences—can be used as an objective measure of the subjective magnitude of the sensation. In this way, we are measuring the stimulus values necessary to give rise to a difference between two sensations.

Fechner suggested that for each sense modality there is a certain relative increase in the stimulus that always produces an observable change in the intensity of the sensation. Thus, the sensation (the mind quality) as well as the excitatory stimulus (the body or material quality) can be measured and the relationship between the two stated in the form of an equation: $S = K \log R$, in which S is the magnitude of the sensation, K is a constant, and R is the magnitude of the stimulus. The relationship is logarithmic; one series increases arithmetically and the other geometrically.

Fechner wrote that this notion was not suggested by a knowledge of Weber's work (with which it is consonant), even though Weber was also at Leipzig and had written about this matter only four years earlier. Heidbreder (1933) noted that Fechner did not discover Weber's work until after he had begun the series of experiments designed to test his hypothesis. Fechner later realized that his principle was essentially what Weber's work had demonstrated, and he gave mathematical form to the relationship.

Methods of Psychophysics

The immediate result of Fechner's insight was the development of a program of research on what he later called *psychophysics*. (The word defines itself— psycho–physics, the relationship between the mind and the material world.) In the course of this research, with its classic experiments on lifted weights, visual brightness, and tactile and visual distances, Fechner developed one and systematized two of the three fundamental methods of psychophysics that are still used today—the method of average error, the method of constant stimuli, and the method of limits.

Fechner developed the method of average error (also called the method of

The Beginnings of Experimental Psychology

adjustment) in cooperation with A. W. Volkmann, a professor of physiology at the University of Halle in Germany. It consists in having subjects adjust a variable stimulus until they perceive it to be equal to a constant standard stimulus. Over a number of trials, the mean value of the differences between the standard stimulus and the subjects' setting of the variable stimulus represents the error of observation. The method assumes that our sense organs are subject to variability, which prevents the obtaining of a true measure. Accordingly, we obtain a large number of approximate measures, the mean of which represents the best single approximation that can be made of the true value. The technique is useful for measuring reaction time, visual and auditory discriminations, and the extent of illusions. In an extended form it is fundamental to much current psychological research. Every time we calculate a mean we are, in essence, using the method of average error.

The method of constant stimuli, first called the method of right and wrong cases, was originated by Karl von Vierordt, a physiologist, in 1852, but developed as a tool by Fechner. It was used for his elaborate work with lifted weights, research which consisted of more than 67,000 comparisons. The technique involves two constant stimuli and the aim is to measure the stimulus difference that is required to produce a given proportion of "right" judgments. For example, subjects first lift the standard weight of 100 grams and then lift a comparison weight of, say, 88, 92, 96, 104, or 108 grams. They must judge whether the second weight is heavier, lighter, or equal to the first. The procedure is continued until a certain number of judgments have been made for each comparison. For the heavier weights, subjects almost always report a judgment of "heavier," and the lightest weights almost always are reported as "lighter." From these data, the stimulus difference (standard versus comparison weights) is determined for that point at which subjects correctly report "heavier" 75 percent of the time. A number of variations of the basic procedure render the technique useful for a range of measurement problems in the determination of sensory thresholds and in aptitude measurement.

The third of Fechner's psychophysical methods was originally known as the method of just noticeable differences, and later came to be called the method of limits. The technique has been traced back to 1700, and was formalized by C. Delezenne in 1827. Weber also used the method of just noticeable differences, as we have noted, but it was given more formal development by Fechner in connection with his work on vision and temperature sensations. The method involves presenting two stimuli and increasing or diminishing one of them until subjects report that they detect a difference. Fechner recommended starting the variable stimulus at an intensity clearly higher than the standard stimulus at one time, and clearly lower than the standard the next time. Data from a number of such trials are obtained, and the just noticeable differences are averaged to determine the differential threshold. A variation, using a single stimulus presented in the ascending and descending approaches, is used to determine the absolute threshold.

Comment

Fechner carried on his research for seven years, publishing part of it for the first time in two short papers in 1858 and 1859. In 1860 the formal and complete exposition of his work appeared in the *Elemente der Psychophysik* (*Elements of Psychophysics*), a text of the exact science "of the functionally dependent relations . . . of the material and the mental, of the physical and psychological worlds" (1966, p. 7). The book is considered one of the outstanding original contributions to the development of the science of psychology.

Fechner failed in his attempt to found a philosophy on exact science, and his research findings have not withstood later criticism. At the time, however, Fechner's statement of the quantitative relationship between stimulus intensity and sensation was considered comparable to Galileo's discovery of the laws of the lever and of falling bodies (Müller-Freienfels, 1935). Fechner's efforts made it possible, for the first time, to measure the impalpable mind—a truly remarkable breakthrough.

At the beginning of the nineteenth century the German philosopher Immanuel Kant had insisted that psychology could never become a science because it was impossible to experiment on or measure psychological phenomena and processes. Because of Fechner's work, such an assertion could no longer be regarded seriously.

It was largely because of Fechner's psychophysical research that Wilhelm Wundt conceived the plan of his experimental psychology. More important, Fechner's methods have proved applicable to a wider range of psychological problems than Fechner ever imagined, and, with only minor modifications, these methods are still in use in psychological research. Boring (1950b) commented that without Fechner there would have been

> little of the breath of science in the experimental body, for we hardly recognize a subject as scientific if measurement is not one of its tools. Fechner, because of what he did and the time at which he did it, set experimental quantitative psychology off upon the course which it has followed. (pp. 294–295)

Although Weber's work preceded Fechner's, accolades have been heaped upon the latter. Fechner seems to have used and built upon Weber's work, but he did much more than extend it. Weber's aims were limited; he was a physiologist working on just noticeable differences. The larger significance of this work escaped him. As R. I. Watson (1978) noted, Weber was an "eventful" man, whereas Fechner was an "event-making" man. Fechner sought a mathematical statement of the relationship between the physical and the spiritual worlds. His brilliant and independent insights about measuring sensations and relating them to their stimulus measures were necessary before the implications and consequences of Weber's earlier work could be recognized and applied to make psychology an exact science.

THE FORMAL "FOUNDING" OF THE NEW SCIENCE

By the mid-nineteenth century the methods of natural science were being applied to purely mental phenomena. Techniques and methods of investigation had been developed, apparatus devised, important books written, and widespread interest aroused. British empiricism and the work in astronomy emphasized the importance of the senses, and the German scientists were describing how the senses worked. The positivistic spirit of the times encouraged the convergence of these two lines of thought. Still lacking, however, was someone to bring them together, in a word, to "found" the new science. This final touch was provided by Wilhelm Wundt.

Wundt is the "founder" of psychology as a formal academic discipline, the first person in the history of psychology to be designated properly and unreservedly a *psychologist*. Moreover, structuralism, the Wundtian approach, constituted psychology's first school of thought.

As the first experimental psychologist, Wundt founded the first laboratory, edited the first journal, and began experimental psychology as a science. The areas he investigated—including sensation and perception, attention, feeling, reaction, and association—became basic chapters in textbooks that were yet to be written. That so much of the history of psychology following Wundt consists of opposition to his view of psychology does not detract from his achievements and contributions.

Why have the honors for founding the new psychology fallen to Wundt and not to Fechner? Fechner's *Elements of Psychophysics* was published in 1860, at least 15 years before Wundt is said to have begun psychology. Wundt himself wrote that Fechner's work represented the "first conquest" in experimental psychology (Wundt, 1888, p. 471). Historians seem to agree on Fechner's monumental importance; some even question whether psychology could have begun when it did were it not for Fechner's work.

Why, then, does history not credit Fechner with founding psychology? The answer lies in the nature of the process of founding.

Founding is a deliberate, intentional act involving abilities and characteristics that exceed those necessary for brilliant scientific achievement. It requires the organization and integration of a great deal of work that has gone on before, and then the publication and promotion of the newly organized material. Boring (1950b) described founding in these terms: "When the central ideas are all born, some promoter takes them in hand, organizes them, adding whatever else seems to him essential, publishes and advertises them, insists upon them, and in short 'founds' a school" (p. 194).

Founding is thus quite different from originating, though we need not make the distinction a disparaging one. Both originators and founders are essential to the formation of a science, as indispensable as are the architect and the builder in constructing a house.

With this distinction in mind, we can see why Fechner is not called the founder of psychology; stated simply, he was not trying to found a new science. His quest was to understand the nature of the relationship between the material and spiritual worlds. He sought to demonstrate a unified concept of mind and body that, although starting from mystical speculation, had a scientific basis.

Wundt, however, set out quite deliberately to found a new science. In the preface to the first edition of his *Principles of Physiological Psychology,* published in 1874, he wrote: "The work I here present to the public is an attempt to mark out a new domain of science." Wundt was greatly interested in promoting the idea of psychology as an independent science. Nevertheless, it bears repeating that although Wundt is considered to have founded psychology, he did not originate it. It emerged from a long line of creative efforts.

During the last half of the nineteenth century the *Zeitgeist* was ready for the development and application of the experimental approach to problems of the mind. Wundt was a vigorous agent and promoter—of the inevitable.

SUGGESTED READINGS

EARLY EXPERIMENTAL PHYSIOLOGY

Brazier, M. The historical development of neurophysiology. In J. Field (Ed.), *Handbook of physiology* (Vol. 1). Baltimore: Williams & Wilkins, 1959. Pp. 1–58.

Fearing, F. *Reflex action: A study in the history of physiological psychology.* Baltimore: Williams & Wilkins, 1930.

Kirsch, I. The impetus to scientific psychology: A recurrent pattern. *Journal of the History of the Behavioral Sciences,* 1976, 12, 120–129. (A brief discussion of the work of Maskelyne and Bessel; this is discussed at greater length in Boring, 1950b, pp. 134–138.)

Lachman, S. *History and methods of physiological psychology.* Detroit: Hamilton, 1963.

Ladd, G. T., & Woodworth, R. S. *Physiological psychology* (Rev. ed.). New York: Scribner's, 1911.

FECHNER

Boring, E. G. Fechner: Inadvertent founder of psychophysics. *Psychometrika,* 1961, 26, 3–8.

Fechner, G. A mysterious illness. In G. Fechner, *Religion of a scientist.* (W. Lowrie, Ed. and trans.). New York: Pantheon Books, 1946. Pp. 36–42.

Fechner, G. *Elements of psychophysics* (H. E. Adler, Trans.) (Vol. I). New York: Holt, 1966. (Originally published, 1860.)

Marshall, M. E. Gustav Fechner, Dr. Mises, and the comparative anatomy of angels. *Journal of the History of the Behavioral Sciences*, 1969, 5, 39–58.

Stevens, S. S. To honor Fechner and repeal his law. *Science*, 1961, 133, 80–86.

Woodward, W. R. Fechner's panpsychism: A scientific solution to the mind–body problem. *Journal of the History of the Behavioral Sciences*, 1972, 8, 367–386.

HELMHOLTZ

Koenigsberger, L. *Hermann von Helmholtz*. New York: Dover, 1965.

Warren, R. M., & Warren, R. P. *Helmholtz on perception: Its physiology and development*. New York: Wiley, 1968.

58

*Physiological Influences on
Psychology*

THE NEW PSYCHOLOGY: STRUCTURALISM AND ITS EARLY OPPONENTS

STRUCTURALISM: AN OVERVIEW

Wundt's founding of the new experimental science of psychology marked the beginning of the first systematic position or school of thought in psychology—structuralism. In the United States, it has become customary to consider Wundt the forerunner of structural psychology and to accord the honors for formally developing the school to the English psychologist E.B. Titchener, who worked at Cornell University in New York. Wundt, however, is certainly more than an antecedent of the structuralists; we shall see that Titchener's position was similar to that of Wundt. Wundt mapped out the field of structural psychology, though at the time there was no reason to call it anything other than "psychology." It remained for Titchener to coin the term *structural psychology* in 1898, for reasons we will discuss in Chapter 5.

What is structuralism and why did it develop as the first systematic position in psychology? The subject matter of the new psychology, conscious experience, and the task, the experimental investigation of the structure of consciousness, were determined by the *Zeitgeist*. The dual influence of British empiricism and German experimental physiology was evident. The new psychology absorbed the experimental methods and basic approach of the older natural sciences. It adapted the scientific methods of investigation for its own use and proceeded to study its subject matter in the same way the natural sciences were studying theirs. The spirit of the times helped to shape both the subject matter and the methods of investigation of the new psychology.

The task of the early structuralists was to discover the nature of elementary conscious experiences, that is, to analyze consciousness into separate parts, and by so doing discover the structure of consciousness. We shall see how they succeeded in their task and, more important, how this initial systematic position influenced the later development of psychology.

WILHELM WUNDT
(1832–1920)

The Life of Wundt

Wundt was born and spent his early years in a small town in Germany, a childhood that was marked by intense loneliness. He got poor grades in school and he lived the life of an only child (his older brother was at boarding school). His only friend his own age was a mentally retarded boy who was good natured but could barely speak.

Wundt's father was a clergyman, and though both parents seem to have been jovial and sociable, Wundt's early memories of his father were not pleasant. When Wundt was in his 80s, he could still vividly recall falling down a flight of stairs while trying to follow his father. He also remembered that his father visited his school one day and hit him across the face for not paying attention to the teacher.

Beginning in the second grade, Wundt's education was undertaken by his father's assistant, a young vicar to whom the boy felt a stronger emotional attachment than to his parents. When the vicar was transferred to another town, Wundt became so upset that he was allowed to go to live with the vicar, with whom he remained until the age of 13.

There was a strong tradition of scholarship in the Wundt family, with ancestors of note in virtually every discipline. It has been said that "virtually no family tree in Germany contains as many intellectually active and productive individuals as that of Wundt" (Bringmann, Balance, & Evans, 1975, p. 288). Nonetheless, it appeared for a time that this impressive family tradition would not be continued by young Wundt.

He spent much more time daydreaming than studying, and failed in his first year at *Gymnasium*. He did not get along well with his classmates, was frequently slapped by one of his teachers and ridiculed by others, and once ran away from the school. It was not a promising beginning.

Gradually Wundt learned to control his daydreaming and even became more popular. Although he always disliked school, he nevertheless developed his intellectual interests and abilities. By the time he graduated at the age of 19, he was ready for the university.[1]

To earn a living and study science at the same time, Wundt decided to become a physician. His medical studies took him for one year to the University of Tübingen and for the next three and one half years to Heidelberg, where he studied anatomy, physiology, physics, medicine, and chemistry, and was strongly influenced in the latter field by the famous Robert Bunsen. He slowly came to realize that the practice of medicine was not for him, so he shifted to physiology.

After a semester of study in Berlin with the great physiologist Johannes

---

[1] Much of this material on Wundt's life is drawn from Bringmann et al. (1975).

Müller, Wundt returned to Heidelberg to take his doctorate in 1855. He held an appointment as *Dozent* (lecturer) in physiology at Heidelberg from 1857 to 1864. In 1858 he was appointed assistant to Helmholtz, but found the work of drilling new students in their laboratory fundamentals a dreary task, so he resigned after a few years of this routine. In 1864 he was made associate professor and continued at Heidelberg until 1874.

While doing research in physiology at Heidelberg, Wundt's conception of psychology as an independent and experimental science began to emerge. His initial proposal for a new science of psychology appeared in the book entitled *Beiträge zur Theorie der Sinneswahrnehmung (Contributions to the Theory of Sensory Perception)*, various sections of which were published between 1858 and 1862. In addition to reporting his own original experiments, which he conducted in a crude laboratory in his home, the book contained his views on the methods of the new psychology. Wundt wrote of "experimental psychology" for the first time. Along with Fechner's *Elements* (1860), this work is often considered to mark the literary birth of the new science.

The *Beiträge* was followed in 1863 by another and perhaps more important book, *Vorlesungen über die Menschen- und Thierseele (Lectures on the Minds of Men and Animals)*. An indication of its importance was its revision almost 30 years later with an English translation and repeated reprintings until after Wundt's death in 1920. It discussed many problems that were to occupy the attention of experimental psychologists for a number of years.

Beginning in 1867, Wundt gave a course on physiological psychology at Heidelberg, the first formal offering of such a course. Out of this work came what is often considered the most important book in the history of psychology, *Grundzüge der physiologischen Psychologie (Principles of Physiological Psychology)*, published in two parts in 1873 and 1874. Six editions appeared in 37 years, with the last published in 1911. Undoubtedly Wundt's masterpiece, this book firmly established psychology as a laboratory science with its own problems and methods of experimentation. For many years the *Grundzüge* served experimental psychologists as a storehouse of information and a record of the progress of the new psychology. It was in the preface to this book that Wundt stated his goal of attempting "to mark out a new domain of science." That this book uses "physiological psychology" in its title is of great significance. Wundt intended his psychology to use the methods of research developed in physiology.

Wundt began the longest and most important phase of his career in 1875 when he became professor of philosophy at Leipzig, where he worked prodigiously for 45 years. He established his laboratory at Leipzig shortly after his arrival, and in 1881 began the journal *Philosophische Studien (Philosophical Studies)*, the official organ of the new laboratory and the new science. With Wundt's handbook, laboratory, and scholarly journal, the new psychology was well under way.

Wundt's spreading fame and the laboratory drew a large number of students to Leipzig to work with him. Among these students were many subsequent contributors to psychology, including several Americans, most of whom returned to the United States to begin laboratories of their own. Through these students, the Leipzig laboratory exerted an immense influence on the development of psychology. It served as the model for the many new laboratories that were developed in the latter part of the nineteenth century. The students who flocked to Leipzig, united in point of view and purpose, at least initially, constituted a school of thought in psychology.

Wundt's lectures at Leipzig were very popular and extremely well attended. At one time he had over 600 students in a class. His classroom manner has been described by Titchener as follows:

> Wundt would appear at exactly the correct minute—punctuality was essential—dressed all in black and carrying a small sheaf of lecture notes. He clattered up the side aisle to the platform with an awkward shuffle and a sound as if his soles were made of wood. On the platform was a long desk where demonstrations were performed. He made a few gestures—a forefinger across his forehead, a rearrangement of his chalk— then faced the audience and placed his elbows on the bookrest. His voice was weak at first, then gained in strength and emphasis. As he talked his arms and hands moved up and down, pointing and waving, in some mysterious way illustrative. His head and body were rigid, and only the hands played back and forth. He seldom referred to the few jotted notes. As the clock struck the end of the hour he stopped and, stooping a little, clattered out as he had clattered in. (Miller & Buckhout, 1973, p. 29)

At the first conference with each new group of graduate students, Wundt appeared with a list of research topics, which he assigned to the students in the order in which they stood. (There was, apparently, no thought of their sitting down in his presence.) Research was thoroughly supervised and Wundt held absolute power of acceptance or rejection upon completion of the thesis. The spirit of German scientific dogmatism flourished openly at the Leipzig laboratory.

In his personal life Wundt was quiet and unassuming, and his days followed a carefully regulated pattern. In the morning he worked on a book or article, read student theses, and edited his journal. In the afternoon he attended examinations or visited the laboratory. Cattell (1928) remarked that Wundt's laboratory visits were limited to five or ten minutes. Apparently, despite his great faith in laboratory research, "he was not himself a laboratory worker" (p. 545). After this, he would walk while thinking about his lecture for the afternoon, always given at 4 P.M. In view of this rigorous life of scholarship, it may be surprising to learn that many of his evenings were occupied by music and current affairs.

A laboratory and a journal established, an immense amount of research under direction, Wundt turned his tremendous energy to philosophy in the years 1880–1891, writing on ethics, logic, and systematic philosophy. He published the second edition of *Principles of Physiological Psychology* in 1880 and the third edition in 1887, all the while contributing articles to the *Studien*.

Another field on which Wundt focused his considerable talent was outlined in the *Beiträge* in 1862—the creation of a social psychology. Toward the end of the nineteenth century he returned to this project, which culminated in the ten volumes of his *Völkerpsychologie (Folk Psychology)* published between 1900 and 1920. Folk psychology was concerned with the investigation of the various stages of mental development as manifested in language, art, myths, social customs, law, and morals. The implications of this work for psychology are of far greater significance than its content; it served to divide the new science of psychology into two parts, the experimental and the social. The simpler mental functions, such as sensation and perception, can and must be studied by laboratory investigation, Wundt believed. But he argued that scientific experimentation is impossible in the study of the higher mental processes because they are so thoroughly conditioned by linguistic habits and other aspects of cultural training.[2] Thus, according to Wundt, the higher thought processes could be studied effectively only by the nonexperimental approaches of sociology, anthropology, and social psychology. This contention that social forces play a major role in the development of the complicated higher mental processes is both true and important. However, Wundt's conclusion—that the higher mental processes cannot be studied experimentally—was refuted not long after he stated it.

Wundt's enormous productivity continued without a break for 63 years until his death in 1920. Consistent with his nearly lifelong systematic habits, he died shortly after completing his psychological reminiscences. Boring (1950b) noted that Wundt wrote 53,735 pages in all, an output of 2.2 pages a day from 1853 to 1920. "This achievement is even more remarkable if one bears in mind that Wundt was half blind for a major part of his life and had to depend on others for his vast reading and writing" (Bringmann et al., 1975, p. 293). Few persons have accomplished so much at such a high level of competence in so short a time.

Wundt's System

The Subject Matter of Psychology

Wundt stated that the subject matter of psychology is immediate experience rather than mediate experience. Mediate experience provides us with information or knowledge about something other than the experience itself. This is the usual form in which we use experience to acquire knowledge about our experiential world. When we look at a flower and say, "The flower is

---

[2] Wundt's emphasis on language in the *Völkerpsychologie* can be seen as a precursor to contemporary work in psycholinguistics.

Wilhelm Wundt (1832–1920) founded the experimental science of psychology, established its first laboratory at Leipzig, and developed structuralism, its first school of thought.
(National Library of Medicine)

The New Psychology:
Structuralism

red," the statement implies that our primary interest is in the flower and not in the fact that we are experiencing red. According to Wundt, the immediate experience of looking at this flower is not in the object itself (the flower), but rather in the experience of red. Thus, immediate experience, for Wundt, is experience per se, free and unbiased by any higher-level interpretations (as in describing this experience of red as a flower). When we describe the various experiences we "feel" when we have a toothache, our concern is with immediate experience. However, when we say "I have a toothache," we are concerned with mediate experience.

To Wundt, it was the basic experiences such as red (the experience of red) that formed the basic states of consciousness or elements of the mind. Wundt wanted to analyze or break down the mind or consciousness into its most elemental components, just as the natural scientists were breaking down their subject matter, the material universe. Marx and Hillix (1979) suggest that the work of the chemist Mendeleev, who developed the periodic table of chemical elements, supported Wundt's aim, and that he wanted to develop a "periodic table of the mind" (p. 67).

The Method of Study

Because, according to Wundt, psychology is the science of experience, the method of psychology must involve observation of experience. No one can observe an experience except the person having it, so the method must involve self-observation or *introspection*. The use of introspection was not new with Wundt; even a cursory review can trace its use back to Socrates. What was a major innovation was Wundt's application of precise experimental control over the conditions of introspection.

The use of introspection in psychology was derived from physics, in which introspection had been used to study light and sound, and physiology, in which it had been used to study the sense organs. To obtain information about the operations of the sense organs, for example, the investigator would apply a stimulus to a sense organ and ask the subjects to report on the sensation produced.

Wundt set forth explicit rules for the proper use of introspection in his laboratory: (1) observers must be able to determine when the process is to be introduced; (2) they must be in a state of readiness or "strained attention"; (3) it must be possible to repeat the observation several times; and (4) the experimental conditions must be capable of variation in terms of controlled manipulation of stimuli. The last condition invokes the essence of the experimental method—varying the conditions of the stimulus situation and observing the resulting changes in the experiences of the subjects.

Introspection, as practiced at Leipzig, was a skill acquired by Wundt's students only after a long period of rigorous apprenticeship. To be able to report on the basic elements of an experience required arduous training. Boring (1953b) reported that observers in Wundt's reaction-time experiments had to perform approximately 10,000 introspective observations before they were considered skilled enough to provide valid data.

The Goals of Psychology

Having defined psychology's subject matter and method, Wundt then considered its goal. The problem of psychology was threefold: *(1)* to analyze the conscious processes into their basic elements; *(2)* to discover how these elements are connected; and *(3)* to determine their laws of connection.

The Elements of Experience

Wundt considered *sensations*—aroused whenever a sense organ is stimulated and the resulting impulse reaches the brain—to be one of the elementary forms of experience. He classified sensations according to modality (vision, hearing, and so on), intensity, and duration. Wundt recognized no fundamental difference between sensations and images because images are also associated with cortical excitation. In keeping with his physiological orientation, he assumed the existence of a direct correspondence between the excitation of the cerebral cortex and the corresponding sensory experience. He regarded the mind and body as parallel but not interacting systems. The mind did not depend on the body so it could be studied effectively by itself.

Feelings were the other elementary form of experience. Wundt thought that sensations and feelings are simultaneous aspects of immediate experience. Feelings are the subjective complements of sensations, but they do not arise directly from a sense organ. Sensations are accompanied by certain feeling qualities, and when sensations combine to form a more complex state, a feeling quality will result from this combination of sensations.

Wundt developed his famous and controversial *tridimensional theory of feeling* from his own introspective observations. Working with a metronome (which produces audible clicks at regular intervals), Wundt reported that after he experienced a row of clicks, some rhythmic patterns appeared to be more pleasant or more agreeable than others. He concluded that part of the experience of any such pattern is a subjective feeling of pleasure or displeasure. (Note that this subjective feeling is a simultaneous aspect of the sensation of the clicks.) He then suggested that this feeling state can be placed at a point along a continuum ranging from agreeable to disagreeable.

A second kind of feeling was detected while listening to the clicks. Wundt reported a slight tension while waiting for each successive click, followed by relief after the occurrence of the anticipated click. From this he concluded that in addition to a pleasure–displeasure continuum, his feelings seemed to have a tension–relief dimension. Moreover, he reported a mildly excited feeling when the click rate was increased, and a more quiet feeling when the rate was reduced.

Through this laborious procedure of patiently varying the speed of the metronome and meticulously noting his experiences (his sensations and feelings), Wundt arrived at three independent dimensions of feeling: pleasure–displeasure, tension–relaxation, and excitement–depression. Every feeling, he stated, can be located somewhere within this three-dimensional space.

Wundt believed that emotions are complex compounds of these elementary feelings, and that elementary feelings could be effectively described by defining their position on each of the three dimensions. Thus, emotions were reduced to conscious contents of the mind. Wundt's theory of feelings stimulated a great deal of research in the Leipzig and other laboratories, but has not stood the test of time.

The Doctrine of
Apperception

Despite his interest in the elements of experience, Wundt recognized that when we look at the real world we see a unity of perceptions. For example, we see a tree as a unity; we do not "see" the many and varied sensations of brightness, hue, shape, and so on, that his observers reported in the laboratory. Our visual experience comprehends the tree as a unity and not as each of the numerous elementary sensations and feelings that constitute the tree.

How is this totality of conscious experience compounded or built up from elementary component parts? Wundt postulated the doctrine of apperception to account for our unified conscious experiences. He designated the actual process of relating or combining the various elements into a unity as the principle of *creative synthesis* or the *law of psychic resultants*. The many elementary experiences are organized into a whole by this process of creative synthesis, which asserts, in essence, that the combination of elements creates new properties. As Wundt stated it, "Every psychic compound has characteristics which are by no means the mere sum of the characteristics of the elements" (1896, p. 375). Something new is created out of the synthesis of the elemental parts of experience. We might say, as the Gestalt psychologists have said since 1912, that the whole is different from the sum of its parts.

This notion of creative synthesis has a counterpart in chemistry. The combination of chemical elements produces resultants that contain properties that were not properties of the original elements. Apperception is an active process. The mind is not merely acted upon by the experienced elements; rather, it acts on them in the creative synthesis of the parts to make up the whole. Thus, Wundt did not treat association only in mechanical terms, as did James Mill.

Wundt gave the larger share of his attention to the opposite of creative synthesis, to the analysis of mind, the reduction of conscious experience to its elementary component parts. Yet the fact that he made synthesis a feature of his formal system is historically significant because the notion was to have important repercussions.

The Research Topics of
the Leipzig Laboratory

Wundt himself determined the problems for experimental psychology during the early years of the Leipzig laboratory. The great man assigned to his students research topics that coincided with his own aims. For a number of years the problems with which the new experimental psychology concerned itself were defined by the work done at the Leipzig laboratory. More important, the extensive research performed there demonstrated that an experimentally based science of psychology was possible.

Because the methods and subject matter of the Leipzig laboratory formed the foundation for the new science, it is necessary to understand the nature of the work during the early years. Wundt believed that his new science should initially be concerned with research problems that had already been investigated and reduced to some kind of empirical and quantitative form. For the most part, he did not occupy himself with new areas of research, but rather with the extension and more formal development of current research problems.

Almost all the work emerging from the laboratory was published in the *Studien*. This journal published very little research that had not been done either at Leipzig or by Wundt's students so soon after leaving Leipzig that it still bore the imprint of the master. Over 100 studies were performed in the first 20 years of the laboratory's existence.

The first series of studies involved the psychological and physiological aspects of vision, hearing, and, to some extent, the so-called minor senses. Typical problems investigated in the area of visual sensation and perception included the psychophysics of color, color contrast, peripheral vision, negative afterimages, visual contrast, color blindness, visual size, and optical illusions. Psychophysical methods were used to investigate auditory sensations. Tactile sensations were studied as well as the time-sense, that is, the perception or estimation of intervals of varying lengths of time.

A topic that claimed a great deal of attention in the laboratory was reaction time, a subject that arose from the work of Bessel on the speed of reaction among astronomers. The speed of a reaction had been a topic of investigation since the end of the eighteenth century and had been studied by Helmholtz and by J. C. Donders, a Dutch physiologist. Wundt believed that he could demonstrate experimentally the three stages that he thought were present in a person's response to a stimulus: perception, apperception, and will.

After a stimulus is presented, subjects first perceive it, then apperceive it, and finally will to react, from which muscular movement results. Wundt hoped to develop a "chronometry of the mind" by succeeding in measuring the times for the various mental processes such as cognition, discrimination, and will. The promise of the method was not to be realized because in practiced subjects the three stages were not clearly apparent, and the times for the separate processes were not constant from person to person or from study to study.

Studies on reaction time were replaced by research on attention and feeling. Wundt considered attention to be the most vivid perception of only a small portion of the entire content of consciousness at any one time. The reference is to what is commonly called the focus of attention. Those stimuli in this focus are the most clearly perceived and are quite distinct and separate from the rest of the visual field. A simple example is the words you are now reading relative to the rest of this page and objects in the surrounding environment that are perceived less clearly. In addition to studies on the range and the fluctuation of attention in the Leipzig laboratory, one of Wundt's students, James McKeen Cattell, performed a classic study of attention span and found that four, five, or six units could be perceived in one short exposure.

Studies of feeling were undertaken in the 1890s to attempt to support the tridimensional theory. Wundt used the method of paired comparisons, which requires the comparison of stimuli in terms of the subjective feeling aroused. Other studies attempted to relate bodily changes, such as pulse rate and breathing, to corresponding feeling states.

Another area of investigation was the analysis of verbal associations, which had been begun by Sir Francis Galton (Chapter 6). Subjects were asked to respond with a single word when presented with the stimulus word. Wundt proceeded to classify the types of word association discovered when single-word stimuli were presented, to determine the nature of all verbal association.

The experimental areas of the psychophysiology of the senses, reaction time, psychophysics, and association constituted more than half of all the work published in the first few years of the *Studien*. Wundt showed some slight concern with child psychology and animal psychology, but apparently undertook no experimentation in these areas, believing that the conditions of study could not be adequately controlled.

In Retrospect

Wolman (1960) suggested that the act of establishing the first psychological laboratory at Leipzig required a great deal of courage. To do so at that time required a person well versed in both contemporary physiology and philosophy, and capable of combining these disciplines effectively. To accomplish his goal of establishing a new science, Wundt had to get rid of the nonscientific past and cut the ties between the new scientific psychology and the old mental philosophy.

By postulating that the subject matter of psychology was experience, and that psychology was a science based on experience, Wundt was able to avoid discussions about the nature of the immortal soul and its relationship to the mortal body. He said simply, though emphatically, that psychology does not deal with this issue. This assertion was a great step forward.

One cannot help but marvel at Wundt's outstanding energy and endurance over a period of more than 60 years. His creation of a scientific experimental psychology commands immense respect and is the source of his greatest influence. He began (as he had announced his intention of doing) a new domain of science, and conducted purely psychological research in a laboratory he designed exclusively for that purpose. He published the results in his own journal and tried to develop a systematic theory of the human mind. His thoroughly trained students founded additional laboratories and continued experimenting on the problems and with the techniques set forth by the great man. Thus, Wundt provided psychology with all the accouterments of a modern science.

Murphy (1949) noted, "Before Wundt published his *Physiological Psychology* and established his laboratory, psychology was little more than a waif knocking now at the door of physiology, now at the door of ethics, now at the door of epistemology. In 1879, it set itself up as an experimental science with a local habitation and a name" (p. 159). The times were, of course, ready for the Wundtian movement, which was the natural outcome of the development of the physiological sciences, particularly in the German universities. That Wundt was the culmination of this movement and not its originator does not diminish his stature. It did, after all, require a kind of genius, and a firm sense of dedication, courage, and vigor, to bring such a movement to fulfillment. The results of his efforts represent an achievement of such overwhelming importance that Wundt is accorded a position unique among psychologists of the modern period.

Like any great man, Wundt was subject to criticism with regard to many points of his systematic position and his experimental technique of introspection. It is hard to verify research findings obtained by introspection. When introspection by different persons gives different results, how can we decide who is right? Experiments using introspection, unlike more objective experimentation, do not ensure agreement among experimenters because introspective observation is a strictly private affair. As such, disagreements cannot be settled by repeated observations. It was thought, however, that with more training and experience of observers, the method could be improved. (We will discuss additional criticisms of structuralism at the end of Chapter 5.)

It was difficult to criticize Wundt's total system during his lifetime, primarily because he wrote so much and so fast. By the time a critic had prepared an attack on a particular point, Wundt had changed his argument in a new edition or was writing on a different topic. An opponent would be outwritten and buried under volumes of highly detailed and complex writings.

Further, since Wundt's theories were like classificatory schemes, they tended to be somewhat loosely knit and almost impossible to verify. There was no vital center to his program, no point at which a critic might damage him with a single stroke. As William James noted, "Cut him up like a worm, and each fragment crawls; there is no *nœud vital* in his mental medulla oblongata, so that you can't kill him all at once" (Perry, 1935, p. 68).

The Wundtian position, as boldly and forcefully advanced by his student Titchener (Chapter 5), has not stood the test of time. Structuralism is no longer an active issue in contemporary psychology and has not been for many years. Contemporary psychologists have voiced complaints about what they now see as the narrowness of Wundt's position. However, as we shall see in the following chapters:

> *Almost all the new schools have been founded as a protest against some one or other characteristic of Wundt's psychology, but we may welcome the schools without condoning the complaint. At any one time a science is simply what its researches yield, and the researches are nothing more than those problems for which effective methods have been found and for which the times are ready. (Boring, 1950b, p. 343)*

Wundt's achievements are not diminished by the fact that much of the history of psychology after him has consisted of rebellion against some of the limitations he placed on the field. Indeed, that fact enhances his achievements. Forward movement must have something to push against, and Wilhelm Wundt provided a compelling and magnificent beginning to modern experimental psychology.

OTHER EARLY EUROPEAN PSYCHOLOGISTS

Wundt had a monopoly on the new psychology for only a short time. At other laboratories in Germany the science was also beginning to flourish. Although he was obviously the most important organizer and systematizer in the early days of psychology, there were others who began to influence the new science. Some of these early psychologists disagreed with Wundt on a number of points, but all shared his belief that introspection was the proper method to be used in psychology. Some of them paradoxically came to influence structural psychology by their opposition to it rather than by any direct, positive contributions to the position. Although these early non-Wundtian psychologists had different points of view, all were engaged in the common enterprise of developing the new psychology. Their endeavors made Germany the undisputed center of the new movement.

There were, however, simultaneous developments in England that were to give psychology an entirely new theme and direction. Charles Darwin proposed his theory of evolution and Sir Francis Galton began work on the psychology of individual differences. These forces would influence the development of American psychology at least as much as the work of Wundt. In addition, early American psychologists, most of whom had studied at Leipzig, returned home and made of the Wundtian psychology something uniquely American in form and temperament. But more of these developments later. The important point for now is that very shortly after its founding, psychology became divided into factions. Although Wundt had developed "the" psychology, it shortly became only one of several varieties. Let us turn to a discussion of Wundt's contemporaries in Germany.

Hermann Ebbinghaus
(1850–1909)

Just a few years after Wundt had stated that it was not possible to experiment on the higher mental processes, a then unknown psychologist who worked alone, isolated from any center of psychology, began successfully to experiment on these processes. Hermann Ebbinghaus became the first psychologist to investigate learning and memory experimentally. In doing so, he not only challenged Wundt, but changed radically the way in which association or learning could be dealt with as well.

Before Ebbinghaus, most notably in the work of the British empiricists and associationists, the customary way to study association was to deal with associations that were already formed. The investigator would, in a sense, work backward, attempting to determine how the associations had been formed. Ebbinghaus began at a different starting point—the development of associations. In this way, it was possible to control the conditions under which the associations were formed and thus to make the study of learning considerably more objective.

Accepted as one of the great manifestations of original genius in experimental psychology, Ebbinghaus's investigation of learning and forgetting was the first venture into a truly *psychological* problem area, one that was not a part of physiology, as was the case with so much of Wundt's research. As a result, experimental psychology was considerably widened in scope.

Born near Bonn in 1850, Ebbinghaus undertook his university studies first at Bonn in history and philology and then at Halle and Berlin. In the course of his academic training his interests shifted to philosophy, in which he received his degree in 1873, following military service during the Franco–Prussian War. The next seven years were devoted to independent study in Berlin, England, and France, where his interests shifted toward science. About 1876, three years before Wundt established his laboratory, Ebbinghaus bought a secondhand copy of Fechner's *Elemente der Psychophysik* at a bookstall in Paris. This chance encounter influenced him and the

*The New Psychology:
Structuralism*

the new psychology profoundly. Fechner's mathematical approach to psychological phenomena was an exciting disclosure to the young Ebbinghaus, and he resolved to do for the study of memory what Fechner had done for psychophysics, through rigid and systematic measurements. He wanted to apply the experimental method to the higher mental processes and decided, probably as a result of the influence of the British associationists, to make the attempt in the field of memory.

Consider Ebbinghaus's course of action in light of the problem he chose and his own situation. Learning and memory had never been studied experimentally. Indeed, the eminent Wundt had stated that they could not be.[3] Further, Ebbinghaus had no academic appointment, no university setting in which to conduct his work, no teacher, and no laboratory. Nevertheless, he carried out alone, over a period of five years, a long series of carefully controlled and thorough studies, using himself as the only subject.

For the basic measure of learning he adapted a technique from the associationists, who were emphasizing the principle of frequency of associations as a condition of recall. He reasoned that the difficulty of learning material could be measured by simply counting the number of repetitions needed for one perfect reproduction of the material.[4]

Ebbinghaus used similar, though not identical, lists of syllables as the material to be learned, and repeated the task frequently to be sure of the accuracy of his results. In this way he could cancel out variable errors from trial to trial, and then take an average measure. So systematic was Ebbinghaus in his experimentation that he even regulated his personal habits, keeping them as constant as possible and following a rigid daily pattern, always learning the material at the same time each day.

For the subject matter of his research—the material to be learned—Ebbinghaus invented the nonsense syllable, which revolutionized the study of association or learning. Titchener later commented that the use of nonsense syllables marked the first significant advance in the area of association since Aristotle (Shakow, 1930). Ebbinghaus recognized an inherent difficulty in using prose or poetry. Meanings or associations are already attached to words by those who know the language. These existing associations can facilitate the learning of material and, because they are present at the time of experimentation, they cannot be meaningfully controlled. Ebbinghaus sought material that would be uniformly unassociated, completely homogeneous, and equally unfamiliar—material with which

[3] Boring (1950b) notes that Ebbinghaus must surely have known of this work.

[4] This is an example of the strong influence of Fechner. As noted in Chapter 3, Fechner measured sensations indirectly by measuring the stimulus intensity necessary to produce a just noticeable difference in sensation. Ebbinghaus approached the problem of measuring memory in a similar way, that is, indirectly, in terms of the number of trials or repetitions needed to learn the material (Postman, 1968).

there could be no past associations. Nonsense syllables, formed of two consonants with a vowel in between, as in *lef*, *bok*, or *yat*, satisfied these criteria. He put all possible combinations of consonants and vowels on cards, yielding a supply of 2300 syllables from which to draw at random those to be learned.

Ebbinghaus designed a number of experiments to determine the influence of various conditions on learning and retention. One of these studies investigated the difference between his speed in memorizing lists of nonsense syllables and in memorizing meaningful materials. To determine this difference, he memorized stanzas of Byron's *Don Juan*. Each stanza has 80 syllables, and Ebbinghaus found that it required about nine readings to memorize one stanza. He then memorized a list of 80 nonsense syllables and discovered that this task required almost 80 repetitions. He concluded that meaningless material is approximately nine times harder to learn than meaningful material.

He also investigated the effect of the length of the material to be learned on the number of repetitions necessary for a perfect reproduction. He concluded that longer material requires more repetitions and, consequently, more time to learn. He found that the average time per syllable was markedly increased by lengthening the number of syllables to be learned. These results are predictable in a general way: the more we have to learn, the longer it will take us. The significance of Ebbinghaus's work is in the careful control of conditions, the quantitative analysis of the data, and the finding that both total learning time and time per syllable increase with longer lists of syllables.

Ebbinghaus studied a number of other variables thought to influence learning and retention, such as the effect of overlearning (repeating the lists more times than necessary for one perfect reproduction), near and remote associations within lists, repeated learning or review, and the influence of time between learning and recall. His research on the effect of time produced the famous Ebbinghaus curve of forgetting. This curve, as every psychology student knows, demonstrates that material is forgotten very rapidly in the first few hours after learning, and more and more slowly thereafter.

In 1880 Ebbinghaus received an academic appointment at the University of Berlin, where he continued his research on memory, repeating and verifying his earlier studies. He published the results of all his research in the important *Über das Gedächtnis (On Memory)* in 1885. "It was epoch-making, not merely because of its scope and style, although these features must have helped, but because it was seen at once to be a breach by experimental psychology in the barrier about the 'higher mental processes.' Ebbinghaus had opened up a new field" (Boring, 1950b, p. 388).

This book represents what is perhaps the most brilliant single investigation in the history of experimental psychology. In addition to beginning a whole new field of study, which is still vital today, it provides a striking

The New Psychology:
Structuralism

example of technical skill, perseverance, and ingenuity. It is not possible to find in the history of psychology any other investigator working alone who subjected himself to such a rigid regimen of experimentation. The research was so exacting, thorough, and systematic that it is still cited in contemporary textbooks.

Ebbinghaus did not continue research on memory but instead let others develop the field and extend and refine the methodology. He published relatively little after 1885, and a year later he was promoted to assistant professor at Berlin. He founded a laboratory and a journal (the latter with Arthur König, a physicist), the *Zeitschrift für Psychologie and Physiologie der Sinnesorgane (Journal of Psychology and Physiology of the Sense Organs)* in 1890. A new journal was needed in Germany because Wundt's *Studien*, the exclusive organ of the Leipzig laboratory, could not present all the research being conducted at that time. The need for a new journal, just nine years after Wundt had begun his, is significant testimony to the phenomenal growth in size and diversity of the new psychology.

Apparently because of his lack of publications, Ebbinghaus was not promoted again at Berlin, and in 1894 he moved to a lesser post in the university hierarchy at Breslau, where he remained until 1905. There, in 1897, he developed a sentence completion test, probably the first successful test of the so-called higher mental capacities, a modified form of which is used in many tests of general intelligence today.

In 1902 Ebbinghaus published a highly successful general textbook, *Die Grundzüge der Psychologie (The Principles of Psychology)*, dedicated to the memory of Fechner, and in 1908 a more popular text, *Abriss der Psychologie (A Summary of Psychology)*. Both books appeared in several editions and were revised by others after Ebbinghaus's death. Ebbinghaus left Breslau for Halle in 1905, and died suddenly of pneumonia a few years later, at the age of 59.

Ebbinghaus did not make any theoretical or systematic contributions to psychology; he created no formal system and had no disciples of importance to psychology. He did not found a school, nor did he seem to want to. Yet he is of great importance not only to the study of learning and memory, which he began, but also to experimental psychology as a whole. Boring commented that he was influential "because he helped to make articulate and effective the spirit of the times that called for an emancipation of psychology from philosophy" (1950b, p. 392).

One measure of the overall historical worth of a scientist is how well the position and research findings stand the test of time. By that standard, one might suggest that Ebbinghaus was more important than Wundt. His research brought objectivity, quantification, and experimentation to the study of association or learning, a topic that has become a central one in contemporary psychology. It is because of Ebbinghaus that work on the concept of association changed from mere speculation about its attributes to its investigation with the aid of the scientific method. Many of his findings on learning and memory remain valid a century after he published them. There are few psychologists about whom this can be said.

Georg Elias Müller
(1850–1934)

A physiologist and philosopher by training, Müller had a strong interest in psychology, which he expressed during a 40-year career at Göttingen. From 1881 until 1921 his well-equipped laboratory rivaled that at Leipzig and attracted many students from Europe and America.

Müller's research contributions were so substantial that Titchener delayed for two years the second volume of his *Experimental Psychology* so that he could incorporate material from Müller's latest book.

Müller did considerable work on color vision, and extensively criticized and elaborated on Fechner's work in psychophysics. He was one of the first to work in the area begun by Ebbinghaus, the experimental study of learning and memory. His careful research verified and extended many of Ebbinghaus's findings. Ebbinghaus's approach had been strictly objective; he had not recorded introspections about his mental processes while engaged in his learning tasks. Müller believed that these reports tended to make learning appear too mechanical or automatic a process. He thought that the mind was more actively involved in the learning process, and although Müller used the objective methods of Ebbinghaus, he added introspective report. His results indicated that learning did not proceed mechanically, that the subjects were actively involved in it. They seemed to be consciously organizing and grouping the material, and even finding meanings in the nonsense syllables.

On the basis of this research, Müller concluded that association by contiguity alone cannot adequately account for learning because the subjects appeared to be actively seeking relationships among the stimuli to be learned. He suggested that there is a set of mental phenomena, such as readiness, hesitation, and doubt (the so-called conscious attitudes), that actively influence learning. Similar findings soon followed from the work of the Würzburg laboratory.

One final contribution to the study of learning deserves mention. Along with Friedrich Schumann, Müller developed the memory drum, a revolving drum that makes possible the uniform presentation of material to be learned. By now a familiar piece of laboratory equipment, this apparatus is significant because it increased the precision and objectivity of research on learning.

Franz Brentano
(1838–1917)

At about age 16 Brentano began his training for the priesthood, studying at Berlin, Munich, and Tübingen, where he received his degree in philosophy in 1864. He was ordained the same year, and two years later began teaching philosophy at Würzburg, writing and lecturing on Aristotle.

In 1870 the Vatican Council accepted the doctrine of papal infallibility, with which Brentano could not agree. He resigned his professorship (to which he had been appointed as a priest) and left the Church.

Non-Wundtian Franz Brentano (1838–1917) contended that psychology should be empirical, studying the activity rather than the content, of the mind.
(National Library of Medicine)

Other Early European
Psychologists

Brentano's most famous work, *Psychologie vom empirischen Standpunkte (Psychology from an Empirical Standpoint)*, was published in 1874, the year in which the second part of the first edition of Wundt's *Principles of Physiological Psychology* was published. Brentano's book was in direct opposition to the Wundtian view, attesting to the dissent apparent in the new psychology. Also in 1874 Brentano was appointed professor of philosophy at the University of Vienna, where he remained for 20 years, during which time his influence grew considerably. He was a popular lecturer, and among his students were several men who achieved their own prominence in the history of psychology—Carl Stumpf, Christian von Ehrenfels, and Sigmund Freud. In 1894 Brentano retired and spent his remaining years in Italy and Switzerland, engaged in study and writing.

Brentano was one of the more important non-Wundtians because of his diverse influences within psychology. (We will see that he is one of the intellectual precursors of Gestalt psychology and of humanistic psychology.)

Brentano shared with Wundt the goal of making psychology a science. However, whereas Wundt's psychology was experimental, Brentano's was empirical. The primary method of psychology for Brentano was observation, not experimentation, though he did not reject the utility of the experimental method. An empirical approach generally is broader in scope in that it obtains its data from observation and individual experience as well as from experimentation.

Brentano opposed one of Wundt's fundamental points—that psychology should study the content of conscious experience. He argued that the proper subject matter of psychology is mental activity; for example, the mental act of seeing rather than the study of the mental content (that which is seen).

Thus, Brentano's *act psychology* countered the Wundtian view that the psychic processes are contents. He argued that the distinction must be drawn between experience as a structure and experience as an activity. The sensory content of red is quite different from the activity of sensing red. Brentano urged that this act of experiencing is the true subject matter for psychology. He stated that a color is not a mental quality but strictly a physical quality. The act of seeing the color, however, is mental. Of course, the act always involves an object, that is, a content is always present because the act of seeing is meaningless unless something is seen.

This new subject matter necessitated a different method of study because acts, unlike sensory contents, are not accessible through analytical introspection as practiced at Wundt's Leipzig laboratory. The study of mental acts requires observation on a larger scale than that used by orthodox introspectionists. For this reason, act psychology, as we have noted, is more empirical than experimental in its methodology. This does not imply that Brentano's psychology was a return to speculative philosophy; though not experimental in nature, it did rely on careful observation.

Brentano's position had its loyal adherents, but the Wundtian psychology of content maintained its prominence in the new psychology. Because

Wundt published much more than Brentano, his position was better known. Also, it was easier to study sensations or contents with the new methods of psychophysics than to study the more elusive acts.

Carl Stumpf (1848–1936)

Born into a medical family, Stumpf came into contact with science at an early age but developed a greater interest in music. At the age of 7 he began studying the violin, and by age 10 was composing music. As a student at Würzburg he was captivated by Brentano and turned his attention to philosophy and science. At Brentano's suggestion he went to Göttingen, were he received his doctorate in 1868. He held a number of academic appointments over the following years, during which time he began his work in psychology.

In 1894 Stumpf was awarded an appointment at the University of Berlin, the most prized professorship in German psychology.[5] The years spent at Berlin were extremely productive, and his original laboratory of three small rooms grew into a large and important institute. Although the laboratory never rivaled Wundt's in scope or intensity of research, Stumpf is often considered to be Wundt's major competitor.

Stumpf's early psychological writings were concerned with space perception, but his most influential work is *Tonpsychologie (Psychology of Tone)*, which appeared in two volumes in 1883 and 1890. This work, and his other studies of music, earned him a place second only to Helmholtz's in the field of acoustics and were a pioneering effort in the psychological study of music.

The influence of Brentano may explain Stumpf's acceptance of a less rigorous form of introspection than that considered necessary at Leipzig. Stumpf argued that the primary data of psychology are phenomena. Phenomenology, the kind of introspection he favored, refers to the examination of unbiased experience—experience just as it occurs. He did not agree with Wundt on breaking experience down into elements. To do so, Stumpf argued, is to render the experience artificial and abstract, no longer "natural."[6] The phenomenological movement in Germany was a precursor of other forms of psychology, notably Gestalt psychology (Chapter 12).

Wundt and Stumpf, in a series of publications, waged a bitter controversy about the introspection of tones. The debate was started by Stumpf on a theoretical level but was personalized by Wundt. Essentially, the issue involved the question of which introspectionist's reports were the more credible. When dealing with tones, should one accept the results of highly trained introspectionists (Wundt) or of expert musicians (Stumpf)? Stumpf

[5] Wundt, who at that time was the dean of German psychologists, would have seemed the logical choice for the position. It has been suggested that the influential Helmholtz opposed his appointment.

[6] A student of Stumpf's, Edmund Husserl, later developed the philosophy of phenomenology.

would not accept the results obtained at Wundt's laboratory on this problem.

While continuing to write on music and acoustics, Stumpf established a center for the collection of recordings of primitive music from all over the world, founded the Berlin Association for Child Psychology, and published a theory of feeling in which he attempted to reduce feeling to sensation. Stumpf was one of a number of German psychologists who maintained their independence from Wundt, and so strove to expand the boundaries of psychology.

Oswald Külpe (1862–1915) and the Würzburg School

Initially a student, disciple, and follower of Wundt, Külpe in the course of his career led a group of students in a movement to break away from what he considered the limitations of the master's work. Although Külpe's movement was not a revolution, it was a declaration of freedom from the narrowness of some of Wundt's views. Külpe worked on a number of problems that Wundt's brand of structuralism had disregarded.

At the age of 19 Külpe began his university training at Leipzig. His intention was to study history, but under the influence of Wundt he switched, for a while at least, to philosophy and to experimental psychology, which at that time (1881) was still in its infancy. History maintained a strong attraction for Külpe, however, because after a year with Wundt he resumed its study at Berlin for a semester. Two further academic forays into psychology and history followed before he returned to Wundt and Leipzig in 1886 for eight years. After receiving his degree at Leipzig, he stayed on as *Dozent* and assistant to Wundt, carried on research in the laboratory, and wrote a psychology textbook, *Grundriss der Psychologie (Outline of Psychology)*. This text, published in 1893 and dedicated to Wundt, defined psychology as the science of the facts of experience as dependent on the experiencing individual.

In 1894 Külpe became a professor at Würzburg, where two years later he established a laboratory that before long became almost as important as Wundt's Leipzig laboratory. Among the students attracted to Würzburg were several Americans, one of whom, James Rowland Angell, was an important figure in the development of functionalism (Chapter 8). Apparently, Külpe was more concerned with philosophy and esthetics than with psychology during the laboratory's early years. Although his own writings are philosophical in nature, a great deal of research performed under his direction in the laboratory was published. Külpe served not only as the inspiration for his students' research, but also as observer in most of the laborious and routine introspective experiments.

In the *Grundriss* Külpe did not discuss the higher mental process of thought. In this respect his position was congruent with that of Wundt, in whose shadow he still moved. By the turn of the century, however, Külpe was convinced that the thought processes could be studied experimentally. Memory, another higher mental process, had already been studied experimentally by Hermann Ebbinghaus in 1885, as we have seen. If memory could be studied in the laboratory, why not thought? For the first time experimentation was consistently applied to the higher mental processes. Posing this question put Külpe into direct opposition to his former mentor, because Wundt had stated most emphatically that the higher mental processes could not be studied experimentally.

A second point of difference between the Würzburg school (as it came to be called) and Wundt's system relates to the method of introspection. For Wundt, introspection involved having an experience and then describing it. Külpe developed a method called *systematic experimental introspection* that involved the performance of a complex task—such as the establishment of logical connections between concepts—after which subjects were required to render a retrospective report of their experiences during the task. In other words, subjects had to perform some mental process, such as thinking or judging, and then examine how they thought or judged. The method is systematic in that the whole experience is described precisely by fractionating it into time periods. Similar tasks were repeated many times so that the introspective accounts could be corrected, corroborated, and amplified. Introspective reports were often supplemented by questioning to direct the subjects' attention to particular points.

The two forms of introspection also differed in that Külpe's subjects did not know in advance what they were to observe, whereas Wundt's subjects did. Thus, there were vast differences in both subject matter and method between the two laboratories.

Külpe did not reject Wundt's focus on conscious experience, his research tool of introspection, or his fundamental task of analyzing consciousness into its basic structure. The Würzburg school did not so much revolt against the master as attempt to expand the conception of psychology's subject matter to include the higher mental processes, and to refine the method of introspection.

What were the results of this attempted expansion and refinement? Wundt's point of view stressed that conscious experience could be reduced to its component sensory or imaginal elements. All experience, Wundt had said, is composed of sensations or images. Külpe's program of direct introspection of thought processes found evidence supporting the opposite point of view—that thinking can occur without any sensory or imaginal content! This finding came to be identified as *imageless thought,* to represent the notion of meanings in thought that do not seem to involve any specific images. Thus, a nonsensory form or aspect of consciousness was identified.

The first important contribution from the Würzburg school was a study by Karl Marbe on the comparative judgment of weights. Marbe found that although sensations and images are indeed present during the task, they

Trained at Leipzig, Oswald Külpe (1862–1915) and his Würzburg school extended psychology's subject matter to include higher mental processes.
(Archives of the History of American Psychology)

seem to play no part in the process of judgment itself. Subjects do not know how the judgments (of lighter or heavier) come into their minds. This finding contradicted the belief about thought that had been held for centuries. It had been supposed that in making a judgment of this kind, subjects retained a mental image of the first object and compared it with the sensory impression of the second object. Marbe's experiment demonstrated that there is no such comparison of image and impression, and that the process of judgment is much more elusive than had been supposed.

These and related experiments conducted at Würzburg demonstrated that although the conscious elements usually considered necessary are not essential for thought, there are apparently other conscious states present that had not been previously suspected. These additional states, such as hesitation, doubt, confidence, searching, or waiting for an answer, were considered to be neither sensations, images, nor feelings, and were initially called "conscious attitudes." In a subsequent work J. Orth suggested that Wundt's feelings of tension–relaxation and excitement–depression could be reduced to these same intangible and obscure conscious attitudes.

The Würzburg group also dealt with association and will. A classic study by Henry Watt demonstrated that in an associative task (for example, asking subjects to find a subordinate or superordinate of a particular word), subjects have little relevant information to report about their conscious process of judgment. This finding provided a further demonstration of conscious experience that could not be reduced to Wundt's sensations and images. Watt found that his subjects were able to respond correctly without being consciously aware of intending to do so during the time of response. He concluded that the conscious work was done before the task was performed, at the time when the instructions were given and understood. According to Watt, subjects, after receiving these instructions, determined to react in the manner required. When presented with the stimulus word, subjects carried out the instructions without any further conscious effort. Through the instructions, subjects had apparently established an unconscious set or *determining tendency* to respond in the way the instructions directed. Once the task had been understood and this determining tendency adopted, the actual task was performed with little, if any, conscious effort. What the Würzburg group suggested is that predispositions outside of consciousness are somehow able to control conscious activities.

A new period in the Würzburg school began in 1907 with the work of Karl Bühler, whose method involved presenting to subjects a question that required some thought before it could be answered. Subjects then gave as complete an account as possible of the steps involved in reaching the answer, with the experimenter interjecting questions about the process. Bühler's importance lies in his careful demonstration of the existence of nonsensory thought processes. This notion had already been uncovered, as we have seen, but it had been only one aspect and not a major focus of the earlier Würzburg work. Bühler stressed the notion of elements of experience that are not sensory in nature. He asserted explicitly that these new types of structural elements, these thought elements, are vital to the process of thought and must be given serious consideration.

Not unexpectedly, Külpe's refinement of Wundt's method of introspection and the attempt to add to the list of elements evoked strong criticism from the more orthodox Wundtian structuralists. It came in the form of vigorous and scathing attacks from Wundt and his pupil Titchener. Wundt called the Würzburg form of introspection "mock" experiments and said that their method did not really involve experimentation or introspection. Through it all, Külpe maintained the highest regard for both of his critics.

In a way it is strange that the Wundtians so strongly opposed the Würzburg notion of nonsensory mental life. After all, Külpe was proceeding along paths that Wundt had opened. And had not Wundt himself thought along not too dissimilar lines? Was not his notion of feelings a recognition of nonsensory elements of conscious experience? It was certainly no accident that Külpe, a product of Wundtian training, had instigated this movement.

Were there really fundamental points of difference between the schools at Würzburg and Leipzig? In terms of basic emphasis, goals, and methods, probably not. Külpe and his followers were trying to find the elements of conscious experience through introspective report. They were, like Wundt, analytical in their approach and structuralist in their basic orientation.

The 15 years that Külpe remained at Würzburg were his most influential for the history of psychology. In 1909 he went to Bonn, where he founded a laboratory, and in 1913 he moved to Munich. His interest in philosophical problems, particularly esthetics, came to the fore in his post-Würzburg years. Külpe wrote very little concerning his students' work at Würzburg, and his planned description of the nature of the thought processes was never written. Boring commented that Külpe "did not in his life-time convince his critics. At the dramatic moment in this work he died, too early, at the age of 53, without having yet convincingly demonstrated to the world that Wundt was wrong, or that Wundt was right, when he said that one can not experiment upon thought" (Boring, 1950b, p. 409). Still, the notions developed by the Würzburg group were to some degree influential for the later Gestalt psychologists.

A major contribution to modern psychology is the Würzburg emphasis on the topic of motivation. Their key concept of determining tendency or set has a bearing on motivation as it is treated in today's psychology. Also, their demonstration that experience depended not only on conscious elements, but also on unconscious determining tendencies, suggests the role of unconscious determinants of behavior, which forms a major part of Freud's systematic position (Chapter 13).

COMMENT

We see, then, division and controversy enveloping psychology almost as soon as it was founded. But it must be emphasized that for all their differences, these early psychologists were united in theme and purpose.

Wundt, Ebbinghaus, Brentano, Stumpf, and others had irrevocably changed the study of human nature. Because of their efforts, the new psychology was no longer

> a study of the soul, certainly not an inquiry by rational analysis into its simplicity, substantiality and immortality. It was a study, by observation and experiment, of certain reactions of the human organism not included in the subject matter of any other science. The German psychologists, in spite of their many differences, were to this extent engaged in a common

enterprise; and their ability, their industry, and the common direction of their labors all made the developments in the German universities the center of the new movement in psychology. (Heidbreder, 1933, p. 105)[7]

One should not conclude that orthodox Wundtian structuralism was dead by the end of the nineteenth century. This was decidedly not the case, as we shall see from our discussion of Wundt's stalwart standard-bearer, E. B. Titchener.

SUGGESTED READINGS

WUNDT

Blumenthal, A. L. A reappraisal of Wilhelm Wundt. *American Psychologist,* 1975, *30,* 1081–1088.

Boring, E. G. On the subjectivity of important historical dates: Leipzig 1879. *Journal of the History of the Behavioral Sciences,* 1965, *1,* 5–9.

Bringmann, W., Balance, W., & Evans, R. Wilhelm Wundt 1832–1920: A brief biographical sketch. *Journal of the History of the Behavioral Sciences,* 1975, *11,* 287–297.

Cattell, J. McK. The psychological laboratory at Leipzig. *Mind,* 1888, *13,* 37–51.

Danziger, K. The positivist repudiation of Wundt. *Journal of the History of the Behavioral Sciences,* 1979, *15,* 205–230.

Leahey, T. H. Something old, something new: Attention in Wundt and modern cognitive psychology. *Journal of the History of the Behavioral Sciences,* 1979, *15,* 242–252.

Mischel, T. Wundt and the conceptual foundations of psychology. *Philosophical and Phenomenological Research,* 1970, *31,* 1–26.

Titchener, E. B. Wilhelm Wundt. *American Journal of Psychology,* 1921, *32,* 161–178.

EBBINGHAUS

Postman, L. Hermann Ebbinghaus. *American Psychologist,* 1968, *23,* 149–157.

Shakow, D. Hermann Ebbinghaus. *American Journal of Psychology,* 1930, *42,* 505–518.

MÜLLER

Boring, E. G. Georg Elias Müller, 1850–1934. *American Journal of Psychology,* 1935, *47,* 344–348.

BRENTANO

Puglisi, M. Brentano: A biographical sketch. *American Journal of Psychology,* 1924, *35,* 414–419.

Rancurello, A. C. *A study of Franz Brentano.* New York: Academic Press, 1968.

---

[7] This and all subsequent quotations credited to Heidbreder, 1933, are from Edna Heidbreder, *Seven Psychologies,* © 1933, renewed 1961. Reprinted by permission of Prentice-Hall, Inc., Englewood Cliffs, New Jersey.

Titchener, E. B. Brentano and Wundt: Empirical and experimental psychology. *American Journal of Psychology,* 1921, *32,* 108–120.

STUMPF

Langfeld, H. S. Carl Stumpf: 1848–1936. *American Journal of Psychology,* 1937, *49,* 316–320.

KÜLPE AND THE WÜRZBURG SCHOOL

Lindenfeld, D. Oswald Külpe and the Würzburg school. *Journal of the History of the Behavioral Sciences,* 1978, *14,* 132–141.

Ogden, R. M. Oswald Külpe and the Würzburg school. *American Journal of Psychology,* 1951, *64,* 4–19.

5 STRUCTURALISM: FINAL FORM

The orthodox Wundtian brand of the new psychology was transplanted to the United States by Wundt's most devoted pupil, E. B. Titchener, and underwent its fullest development at his hands. A knowledge of Wundt's psychology provides a reasonably accurate picture of Titchener's system. Although the pupil did differ with the teacher on some points, the Titchenerian system is unmistakably Wundtian in method, content, and spirit.

EDWARD BRADFORD TITCHENER (1867–1927)

The Life of Titchener

Titchener, a fascinating man who was English by birth but German in professional and personal temperament, spent his most productive years at Cornell University in New York. For Titchener, who is often pictured clad in the academic gown he invariably wore to class, every lecture was a dramatic production. The staging was carefully prepared by assistants under Titchener's watchful eye. The staff and junior faculty, who attended all his lectures, entered through one door to take front-row seats, and the professor came through another that led directly to the lecture platform. Afterward, the lecture was solemnly discussed by the faculty and graduate students.

As Titchener put it, his Oxford gown gave him the right to be dogmatic. Although he spent only two years with Wundt, Titchener resembled his mentor in many respects, including his autocratic nature, his formal lectures, and even his bearded appearance.

Born in Chichester, England, into an old family that had little money, Titchener relied on his considerable intellectual abilities to win scholarships to further his education. He attended Malvern College and then Oxford, where he studied philosophy and the classics for four years and became a research assistant in physiology for the fifth year.

While at Oxford, Titchener became interested in Wundt's new psychology, an interest that was not shared or encouraged by anyone at the university. It was natural, then, that he should journey to Leipzig, the mecca for scientific pilgrims, to study under Wundt for two years, receiving his degree in 1892. There seems no doubt that Wundt made a lifelong impression on the young student, though Titchener apparently saw little of him (Wundt was 35 years older and somewhat aloof). The years at Leipzig determined Titchener's future in psychology, that of his many students, and to a certain extent, the course of American psychology for a number of years. For most of his career Titchener was a zealous disciple of Wundt's, with all the ardor and narrowness of view that characterize a convert to any faith. As Arthur Koestler so perceptively noted:

> *Disciples tend to be more fanatical than their masters; they have committed themselves to his system, invested years of labour and staked their reputation on it; they fought the opposition and cannot tolerate the idea that the system might be at fault. [This is] as common among scientists devoted to their theory as it is among politicians or theologians devoted to a doctrine. (1971, p. 33)*

Such faithful and fanatical stewardship on the part of Titchener was both his greatest strength and his ultimate undoing, although, as we shall see, he began to move away from the orthodox Wundtian view toward the end of his life.

After receiving his degree, Titchener wanted to become the pioneer of the new experimental psychology in England. The British, however, were skeptical of a scientific approach to one of their favorite philosophical subjects. Therefore, after a few months as an extension lecturer in biology at Oxford, Titchener went to the United States to teach psychology and direct the laboratory at the new Cornell University. He was then 25 years old, and he remained at Cornell for the rest of his life.

The years 1893–1900 were spent in developing the laboratory, acquiring equipment, conducting research, and writing some 62 articles. As more students were attracted to Cornell, Titchener relinquished the time-consuming task of participating personally in every research study and in later years the research was conducted almost entirely by his students.

It was through direction of his students' research that his systematic position reached fruition. Titchener supervised more than 50 doctoral candidates in psychology in 35 years, and most of their dissertations bear the stamp of his personal thought. He exercised great authority in the selection of the students' research problems, assigning topics that were relevant to the issues with which he was concerned at the time. In this way, Titchener built a unified systematic position, and all graduate students at a given time were expected to work collectively on his ideas. Roback (1952) noted that "Titchener thus erected an ivory tower in which he was to sit aloft and direct the course of what he considered to be the only scientific psychology worthy of the name" (p. 184).

Titchener's own bibliography includes 216 articles and notes and a number of books. He translated the master, Wundt, and when he had completed the third edition of *Principles of Physiological Psychology*, he found that Wundt had finished another new edition. Titchener then translated this fourth edition, only to learn that the tireless Wundt had published a fifth edition!

Titchener wrote *An Outline of Psychology* in 1896, *Primer of Psychology* in 1898, and the four-volume *Experimental Psychology* in 1901–1905. Külpe is said to have described the last as "the most erudite psychological work in the English language" (Boring, 1950b, p. 413). These "Manuals" as the volumes of *Experimental Psychology* came to be called, helped to speed the growth of laboratory work in psychology and influenced a generation of American experimental psychologists, including John B. Watson, the founder of behaviorism (Chapter 10). The textbooks enjoyed wide popularity and some were translated into Russian, Italian, German, Spanish, and French.

Titchener engaged in several hobbies that tended to divert time and energy from psychology. He became so proficient in music that he conducted a small ensemble at his home every Sunday evening, and at one time substituted for a music professor at Cornell. His avid interest in coin collecting led him, with typical thoroughness, to learn such difficult languages as Chinese and Arabic to master the characters on the coins. In addition to his knowledge of classical languages, he was conversant in a half-dozen modern languages, including Russian. Throughout his career he maintained a voluminous correspondence with colleagues; the majority of these letters were typewritten by Titchener and contain additional hand-written material.

As he grew older, Titchener withdrew more and more from social and university life. He had become a living legend at Cornell, though a number of faculty members had never met him. He did a great deal of his work at home and spent relatively little time at the university. After 1909 he lectured only on Monday evenings of the spring semester of each year. He was well protected in his study at home from intrusions from the outside world. His wife screened all callers and it was understood that no student would telephone him except in an extreme emergency.

Although he did tend to be autocratic, in the mold of the German professor, he was also kind and helpful to students and colleagues, so long as they paid him the deference and respect he felt were his due. Stories are told of how junior faculty members and students washed his car and installed his window screens in the summer, not on command, but out of respect and admiration.

Karl Dallenbach (1967), a former student, quotes Titchener as saying, "A man could not hope to become a psychologist until after he had learned to smoke." Accordingly, most of his students took to cigars, at least in his presence.[1]

---

[1] Ludy Benjamin offers the following anecdote: "Cora Friedline, one of Titchener's doctoral students, was discussing her research in Titchener's office when his ever-present cigar caught his beard on fire. He was talking at the time and his imposing manner made her reluctant to interrupt. Finally she said, "I beg your pardon, Dr. Titchener, but your whiskers are on fire." By the time he extinguished the flames, the fire had burned through his shirt and his underwear." (From the Cora Friedline papers, Archives of the History of American Psychology, University of Akron.)

Titchener's concern for his students did not end when they left Cornell, nor did his impact on their lives. Dallenbach, upon receiving his Ph.D., intended to go to medical school, but Titchener obtained a teaching position for him at the University of Oregon. Dallenbach thought that Titchener would approve of his going to medical school, "but he did not. I had to go to Oregon, as he did not intend to have his training and work with me wasted" (1967, p. 91).

Titchener's relations with psychologists outside his own group were never very close. Elected to the American Psychological Association by the charter members in 1892, he resigned shortly thereafter because the association would not expel a member he accused of plagiarism. It is said that a friend paid Titchener's dues for a number of years so that his name might be listed.

In 1904 a group of psychologists called the "Titchener experimentalists" was formed and met regularly to compare research notes. As might be suspected, Titchener selected both the topics and the guests, and generally dominated these meetings.

Around 1910 Titchener began work on what was intended to be a thorough exposition of his systematic point of view. Unfortunately, it was never completed, though a few sections were published in a journal and reprinted posthumously in a book in 1929. He died of a brain tumor at age 60.

Titchener's System

The Subject Matter of Psychology

According to Titchener, the subject matter of psychology is experience. All sciences, he noted, share this subject matter—some aspect of the world of human experience—but each deals with a different aspect. The subject matter of psychology is experience as it is dependent on experiencing persons. This kind of experience is vastly different from that studied by other scientists. For example, light and sound may be studied by both a physicist and a psychologist, but the physicist looks at the phenomena from the viewpoint of the physical processes involved, and the psychologist views them in terms of how they are experienced by human observers.

The other sciences, Titchener said, are independent of experiencing persons. The temperature in a room may be 85 degrees whether anyone experiences the level of heat or not. When observers stand in a room and report that they feel uncomfortable, however, this feeling is experienced by and is dependent on the experiencing individuals. This experience alone is the subject matter of psychology.

Titchener cautioned that in the study of experiencing one must not commit what he called the *stimulus error*, that is, confusing the mental process with the object being observed. For instance, observers who see an apple and describe it as an apple, instead of reporting the hues, brightnesses, and spatial characteristics they are experiencing, are committing the stimulus error. The object of observation is not to be described in everyday language, but rather in terms of the conscious content of the experience.

When observers focus on the stimulus object instead of the conscious process, they fail to distinguish what they know about the object (for example, that it is called "apple") from their own immediate experience. The only things observers really know about an object are its color, brightness, and spatial pattern (for example, that the object is red, shiny, and round). When they describe anything other than these characteristics, they are interpreting the object, not observing it.

Titchener defined consciousness as the sum total of our experiences as they exist at a given time. Mind is defined as the sum of our experiences accumulated over a lifetime. Thus, mind and consciousness are similar, except that consciousness involves mental processes occurring at the moment instead of the total accumulation of processes.

Titchener argued that psychology must study the generalized human mind, not individual minds, and certainly not individual differences among minds. The purpose of this study is solely that of understanding the mind. Titchener's psychology was a pure science. He agreed wholeheartedly with Wundt that psychology has no applied or utilitarian concerns. Psychology was not, he said, in the business of curing "sick minds" or reforming individuals or society. Its only legitimate purpose is to discover the facts of the mind.

He believed that scientists have to remain free of any concern for the practical worth of their work. He opposed child psychology, animal psychology, and any other area of the science that did not fit in with his introspective experimental psychology of the content of consciousness.

The Method of Study

Psychology, like all sciences, depends on observation, but it depends on observation of conscious experience, or introspection. Titchener's form of introspection was even more highly developed and formalized than Wundt's. Titchener believed that introspection could be performed only by well-trained observers. He realized that everyone learns to describe experience in terms of the stimulus, and that in everyday life this is beneficial and necessary. In the laboratory, however, this habit must be unlearned through intensive training. His introspectors were required to relearn how to perceive so as to be able to describe the conscious state and not the stimulus. (The difficulties in specifying precisely what observers learned to do are discussed in the section "Criticisms of Structuralism.")

The influence of the mechanistic spirit is evident in the image developed by structuralists of the human subjects who supplied the data. In the journal articles of the day subjects were called "reagents," a term used by scientists to denote substances that, because of their capacity for certain reactions, are used to detect, examine, or measure other substances. A reagent is generally a passive agent, one that is applied to something to elicit certain reactions. The parallel with chemistry is obvious.

Transposing this concept to the human subject in Titchener's laboratory, we see that subjects were used as recording instruments, objectively noting the characteristics of the object being observed. Human subjects were nothing more than impartial and detached machines. Titchener wrote of trained observation becoming mechanized or habitual, that is, no longer a conscious process.

If human subjects are considered to be machines, then it is easy to think that all human beings are machines. The point deserves mention because it shows the continuing influence of the Galilean–Newtonian mechanical view of the universe, an influence that did not cease with the demise of structuralism. We shall see as the history of psychology unfolds that this image of human-as-machine still characterizes much of experimental psychology.

Titchener believed that observation in psychology must be not only introspective but also experimental. He diligently observed the rigid rules of scientific experimentation, noting that:

> An experiment is an observation that can be repeated, isolated and varied. The more frequently you can repeat an observation, the more likely are you to see clearly what is there and to describe accurately what you have seen. The more strictly you can isolate an observation, the easier does your task of observation become, and the less danger is there of your being led astray by irrelevant circumstances, or of placing emphasis on the wrong point. The more widely you can vary an observation, the more clearly will the uniformity of experience stand out, and the better is your chance of discovering laws. All experimental appliances, all laboratories and instruments, are provided and devised with this one end in view: that the student shall be able to repeat, isolate and vary his observations. (1909–1910, p. 20)

The Aims of Psychology

Titchener's three problems or aims of psychology are similar to those of Wundt. Psychologists seek (1) to reduce conscious processes to their simplest, most basic components; (2) to determine how these elements are combined and their laws of combination; and (3) to bring the elements into

Structuralism was established as the first American science of psychology by Edward Bradford Titchener (1867–1927), who refined Wundt's theory and methods.
(National Library of Medicine)

connection with their physiological conditions. Thus, the aims of psychology coincide with those of the natural sciences. After scientists decide which part of the natural world to study, they proceed to discover its elements, to demonstrate how they are compounded into more complex phenomena, and to formulate the laws governing the phenomena.

We have noted that one of Titchener's goals for psychology was to reduce consciousness to its component elements. How do we know whether a given conscious process is elemental, that is, cannot be broken down into anything simpler? Titchener's answer is that when the process remains unchanged in the face of rigorous and persistent introspection, it is a true element. In essence, his test of the irreducibility of elements into anything simpler is analogous to the chemist's criterion for establishing chemical elements.

Titchener believed that there are three elementary states of consciousness—sensations, images, and affective states. *Sensations* are the basic elements of perception and occur in the sounds, sights, smells, and other experiences occasioned by physical objects present in the environment. *Images* are the elements of ideas and are found in the process that pictures or reflects experiences not actually present at the moment, such as a memory of a past experience. It is not clear from Titchener's writings whether he thought sensations and images belonged to mutually exclusive categories. He emphasized the similarity between the two while arguing that they could be distinguished. *Affections* are the elements of emotion and are found in experiences such as love, hate, or sadness.

In *An Outline of Psychology* (1896) Titchener presented a list of his discovered elements of sensation; it comprises more than 44,000 sensation qualities, the majority of which were visual (32,820) and auditory (11,600). Each element was believed to be conscious and distinct from all others, and each could be blended or combined with others to form perceptions and ideas.

Although basic and irreducible, these elements could still be categorized, just as chemical elements are grouped into various classes. Despite their simplicity, elements have characteristics that enable us to distinguish among them. To the Wundtian attributes of quality and intensity, Titchener added duration and clearness. He considered these four attributes to be basic characteristics of all sensations that are present, to some degree, in all experience.

Quality is the characteristic that clearly distinguishes each element from every other, such as cold or red. *Intensity* refers to the strength or weakness, loudness or brightness, of a sensation. *Duration* refers to the course of a sensation over time, and *clearness* refers to the role of attention in conscious experience. That which is the focus of attention is more dominant than that toward which attention is not directed.

Sensations and images possess all four of these attributes, but affection has only three; it lacks clearness. Titchener thought that it was not possible to focus attention directly on the quality of pleasantness, for example. When we try to do so, the affective quality disappears. Some sensory processes, particularly vision and touch, also possess the attribute of *extensity*, in that they spread out in space.

All conscious processes are reducible to one of these categories. The findings of the Würzburg school did not cause Titchener to modify his position. He recognized that obscure and ill-defined qualities may occur during thought, but he held that these were still sensory or imaginal elements. The subjects in the Würzburg laboratory had, Titchener said, succumbed to the stimulus error because they paid more attention to the object than to their conscious processes.

A good deal of research on affection or feeling was carried out in the Cornell laboratory and resulted in the rejection of Wundt's tridimensional theory. We stated that affection has only three attributes—quality, intensity, and duration. Thus, sensations and affections are processes of the same general type and have these three attributes in common, differing, as noted, in that affection lacks the attribute of clearness. Titchener believed that affection had only one of the dimensions in Wundt's theory, pleasure–displeasure, denying the other two dimensions of tension–relaxation and excitement–depression.

Titchener began to alter his system in major ways toward the end of his life (Evans, 1972; Henle, 1974). Although he never formalized these modifications into a new system—he died before being able to do so—the nature of the changes is nevertheless clear from studies of his lectures and correspondence.

His system began to change as early as 1918. Dropping the concept of mental elements from his course, he began to argue that psychology should study not elements, but the dimensional categories or attributes of mental life, which he listed as quality, intensity, protensity (duration), extensity, and attensity (clearness). Later, two years before his death, he wrote to a graduate student that "You must give up thinking in terms of sensations and affections. That was all right ten years ago; but now, as I have told you, it is wholly out of date. . . . You must learn to think in terms of dimensions rather than in terms of systematic constructs like sensation" (Evans, 1972, p. 174). Titchener was also having second thoughts about the rigid, controlled form of introspection that he and Wundt had been practicing for so long. He came to favor a more open, phenomenological approach.

These are dramatic shifts that, had he lived long enough to implement them, would have radically altered the face if not the fate of structural psychology. As well, they clearly suggest a flexibility and openness that scientists like to think they possess, but which not all demonstrate.

It should be remembered that the evidence for these changes was pieced together by Evans (1972) and Henle (1974) from a meticulous examination of Titchener's letters and lectures. The ideas were never incorporated into Titchener's system. They indicate a direction and a goal toward which Titchener was apparently moving, but which his death prevented him from reaching.

ORIGINAL SOURCE MATERIAL ON STRUCTURALISM: FROM *A TEXT-BOOK OF PSYCHOLOGY* BY E. B. TITCHENER

The following material is reprinted from Titchener's popular *A Text-Book of Psychology*, published in 1909–1910.[2] It describes the orthodox structuralist view of the subject matter and methodology of the new science of psychology.

This material supplements our discussion of Titchener and provides an example of the style of exposition that psychology students were studying more than a half century ago.

All human knowledge is derived from human experience; there is no other source of knowledge. But human experience, as we have seen, may be considered from different points of view. Suppose that we take two points of view, as far as possible apart, and discover for ourselves what experience looks like in the two cases. First, we will regard experience as altogether independent of any particular person; we will assume that it goes on whether or not anyone is there to have it. Secondly, we will regard experience as altogether dependent upon the particular person; we will assume that it goes on only when someone is there to have it. We shall hardly find standpoints more diverse. What are the differences in experience, as viewed from them?

Take, to begin with, the three things that you first learn about in physics: space, time and mass. Physical space, which is the space of geometry and astronomy and geology, is constant, always and everywhere the same. Its unit is 1 cm., and the cm. has precisely the same value wherever and whenever it is applied. Physical time is similarly constant; and its constant unit is the 1 sec. Physical mass is constant; its unit, the 1 gr., is always and everywhere the same. Here we have experience of space, time and mass considered as independent of the person who experiences them. Change, then, to the point of view which brings the experiencing person into account. The two vertical lines in Fig. 1 [*Figure 5.1*, this volume] are physically equal; they measure alike in units of 1 cm. To you, who see them, they are not equal. The hour that you spend in the waiting-room of a village station and the hour that you spend in watching an amusing play are physically equal; they measure alike in units of 1 sec. To you, the one hour goes slowly, the other quickly; they are not equal. Take two circular cardboard boxes of different diameter (say, 2 cm. and 8 cm.), and pour sand into them until they both

[2] Reprinted with permission of Macmillan Publishing Co., Inc., from *A Text-Book of Psychology* by E. B. Titchener (pp. 6–9, 15–25, 36–41). Copyright 1909 by Macmillan Publishing Co., Inc. Revised 1937 by Sophia K. Titchener. (Footnotes omitted.)

Structuralism:
Final Form

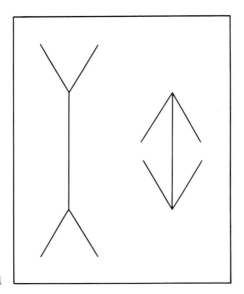

FIGURE 5-1

weigh, say, 50 gr. The two masses are physically equal; placed on the pans of a balance, they will hold the beam level. To you, as you lift them in your two hands, or raise them in turn by the same hand, the box of smaller diameter is considerably the heavier. Here we have experience of space, time and mass considered as dependent upon the experiencing person. It is the same experience that we were discussing just now. But our first point of view gives us facts and laws of physics; our second gives us facts and laws of psychology.

Now take three other topics that are discussed in the physical text-books: heat, sound and light. Heat proper, the physicists tell us, is the energy of molecular motion; that is to say, heat is a form of energy due to a movement of the particles of a body among themselves. Radiant heat belongs, with light, to what is called radiant energy—energy that is propagated by wave-movements of the luminiferous ether with which space is filled. Sound is a form of energy due to the vibratory movements of bodies, and is propagated by wave-movements of some elastic medium, solid, liquid or gaseous. In brief, heat is a dance of molecules; light is a wave-motion of the ether; sound is a wave-motion of the air. The world of physics, in which these types of experience are considered as independent of the experiencing person, is neither warm nor cold, neither dark nor light, neither silent nor noisy. It is only when the experiences are considered as dependent upon some person that we have warmth and cold, blacks and whites and colours and greys, tones and hisses and thuds. And these things are the subject-matter of psychology.

We find, then, a great difference in the aspect of experience, according as it is viewed from the one or the other of our different standpoints.

It is the same experience all through; physics and psychology deal with the same stuff, the same material; the sciences are separated simply—and sufficiently—by their point of view. From the standpoint of physics, we get such sciences as physics (in the narrower sense), chemistry, geology, astronomy, meteorology. From the standpoint of psychology we get, in the same way, a special group of sciences. . . .

It must be clearly understood that we are not here attempting to give a strict definition of the subject-matter of psychology. We assume that everybody knows, at first hand, what human experience is, and we then seek to mark off the two aspects of this experience which are dealt with respectively by physics and psychology. Any further definition of the subject-matter of psychology is impossible. Unless one knows, by experience itself, what experience is, one can no more give a meaning to the term "mind" than a stone can give a meaning to the term "matter." . . .

MENTAL PROCESS, CONSCIOUSNESS AND MIND. The most striking fact about the world of human experience is the fact of change. Nothing stands still; everything goes on. The sun will someday lose its heat; the eternal hills are, little by little, breaking up and wearing away. Whatever we observe, and from whatever standpoint we observe it, we find process, occurrence; nowhere is there permanence or stability. Mankind, it is true, has sought to arrest this flux, and to give stability to the world of experience, by assuming two permanent substances, matter and mind: the occurrences of the physical world are then supposed to be manifestations of matter, and the occurrences of the mental world to be manifestations of mind. Such an hypothesis may be of value at a certain stage of human thought; but every hypothesis that does not accord with the facts must, sooner or later, be given up. Physicists are therefore giving up the hypothesis of an unchanging, substantial matter, and psychologists are giving up the hypothesis of an unchanging, substantial mind. Stable objects and substantial things belong, not to the world of science, physical or psychological, but only to the world of common sense.

We have defined mind as the sum-total of human experience considered as dependent upon the experiencing person. We have said, further, that the phrase "experiencing person" means the living body, the organized individual; and we have hinted that, for psychological purposes, the living body may be reduced to the nervous system and its attachments. Mind thus becomes the sum-total of human experience considered as dependent upon a nervous system. And since human experience is always process, occurrence, and the dependent aspect of human experience is its mental aspect, we may say, more shortly, that mind is the sum-total of mental processes. All these words are significant. "Sum-total" implies that we are concerned with the whole world of experience, not with a limited portion of it; "mental" implies that we are concerned with experience under its dependent aspect, as conditioned by a nervous system; and "processes" implies that our subject-matter is a stream, a perpetual flux, and not a collection of unchanging objects.

It is not easy, even with the best will possible, to shift from the common-sense to the scientific view of mind; the change cannot be made all in a moment. We are to regard mind as a stream of processes? But mind is personal, my mind; and my personality continues throughout my life. The experiencing person is only the bodily organism? But, again, experience is personal, the experience of a permanent self. Mind is spatial, just as matter is? But mind is invisible, intangible; it is not here or there, square or round.

These objections cannot be finally met until we have gone some distance into psychology, and can see how the scientific view of mind works out. Even now, however, they will weaken as you look at them. Face that question of personality. Is your life, as a matter of fact, always personal? Do you not, time and again, forget yourself, lose yourself, disregard yourself, neglect yourself, contradict yourself, in a very literal sense? Surely, the mental life is only intermittently personal. And is your personality, when it is realised, unchanging? Are you the same self in childhood and manhood, in your working and in your playing moods, when you are on your best behaviour and when you are freed from restraint? Surely, the self-experience is not only intermittent, but also composed, at different times, of very different factors. As to the other question: mind is, of course, invisible, because sight is mind; and mind is intangible, because touch is mind. Sight-experience and touch-experience are dependent upon the experiencing person. But common sense itself bears witness, against its own belief, to the fact that mind is spatial: we speak, and speak correctly, of an idea in our head, a pain in our foot. And if the idea is the idea of a circle seen in the mind's eye, it is round; and if it is the visual idea of a square, it is square.

Consciousness, as reference to any dictionary will show, is a term that has many meanings. Here it is, perhaps, enough to distinguish two principal uses of the word.

In its first sense, consciousness means the mind's awareness of its own processes. Just as, from the commonsense point of view, mind is that inner self which thinks, remembers, chooses, reasons, directs the movements of the body, so is consciousness the inner knowledge of this thought and government. You are conscious of the correctness of your answer to an examination question, of the awkwardness of your movements, of the purity of your motives. Consciousness is thus something more than mind; it is "the perception of what passes in a man's own mind"; it is "the immediate knowledge which the mind has of its sensations and thoughts."

In its second sense, consciousness is identified with mind, and "conscious" with "mental." So long as mental processes are going on, consciousness is present; as soon as mental processes are in abeyance, unconsciousness sets in. "To say I am conscious of a feeling, is merely to say that I feel it. To have a feeling is to be conscious; and to be conscious is to have a feeling. To be conscious of the prick of the pin, is merely to have the sensation. And though I have these various modes of naming my sensation, by saying, I feel the prick of a pin, I feel the pain of a prick, I have the sensation of a prick, I have the feeling of a prick, I am conscious of the feeling; the thing named in all these various ways is one and the same."

The first of these definitions we must reject. It is not only unnecessary, but it is also misleading, to speak of consciousness as the mind's awareness of itself. The usage is unnecessary, because, as we shall see later, this awareness is a matter of observation of the same general kind as observation of the external world; it is misleading, because it suggests that mind is a personal being, instead of a stream of processes. We shall therefore take mind and consciousness to mean the same thing. But as we have the two different words, and it is convenient to make some distinction between them, we shall speak of mind when we mean the sum-total of mental processes occurring in the life-time of an individual, and we shall speak of consciousness when we mean the sum-total of mental processes occurring *now,* at any given "present" time. Consciousness will thus be a section, a division, of the mind-stream. This distinction is, indeed, already made in common speech: when we say that a man has "lost consciousness," we mean that the lapse is temporary, that the mental life will shortly be resumed; when we say that a man has "lost his mind," we mean—not, it is true, that the mind has altogether disappeared, but certainly that the derangement is permanent and chronic.

While, therefore, the subject-matter of psychology is mind, the direct object of psychological study is always a consciousness. In strictness, we can never observe the same consciousness twice over; the stream of mind flows on, never to return. Practically, we can observe a particular consciousness as often as we wish, since mental processes group themselves in the same way, show the same pattern of arrangement, whenever the organism is placed under the same circumstances. Yesterday's high tide will never recur, and yesterday's consciousnesses will never recur; but we have a science of psychology, as we have a science of oceanography.

THE METHOD OF PSYCHOLOGY. Scientific method may be summed up in the single word "observation"; the only way to work in science is to observe those phenomena which form the subject-matter of science. And observation implies two things: attention to the phenomena, and record of the phenomena; that is, clear and vivid experience, and an account of the experience in words or formulas. In order to secure clear experience and accurate report, science has recourse to experiment. An experiment is an observation that can be repeated, isolated and varied. The more frequently you can *repeat* an observation, the more likely are you to see clearly what is there

Structuralism:
Final Form

and to describe accurately what you have seen. The more strictly you can *isolate* an observation, the easier does your task of observation become, and the less danger is there of your being led astray by irrelevant circumstances, or of placing emphasis on the wrong point. The more widely you can *vary* an observation, the more clearly will the uniformity of experience stand out, and the better is your chance of discovering laws. All experimental appliances, all laboratories and instruments, are provided and devised with this one end in view: that the student shall be able to repeat, isolate and vary his observations.—

The method of psychology, then, is observation. To distinguish it from the observation of physical science, which is inspection, a looking-at, psychological observation has been termed introspection, a looking-within. But this difference of name must not blind us to the essential likeness of the methods. Let us take some typical instances.

We may begin with two very simple cases. (1) Suppose that you are shown two paper discs: the one of an uniform violet, the other composed half of red and half of blue. If this second disc is rapidly rotated, the red and blue will mix, as we say, and you will see a certain blue-red, that is, a kind of violet. Your problem is, so to adjust the proportions of red and blue in the second disc that the resulting violet exactly matches the violet of the first disc. You may repeat this set of observations as often as you like; you may isolate the observations by working in a room that is free from other, possibly disturbing colours; you may vary the observations by working to equality of the violets first from a two-colour disc that is distinctly too blue, and secondly from a disc that is distinctly too red. (2) Suppose, again, that the chord *c-e-g* is struck, and that you are asked to say how many tones it contains. You may repeat this observation; you may isolate it, by working in a quiet room; you may vary it, by having the chord struck at different parts of the scale, in different octaves.

It is clear that, in these instances, there is practically no difference between introspection and inspection. You are using the same method that you would use for counting the swings of a pendulum, or taking readings from a galvanometer scale, in the physical laboratory. There is a difference in subject-matter: the colours and the tones are dependent, not independent experiences: but the method is essentially the same.

Now let us take some cases in which the material of introspection is more complex. (1) Suppose that a word is called out to you, and that you are asked to observe the effect which this stimulus produces upon consciousness: how the word affects you, what ideas it calls up, and so forth. The observation may be repeated; it may be isolated—you may be seated in a dark and silent room, free from disturbances; and it may be varied—different words may be called out, the word may be flashed upon a screen instead of spoken, etc. Here, however, there seems to be a difference between introspection and inspection. The

*Original Source Material on
Structuralism*

observer who is watching the course of a chemical reaction, or the movements of some microscopical creature, can jot down from moment to moment the different phases of the observed phenomenon. But if you try to report the changes in consciousness, while these changes are in progress, you interfere with consciousness; your translation of the mental experience into words introduces new factors into that experience itself. (2) Suppose, again, that you are observing a feeling or an emotion: a feeling of disappointment or annoyance, an emotion of anger or chagrin. Experimental control is still possible; situations may be arranged, in the psychological laboratory, such that these feelings may be repeated, isolated and varied. But your observation of them interferes, even more seriously than before, with the course of consciousness. Cool consideration of an emotion is fatal to its very existence; your anger disappears, your disappointment evaporates, as you examine it.

To overcome this difficulty of the introspective method, students of psychology are usually recommended to delay their observation until the process to be described has run its course, and then to call it back and describe it from memory. Introspection thus becomes retrospection; introspective examination becomes *post mortem* examination. The rule is, no doubt, a good one for the beginner; and there are cases in which even the experienced psychologist will be wise to follow it. But it is by no means universal. For we must remember (a) that the observations in question may be repeated. There is, then, no reason why the observer to whom the word is called out, or in whom the emotion is set up, should not report at once upon the first stage of his experience: upon the immediate effect of the word, upon the beginnings of the emotive process. It is true that this report interrupts the observation. But, after the first stage has been accurately described, further observations may be taken, and the second, third and following stages similarly described; so that presently a complete report upon the whole experience is obtained. There is, in theory, some danger that the stages become artificially separated; consciousness is a flow, a process, and if we divide it up we run the risk of missing certain intermediate links. In practice, however, this danger has proved to be very small; and we may always have recourse to retrospection, and compare our partial results with our memory of the unbroken experience. Moreover, (b) the practised observer gets into an introspective habit, has the introspective attitude ingrained in his system; so that it is possible for him, not only to take mental notes while the observation is in progress, without interfering with consciousness, but even to jot down written notes, as the histologist does while his eye is still held to the ocular of the microscope.

In principle, then, introspection is very like inspection. The objects of observation are different; they are objects of dependent, not of independent experience; they are likely to be transient, elusive, slippery. Sometimes they refuse to be observed while they are in passage; they must be preserved in memory, as a delicate tissue is preserved in hardening fluid, before they can be examined. And the standpoint of the observer is different; it is the standpoint of human life and of human interest, not of detachment and aloofness. But, in general, the method of psychology is much the same as the method of physics.

It must not be forgotten that, while the method of the physical and the psychological sciences is substantially the same, the subject-matter of these sciences is as different as it can well be. Ultimately, as we have seen, the subject-matter of all the sciences is the world of human experience; but we have also seen that the aspect of experience treated by physics is radically different from the aspect treated by psychology. The likeness of method may tempt us to slip from the one aspect to the other, as when a text-book of physics contains a chapter on vision and the sense of colour, or a text-book of physiology contains paragraphs on delusions of judgment; but this confusion of subject-matter must inevitably lead to confusion of thought. Since all the sciences are concerned with the one world of human experience, it is natural that scientific method, to whatever aspect of experience it is applied, should be in principle the same. On the other hand, when we have decided to examine some particular aspect of experience, it is necessary that we hold fast to that aspect, and do not shift our point of view as the enquiry proceeds. Hence it is a great advantage that we have the two terms, introspection and inspection, to denote observation taken from the different stand-points of psychology and of physics. The use of the word introspection is a constant reminder that we are working in psychology, that we are observing the dependent aspect of the world of experience.

Observation, as we said above, implies two things: attention to the phenomena, and record of the phenomena. The attention must be held at the highest possible degree of concentration; the record must be photographically accurate. Observation is, therefore, both difficult and fatiguing; and introspection is, on the whole, more difficult and more fatiguing than inspection. To secure reliable results, we must be strictly impartial and unprejudiced, facing the facts as they come, ready to accept them as they are, not trying to fit them to any preconceived theory; and we must work only when our general disposition is favourable, when we are fresh and in good health, at ease in our surroundings, free from outside worry and anxiety. If these rules are not followed, no amount of experimenting will help us. The observer in the psychological laboratory is placed under the best possible external conditions; the room in which he works is fitted up and arranged in such a way that the observation may be repeated, that the process to be observed may stand out clearly upon the background of consciousness, and that the factors in the process may be separately varied. But all this care is of no avail, unless the observer himself comes to the work in an even frame of mind, gives it his full attention, and is able adequately to translate his experience into words. . . .

Original Source Material on Structuralism

THE PROBLEM OF PSYCHOLOGY.   Science seeks always to answer three questions in regard to its subject-matter, the questions of what, how, and why. What precisely, stripped of all complications and reduced to its lowest terms, is this subject-matter? How, then, does it come to appear as it does; how are its elements combined and arranged? And, finally, why does it appear now in just this particular combination or arrangement? All three questions must be answered, if we are to have a science. . . .

To answer the question "what" is the task of analysis. Physical science, for example, tries by analysis to reduce the world of independent experience to its lowest terms, and so arrives at the various chemical elements. To answer the question "how" is the task of synthesis. Physical science traces the behaviour of the elements in their various combinations, and presently succeeds in formulating the laws of nature. When these two questions have been answered, we have a description of physical phenomena. But science enquires, further, why a given set of phenomena occurs in just this given way, and not otherwise; and it answers the question "why" by laying bare the cause of which the observed phenomena are the effect. There was dew on the ground last night because the surface of the earth was colder than the layer of air above it; dew forms on glass and not on metal because the radiating power of the one is great and of the other is small. When the cause of a physical phenomenon has thus been assigned, the phenomenon is said to be explained.

So far, now, as description is concerned, the problem of psychology closely resembles the problem of physics. The psychologist seeks, first of all, to analyse mental experience into its simplest components. He takes a particular consciousness and works over it again and again, phase by phase and process by process, until his analysis can go no further. He is left with certain mental processes which resist analysis, which are absolutely simple in nature, which cannot be reduced, even in part, to other processes. This work is continued, with other consciousnesses, until he is able to pronounce with some confidence upon the nature and number of the elementary mental processes. Then he proceeds to the task of synthesis. He puts the elements together, under experimental conditions: first, perhaps, two elements of the same kind, then more of that kind, then elementary processes of diverse kinds: and he presently discerns that regularity and uniformity of occurrence which we have seen to be characteristic of all human experience. He thus learns to formulate the laws of connection of the elementary mental processes. If sensations of tone occur together, they blend or fuse; if sensations of colour occur side by side, they enhance one another: and all this takes place in a perfectly regular way, so that we can write out laws of tonal fusion and laws of colour contrast.

If, however, we attempted to work out a merely descriptive psychology, we should find that there was no hope in it of a true science of mind. A descriptive psychology would stand to scientific psychology very much as the old-fashioned natural histories stand to modern text-books of biology, or as the view of the world which a boy gets from his cabinet of physical experiments stands to the trained physicist's view. It would tell us a good deal about mind; it would include a large body of observed facts, which we might classify and, in large measure, bring under general laws. But there would be no unity or coherence in it; it would lack that single guiding principle which biology has, for instance, in the law of evolution, or physics in the law of the conservation of energy. In order to make psychology scientific we must not only describe, we must also explain mind. We must answer the question "why."

But here is a difficulty. It is clear that we cannot regard one mental process as the cause of another mental process, if only for the reason that, with change of our surroundings, entirely new consciousnesses may be set up. When I visit Athens or Rome for the first time, I have experiences which are due, not to past consciousnesses, but to present stimuli. Nor can we, on the other hand, regard nervous processes as the cause of mental processes. The principle of psychophysical parallelism lays it down that the two sets of events, processes in the nervous system and mental processes, run their course side by side, in exact correspondence but without interference: they are, in ultimate fact, two different aspects of the same experience. The one cannot be the cause of the other.

Nevertheless, it is by reference to the body, to the nervous system and the organs attached to it, that we explain mental phenomena. The nervous system does not cause, but it does explain mind. It explains mind as the map of a country explains the fragmentary glimpses of hills and rivers and towns that we catch on our journey through it. In a word, reference to the nervous system introduces into psychology just that unity and coherence which a strictly descriptive psychology cannot achieve.

It is worth while, for the sake of clearness, to dwell on this point in more detail. The physical world, the world of independent experience, just because it is independent of the individual man, is complete and self-contained. All of the processes that make it up are bound together as cause and effect; nowhere is there a gap or break in their connection. Now, among the processes that make up this independent world are the processes of the nervous system. These are linked, as cause and effect, both to one another and also to physical processes, outside the body, which precede and follow them; they have their fixed place in the unbroken chain of physical events; they may themselves be explained, exactly as the occurrence of dew is explained. Mental processes, on the other hand, correspond, not to the whole series of physical events, but only to a small part of them, namely, to certain events within the nervous system. It is natural, then, that mental phenomena should appear scrappy, disconnected, unsystematic. It is also natural that we should seek their explanation in the nervous processes which run parallel to them, and whose causal connection with all the other processes of the independent world ensures the continuity that they so conspicuously lack. Mind lapses every night, and reforms every morning; but the bodily processes go on, in sleep and in waking. An idea drops out of memory, to recur, perhaps quite unexpectedly, many years later; but the bodily processes have been going on without interruption. Reference to the body does not add one iota to the data of psychology, to the sum of introspections. It does furnish us with an explanatory principle for psychology; it does enable us to systematise our introspective data. Indeed, if we refuse to explain mind by body, we must accept the one or the other of two, equally unsatisfactory alternatives: we must either rest content with a simple description of mental experience, or must invent an unconscious mind to give coherence and continuity to the conscious. Both courses have been tried. But, if we take the first, we never arrive at a science of psychology; and if we take the second, we voluntarily leave the sphere of fact for the sphere of fiction.

These are scientific alternatives. Common sense, also, has in its own fashion realised the situation, and has found its own way out. It is precisely because of the incompleteness and disconnectedness of mental experience that common sense constructs a hybrid world, travelling easily from mental to physical and back again, filling up the breaks in the mental by material borrowed from the physical. That way, we may be sure, lies confusion of thought. The truth underlying the confusion is, however, the implicit acknowledgment that the explanatory principle for psychology must be looked for beyond, and not within, the world of dependent experience.—

Physical science, then, explains by assigning a cause; mental science explains by reference to those nervous processes which correspond with the mental processes that are under observation. We may bring these two modes of explanation together, if we define explanation itself as the statement of the proximate circumstances or conditions under which the described phenomenon occurs. Dew is formed under the condition of a difference of temperature between the air and the ground; ideas are formed under the condition of certain processes in the nervous system. Fundamentally, the object and the manner of explanation, in the two cases, are one and the same.

In fine, just as the method of psychology is, on all essential points, the method of the natural sciences, so is the problem of psychology essentially of the same sort as the problem of physics. The psychologist answers the question "what" by analysing mental experience into its elements. He answers the question "how" by formulating the laws of connection of these elements. And he answers the question "why" by explaining mental processes in terms of their parallel processes in the nervous system. His programme need not be carried out in this order:

he may get the hint of a law before his analysis is completed, and the discovery of a sense-organ may suggest the occurrence of certain elementary processes before he has found these processes by introspection. The three questions are intimately related, and an answer to any one helps towards the answers to the other two. The measure of our progress in scientific psychology is our ability to return satisfactory answers to all three.

THE FATE OF STRUCTURALISM

Boring (1950b) commented that persons often gain prominence in history because they oppose an older thought or position. The situation may be reversed with Titchener, who "stood out in bold relief because every one near him moved away from him" (p. 419). The climate of American and European psychology was changing, but the formal statement of Titchener's system was not, and some came to regard his work as a futile attempt to cling to antiquated principles.

Titchener thought he was establishing the basic pattern for psychology, but his efforts have proved to be only one phase in its history. The era of structuralism collapsed when he died. That it was sustained so long is an effective tribute to the commanding personality of the man himself.

Criticisms of Structuralism

The most severe criticisms of structuralism have been leveled at the method of introspection. Introspection was not new with Wundt and Titchener. The method (though in a more broadly defined sense) had been in use for a long time. The attack on introspection was by no means new either. Immanuel Kant had written that an attempt to introspect changes the conscious experience by virtue of introducing an observing element into the content of this conscious experience. The positivist Auguste Comte also attacked the method. Several decades before Wundt founded the new psychology, Comte wrote this telling criticism:

> The mind may observe all phenomena but its own. . . . The observing and observed organ are here the same, and its action cannot be pure and natural. In order to observe, your intellect must pause from activity; yet it is this very activity that you want to observe. If you cannot effect that pause, you cannot observe; if you do effect it, there is nothing to observe. The results of such method are in proportion to its absurdity. After two thousand years of psychological pursuit, no one proposition is established to the satisfaction of its followers. (1830–1842, Vol. I, p. 9)

Turner (1967, p. 11) lists additional criticisms leveled against introspection by the Englishman Henry Maudsley in 1867, a few years before the new science of psychology was launched.

1. There is little agreement among introspectionists.

2. Where agreement does occur, it can be attributed to the fact that introspectionists must be meticulously trained, and thereby have a bias built into their observations.

3. A body of knowledge based on introspection cannot be inductive; no discovery is possible from those who are trained specifically on what to observe.

4. Due to the extent of the pathology of mind, self-report is hardly to be trusted.

5. Introspective knowledge cannot have the generality we expect of science. It must be restricted to the class of sophisticated, trained adult subjects.

6. Much of behavior (habit and performance) occurs without conscious correlates.

Important

There was, then, substantial criticism of introspection before Wundt and Titchener sharpened and modified the method to bring it into line with the requirements of experimentalism. The modifications did not reduce the amount of criticism. As the method was made more specific, so were the attacks against it.

One criticism relates to the definition of introspection. Titchener seems to have had a difficult time defining introspection with any degree of rigor, and apparently attempted to do so by relating it to the particular experimental conditions. "The course that an observer follows will vary in detail with the nature of the consciousness observed, with the purpose of the experiment, with the instruction given by the experimenter. Introspection is thus a generic term, and covers an indefinitely large group of specific methodological procedures" (Titchener, 1912, p. 485). With so much variation, it is difficult to find similarities among the uses of the term.

A point mentioned earlier relates to the question of precisely what the structuralist introspectors were trained to do. Observers learning to introspect had to ignore certain classes of words—the so-called meaning words—that had become an established part of their vocabulary. The phrase, "I see a table," for example, had no scientific meaning to a structuralist; the word "table" is a meaning word, based on previously established and generally agreed-upon knowledge about the specific conglomeration of sensations we have learned to identify and label as "table." The observation, "I see a table," told the structuralist nothing about the observers' conscious experience. The structuralist was interested not in the aggregate of sensations summarized in a meaning word, but in the specific elementary forms of the experience. Observers who said "table" were committing the stimulus error.

If these ordinary words were stricken from the vocabulary, how was the experience to be described? An introspective language or vocabulary had to be developed. Because Wundt and Titchener emphasized that the external conditions of the experiment must be carefully controlled so that the conscious contents could be precisely determined, two observers should have the identical experience and their results should corroborate one another. Because of these highly similar experiences under controlled conditions, it seemed possible, theoretically, to develop a working vocabulary devoid of meaning words. It is, after all, because of commonalities of experience in everyday life that we are able to agree on conventional meanings for customary words.

Although the development of such a vocabulary may be possible in principle, it was never realized. There was frequent disagreement among introspectors, even under the most rigidly controlled conditions of observation. Introspectors at different laboratories obtained different results. Even those at the same laboratory often failed to agree. Titchener nevertheless maintained that agreement would be reached eventually. It is possible that had there been sufficient agreement on introspective findings, structuralism might have lasted longer than it did.

There were other criticisms of the method of introspection. It was charged that introspection was, in reality, retrospection, because some period of time elapsed between the experience itself and the reporting of it. Because forgetting is most rapid immediately after an experience, it seemed likely that some of the experience was lost. The structuralist answer to this criticism was to specify that the observers work with very short time intervals. The structuralists postulated the existence of a primary mental image that was alleged to maintain the experience for the observer until it could be reported.

Another difficulty is that the act of minutely examining an experience in introspective fashion may radically change that experience. Consider the difficulty in introspecting the conscious state of anger. In the process of rationally attending to and trying to dissect the experience into its elementary components, the anger may subside or disappear. Titchener believed, however, that experienced, well-trained introspectors became unconscious of their observational task with continued practice.

A final criticism of introspection relates to the large and growing body of data that seemed to belong within the province of psychology, but that were not available to introspectors. Animal psychologists, for example, were rapidly accumulating useful knowledge, obviously without the use of introspection. The psychoanalysts were pointing to the importance of unconscious determinants of behavior, which were not accessible to introspection.

The method of the structuralists was not the only target of criticism. The movement was accused of artificiality and sterility because of its attempt to analyze conscious processes into elements. Critics agree that the whole of an experience cannot be recovered by any synthesis or compounding of the elemental parts. Experience, they argue, does not come to human beings in sensory, imaginal, or affective elements, but rather in unified wholes.

Something of the experience must inevitably be lost in what is essentially an artificial breakdown of the conscious experience. The Gestalt school (Chapter 12) made effective use of this criticism in launching their new psychology, their revolt against structuralism.

The structuralists' narrow definition of psychology came under attack. Psychology was growing in a number of areas and the structuralists, in the person of Titchener, preferred to exclude those areas that were not congruent with their definition and method of psychology. Titchener regarded animal and child psychology as not really psychology at all. His conception of psychology was too circumscribed to contain the new work being carried out by a rapidly increasing number of psychologists. Psychology was moving beyond Titchener, and moving very quickly.

Contributions of Structuralism

There is no denying that structuralism made important contributions to psychology. As Heidbreder (1933) stated, "It is a simple historical fact that it was the kind of psychology which Titchener taught, the enterprise which centered in the German laboratories, that first gained recognition for psychology as a science" (p. 148). For the first time, psychology achieved a formal academic identity and stature clearly separate from philosophy and physiology.

The subject matter of the structuralists—conscious experience—was sharply defined. Their research methods were certainly in the best tradition of science, involving observation, experimentation, and measurement. Because consciousness was best perceived by the person having the conscious experience, the best method for that subject matter was self-observation.

Although the subject matter and aims of the structuralists are no longer vital issues, introspection—defined as the giving of a verbal report based on experience—continues to be used in many areas of psychology. Researchers in psychophysics, for example, ask a subject whether a second tone sounds louder or softer than the first. Verbal reports are rendered by persons describing their experiences in an unusual experimental environment, such as a sensory deprivation cubicle. Clinical reports from patients and responses on personality tests or attitude scales are introspective in nature. These examples, and many more, involve a verbal report based on experience and are acceptable and legitimate forms of data collecting. Obviously the modern use of introspection is not of the structuralists' sort; the verbal reports are in the language of behavior, not in the vocabulary of the structuralists.

Perhaps another contribution of structuralism is its service as a target of criticism. It provided a strong orthodoxy against which the newly developing functional, Gestalt, and behaviorist movements could marshal their forces. These newer schools owed their existence in no small measure

*Structuralism:
Final Form*

to their progressive reformulation of the psychology the structuralists began. As we noted earlier, forward movement requires something against which to push. With the help of the structuralist position, psychology advanced far beyond this initial boundary. "Beyond question, the psychology of Titchener played a major role in the development of American psychology, not only as a distinct and lasting achievement, but also as a gallant and enlightening failure" (Heidbreder, 1933, p. 151).

SUGGESTED READINGS

TITCHENER

Boring, E. G. The stimulus-error. *American Journal of Psychology*, 1921, *32*, 449–471.

Boring, E. G. Edward Bradford Titchener: 1867–1927. *American Journal of Psychology*, 1927, *38*, 489–506.

Evans, R. E. B. Titchener and his lost system. *Journal of the History of the Behavioral Sciences*, 1972, *8*, 168–180.

Henle, M. E. B. Titchener and the case of the missing element. *Journal of the History of the Behavioral Sciences*, 1974, *10*, 227–237.

Henle, M. Did Titchener commit the stimulus error? The problem of meaning in structural psychology. *Journal of the History of the Behavioral Sciences*, 1971, *7*, 279–282.

INTROSPECTION

Bakan, D. A consideration of the problem of introspection. *Psychological Bulletin*, 1954, *51*, 105–118.

Boring, E. G. A history of introspection. *Psychological Bulletin*, 1953, *50*, 169–186.

McKellar, P. The method of introspection. In J. Scher (Ed.), *Theories of the mind*. New York: Free Press, 1962. Pp. 619–644.

GENERAL

Bentley, M. The psychologies called "Structuralism": Historical derivation. In C. Murchison (Ed.), *Psychologies of 1925*. Worcester, Mass.: Clark University Press, 1926. Pp. 383–393.

Bentley, M. The work of the structuralists. In C. Murchison (Ed.), *Psychologies of 1925*. Worcester, Mass.: Clark University Press, 1926. Pp. 395–404.

Boring, E. G. A psychological function is the relation of successive differentiations of events in the organism. *Psychological Review*, 1937, *44*, 445–461.

6

FUNCTIONALISM: ANTECEDENT INFLUENCES

INTRODUCTION

Functional psychology, as the name suggests, is concerned with the mind as it functions or is used in the adaptation of the organism to its environment. The movement focused on a practical question: What do mental processes accomplish? Functionalists studied the mind, not from the standpoint of its composition—that is, a structure of elements—but rather as a conglomerate of activities or functions that lead to practical consequences in the real world.

The study of the mind undertaken by the structuralists revealed nothing of the consequences or accomplishments of mental activity. Nor did it aspire to, of course; such a utilitarian goal was anathema to the pure science approach of Wundt and Titchener.

Functionalism was the first uniquely American system of psychology. It was a deliberate protest against structuralism, the establishment of the day. The psychology of structure was viewed as too narrow and restrictive. It could not answer the questions the functionalists wished psychology to answer. What does the mind do? How does it do it?

Functionalism was not a protest against the methods and topics of research at Leipzig and Cornell. The functionalists adopted many of the older school's findings. They did not object to introspection, nor did they argue against the experimental study of consciousness. What they did oppose was the structuralists' definition of psychology, a definition that ruled out any consideration of the useful and practical functions of the mind, the ongoing activities or operations of consciousness.

Although functionalism was a protest against the current school of thought, it did not intend to become a full-fledged school. The primary reason for this seems to have been personal rather than ideological. None of the proponents of the functionalist position had the ambition to lead a formal movement. In time, functionalism did gain many of the characteristics of a new school of thought, but such was not its aim. The leaders appeared content to challenge structuralism and to broaden the base and scope of the new psychology, which they did with considerable success. They modified the existing orthodoxy without striving to replace it.

As a result, functionalism was never as rigid or formally differentiated a systematic position as structuralism. It cannot, therefore, be described as neatly or precisely as the earlier school. There was not a single functional psychology, as there was a single structural psychology. Several functional psychologies existed, each differing somewhat from the others, but all shared an interest in the functions of consciousness.

Because of this emphasis on the functioning of an organism in its environment, functionalists became interested in the possible applications of psychology. Thus, applied psychology developed rapidly in the United States.

FUNCTIONALISM: AN OVERVIEW

Functionalism has a long history, ranging from the mid-1850s to the present, at least in modified form. Its historical development, unlike that of structuralism, was influenced by intellectual leaders with various interests and backgrounds. Perhaps it is partly because of this diversified base that functionalism, unlike structuralism, did not stultify and decline.

We will consider the antecedent influences on the functional psychology movement, including the works of Charles Darwin, Sir Francis Galton, and early students of animal behavior. Although these initial sources of influence were British, functionalism, as we have mentioned, formally began and flourished in America (Chapter 7).

It is important to note the time when the British precursors of functionalism were developing their ideas—the period before and during the years in which structuralism was developing. Darwin's famous *On the Origin of Species* (1859) was published one year before Fechner's *Elements of Psychophysics* (1860), and appeared approximately 20 years before Wundt's Leipzig laboratory was established. Galton began his work on individual differences in 1869, before Wundt wrote his *Principles of Physiological Psychology* (1874). Animal psychology experiments were conducted in the 1880s, before Titchener had journeyed to Leipzig and come under Wundt's influence. This major work on the functions of consciousness, individual differences, and animal psychology was being done at the time Wundt and Titchener were excluding these areas from the province of psychology. It remained for the new American psychologists, with their different temperament, to bring function, individual differences, and the white rat to positions of prominence in psychology.

American psychology today is functionalist in orientation and attitude. This is evident in the emphasis placed on testing, and on learning, perception, and other functional processes that aid our adaptation and adjustment to our environment.

THE EVOLUTION REVOLUTION: CHARLES DARWIN (1809–1882)

Charles Darwin's *On the Origin of Species by Means of Natural Selection*, published in 1859, is considered one of the most important books in the history of Western civilization. The theory of evolution presented in this work freed scholars from constraining traditions and superstitions and ushered in the era of maturity and respectability for the life sciences. The theory of evolution was also to have a tremendous impact on contemporary psychology. American psychology today owes its form and substance as much to the influence of evolutionary theory as to any other idea or individual.

The suggestion that living things change with time, which is the fundamental notion of evolution, did not originate with Darwin. Though intellectual anticipations of this general idea can be traced to the fifth century B.C., not until the late eighteenth century was the theory first investigated systematically. Erasmus Darwin (grandfather of both Charles Darwin and Sir Francis Galton) expressed the belief that all warm-blooded animals had evolved from a single living filament, given animation by the Creator. In 1809 Lamarck formulated a behavioral theory of evolution that emphasized the modification of animal bodily form through the organism's efforts to adapt to its environment, modifications that were inherited by succeeding generations. For example, the giraffe developed its long neck over generations by reaching for higher and higher branches to find food. In the mid-1800s Sir Charles Lyell introduced the notion of evolution into geological theory, arguing that the earth had passed through various stages of development in evolving to its present structure.

Why, after so many centuries of acceptance of the biblical account of creation—"every species after its own kind"—were scholars driven to seek an alternative explanation? One reason is that more was being learned about the other species that inhabited the earth. Many new kinds of animal life were being reported by explorers on several continents. It was inevitable that some thinkers should begin to ask: How could Noah have put a pair of all these animals into the ark? There were too many species to continue to believe in the legend.

Explorers and scientists had also discovered fossils and bones of animals that did not match those of existing species. They apparently belonged to creatures that had once roamed the earth and then disappeared. Thus, living forms were no longer believed to be constant, unchanged since creation, but subject to modification. Old species became extinct and new species appeared, some of them alterations of current forms. Perhaps, it was speculated, all of nature is a result of change and is still in the process of evolution.

The impact of continuing change was being observed not only in the

Functionalism:
Antecedent Influences

intellectual and scientific realm, but also in everyday life. Society was being transformed by the forces of the Industrial Revolution. Values, social relationships, and cultural norms that had remained constant for generations were being torn apart as people migrated from rural areas and small towns to the huge urban manufacturing centers.

Above all, there was the growing influence of science. People were less content to base their knowledge of themselves and their world on what the Bible and ancient authorities had stated to be true. They were ready to put their faith in science.

Change was the *Zeitgeist* of the day. It affected the peasant farmer, whose life now pulsed to the rhythm of the machine instead of the seasons, as much as the scientist, whose time was spent puzzling over a newly found set of bones. The intellectual and social climate rendered the notion of evolution scientifically respectable. There was a great deal of speculating and theorizing, but little in the way of supporting evidence. Then *On the Origin of Species* provided so much well-organized data that evolution could no longer be ignored. The times demanded such a theory, and Charles Darwin became its agent.

The Life of Darwin

As a boy,[1] Darwin gave little indication of becoming the keen, hard-working scientist the world later came to know. Indeed, he showed little indication of becoming anything other than an idler and a gentleman-sportsman. In his early years he showed so little promise that his father, a wealthy physician, worried that young Charles would be a disgrace to the family.

Though he never liked school and, probably as a result, never did well in it, he displayed an early interest in natural history and in collecting coins, shells, and minerals. Sent by his father to Edinburgh to study medicine, Charles found it dull. Aware that the young man was doing poorly, his father decided that Charles should become a clergyman instead.

He spent three years at Cambridge, and described the experience as "entirely wasted" from an academic standpoint. He did, however, have a marvelous time, and later referred to the Cambridge period as the happiest of his life. He collected beetles, went shooting and hunting, and spent a great deal of time drinking, singing, and playing cards with a group of young men he referred to as dissipated and "low-minded."

One of his instructors, the noted botanist John Stevens Henslow, promoted Darwin's appointment as a naturalist aboard *H.M.S. Beagle*, which the British government was preparing for a scientific voyage around the world. This famous excursion, lasting from 1831 to 1836, began in South American waters, proceeded to Tahiti and New Zealand, and returned to

[1] Material on Darwin's early life is drawn from his autobiography (1892) and from Pickering (1974).

England by way of Ascension Island and the Azores. The trip afforded him a unique opportunity to observe a variety of plant and animal life, and Darwin was able to collect an immense amount of data. The voyage altered Darwin's character. No longer the pleasure-loving dilettante, he returned to England a dedicated, committed, serious scientist with but one passion and aim in life—the promulgation of the theory of evolution.

In 1839 he married, and three years later he moved to Down, 16 miles from London, so that he could concentrate on his work without the distractions of city life. It was then that he began to be plagued by the physical disturbances, including vomiting, flatulence, and eczema, from which he would suffer for most of his long life. The illnesses were apparently neurotic, brought on by any change in his rigid daily routine. Whenever the outside world intruded, preventing Darwin from working, he would suffer another attack. Illness became a useful device, protecting him from mundane affairs and allowing him the intense solitude and concentration he needed to create his theory. Pickering (1974) aptly described Darwin's condition as a "creative malady."

From the time of his return with the *Beagle* Darwin was convinced of the validity of the theory of the evolution of species. Why, then, did he wait 22 years before presenting his work to the world? The answer seems to lie in his extremely conservative attitude, a temperamental requisite for a scientist. He knew his theory would have a revolutionary impact, and he wanted to be certain that it was buttressed with sufficient supporting data. So he proceeded with painstaking caution. It was not until 1842 that he felt prepared to write a brief 35-page summary of the development of his theory. Two years later he expanded this into a 200-page essay, but still he was not satisfied. He continued to keep his ideas from the public, sharing them only with Lyell and with Joseph Hooker, a botanist. For 15 more years Darwin pored over the data, checking, elaborating, revising, to be sure that when he did finally publish, the theory would be unassailable.

Who knows how much longer Darwin might have worked over his findings if in June of 1858 he had not received a shattering letter from a young naturalist, Alfred Russel Wallace? Wallace, while staying in the East Indies to recover from an illness, had developed the outline of a theory of evolution that was amazingly similar to Darwin's. His work had taken three days! In his letter to Darwin, Wallace asked the older man's opinion of the theory and for help in getting it published. One can imagine Darwin's feelings after more than two decades of laborious and painstaking work. It must be noted, however, that Wallace's theory did not rest on the wealth of data that Darwin's did.

Darwin possessed another characteristic—personal ambition—not unknown among scientists. Sometime before his explorations on the *Beagle* he had written in his diary that he was "ambitious to take a fair place among scientific men." Later he wrote: "I wish I could set less value on the bauble fame," and, "I rather hate the idea of writing for priority, yet I certainly should be vexed if any one were to publish my doctrines before me" (Merton, 1957, pp. 647–648).

With an enviable sense of fair play, Darwin considered Wallace's letter and decided that "It seems hard on me that I should lose my priority of many years' standing, but I cannot feel at all sure that this alters the justice of the case. . . . it would be dishonourable in me now to publish" (Merton, 1957, p. 648). At this moment of apparent defeat Darwin's mentally retarded son died, throwing him into a greater despair. His friends Lyell and Hooker suggested that he read Wallace's paper and portions of his own forthcoming book at a meeting of the Linnean Society on July 1, 1858. The rest is history.

Every one of the 1250 copies of the first printing of *On the Origin of Species* was sold on the day of publication. The work generated immediate excitement and controversy, and Darwin, though subjected to much abuse and criticism, nevertheless won "the bauble fame."

The Works of Darwin

The Darwinian theory of evolution is so well known that only an overview of the fundamental points is necessary here. Starting with the obvious fact of variation among individual members of a species, Darwin reasoned that this spontaneous variability was inheritable. In nature there is a process of natural selection that results in the survival of those organisms best suited for their environment and the elimination of those not fit. A continuing struggle for survival takes place in nature, Darwin wrote, and those forms that survive are the ones that have made successful adaptations or adjustments to the environmental difficulties to which they have been exposed. Species that cannot adapt do not survive.

Darwin formulated the notion of a struggle for survival after reading *Essay on the Principle of Population*, written by Thomas Malthus in 1789. Malthus had argued that the world's food supply increases arithmetically, while the human population tends to increase geometrically. The inevitable result, which Malthus described as having "a melancholy hue," is that many human beings will live under conditions of near starvation. Only the most forceful and cunning will survive.

Darwin extended this principle to all living organisms and developed the concept of natural selection. Those forms that survive the struggle and reach maturity tend to transmit to their offspring the skills or advantages that enabled them to survive. Further, since variation is another general law of heredity, offspring will show variation among themselves; some will possess the advantageous qualities developed to a higher level than their parents. These qualities tend to survive, so in the course of many generations great changes in form may develop. These changes can be so extensive as to account for the differences among species that exist today.

Herrnstein and Boring (1965) noted that natural selection was not the only mechanism of evolution allowed by Darwin. He also believed in the

The theory of human evolution proposed by Charles Darwin (1809–1882) set the stage for functional psychology, which studied the adaptive role, rather than the content, of consciousness.
(National Library of Medicine)

Lamarckian doctrine that changes in form brought about by experience during an animal's lifetime can be passed to subsequent generations.

Many religionists saw the theory of evolution as a threat because they believed it to be inconsistent with the biblical account of creation. White noted these comments made by distinguished clergymen of the time: "an attempt to dethrone God"; "a huge imposture from the beginning"; "If the Darwinian theory is true, Genesis is a lie . . . and the revelation of God to

Functionalism:
Antecedent Influences

man, as we Christians know it, is a delusion and a snare"; even "God is dead" (1965, p. 93). The controversy raged for many years.

Within a year of the book's publication, a debate took place at Oxford, at a meeting of the British Association for the Advancement of Science, between the biologist Thomas Henry Huxley, who defended Darwin and evolution, and Bishop Wilberforce, defending the Book of Genesis.

> *Referring to the ideas of Darwin, [Wilberforce] congratulated himself . . . that he was not descended from a monkey. The reply came from Huxley: "If I had to choose, I would prefer to be a descendant of a humble monkey rather than of a man who employs his knowledge and eloquence in misrepresenting those who are wearing out their lives in the search for truth." (White, 1965, p. 92).*

During the debate a man walked about the hall holding a Bible over his head, shouting, "The Book, the Book." He was Robert Fitzroy, captain of the *Beagle* during Darwin's voyage. A religious fundamentalist, Fitzroy blamed himself for his part in the development of the theory of evolution. Five years after the Oxford debate he committed suicide (Gould, 1976, p. 34).

The battle was not yet finished. In 1925, at the famous Scopes "monkey trial" in Dayton, Tennessee, a high school teacher (John T. Scopes) was prosecuted for teaching evolution. Almost half a century later, in 1972, a poll showed that 75 percent of that town's high school students believed the biblical version of creation. In a debate between Francis Darwin (great-grandson of Charles) and local clergy, one minister said that Darwin's theory "breeds corruption, lust, immorality, greed and such acts of criminal depravity as drug addiction, war and atrocious acts of genocide" (*New York Times*, October 1, 1972).

Several state legislatures and boards of education entered the evolution controversy in 1980, discussing demands that classroom lectures and text-books for state schools offer the biblical account of creation as well as Darwinian theory. In 1978 a federal judge, responding to a complaint by two religious groups, ruled that the Smithsonian Institution in Washington, D.C., did not have to publicize the Bible alongside a museum exhibit on evolution. Science and religion are still at odds over the theory of evolution.

Darwin remained aloof from the disputes of his time and wrote other books of interest to psychologists. His second major report on evolution, *The Descent of Man* (1871), marshaled the evidence for human evolution from lower forms of life, emphasizing the similarity between animal and human mental processes and stressing the importance of natural selection as a factor in evolution.

Darwin made an intensive study of emotional expression in humans and animals, and suggested that the changes of gesture and posture that characterize the major emotions could be interpreted in evolutionary terms. In *The Expression of the Emotions in Man and Animals* (1872) he argued that

*The Evolution Revolution:
Charles Darwin*

emotional expressions were remnants of movements that at one time had served some practical function.

Beginning in 1840, Darwin kept a diary of his infant son, recording the child's development. He published "A Biographical Sketch of an Infant" in the journal *Mind* in 1877, and the article was one of the early sources for modern child psychology.

The importance of mental factors in the evolution of species was apparent in Darwin's theory, and he frequently cited conscious reactions in humans and animals. Because of this role accorded consciousness in evolutionary theory, psychology was compelled to accept an evolutionary point of view.

The Influence of Darwin on Psychology

Darwin's work in the last quarter of the nineteenth century was a major force in shaping modern psychology. The theory raised the intriguing possibility of a continuity in mental functioning between animals and humans. The evidence was largely anatomical, but it strongly suggested continuities in the development of behavior and mental processes. If the human mind had evolved from more primitive minds, it would follow that similarities in mentality might exist between animals and humans. The gap between animals and humans posited two centuries earlier by Descartes was thus open to serious question for the first time. Scientists turned to the investigation of animal mental functioning, introducing a new subject into the psychological laboratory. Animal psychology, a field with far-reaching implications, was the result.

Darwin's work also brought a change in the subject matter and goal of psychology. The focus of the structuralists was the analysis of conscious content. Darwin influenced some psychologists, particularly Americans, to consider the functions that consciousness might serve. This seemed to many researchers to be a more important task than determining the elements of consciousness. Thus, psychology came to be more concerned with the adaptation of the organism to its environment, and the detailed investigation of mental elements began to lose its appeal.

A third point of influence of Darwin's theory on psychology was the broadening of the methodology the new science could legitimately use (Mackenzie, 1976). The methods of structuralism were derived primarily from physiology, notably the psychophysical methods of Fechner. Darwin's methods, which produced results applicable to both humans and animals, bore no resemblance to physiologically based techniques.

His data came from a variety of sources—geology, paleontology, archeology, demography, observations of wild and domesticated animals, research on breeding, among others. The information from all these sources provided support for his theory, confirming "the assumption that a wide variety of

Functionalism:
Antecedent Influences

kinds of evidence could legitimately be applied to the study of fundamental problems about living organisms" (Mackenzie, 1976, p. 334).

Here was tangible and impressive evidence that scientists could study human nature by means of techniques other than experimental introspection. Following Darwin's example, the psychologists who were influenced by evolutionary theory and, its emphasis on the functions of consciousness became much more eclectic with regard to the methods of psychology. As a result, the kinds of data psychologists collected were broadened considerably.

A fourth effect of evolution on psychology was seen in the growing focus on individual differences. The fact of variation among members of the same species was obvious to Darwin as a result of his five-year observation of so many species and forms. Evolution could not occur if each generation were identical to its forebears. Hence, variation was an important ingredient of evolutionary theory. While the structuralists continued their search for general laws to encompass all minds, the psychologists influenced by Darwin began to search for ways in which individual minds could differ from one another. The psychology of the structuralists had little room for the consideration of animal minds and individual differences. It remained for scientists of a functionalist persuasion to pursue these problems.

INDIVIDUAL DIFFERENCES: SIR FRANCIS GALTON (1822–1911)

Galton effectively brought the spirit of evolution to bear on psychology with his work on the problems of mental inheritance and individual differences in human capacity. Before Galton's efforts, the phenomenon of individual differences had not been considered a subject for serious study in psychology; this was a serious omission. Only a few isolated attempts had been made, notably by Weber, Fechner, and Helmholtz, who had reported individual differences in their experiments but had not investigated them systematically. Wundt and Titchener did not consider individual differences to be a part of psychology.

The Life of Galton

Galton possessed an extraordinary intelligence (an estimated IQ of 200) and a wealth of novel ideas. He is perhaps without equal in the history of modern psychology. His creative curiosity and genius attracted him to a variety of problems, the details of which he left to be filled in by others. A few of the areas he investigated are fingerprints (which Scotland Yard adopted for identification purposes), fashions, the geographical distribution of beauty, weight lifting, the future of the race, and the efficacy of prayer. There was little that did not interest this versatile and inventive man.

Galton was born in 1822 near Birmingham, England, the youngest of nine children. His father was a prosperous banker whose wealthy and socially prominent family included important persons in all spheres of influence—Parliament, the clergy, and the military. From an early age Galton was acquainted with influential persons through his family connections.

At the age of 16, at his father's insistence, Galton began the study of medicine as a house pupil at the Birmingham General Hospital. He worked as an apprentice to the hospital physicians, dispensed pills, studied medical

Evolution left its first imprint on psychology in the work of Sir Francis Galton (1822–1911) on mental inheritance and individual differences.
(*National Library of Medicine*)

Functionalism:
Antecedent Influences

books, set broken bones, amputated fingers, pulled teeth, vaccinated children, and found diversion in reading Horace and Homer. It was not a pleasant existence and only the continued pressure from his father kept him there.

One incident during this medical apprenticeship reflects his ever-present curiosity. Wanting to learn for himself the effects of the various medicines in the pharmacy, Galton began taking small doses of each, beginning in systematic fashion with those under the letter A. This scientific venture ended at the letter C when he took a dose of croton oil, a powerful purgative.

After a year at the hospital Galton continued his medical education at King's College in London. A year later he changed his plans and enrolled in Trinity College, Cambridge, where, with a bust of Newton opposite his fireplace, he studied mathematics. Although his studies were interrupted by a severe mental breakdown, he did manage to graduate. He returned briefly to the study of medicine until the death of his father released him from this profession, which he had come to dislike intensely.

Travel and exploration claimed Galton's attention. He journeyed to the Sudan in 1845 and to Southwest Africa in 1850. (In 1850 he also invented a teletype printer). He published accounts of his travels and was awarded a medal from the Royal Geographic Society for his exploration of Southwest Africa, then an unknown land.

In the 1850s he stopped his travels because of marriage and poor health, but he continued to serve on scholarly committees and wrote a guide for explorers *(The Art of Travel)*. He also organized expeditions for others, and gave lectures on camp life to soldiers training for duty in the Crimean War.

His spirited restlessness led him next to meteorology and the design of instruments with which to plot weather data. His meteorological findings were summarized in a book that is considered the first attempt to chart weather patterns on an extensive scale.

When his cousin Charles Darwin published *On the Origin of Species*, Galton immediately became interested in the new theory. The biological aspect of evolution captivated him at first and he investigated the effects of blood transfusions between rabbits to determine whether acquired characteristics could be inherited. Although the genetic side of evolution did not hold his attention for long, the social implications guided Galton's work and determined his influence on modern psychology.

The Works of Galton

Mental Inheritance

Galton's first important work for psychology was *Hereditary Genius*, published in 1869. His purpose was to demonstrate that individual greatness or genius occurred in families far too often to be explained by environmental influences—hence his thesis that eminent men have eminent sons. For the most part, the biographical studies reported in this book were investigations into the ancestries of influential persons such as scientists and physicians. Galton's data showed that each famous person inherited not only genius but a specific form of genius. A great scientist, for example, was born into a family that had attained eminence in science.

Galton's ultimate aim was to encourage the birth of the more eminent or fit individuals and to discourage the birth of the unfit. To help achieve this end, he founded the science of *eugenics* and argued that the human strain, not unlike livestock, could be improved by artificial selection. He believed that if men and women of considerable talents were selected and mated generation after generation, a highly gifted race would be the result.[2]

In attempting to verify his eugenic thesis, Galton became involved in problems of measurement and statistics. In *Hereditary Genius* he applied statistical concepts to the problems of heredity and sorted the celebrated men in his sample into classes or categories according to the frequency with which their level of ability occurred in the population. He found that eminent men have a higher probability of fathering eminent sons than do average men. His sample consisted of 977 famous men, each so outstanding as to be one in 4000. On a chance basis this group would be expected to have only one prominent relative; instead it had 332. The probability of eminence in certain families was high, but not high enough for Galton to consider seriously any possible influence of superior environment, education, or opportunity open to the sons of the outstanding families he studied. Eminence, or the lack of it, was a function of heredity, he argued, not of opportunity.

Galton wrote *English Men of Science* (1874), *Natural Inheritance* (1889), and more than 30 papers on problems of inheritance. His interest in heredity grew in scope from the individual and the family to the race as a whole. As he became more concerned with the possibility of improving the race by selective breeding, he made formal his proposal for a science of heredity (eugenics). This was followed by the creation of the journal *Biometrika* in 1901, the establishment of the Eugenics Laboratory at University College, London, in 1904, and the founding of an organization for promoting the idea of racial improvement, all of which are in existence today.

Statistical Methods

We noted Galton's interest in measurement and statistics. Throughout his career he never seemed fully satisfied with a problem unless he had found some means of quantifying the data and analyzing them statistically. He not only applied statistical methods, but he also developed several techniques.

Adolph Quetelet (1796–1874), a Belgian astronomer, had been the first to

---

[2] It is interesting that Galton, who founded the science of eugenics and believed that only the very intelligent should reproduce, did not have any children. The problem was apparently genetic; neither of Galton's brothers fathered children (Forrest, 1974).

apply statistical methods and the normal probability curve to biological and social data. The normal curve had been discovered and used in work on the distribution of measurements and errors in scientific observation, but the principle of normal distribution had not been applied to human variability until Quetelet demonstrated that anthropometric measurements of unselected samples of persons typically yield a normal curve. He demonstrated that measures of stature of 10,000 subjects approximated the normal curve of distribution, and he used the phrase *l'homme moyen* (the average man) to express the finding that most individuals cluster around the average or center of the distribution, and fewer and fewer are found as one moves from the center toward either extreme.

Galton was impressed by Quetelet's data and assumed that similar results would be obtained for mental characteristics. He found, for instance, that the marks given on university examinations followed the same normal curve distribution as Quetelet's physical measurement data. Because of the simplicity of the normal curve and its consistency over a number of traits, Galton proposed that a range of measurements could be meaningfully defined and summarized by two numbers—the average value of the distribution and the dispersion or range of variation around this average value (essentially, the mean and the standard deviation). Thus, a large set of measurements or values on human traits could be reduced to these two figures.

Galton's work in statistics yielded one of science's most important measures, the *correlation*. The first report of what he called "co-relations" appeared in 1888. Modern techniques for determining the validity and reliability of tests, as well as factor analytic methods, are direct outgrowths of Galton's discovery of correlation, which resulted from his observation that inherited characteristics tend to regress toward the mean. For example, he observed that tall men are, on average, not as tall as their fathers, while the sons of very short men are, on average, taller than their fathers. He devised the graphic means to represent the basic properties of the correlation coefficient and developed a formula for its calculation, though the formula has not remained in use.

Galton applied the correlational method to variations in physical measurements, demonstrating, for example, a correlation between body height and head length. With Galton's encouragement, his student Karl Pearson developed the mathematical formula used today for the precise calculation of the correlation coefficient—the Pearson product–moment coefficient of correlation. The traditional symbol for correlation coefficient, r, is taken from the first letter of the word "regression," in recognition of Galton's discovery of the tendency of inherited human traits to regress toward the average or mean.

Correlation is a fundamental tool in the social and behavioral sciences, as well as in engineering and the natural sciences. Many other statistical techniques have been developed on the basis of Galton's pioneering work.

Mental Tests

With the development of specific mental tests, Galton may properly be called the first practitioner of psychology. It has been said that he originated mental tests, although the term itself came from Cattell, an American disciple of Galton's. Galton began by assuming that intelligence could be measured in terms of a person's level of sensory capacity—the higher the intelligence, the higher the level of sensory discrimination.

He needed to invent the apparatus with which psychological measurements could be made quickly and accurately for large numbers of people. With characteristic ingenuity and enthusiasm, he devised several instruments. To determine the highest frequency of sound that could be heard, he invented a whistle, with which he tested animals as well as people. (He tested animals by walking through the streets of London and the Royal Zoological Gardens with the whistle fixed in the lower end of a hollow walking stick with a rubber bulb at the other end.) The "Galton whistle," in improved form, was a standard piece of psychological laboratory equipment until it was replaced by more sophisticated electronic apparatus in the 1930s.

Galton's other devices included a photometer to measure the precision with which a subject could match two spots of color, a calibrated pendulum to measure reaction time to sounds and lights, a series of weights to be arranged in order of heaviness to measure kinesthetic sensitivity, a bar with a variable distance scale to test estimation of visual extension, and sets of bottles containing different substances to test olfactory discrimination. Most of his tests were prototypes for the standard equipment used in psychological laboratories today.

Armed with his new tests, Galton proceeded to obtain a mass of data. He established the Anthropometric Laboratory in 1884 at the International Health Exhibition, later moved to the South Kensington Museum in London. The laboratory remained active for six years, and data from more than 9000 people were collected. Instruments for the anthropometric and psychometric measurements were arranged on a long table at one end of a narrow room. For a threepence admission fee, a person could pass along the table while an attendant took the measurements and wrote the data on a card. In addition to those noted above, measurements included height, weight, breathing power, strength of pull and squeeze, quickness of blow, hearing, vision, and color sense.

The aim of this large-scale testing program was to determine the range of human capacities. Galton wanted to test the entire population of Great Britain so that the people would know the exact level of their collective mental resources.

Association

Galton worked on two problems in the area of association—the diversity of associations of ideas, and the time required to produce associations. One of

In his laboratory at South Kensington Museum Galton used a variety of novel devices to conduct the first large-scale psychological testing.

his methods for studying the diversity of associations was to walk 450 yards along Pall Mall, the street in London running between Trafalgar Square and St. James Palace, focusing his attention on an object until it suggested one or two associated ideas to him. The first time he did this, he was amazed at the number of associations that developed from the nearly 300 objects he had seen. (Galton made a habit of counting things whenever possible.) He found that many of these associations were recollections of past experiences, including incidents long forgotten. Repeating the walk a few days later, he found considerable repetition of the associations that had occurred during the first walk. This greatly diminished his interest in the study of the diversity of associations, and he turned to reaction-time experiments instead, which produced more useful results.

Galton prepared a list of 75 words, writing each on a slip of paper. After a week he viewed them one at a time, using a chronometer to record the time necessary to produce two associations for each word. Many of the associations were single words, but several appeared as images or mental pictures that required a number of words to describe.

His next task was to determine the origin of these associations. He discovered that about 40 percent of them could be traced to events in his childhood and adolescence, an early demonstration of the influence of childhood experiences on the adult personality.

Of greater importance was the introduction of the experimental study of association. Galton's invention of the *word association test* marked the first attempt to subject association to laboratory experimentation. Wundt adapted the technique, limited the response to a single word, and used it at Leipzig. Carl Jung elaborated on it for his own word association studies (Chapter 14).

Mental Imagery

Galton's investigation of mental imagery marks the first extensive use of the psychological questionnaire. Subjects were asked to recall a scene—such as their breakfast table that morning—and to try to elicit images of it. They were instructed to indicate whether the images were dim or clear, bright or dark, colored or not colored, and so on.

To Galton's amazement, his first group of subjects, scientific acquaintances, reported no clear imagery at all. Some were not even sure what Galton was talking about when he questioned them about images. Further investigation, using subjects of more average ability, resulted in reports of clear and distinct images that were often full of detail and color. He found that the imagery of women and children was particularly concrete and detailed. As more people were questioned, it became clear that imagery is more or less normally distributed in the population.

Galton's work began a long line of research on imagery; in general, his results have been supported. As with most of his research, the interest in imagery was rooted in his attempt to demonstrate hereditary similarities. For example, he found that similarity in imagery is greater between siblings than between individuals who are unrelated.

Additional Studies

The areas of research discussed thus far constitute Galton's chief sources of influence on psychology. Because he performed many other studies, we will discuss a few of them to indicate the richness and variety of his talent.

Galton tried to put himself into the state of mind of the insane by imagining that everyone or everything he saw while he was taking a walk was a spy. "By the end of the morning stroll, every horse seemed to be watching him either directly or, just as suspicious, disguising their espionage by elaborately paying no attention" (Watson, 1978, pp. 328–329).

Galton lived at a time when the debate between evolution and theology was acute. With great objectivity, he investigated the problem and concluded that although large numbers of people hold intense religious beliefs, this is not evidence that such beliefs are valid. He discussed the power of prayer to produce results and concluded that it was of no use to physicians in curing patients, or to meteorologists in invoking weather changes, or to clergy in conducting their worldly affairs.

Galton believed that there was little difference between persons who profess a belief in one of the many brands of religion and those who do not, in terms of their dealings with others or in their own emotional lives. He would have liked to give the world a new set of beliefs, structured in terms of science, as a substitute for religious dogma. He thought that the evolutionary development of a finer and nobler race through eugenics should be our goal, rather than a place in heaven.

Galton always seemed to be counting something. He occupied himself at lectures or at the theater by counting the yawns and fidgets of the audience, using the results as a measure of boredom. When he was having his portrait painted, he counted the number of brush strokes—some 20,000. At one time, he decided to try to count by odors instead of numbers. After training himself to forget what the numbers 1, 2, 3, and so on, meant, he assigned number values to odors such as camphor and peppermint. He learned to add and subtract by thinking of odors instead of numbers. Out of this intellectual exercise came a paper entitled "Arithmetic by Smell," which was published in the first issue of the American journal *Psychological Review.*

Comment

Galton spent only 15 years engaged in investigating activities of a psychological nature, yet his efforts during this short period strongly affected the direction psychology would take. He was not truly a psychologist, any more than he was a eugenicist or an anthropologist. He was an extremely gifted individual whose talent and temperament could not be bound by the confines of any one discipline. Consider again the studies that Galton initiated in which psychologists (especially American psychologists) became interested: adaptation, heredity versus environment, comparison of species, child development, the questionnaire method, statistical techniques, individual differences, and mental tests. Galton's work influenced American psychology much more than did Wundt's. Flugel and West (1964) commented: "Never again in the history of the science . . . do we meet an investigator so brilliant, so versatile, so wide in his interests and abilities, so little bound by prejudice or preconception. Compared with him, all others (with the one exception perhaps of William James) are apt to appear a little ponderous and pedantic, a little blinkered in their outlook" (p. 111).

THE INFLUENCE OF ANIMAL PSYCHOLOGY ON FUNCTIONALISM

The evolutionary theory of Charles Darwin provided the impetus for animal psychology. Before Darwin published his theory, there was no reason for scientists to be interested in the animal mind because animals were considered to be soulless or mindless automata, possessing no similarity with humans, a point stressed by Descartes.

On the Origin of Species radically altered this notion. It became clear that there was no sharp break between the human and animal minds. Instead, a continuity between all aspects—mental and physical—of humans and animals was postulated, because we were believed to be derived from animals by the continuous evolutionary process of change and development. If mind could be demonstrated to exist in animals, and if continuity between the animal mind and the human mind could be shown, such evidence would serve as a defense of Darwin's theory against the human–animal dichotomy espoused by Descartes. A quest was begun for evidence of mind in animals.

Darwin undertook the defense of his theory in *Expression of the Emotions in Man and Animals* (1872), in which he argued that our emotional behavior results from the inheritance of behavior once useful to animals, but no longer of any use to humans. One of Darwin's famous examples to demonstrate this point is the way our lips curl when we sneer. Darwin held this to be a remnant of the animal baring of the canine teeth in rage. Many such examples were cited to demonstrate a continuity between animals and humans.

A more systematic and direct approach to the question of mental evolution was taken by a friend of Darwin's, George John Romanes (1848–1894), who applied the notion of evolution to the mind, as Darwin had applied it to the body. In 1883 Romanes published *Animal Intelligence*, generally considered the first book on comparative psychology. Romanes collected data on the behavior of fish, birds, domestic animals, and monkeys. His purpose was to demonstrate the high level of animal intelligence as well as its similarity to human intellectual functioning, thus illustrating a continuity in mental development. His methodology is referred to in somewhat contemptuous terms as the *anecdotal* method—the utilization of observational, often casual, reports about animal behavior. Many of the reports used by Romanes came from uncritical and untrained observers, and, of course, were open to the charges of incorrect observation, careless description, and biased interpretation.

How did Romanes derive his findings on the nature of animal intelligence from anecdotal observations of animal behavior? He worked through a curious and ultimately discarded technique known as *introspection by analogy*. Using this approach, investigators assume that the same mental processes that occur in their own minds also occur in the minds of the animals under observation. The existence of mind and specific mental functions is inferred by observing behavior and then drawing an analogy from human mental processes to those assumed to be taking place in animals.

Romanes described the process of introspection by analogy in these terms: "starting from what I know subjectively of the operations of my own individual mind, and of the activities which in my own organism these operations seem to prompt, I proceed by analogy to infer from the observable activities displayed by other organisms, the fact that certain mental operations underlie or accompany these activities" (Mackenzie, 1977, pp. 56–57).

Through the use of this technique, Romanes concluded that animals were

Functionalism:
Antecedent Influences

capable of the same kinds of rationalization, ideation, complex reasoning, and problem-solving ability as humans. Some of Romanes's followers even credited animals with a level of intelligence far superior to that of the average human being.

In a study of cats, which he considered to be more intelligent than any other animal except monkeys and elephants, Romanes wrote about the behavior of the cat that belonged to his coachman. Through an intricate pattern of movements, the cat was able to open a door leading into the stables. Introspecting by analogy, Romanes reached the following conclusion:

> Cats in such cases have a very definite idea as to the mechanical properties of a door; they know that to make it open, even when unlatched, it requires to be pushed. . . . First the animal must have observed that the door is opened by the hand grasping the handle and moving the latch. Next she must reason, by "the logic of feelings"—If a hand can do it, why not a paw? . . . the pushing with the hind feet after depressing the latch must be due to adaptive reasoning. (Romanes, 1883, pp. 421–422)

Romanes's work fell far short of modern scientific rigor. He did, however, employ certain criteria for judging the reliability of the reports he used, and he adhered to them strictly. Despite these precautions, the line between fact and subjective interpretation in his data is unclear. Although there are deficiencies in his data and method, Romanes is respected for his pioneer efforts in stimulating the development of comparative psychology and preparing the way for the experimental approach that followed. In many areas of science reliance on observational data has preceded the development of refined experimental methodology, and it was Romanes who launched the observational stage of comparative psychology.

The weaknesses inherent in the anecdotal method and introspection by analogy were recognized by C. Lloyd Morgan (1852–1936), who proposed a *law of parsimony* (often called "Lloyd Morgan's canon"), in an effort to counter the tendency to anthropomorphize and thus attribute too much intelligence to animals. The principle states that an animal's behavior must not be interpreted as the outcome of a higher mental process when it can be explained in terms of lower mental processes.

Lloyd Morgan followed essentially the same methodological approach as Romanes. He observed an animal's behavior and tried to explain that behavior through an introspective examination of his own mental processes. Applying the law of parsimony, however, he refrained from ascribing complex, high-level mental processes to animals when their behavior could be explained more simply in terms of lower-level processes. He believed, for example, that most animal behavior could be explained as a result of learning or association based on sense experience; learning is a much lower-level "psychical faculty" than rational thought or ideation. With Lloyd

Morgan's canon, introspection by analogy came to be more restricted in use, and finally was superseded by more objective methods.

Lloyd Morgan was the first to conduct large-scale experimental studies in animal psychology. Although his early experiments were not performed under rigid laboratory conditions, they did involve careful, detailed observations of the behavior of animals in their natural environments, with some artificially induced modifications. These studies did not permit the same degree of control as did laboratory experiments, but they were a great advance over Romanes's anecdotal method.

These early approaches to comparative psychology were British in origin, but leadership in the field rapidly passed to the United States. Reasons for this shift include Romanes's early death and Lloyd Morgan's change from a career in research to one in administration at the University College of Bristol.

Comparative psychology was an outgrowth of the excitement and controversy engendered by Darwin's notion of continuity. Perhaps comparative psychology would have begun without the theory of evolution, but most likely it would not have had such a sound or early start. We shall continue the story of the development of animal psychology in Chapter 9.

COMMENT

Basic to Darwin's theory of evolution are the notion of function and the assertion that as a species evolves, its physical structure is determined by its requirements for survival. This premise caused biologists to regard each anatomical structure as a functioning element in a total living, adapting system. When psychologists began to consider mental processes in the same manner, they created a new movement—functional psychology. Chapters 7 and 8 will consider the development of the new functionalism in the United States.

SUGGESTED READINGS

DARWIN

Angell, J. R. The influence of Darwin on psychology. *Psychological Review,* 1909, *16,* 152–169.

Boring, E. G. The influence of evolutionary theory upon American psychological thought. In S. Persons (Ed.), *Evolutionary thought in America.* New Haven, Conn.: Yale University Press, 1950. Pp. 267–298.

Colp, R. *To be an invalid: The illness of Charles Darwin.* Chicago: University of Chicago Press, 1977.

Cravens, H. *The triumph of evolution: American scientists and the heredity–environment controversy, 1900–1941.* Philadelphia: University of Pennsylvania Press, 1978.

Darwin, F. (Ed.). *The autobiography of Charles Darwin and selected letters.* New York: Dover, 1958. (Originally published, 1892.)

Gruber, H. E. *Darwin on man: A psychological study of scientific creativity.* New York: Dutton, 1974.

Irvine, W. *Apes, angels, and Victorians: Darwin, Huxley, and evolution.* New York: Time, 1955.

Mackenzie, B. Darwinism and positivism as methodological influences on the development of psychology. *Journal of the History of the Behavioral Sciences,* 1976, *12,* 330–337.

Moorehead, A. *Darwin and the Beagle.* New York: Harper, 1969.

Pickering, G. *Creative malady.* London & New York: Oxford University Press, 1974. (Discusses the role of illness in the lives of Darwin and other noted persons.)

Russett, C. E. *Darwin in America: The intellectual response, 1865–1912.* San Francisco: Freeman, 1976.

Vorzimmer, P. J. *Charles Darwin, the years of controversy:* The Origin of Species *and its critics, 1859–1882.* Philadelphia: Temple University Press, 1970.

Young, R. M. The role of psychology in the nineteenth-century evolutionary debate. In M. Henle, J. Jaynes, & J. J. Sullivan (Eds.), *Historical conceptions of psychology.* New York: Springer, 1973. Pp. 180–204.

GALTON

Buss, A. R. Galton and the birth of differential psychology and eugenics: Social, political, and economic forces. *Journal of the History of the Behavioral Sciences,* 1976, *12,* 47–58.

Crovitz, H. *Galton's walk.* New York: Harper, 1970.

Forrest, D. W. *Francis Galton: The life and work of a Victorian genius.* New York: Taplinger, 1974.

Galton, F. *Memories of my life.* London: Methuen, 1908.

Pearson, K. *The life, letters and labors of Francis Galton* (3 vols.). London & New York: Cambridge University Press, 1914–1930.

ANIMAL PSYCHOLOGY,
ROMANES, MORGAN

Lockard, R. B. Reflections on the fall of comparative psychology. *American Psychologist,* 1971, *26,* 168–179.

Warden, C. J. The historical development of comparative psychology. *Psychological Review,* 1927, *34,* 57–85; 135–168.

7
FUNCTIONALISM: AMERICAN PIONEERS

By the turn of the century psychology in the United States was assuming a character all its own, distinct from the German structural psychology. Why did functional psychology develop and thrive in America rather than in England, where the functional spirit originated? The answer seems to lie in the American temperament; the American *Zeitgeist* was ready for evolutionism and the functionalist attitude that derived from it.

ONLY IN AMERICA: HERBERT SPENCER (1820–1903) AND SYNTHETIC PHILOSOPHY

In 1882 a self-taught 62-year-old British philosopher arrived in the United States, where he was hailed as a national hero. He was met at his ship in New York by Andrew Carnegie, the multimillionaire patriarch of the American steel industry, who praised the Englishman as a messiah (Blumenthal, 1977). In the eyes of many leaders of American science, business, politics, and religion, the man was indeed a savior, and he was wined and dined and lavished with honors and appreciation.

His name was Herbert Spencer, the scholar whom Darwin called "our philosopher." His impact on the American scene was monumental; he was a celebrity of the day. His works were serialized in popular magazines, his books sold hundreds of thousands of copies, and his system of philosophy was taught in the universities by scholars in almost every discipline. His ideas, read by people at all levels of society, influenced a generation of Americans (Hofstadter, 1955). Had there been television, Spencer would doubtless have appeared on talk shows and received even greater adulation.

What was the philosophy that brought him so much recognition and acclaim? Briefly stated, it was Darwinism—the notion of evolution and survival of the fittest—carried beyond Darwin.

In the United States interest in Darwin's theory was intense before

Spencer was recognized. The notion of evolution had been accepted more rapidly and fully in America than elsewhere, including England, the country of its birth. Darwin's ideas were discussed and embraced not only in the universities and learned societies, but also in popular magazines and some religious publications.

Spencer pointed out the implications of evolution for human knowledge and experience and argued that the development of all aspects of the universe, including human character and social institutions, is evolutionary, operating in accordance with the principle of survival of the fittest. It was this emphasis on *social Darwinism*, the application of evolution to human nature and human societies, that met with such enthusiasm in the United States. Spencer's utopian view argued that through the survival of the fittest, only the best would survive. Human perfection was inevitable so long as nothing was done to interfere with the natural order of things. He stressed individualism and a laissez-faire economy, and opposed such government attempts to regulate people's lives as subsidized education and housing.

People and organizations were to be left alone to develop themselves and their society in their own way, just as living species were left alone to develop in the world of nature. Any help from the state would interfere with the natural process of evolution. In this view, those individuals or businesses or institutions that could not adapt to the environment were unfit for survival and should be allowed to perish or become extinct, for the betterment of society as a whole. If government continued to support the poor and the weak, they would endure and ultimately weaken the society, in violation of the primary law of nature that states that only the fittest shall survive. Spencer argued that by ensuring that only the strongest survive, human societies can improve themselves and eventually reach a state of human and societal perfection.

This message was highly compatible with America's individualistic creed, and the phrases "survival of the fittest" and "the struggle for existence" became part of the national consciousness. They reflect much of what nineteenth-century American society was all about.

In the closing decades of the nineteenth century the United States was a living example of Spencer's ideas. It was a pioneer nation being settled by hard-working persons who believed in free enterprise, independence from government regulation, and self-sufficiency. And they knew all about the survival of the fittest from their own daily experiences. Land was still freely available to those with the courage, cunning, and ability to take it and wrest a living from it. The principles of natural selection were vividly demonstrated in everyday life, particularly on the Western frontier, where success (and sometimes survival) depended on one's ability to adapt to the demands of an often hostile environment. Those who could not adapt did not survive. The historian Frederick Jackson Turner described nineteenth-century Amer-

Herbert Spencer (1820–1903) was acclaimed for his philosophy of social Darwinism: the utopian view that human character and society, without aid or regulation, would naturally evolve toward perfection. (*National Library of Medicine*)

icans in these terms: "That coarseness and strength combined with acuteness and inquisitiveness; that practical, inventive turn of mind, quick to find expedients; that masterful grasp of material things . . . powerful to effect great ends; that restless, nervous energy; that dominant individualism" (1947, p. 235).

America was oriented toward the practical, the useful, and the functional and American psychology in its pioneering stages reflected these qualities. Thus, America was more amenable to evolutionism than Germany or even England. American psychology became a functional psychology because evolutionary theory and its derived functional spirit were both in keeping with the basic temperament of the United States.

Spencer's views were thus congruent with the American ethos in general. For 20 years his philosophical system influenced every field of learning, including the new psychology.

Spencer had written on the topic of evolution as early as 1850, but these pre-Darwin publications attracted relatively little attention. When Darwin's *On the Origin of Species* was published in 1859, Spencer became associated with the movement, and his own brand of more speculative evolutionism gained strength from Darwin's well-documented position. Their work was complementary; whereas Darwin was cautious about generalizing beyond his detailed data, Spencer was wont to discuss the implications of the theory and to apply evolutionary doctrine universally.

To accomplish this, Spencer developed his *synthetic philosophy*. (The word "synthetic" was used in the sense of "to synthesize" or "to combine," and not to mean something artificial or unnatural.) This all-encompassing system was, as noted, based on the application of evolutionary principles to all human knowledge and experience. Specifically, Spencer argued that the development of all aspects of the universe involves the processes of differentiation followed by integration. Any developing or growing thing is initially homogeneous and simple. Then recognizably distinct parts emerge (*differentiation*), and at a later stage these unique parts are joined or combined in a new, functioning whole (*integration*).

To Spencer, this notion of differentiation followed by integration, in which all things proceed from homogeneity to heterogeneity, was evolutionary. The implication of this view for psychology is that as the nervous system evolves to greater complexity, there is a corresponding increase in the richness and variety of experience to which the organism is exposed, and thus ever higher levels of functioning.

Successive volumes of *The System of Synthetic Philosophy* were published between 1862 and 1893. *The Principles of Psychology*, published first in 1855 and then in 1870–1872, was used by William James as a textbook for the psychology courses he taught at Harvard. In his *Principles of Psychology* Spencer discussed the notion that the mind exists in its present form because of past and continuing efforts to adapt to various environments. He stressed the adaptive nature of nervous and mental processes, and wrote that increasing complexity of experiences, and hence behavior, is part of the evolutionary process of an organism's need to adapt to its environment in order to survive.

Only in America:
Herbert Spencer

ANTICIPATOR OF FUNCTIONAL PSYCHOLOGY: WILLIAM JAMES (1842–1910)

There is much that is paradoxical about William James and his role and stature in American psychology. On the one hand, he was certainly the leading American precursor of functional psychology. He was also the pioneer of the new scientific psychology in the United States and its senior psychologist, and is still considered by many to be the greatest American psychologist. On the other hand, James at times denied that he was a psychologist or that there was a new psychology. He founded no formal system of psychology and had no disciples.

Although the psychology he embodied was scientific and experimental, James was not an experimentalist in attitude or deed. Psychology—he once called it that "nasty little science"—was not a lifelong passion, as it was for Wundt. James worked in psychology for a while and then moved on.

Even when he was actively working in psychology, he remained independent, refusing to be absorbed by any ideology, system, or school. James was neither a follower nor a founder, neither a disciple nor a leader. He was aware of everything that was happening in psychology and was very much a part of it, but he was able to select from among the various positions only those parts that were congenial with his view of psychology, and to reject the rest.

This fascinating man who contributed so greatly to psychology turned his back on it later in life. He said that the field consisted of an "elaboration of the obvious" and allowed it to fumble on without his commanding presence. Still, his place in the history of psychology is both assured and significant.

Although James did not found functional psychology, he wrote and thought most clearly and effectively in the functionalist atmosphere permeating American psychology at that time. In so doing, he influenced the functionalist movement through the inspiration he provided to subsequent generations of psychologists.

The Life of James

William James was born in the Astor House, a New York hotel, into a well-known wealthy family. His father devoted himself with enthusiasm to the education of his five children, alternating between Europe (because of his belief that American schools were too restricted in their outlook) and America (because of an equally strong belief that his children should be educated among their countrymen). James's early formal education, often interrupted by travel, took place in France, England, Switzerland, Germany,

Functionalism:
American Pioneers

The essence of functionalism—the adaptation of living persons to their environment, especially as assisted by consciousness—is expressed in the writings of William James (1842–1910), often considered the greatest American psychologist.
(National Library of Medicine)

Italy, and the United States.[1] The father encouraged intellectual independence among his children, whose family ties remained strong throughout their lives.

The stimulating experiences of his youth exposed James to the intellectual and cultural advantages of England and Europe and made him a man of the

[1] A biography of James contains a chapter on this sporadic education, entitled, appropriately, "Zigzag Voyages" (Allen, 1967).

world. Frequent trips abroad characterized his entire life; his father's method of dealing with illness was to send the ailing family member to Europe rather than to a hospital. Because his health was seldom good, James became a commuter between the United States and Europe.

Although his father seemed to think that none of the children need be concerned with learning a vocation or earning a living, he did try to encourage James's early interest in science. At age 15, James received a microscope as a Christmas gift. He already had a "Bunsen burner and vials of mysterious liquids which he mixed, heated, and transfused, staining his fingers and clothes, to his mother's annoyance, and sometimes even causing alarming explosions" (Allen, 1967, p. 47). James decided, however, at the age of 18, that he wanted to be an artist. Six months at the studio of William Morris Hunt persuaded him that he lacked promise, and in 1861 he entered the Lawrence Scientific School at Harvard. He soon left his first choice, chemistry, apparently because he disdained the painstaking demands of laboratory work, and enrolled in medical school. He had little enthusiasm for the practice of medicine, noting that "there is much humbug therein . . . with the exception of surgery, in which something positive is sometimes accomplished, a doctor does more by the moral effect of his presence on the patient and family, than by anything else. He also extracts money from them" (Allen, 1967, p. 98).

James interrupted his medical studies for a year to assist the zoologist Louis Agassiz on his expedition to Brazil to collect specimens of marine animals in the Amazon. On this trip he sampled another possible career, biology, but found that he could not tolerate the precise and orderly collecting and categorizing that this field required. His reaction to chemistry and biology was prophetic of his subsequent distaste for experimentation in psychology.

Although medicine was no more attractive to him after the 1865 expedition than it had been before, James reluctantly resumed his studies because nothing else appealed to him. He interrupted the work again, however, complaining of depression and physical problems (digestive disorders, insomnia, eye problems, and a weak back).

> It was obvious to everyone that he was suffering from America; Europe was the only cure. In 1867 he went to Dresden and Berlin, where he took baths for his back, read widely in German and other literature, toyed with thoughts of suicide, displayed his loneliness and homesickness by the tremendous volume of his correspondence, and remained just as miserable as he had been at home. (Miller & Buckhout, 1973, pp. 84–85)

He was able to attend lectures on physiology at the University of Berlin and remarked that it was time for "psychology to begin to be a science" (Allen, 1967, p. 140).

James finally obtained his medical degree from Harvard in 1869, but his depression deepened and his will to live was not very strong. In these dark

Functionalism:
American Pioneers

months he began to build a philosophy of life, compelled not so much by intellectual curiosity as by desperation.

After reading a number of essays by the philosopher Charles Renouvier on free will, James became persuaded of its existence and resolved that his first act of free will would be to believe in free will, and to believe that he could cure himself through belief in the efficacy of the will. He apparently succeeded to some extent, because in 1872 he felt well enough to accept a teaching position at Harvard in physiology. After one year he took a year off to travel in Italy, but then returned to teaching.

In 1875–1876 James taught his first course in psychology, called "The Relations between Physiology and Psychology." Harvard thus became the first American university to offer the new experimental psychology. (James had never received formal classroom instruction in psychology; the first psychology lecture he attended was his own.) Also in 1875, the year Wundt established his laboratory at Leipzig, James secured $300 from Harvard to purchase laboratory and demonstration equipment for the course.

In 1878 two important events occurred. The first was his marriage, which would produce five children and a certain amount of much needed order in his life. It was James's father who had first met the 27-year-old schoolteacher James was to marry. He returned from a meeting one night and announced that he had just met his son's future wife. Shortly thereafter, James verified his father's prophecy. The second event was the signing of a contract with the publishing house of Henry Holt, which resulted in one of the classic books in psychology. James believed that it would take him two years to write the book; it took 12. He began the work, to the amusement of his friends, on his honeymoon.

In 1880 James was made assistant professor of philosophy. He was promoted to professor of philosophy in 1885, and his title was changed to professor of psychology in 1889. His book was delayed by travels abroad, where he met many European psychologists of the day, including Wundt, who, he wrote, "made a pleasant and personal impression on me, with his agreeable voice and ready, tooth-showing smile." A few years later he wrote that Wundt "isn't a genius, he is a *professor*—a being whose duty is to know everything, and have his own opinion about everything"(Allen, 1967, p. 251, 304).

The Principles of Psychology finally appeared in two volumes in 1890 and was a tremendous success; it is still considered a major contribution to the field. Almost 80 years after its publication MacLeod wrote: "James' *Principles* is without question the most literate, the most provocative, and at the same time the most intelligible book on psychology that has ever appeared in English or in any other language" (1969, p. iii). One indication of the book's popularity is that it is often read by people who are not required to do so. In 1892 James published a condensed version.

James's reaction to the book on its completion was quite different from MacLeod's opinion. In a letter to his publisher he described the manuscript as "a loathsome, distended, tumefied, bloated, dropsical mass, testifying to nothing but two facts: *1st,* that there is no such thing as a *science* of psychology, and *2nd,* that W.J. is an incapable" (Allen, 1967, pp. 314–315).

With the publication of *The Principles*, James decided that he had said all he knew about psychology and no longer wanted to direct the psychological laboratory. He arranged for Hugo Münsterberg, then at the University of Freiburg in Germany, to become director of the Harvard laboratory and to teach courses in psychology, thus freeing James to turn to work in philosophy. Münsterberg had been criticized by Wundt, and this was high praise in James's eyes. Münsterberg, however, never fulfilled James's intention of providing leadership in experimental research for Harvard; he worked in a variety of fields, such as psychotherapy, legal psychology, and industrial psychology, and paid little attention to the laboratory after his first few years there.

We noted that James was not an experimentalist, although he did begin and equip the laboratory at Harvard. He was never fully convinced of the value of laboratory work in psychology and did not like it personally. "I naturally hate experimental work," he had written to Münsterberg. In 1894 he stated that the United States had too many laboratories, and in *The Principles* he commented that the results of laboratory work were not in proportion to the amount of painstaking effort involved. It is not surprising that James contributed little of importance in the way of experimental work.

James spent the last 20 years of his life refining his philosophical system, and in the 1890s became America's leading philosopher. In 1899 he published *Talks to Teachers*, developed from lectures he had given to teachers, which helped to apply psychology to the classroom learning situation. *The Varieties of Religious Experience* appeared in 1902 and three additional works in philosophy were published in 1907 and 1909.

James's health remained poor and he retired from Harvard in 1907. In 1898, while climbing in the Adirondack Mountains, he had been lost for 13 hours and the ordeal aggravated a heart lesion. The condition grew worse and resulted in his death in 1910, two days after his return from a final trip to Europe.

The Works of James

Since James was neither an experimentalist nor a founder (and not even a psychologist for the last two decades of his life), how did he come to exert such a profound influence on psychology? Why is he often considered the greatest American psychologist?

Boring (1950b) suggested three reasons for his overwhelming stature and influence. First, James wrote with a brilliance and clarity rare in science, then as well as now. There is magnetism, spontaneity, and charm throughout his books. The second reason for his influence is negative, in the sense in which all movements are negative. James opposed the current Wundtian

Functionalism:
American Pioneers

psychology, with its introspective analysis of consciousness into elements. (3) The third reason is positive. He offered an alternative way of looking at the mind, an approach congruent with the new American functional approach to psychology. The times were ready for what James had to tell us.

The concept of functionalism is explicit in James's psychology, in which he presented what subsequently became the central tenet of American functionalism: the study of living persons as they adapt to their environment, not the discovery of elements of experience. The function of consciousness, James wrote, is to guide us to those ends required for survival. Consciousness is thus depicted as an organ particularly appropriate to the needs of complex beings in a complex environment; without it, the process of human evolution could not have occurred.

The Principles of Psychology

> The publication of The Principles was hailed both at home and abroad as an event of the first magnitude in the psychological world. Not only was it a comprehensive survey of a new field of learning, not only was it a new synthesis of the facts of psychology; it was itself a contribution to psychology. From the first, it was recognized as more than a mere book about psychology. Because of its freshness and power, because of its definite attitudes and stimulating suggestions, it was itself an event in the history of psychology. (Heidbreder, 1933, p. 197)

James's book treats psychology as a natural science, specifically a biological science. This was nothing new in 1890, but in James's hands the science of psychology took a different direction from German orthodox psychology. James was concerned with conscious processes as activities of an organism that produced some change in that organism's life. Mental processes were believed by James to be useful, *functional* activities to living creatures as they attempt to maintain and adapt themselves in the world of nature.

A related attitude is James's emphasis on the nonrational aspect of human nature. We are, he noted, creatures of action and passion as well as of thought and reason. Even when discussing purely intellectual processes, James emphasized the nonrational. For instance, he carefully noted that intellect operates under the physiological influences of the body, that one's beliefs are determined by emotional factors, and that reason and the formation of concepts are affected by various wants and needs. James did not consider the human being a wholly rational creature.

Let us briefly survey this important book. The first six chapters of the first volume introduce the reader to the biological foundations that James believed necessary to prepare a base for psychology. He discussed aspects of nervous system activity important to mental functioning. He believed that all of mental life is determined largely by the tendency of the nervous system to undergo modification by each action it makes, so that subsequently the organism will find it easier to perform similar responses. Thus, habit became a vital part of all mental life.

James discussed and criticized all major philosophical conceptions of the relationships between mind and body. He accepted states of consciousness (mind) and brain processes (body) as phenomena in the natural world, and noted a correspondence, term for term, between the succession of conscious states and the succession of brain processes. He believed, however, that psychology as a science could accept whatever mind–body relationships it found, but was under no obligation to explain or account for their existence.

The remainder of the first volume is concerned with the subject matter and methods of investigation for psychology. Here James develops fully his notion of consciousness and its characteristics.

The second volume begins with a treatment of sensation, followed by chapters on perception, belief, reasoning, instinct, and volition. The last two chapters deal with hypnosis and with psychogenesis (the development of the human species and the individual). Several of the major points as expressed in *The Principles* are discussed in the following sections.

Subject Matter for Psychology: A New Look at Consciousness

James stated in the opening sentence of *The Principles* that "psychology is the Science of Mental Life, both of its phenomena and of their conditions." In terms of subject matter, the key words are "phenomena" and "conditions." "Phenomena" indicates that the subject matter is to be found in immediate experience; "conditions" refers to the importance of the body, particularly the brain, in mental life.

According to James, the physical substructures of consciousness form an important part of psychology. He recognized the importance of considering consciousness, the focal point of his interest, in its natural setting—the physical human being. This awareness of biology, of the action of the brain on consciousness, is a unique feature of James's approach to psychology.

James rebelled against what he considered the artificiality and narrowness of the structuralist position, a revolt that anticipated the more general protest subsequently made by the functionalists (as well as the Gestalt psychologists). Experiences are simply what they are, he said, not groups or amalgamations of elements. The discovery of discrete elements through introspective analysis does not demonstrate that these elements exist independently of the observation. He argued that psychologists may read into an experience what their systematic position in psychology tells them should be there.

A tea-taster can be trained to discriminate individual elements in a flavor that may not be perceived by the untrained individual. The latter, sipping tea, experiences a fusion of the alleged flavor elements, a total blend not capable of analysis. Similarly, James argued, the fact that some people can analyze their conscious experiences does not mean that the resulting discrete elements are present in the consciousness of anyone else exposed to the same experience. James considered the making of such an assumption the "psychologists' fallacy."

Striking at the heart of Wundtian–Titchenerian structural psychology, James declared that individual simple sensations (the elements of the structuralists) do not exist in conscious experience. They exist only as a result of a rather tortuous process of inference or abstraction.

In a blunt and characteristically eloquent statement, James wrote: "No one ever had a simple sensation by itself. Consciousness, from our natal day, is of a teeming multiplicity of objects and relations, and what we call simple sensations are results of discriminative attention, pushed often to a very high degree" (1890, p. 224).

In place of the artificial analysis and reduction of conscious experience to alleged elements, James forcefully called for a new positive program for psychology. Mental life is a unity, he argued, a total experience that flows and changes. The basic point of James's conception of consciousness is that it "goes on," it is a stream, and he coined the phrase "stream of consciousness" to express this property. Because consciousness is a continuous flow, any attempt to subdivide it into temporally distinct elements or phases can only distort it.

Another characteristic of consciousness is that it is always changing; one can never have exactly the same state or thought twice. Objects in the environment can occur again and again, but not the identical sensations or thoughts they stimulate. We may think of an object on more than one occasion, but each time we think of it, we do so in a different fashion because of the effect of intervening experiences. Thus, consciousness is cumulative and not recurrent.

The mind is also sensibly continuous, that is, there are no sharp breaks in the stream of consciousness. There may be gaps in time, such as during sleep, but upon awakening, we have no difficulty making connection with the stream of consciousness that was going on before the interruption.

Still another characteristic of the mind is its selectivity. The mind chooses from among the many stimuli to which it is exposed, filtering out some, combining or separating others, selecting or rejecting still others. We can attend to only a small part of our experiential world, and the criterion of selection, according to James, is relevance. The mind selects relevant stimuli so that consciousness may operate in a logical manner and a series of ideas may arrive at a rational end.

Above all, James stressed the purpose of consciousness. He believed that consciousness must have some biological utility or it would not have survived. The purpose or function of consciousness is to enable us to adapt to our environment by enabling us to choose. James distinguished between conscious choice and habit, the latter being involuntary and nonconscious.

When the organism faces a new problem and needs a new mode of adjustment, consciousness comes into play. This emphasis on purposiveness clearly reflects the influence of evolutionary theory.

The Methods of Psychology

The discussion of James's subject matter for psychology provides clues to his methods of study. Because psychology deals with a highly personal and immediate consciousness, introspection must be a basic tool. James believed that it is possible to investigate states of consciousness by examining one's own mind. However, consciousness is not capable of analysis, according to James, so the form of introspection practiced could not be the rigid type used by Wundt and Titchener. James considered introspection to be the exercise of a natural gift, consisting in "catching the very life of a moment as it passed, in a fixing and reporting of the fleeting event as it occurred in its natural setting. It was not the introspection of the laboratory, aided by brass instruments; it was the quick and sure arresting of an impression by a sensitive and acute observer" (Heidbreder, 1933, p. 171).

James was aware of the difficulties and limitations of introspection and he accepted it as a less than perfect form of observation. He thought, however, that introspective results could be verified by appropriate checks and through the comparison of the findings of several observers. And though he was not himself a devotee of the experimental method, he did believe in its use as another possible means to psychological knowledge.

To supplement experimental and introspective methods, James urged the use of the comparative method in psychology. By inquiring into the psychological functioning of animals, children, preliterate peoples, and the insane, James believed that the psychologist would discover meaningful and useful variations in mental life.

This discussion of James's methods points up a major difference between structuralism and the newly developing functionalism. The new American movement was not to be restricted to a single technique—introspection. It would apply other methods as well, and this eclecticism broadened the scope of psychology considerably. As noted in Chapter 6, this more diverse methodology was one of Darwin's important legacies.

James emphasized the value for psychology of pragmatism. The basic tenet of the pragmatic point of view is that the validity of an idea, or of any knowledge, must be tested by its consequences. The popular expression of the pragmatic viewpoint is "anything is true if it works." The notion of pragmatism had been advanced in the 1870s by Charles S. Peirce, a philosopher and lifelong friend of James. Peirce's work, however, remained largely ignored until James wrote his *Pragmatism* (1907), which was one of his major contributions as a philosopher.

Emotions

James's most famous theoretical contribution deals with emotions. His theory, published in an article in 1884 and six years later in *The Principles*, contradicted the current thinking about emotions. The experience of emotion had been assumed to precede the physical or bodily expression. The traditional example—we meet a bear, are frightened, and run—exemplifies this notion that the emotion (fright) precedes the bodily expression (running).

James reversed this and stated that the arousal of the physical response precedes the appearance of the emotion. Thus, we see the bear, run, and then are afraid. In essence, the emotion is nothing but the feeling of the bodily changes as they occur. For supporting evidence, James appealed to the introspective observation that if these bodily changes, such as increased heart rate and muscle tension, did not occur, there would be no emotion.[2] James's theory of emotion led to a great deal of controversy, stimulated considerable research, and is the starting point for much of modern theory on emotions.

Habit

The chapter in *The Principles* dealing with habit is in keeping with James's awareness of physiological influences. He considered habit to involve the functioning of the nervous system and postulated that repeated actions serve to increase the plasticity of neural matter. As a result, the action becomes easier to perform on subsequent repetitions and requires less attention on the part of the individual. James also believed that habit had enormous social implications, as noted in this frequently quoted passage.

> Habit is thus the enormous fly-wheel of society, its most precious conservative agent. It alone is what keeps us all within the bounds of ordinance, and saves the children of fortune from the envious uprisings of the poor. It alone prevents the hardest and most repulsive walks of life from being deserted by those brought up to tread therein. It keeps the fisherman and the deck-hand at sea through the winter; it holds the miner in his darkness, and nails the countryman to his log-cabin and his lonely farm through all the months of snow; it protects us from invasion by the natives of the desert and the frozen zone. It dooms us all to fight out the battle of life upon the lines of our nurture or our early choice, and to make the best of a pursuit that disagrees, because there is no other for which we are fitted, and it is too late to begin again. It keeps different social strata from mixing. Already at the age of twenty-five you see the professional mannerism settling down on the young commercial traveller, on the young doctor, on the young minister, on the young counsellor-at-law. You see the little lines of cleavage running through the character,

[2] As another example of simultaneous discovery, the Danish physiologist Carl Lange published an analogous theory in 1885. The similarity between the two led to the designation "James–Lange theory."

Anticipator of Functional Psychology: William James

the tricks of thought, the prejudices, the ways of the "shop," in a word, from which the man can by-and-by no more escape than his coat-sleeve can suddenly fall into a new set of folds. On the whole, it is best he should not escape. It is well for the world that in most of us, by the age of thirty, the character has set like plaster, and will never soften again. (1890, p. 79)[3]

Comment

Our coverage of James cannot hope to encompass the scope and brilliance of his form of psychology. *The Principles* was of major importance and its publication has legitimately been acclaimed as a great event in the history of psychology.

Perhaps it is easier to admire William James than to attempt to analyze his work. His book influenced thousands of students and his position inspired John Dewey and other functional psychologists to shift the new science of psychology away from the Wundtian view. There is no denying that James is one of the most important psychologists the United States has ever produced.

GRANVILLE STANLEY HALL (1844–1924)

Although William James was the first truly great American psychologist, the tremendous growth of psychology in the United States between 1875 and 1900 was not his work alone. Another remarkable figure in the history of American psychology, and a worthy and influential contemporary of James, was Granville Stanley Hall.

Hall's career was one of the most interesting and varied of any psychologist. He worked in bursts of energy and enthusiasm in a number of areas and then moved on, leaving the details to be investigated by others. He was not a founder of functionalism, but his contributions to new fields and activities had a pronounced functional flavor.

American psychology owes Hall a debt because of his outstanding record of "firsts." He received the first American doctorate in psychology, and he was the first American student in the first year of the first psychology laboratory (at Leipzig). He began what is often considered to be the first psychological laboratory in the United States, as well as the first American journal of psychology. He was the first president of Clark University, and the organizer and first president of the American Psychological Association.

---

[3] From William James, *Psychology (Briefer Course)*. New York: Collier, 1962, pp. 158–159. Reprinted by permission of Alexander R. James, Lit. Exec.

*Functionalism:
American Pioneers*

The Life of Hall

Hall was born on a farm in Massachusetts and developed at an early age a succession of interests that characterized his later life. Also characteristic was his personal ambition. At the age of 14, "he vowed to leave the farm and 'do and be something in the world.' . . . His most intense adolescent

A man of diverse professional interests, American Psychological Association founder Granville Stanley Hall (1844–1924) made notable contributions to educational psychology, applying a basic belief in evolution to problems of human development. *(National Library of Medicine)*

Granville Stanley Hall

fear was the fear of mediocrity" (Ross, 1972, p. 12). In 1863 he entered Williams College, where he investigated many ideas, including evolution, which impressed him greatly and was to influence his career in psychology. By the time he graduated, Hall had won a number of honors and had developed an enthusiasm for philosophy and evolution.

In 1867 he enrolled in the Union Theological Seminary in New York City, without much of a call to the ministry. His interest in evolution was no advantage in the seminary and he was not noted for his religious orthodoxy. The story has been told that when Hall gave his trial sermon to the faculty and students, the seminary president, whose job it was to criticize such speeches, instead knelt and prayed for Hall's soul.

On the advice of the preacher Henry Ward Beecher, Hall went to Bonn to study philosophy and theology. From there he went to Berlin, where he added studies in physiology and physics. This phase of his education was supplemented by romantic interludes and the frequenting of beer gardens and the theater, all daring experiences for a young man of Puritan upbringing.

He returned home in 1871, 27 years old, with no degree and heavily in debt. He completed his divinity studies and preached in a country church for all of ten weeks. After working as a private tutor for more than a year, Hall secured a teaching job at Antioch College in Ohio. He taught English literature, French and German languages and literature, and philosophy, served as librarian, led the choir, and even preached. In 1874 he read Wundt's *Physiological Psychology*, and his interest in the new psychology was aroused, causing him some uncertainty about his future career. He took a leave of absence from Antioch, settled in Cambridge, Massachusetts, in 1876, and became a tutor in English at Harvard.

In addition to the monotonous and time-consuming work of teaching sophomore English, Hall managed to conduct research at the medical school. In 1878 he presented his dissertation on the muscular perception of space for his doctorate, the first degree in psychology awarded in America. He got to know William James very well. The two were close in age, but far apart in background and temperament.

Immediately after receiving his degree, Hall left for Europe, first to study physiology at Berlin and then to become Wundt's first American student at Leipzig. The anticipation of working with Wundt was apparently greater than the reality. Although he attended Wundt's lectures and dutifully served as a subject in the laboratory, his own research was conducted along more physiological lines. His career demonstrated that he was little influenced by the founder of structural psychology. When Hall returned to America in 1880 he had no prospect of a job, yet within a span of only ten years he would become a figure of national renown and a leading American psychologist, second only to William James.

The first step in Hall's rise from obscurity was an invitation from the president of Harvard to give a series of Saturday morning talks on education. These well-received lectures brought Hall much favorable publicity and an invitation to lecture at Johns Hopkins University, which had been established five years earlier as the first graduate school in the United States.

His lectures were successful and he was given a professorship in 1884. During his years at Johns Hopkins, Hall began what is usually considered to be the first American psychology laboratory (in 1883) and taught a number of students who later became prominent psychologists, among them Cattell and Dewey. In 1887 Hall founded the *American Journal of Psychology*, the first journal of psychology in the United States and still an important publication. This journal provided a platform for theoretical and experimental ideas and a sense of solidarity and independence for American psychology. (In a burst of enthusiasm Hall had an excessive number of copies printed of the first issue. It took five years for the journal and Hall to pay back those initial costs.)

In 1888 Hall accepted the invitation to become the first president of the new Clark University. He aspired to make Clark a graduate university along the lines of Hopkins and the German universities, with the primary emphasis on research rather than teaching. Unfortunately, the founder, wealthy merchant Jonas Gilman Clark, had different ideas, and did not provide as much money as Hall had been led to expect. When Clark died in 1900, the endowment was devoted to the founding of an undergraduate college, which had been opposed by Hall but long advocated by Clark.

Hall was professor of psychology as well as university president, and taught in the graduate school for several years. He also found time in 1891 to establish at his own expense another journal, the *Pedagogical Seminary* (now the *Journal of Genetic Psychology*), to serve as an outlet for research in child study and educational psychology.

The American Psychological Association was founded in 1892, largely through Hall's efforts. At his invitation, approximately a dozen psychologists met in his study to plan the organization, and they elected him its first president. By 1900 the organization included 127 members.

Hall's interest in religion persisted. He began the *Journal of Religious Psychology* (1904), which ceased publication after a decade, and in 1917 published a book entitled *Jesus the Christ in the Light of Psychology*. His portrayal of Jesus as "a kind of adolescent superman" (Ross, 1972, p. 418) was not well received by organized religion. In 1915 he founded the *Journal of Applied Psychology*, bringing the number of American psychology journals to 16.

Psychology prospered at Clark under Hall; during his 36 years there, 81 doctorates were awarded in psychology. Perhaps the best known of these students is Lewis Terman, a leader in testing and individual differences. At one time it could be claimed that the majority of American psychologists had been associated with Hall either at Clark or at Johns Hopkins, though he was not the primary source of inspiration for them all. Perhaps his personal influence is reflected best in the fact that one-third of his doctoral students eventually went into administration, as he had done.

Hall was one of the first Americans to become interested in psychoanalysis, and was in large part responsible for the attention it received in the United States. To celebrate the twentieth anniversary of Clark University in 1909, he invited Sigmund Freud and Carl Jung to participate in a series of conferences. This was Freud's only visit to the United States, and Hall's invitation was courageous because of the suspicion with which many American psychologists viewed psychoanalysis.

Hall continued to write after his retirement from Clark University in 1920. He died four years later, a few months after his election for a second term as president of the American Psychological Association.

The Works of Hall

Unlike Wundt, who had a single focus, Hall was interested in many areas. However, his intellectual wanderings had a guiding theme—evolutionary theory. His work on a variety of psychological topics was governed by the conviction that the normal growth of the mind involves a series of evolutionary stages. Hall used the theory of evolution as a framework for broad theoretical speculations.

Hall contributed more to educational psychology than to experimental psychology. Only in the early phases of his productive career did he focus on experimental psychology; although he remained favorable toward it, he became impatient with its limitations. Laboratory work in the new psychology proved too narrow for Hall's more general goals and efforts.

Hall is often called a genetic psychologist because of his concern with human and animal development, and with the related problems of adaptation and development. At Clark, Hall's geneticism led him to the psychological study of childhood, and, later, of adolescence. In his child studies he made extensive use of questionnaires, a procedure he had learned in Germany. By 1915 Hall and his students had developed and used 194 questionnaires covering many topics. So extensive was his use of questionnaires that for a time the method came to be associated in America with Hall's name, even though the technique had been used earlier by Galton.

These early studies of children created great public enthusiasm, leading to the so-called child study movement. Although it disappeared in a few years because of poorly executed studies, the movement served to establish the importance of both the empirical study of the child and the concept of psychological development.

Hall's most influential work is the lengthy (about 1300 pages) two-volume *Adolescence: Its Psychology, and Its Relations to Physiology, Anthropology, Sociology, Sex, Crime, Religion, and Education*, published in 1904. This encyclopedia contains the most complete statement of Hall's recapitulation theory of development. He believed that children in their individual development repeat the life history of the race. When children play cowboys and Indians, for example, they are recapitulating the level of preliterate human beings. The book included much material of interest to child psychologists and educators, and went through several printings, one 20 years after initial publication.

As Hall grew older, he became interested in a later stage of development—old age. At the age of 78 he published the two-volume work *Senescence* (1922), the first large-scale geriatric survey of a psychological nature. In the last few years of his life he also wrote two autobiographical books, *Recreations of a Psychologist* (1920) and *The Life and Confessions of a Psychologist* (1923).

Comment

G. Stanley Hall was once introduced to an audience as "the Darwin of the mind." It was a characterization that evidently pleased him and vividly expressed his aspirations and the basic attitude that flavored his work. Throughout his amazing career he remained versatile and agile. His seemingly limitless enthusiasm was bold, diverse, and nontechnical, and it is perhaps this characteristic that made him so stimulating and influential.

In his autobiography he wrote: "All my active conscious life has been made up of a series of fads or crazes, some strong, some weak; some lasting long . . . and others ephemeral" (1923, pp. 367–368). It was a perceptive observation—he was mercurial, aggressive, quixotic, often at odds with his colleagues, but never dull. Hall once noted that Wundt would rather have been commonplace than brilliantly wrong. It has been suggested that Hall would rather have been brilliantly wrong than commonplace.

JAMES McKEEN CATTELL (1860–1944)

The functionalist spirit of American psychology may be best represented in the life and work of Cattell, another contemporary of James. Cattell is generally credited with influencing the movement in American psychology toward a practical, test-oriented approach to the study of mental processes. His psychology was concerned with human abilities rather than conscious content, and in this respect he comes close to being a functionalist, though, like Hall and James, he was never formally associated with the movement. He represented the American functionalist spirit, however, in his emphasis on mental processes in terms of their utility to the organism.

The Life of Cattell

Cattell was born in Easton, Pennsylvania, and received his bachelor's degree in 1880 from Lafayette College, whose president was his father. Following the custom of going to Europe for graduate study, Cattell first went to Göttingen and then to Leipzig and Wundt.

A paper in philosophy won him a fellowship at Johns Hopkins in 1882. At the time, his major interest was philosophy, and during his first semester at Johns Hopkins no psychology courses were even offered. It appears that Cattell became interested in psychology as a result of personal experimentation with drugs. While under the influence of such substances as cannabis and hashish, he observed the changes taking place in his behavior. "These observations marked his first concern with psychology as such" (Sokal, 1971, p. 632).

During Cattell's second semester G. Stanley Hall began to teach psychology at Johns Hopkins, and Cattell (along with John Dewey) enrolled in Hall's laboratory course. Shortly thereafter, Cattell began his research on the time required for different mental activities, work that reinforced his desire to become a psychologist.

Cattell's return to Wundt in 1883 is the subject of some well-known anecdotes in the history of psychology. Cattell appeared at the Leipzig laboratory and boldly announced, "Herr Professor, you need an assistant, and I shall be your assistant" (Cattell, 1928, p. 545). He made it clear to Wundt that he would choose his own research project, on the psychology of individual differences, a topic that was hardly central to Wundtian psychology. Wundt is said to have characterized both Cattell and his project as *ganz Amerikanisch* (typically or completely American), a prophetic remark. The interest in individual differences, a natural outcome of an evolutionary point of view, has since been a feature of American and not German psychology.

Cattell supposedly gave Wundt his first typewriter, on which most of Wundt's books were written. For this gift, Cattell was criticized in jest for having "done a serious disservice . . . for it had enabled Wundt to write twice as many books as would otherwise have been possible" (Cattell, 1928, p. 545).

Careful historical research by Sokal (1980) on Cattell's letters and journals indicates that these stories are questionable. Cattell's account of these events, written many years later, is not supported by his correspondence and journal entries. For example, Sokal points out that Wundt thought highly of Cattell and appointed him as his laboratory assistant in 1886. Also, there is no evidence that Cattell wanted to study individual differences. Third, Cattell introduced Wundt to the use of the typewriter, but he did not give him one.[4]

Cattell found that he was incapable of Wundtian introspection—fractionating the reaction time into various activities, such as perception or choice—

---

[4] I am grateful to Michael M. Sokal for providing this information from *An education in psychology: James McKeen Cattell's journal and letters from Germany and England, 1880–1888* (Cambridge, Mass.: MIT Press, 1980).

154

Functionalism:
American Pioneers

and questioned whether anyone was equal to the task. This attitude did not ingratiate him with Wundt, who did not allow in his laboratory anyone who was unable to benefit from his method. Consequently, Cattell conducted some of his research in his own room.

In spite of their differences, Wundt and Cattell did agree on the value of studying reaction time. Cattell believed it to be useful for the study of the time necessary for various mental operations, and for research on individual differences. Many of the classic reaction-time studies were carried out by Cattell during his three years at Leipzig and he published several articles on reaction time before leaving there.

After obtaining his degree in 1886 Cattell lectured in psychology at Bryn Mawr and at the University of Pennsylvania. He then became a lecturer at Cambridge University in England, where he met Sir Francis Galton. The two men had similar interests and views on individual differences, and Galton, who was then at the zenith of his fame, broadened Cattell's horizons. Cattell admired Galton's versatility and was impressed by his emphasis on measurement and statistics. As a result, Cattell became one of the first American psychologists to stress quantification, ranking, and ratings. He later developed the order of merit or ranking method, which has been widely used in psychology, and was the first psychologist to teach statistics in his courses and to stress the statistical analysis of experimental results (Diamond, 1977).[5]

Cattell was also influenced by Galton's work in eugenics. He argued for sterilization of delinquents and defectives and for giving incentives to the brightest and healthiest people to marry their own kind. He offered his seven children $1000 each if they would marry the sons or daughters of college professors (Sokal, 1971).

In 1888 Cattell was appointed professor of psychology at the University of Pennsylvania. This appointment was significant because, as the first professorship of psychology in the world, it represented formal recognition of psychology's separate status. Earlier academic appointments of psychologists had been in departments of philosophy. Cattell left Pennsylvania in 1891 to become professor of psychology and head of the department at Columbia University, where he remained for 26 years.

Because of his dissatisfaction with Hall's *American Journal of Psychology*, Cattell began *The Psychological Review* in 1894 with J. Mark Baldwin. In 1894 Cattell acquired from Alexander Graham Bell the weekly journal *Science*, which was ceasing publication for lack of funds. Five years later it became the official journal of the American Association for the Advancement of Science. Cattell began in 1906 a series of reference works including *American Men of Science* and *Leaders in Education*. He bought *Popular Science Monthly* in 1900; after selling the name in 1915, he continued to publish it as *Scientific*

---

[5] Wundt did not favor the use of statistical techniques. The influence of Galton on Cattell is one reason the new American psychology came to resemble Galton's work more than Wundt's.

Monthly. Another weekly, *School and Society,* was established in 1915. The phenomenal organizing and editing work required a great deal of time and, not surprisingly, Cattell's research productivity declined.

During his career at Columbia more doctorates in psychology were awarded there than at any other graduate school in the United States. Cattell stressed the importance of independent work and gave his students considerable freedom to do research on their own. He believed that a professor should be independent of both the university and the students, and to make this point, he lived 40 miles from the campus, opposite the military academy at West Point. He set up a laboratory and editorial office at home and went to the university only certain days each week. Thus, he was able to avoid the frequent distractions common to academic life.

This independence was only one of several factors that strained relations between Cattell and the university administration. He urged increased faculty participation in university affairs, arguing that many decisions should be made by faculty and not by administrators. To this end, he helped to found the American Association of University Professors.

Cattell was not tactful in his dealings with the Columbia University administration. He has been described as "a difficult man to get along with . . . 'ungentlemanly,' 'irretrievably nasty,' and 'lacking in decency' "(C. Gruber, 1972, p. 300). He did not play by the rules of social conduct, preferring slashing satire to gentlemanly argument in his attacks on the administration. Cattell's days at Columbia were numbered. On three occasions between 1910 and 1917 the trustees considered "retiring" him. The final blow came during World War I, when Cattell wrote letters to Congress protesting the practice of sending conscientious objectors into combat. This was an unpopular position to take, but Cattell, characteristically, remained adamant. He was dismissed from Columbia in 1917 on the grounds that he had been disloyal to his country. He sued the university for libel, and although he was awarded $40,000, he was not reinstated.

Cattell never returned to academic life. He devoted himself with greater zest to his publications and to the American Association for the Advancement of Science and other learned societies. His promotional efforts as a spokesman for psychology to the other sciences elevated psychology to a higher standing in the scientific community.

In 1921 Cattell realized one of his greatest ambitions—the promotion of the application of psychology. He organized the Psychological Corporation, with stock purchased by members of the American Psychological Association, to provide psychological services to industry, the psychological community, and the public. This organization has grown considerably and is today an international enterprise.

Cattell remained active as an editor and a spokesman for psychology until his death in 1944. His extremely rapid rise in American psychology deserves mention. He was a professor at the University of Pennsylvania at 28, chairman of the department at Columbia at 31, president of the American

Psychological Association at 35, and, at 40, the first psychologist elected to the National Academy of Sciences.

The Works of Cattell

We have already mentioned Cattell's early work on reaction time and his interest in the study of individual differences. The scope of his work was illustrated in 1914, when a group of his students assembled his numerous short papers. In addition to reaction time and individual differences, his research dealt with reading and perception, association, psychophysics, and the order of merit method. Although the importance of all of these areas cannot be denied, it can be said that Cattell influenced psychology most through his work on individual differences and mental tests. The theme of all his research was the problem of individual differences. By the time he went to Columbia in 1891, his interest in the development and promotion of mental tests had become paramount. (Again we see the influence of Galton.) A few years earlier he had administered a series of tests to students at the University of Pennsylvania, and in a paper published in 1890 had coined the term *mental tests*. He continued the testing program at Columbia and collected data from several classes of entering students.

It is instructive to consider the kinds of tests Cattell used in trying to measure the range and variability of the human capacity. Different from the later *intelligence* tests, which used more complex tasks of mental ability, Cattell's tests, like Galton's, dealt with elementary bodily or sensory–motor measures. These included dynamometer pressure, rate of movement (how quickly the hand can be moved 50 centimeters), sensation (using the two-point threshold), pressure causing pain (amount of pressure on the forehead necessary to cause pain), just noticeable differences in weight, reaction time for sound, time for naming colors, bisection of a 50-centimeter line, judgment of a ten-second period of time, and the number of letters remembered after one presentation.

By 1901 enough data had been collected to correlate the test scores with the students' academic performance. The correlations proved disappointingly low, as did intercorrelations among individual tests. Since similar results had been obtained in Titchener's laboratory using sensory–motor tests, it seemed that tests of this type were not valid predictors of intellectual ability.

As every student of psychology knows, in 1905 the French psychologist Alfred Binet, together with Victor Henri and Theodore Simon, developed an intelligence test using more complex measures of higher mental abilities. This approach provided an effective measure of intelligence and marked the beginning of the phenomenal growth of intelligence testing.

Cattell's influence on the mental test movement was strong. His student E. L. Thorndike (Chapter 9) was a leader in the psychology of mental tests, and Columbia was for years the center of the testing movement.

Building on Galton's work, Cattell undertook a series of studies to investigate the nature and origin of scientific ability using the technique he had developed in 1902, the method of order of merit. Stimuli ranked by a number of judges were arranged in a final rank order by calculating the average rating given to each stimulus item. The method was applied to eminent American scientists by having competent persons in each scientific field rank in order a number of their outstanding colleagues. The source book *American Men of Science* emerged from this work.

Comment

Cattell's impact on American psychology was made not through the development of a system of psychology (he had little patience with theory), or through an impressive list of publications. Rather, his influence was exerted most strongly through his work as an organizer, executive, and administrator of psychological science and practice, and as a spokesman for psychology to the scientific community. Cattell became something of an ambassador of psychology, giving lectures, editing journals, and promoting the practical application of psychology.

He also contributed to the development of psychology through his students. During his years at Columbia he trained more graduate students in psychology than anyone else in the United States, and a number—Woodworth and Thorndike were among them—became prominent in the field. Through his work on mental testing, the measurement of individual differences, and the promotion of applied psychology, Cattell energetically reinforced the functionalist movement in American psychology.

GANZ AMERIKANISCH

Evolutionary doctrine rapidly took hold in America toward the end of the nineteenth century, and American psychology was influenced, indeed guided, much more by Darwin and Galton than by Wundt. This was a curious phenomenon. Wundt had trained virtually all of the first generation of American psychologists in his form of psychology. Yet "very little of Wundt's actual system of psychology ever survived the return passage back across the Atlantic with those young Americans who traveled abroad around the turn of the century" (Blumenthal, 1977, p. 13). When they came back to the United States, these new psychologists set about establishing a kind of psychology that bore little resemblance to what Wundt had taught them. The new science, not unlike a living species, had to adapt itself to its environment. Structuralism could not survive in the American *Zeitgeist*. It evolved into functionalism.[6]

Structuralism was not a practical kind of psychology. It did not deal with the mind in use; it could not be applied to the everyday demands and problems of life. American culture was oriented toward the practical and

---

[6] Structuralism did survive at Cornell, but Titchener was not an American and he deliberately remained aloof from American culture.

the pragmatic, and people valued what worked. The country wanted a utilitarian, shirt-sleeves form of psychology, and through the efforts of James, Hall, Cattell, and other American pioneers, it got it.

When the newly trained American psychologists returned from Germany, in typically direct, aggressive American fashion they transformed the uniquely German species of psychology into a uniquely American one. They began to study not what the mind is but what it does. They took their psychology into the real world, into education, industry, advertising, child development, clinics, and testing centers, and made of it something functional in subject matter and application.

Psychology grew and prospered in America, along with the country. The vibrant and dynamic development of American psychology during the period 1880–1900 is a striking event in science. In 1880 there were no laboratories; by 1895 there were 24. In 1880 there were no journals; by 1895 there were three. In 1880 Americans were going to Germany to study psychology; by 1900 they could study it at many of their own universities. Less than 40 years after psychology had begun in Europe, American psychologists had assumed leadership of the field.

Jonçich (1968) noted that the English publication *Who's Who in Science* showed, in 1913 "the United States [was] already doing the heaviest volume of the world's psychological work. With eighty-four of the world's leading psychologists (more than Germany, England and France combined), among all the sciences only in psychology does this nation hold predominance" (p. 444).

Psychology made its debut before the general public at the Chicago World's Fair in 1893. Hugo Münsterberg and Joseph Jastrow, in a program reminiscent of Galton's Anthropometric Laboratory, set up exhibits of psychological apparatus and a testing laboratory in which, for a fee, people could measure and learn about their capacities. William James called it "Münsterberg's circus." Such popular display would not have found favor with Wundt. He would, no doubt, have characterized this attempt at propagandizing psychology as *ganz Amerikanisch*. And so it was, again reflecting the American temperament that transformed structural psychology into functional psychology.

Psychology became firmly established in America, not only in college catalogues, but also in our daily lives. We have all been influenced and affected by its practical application to a degree not thought possible by the American pioneers of functionalism.

SUGGESTED READINGS

EARLY PSYCHOLOGY IN
AMERICA

Camfield, T. M. The professionalization of American psychology: 1870–1917. *Journal of the History of the Behavioral Sciences*, 1973, 9, 66–75.

Jastrow, J. American psychology in the '80s and '90s. *Psychological Review*, 1943, *50*, 65–67.

Sokal, M. M., Davis, A. B., & Merzbach, U. C. Laboratory instruments in the history of psychology. *Journal of the History of the Behavioral Sciences*, 1976, *12*, 59–64.

INFLUENCE OF EVOLUTION
ON AMERICAN
PSYCHOLOGY

Blumenthal, A.L. Wilhelm Wundt and early American psychology: A clash of two cultures. *Annals of the New York Academy of Sciences*, 1977, *291*, 13–20. (See pp. 16–17 for a discussion of the influence of Spencer.)

Boring, E. G. The influence of evolutionary theory upon American psychological thought. In S. Persons (Ed.), *Evolutionary thought in America*. New Haven, Conn.: Yale University Press, 1950. Pp. 267–298.

Hofstadter, R. *Social Darwinism in American thought* (Rev. ed.). New York: Braziller, 1955.

JAMES

Allen, G. W. *William James*. New York: Viking Press, 1967.

Allport, G. W. The productive paradoxes of William James. *Psychological Review*, 1943, *50*, 95–120.

Allport, G. W. William James and the behavioral sciences. *Journal of the History of the Behavioral Sciences*, 1966, *2*, 145–147.

Harper, R. S. The first psychological laboratory. *Isis*, 1950, *41*, 158–161.

MacLeod, R. B. *William James: Unfinished business*. Washington, D.C.: American Psychological Association, 1969.

Perry, R. B. *The thought and character of William James: As revealed in unpublished correspondence and notes, together with his published writings*. (Vols. 1 & 2). Boston, Mass.: Little, Brown, 1935.

HALL

Burnham, W. H. The man, G. Stanley Hall. *Psychological Review*, 1925, *32*, 89–102.

Dennis, W., & Boring, E. G. The founding of APA. *American Psychologist*, 1952, *7*, 95–97.

Hall, G. S. *The life and confessions of a psychologist*. New York: Appleton, 1923.

Ross, D. *Granville Stanley Hall: The psychologist as prophet*. Chicago: University of Chicago Press, 1972.

CATTELL

Kuna, D. P. Early advertising applications of the Gale–Cattell Order-of-Merit method. *Journal of the History of the Behavioral Sciences*, 1979, *15*, 38–46.

Poffenberger, A. T. (Ed.). *James McKeen Cattell—Man of science* (Vols. 1 & 2). Lancaster, Pa.: Science Press, 1947.

Sokal, M. M. The unpublished autobiography of James McKeen Cattell. *American Psychologist*, 1971, *26*, 626–635.

Woodworth, R. S. J. McKeen Cattell, 1860–1944. *Psychological Review*, 1944, *51*, 201–209.

FUNCTIONALISM: FORMAL DEVELOPMENT

8

THE FOUNDING OF FUNCTIONALISM

In Chapters 6 and 7 we discussed the major themes of the functionalist movement and how they evolved from the work of Darwin and Galton. Functionalism is concerned with the operation and processes of conscious phenomena rather than with their structure. Its interest is the utility or purpose of mental processes to the living organism in its continuing attempt to adapt to the environment. Mental processes are regarded as activities leading to practical consequences, not as elements in some kind of composition. Functionalism's practical cast inevitably led to an interest in the application of science to the affairs of the world. Thus, applied psychology, disdained by Wundt and Titchener, was accepted and practiced by the functionalists.

These themes of functionalism were developed in the laboratory and in the real world by American psychologists such as Hall, Cattell, and James. They shaped this new movement from the works of Darwin, Galton, and, to some extent, Wundt without feeling the need to formalize it, to make of it a firm doctrine.

Although there was no formal school of functionalism by the end of the nineteenth century, functionalist ideas had permeated American psychology. How did this general attitude or approach, loosely structured around several universities and individuals, take on the characteristics of a formal school of thought?

The scholars associated with the "founding" of functionalism were not ambitious to start a new school of psychology in the sense that Wundt had been. They did protest against the strictures of structuralism, but they did not aim to replace it with another "ism" characterized by the rigidity and narrowness formalization usually entails. The formalization of their movement of protest—the founding of functionalism—was partly imposed on them by E. B. Titchener.

Paradoxically, it was Titchener who may have "founded" functional psychology when he adopted the word *structural* as opposed to *functional* in a paper published in the *Philosophical Review* in 1898 entitled "The Postulates of a Structural Psychology." In this paper he pointed out the differences between a structural psychology and a functional psychology, and argued that structuralism was the only proper province of psychology. But by viewing functionalism as an opponent, Titchener unwittingly served to bring it into clearer focus. "What Titchener was attacking was in fact nameless until he named it; hence he thrust the movement into high relief and did more than anyone else to get the term *functionalism* into psychological currency" (Harrison, 1963, p. 395).

Of course, not all the credit for founding functionalism can go to Titchener, but those whom history has labeled the founders of the school, to whom we now turn, were reluctant founders at best.

THE CHICAGO SCHOOL

In 1894 John Dewey and James Rowland Angell came to the newly organized University of Chicago. Their combined influence was largely responsible for that university's becoming a leading center of functionalism, but the university itself played a role in the founding of the new school of psychology.

> It is appropriate, surely, that the first distinctively American school of psychology arose at the new university that was itself an expression of so much that is characteristically American. The almost incredible feat of creating a great university outright—of actualizing a plan, of assembling a distinguished faculty, of bringing into being the whole complex organization, body and soul—gave the place an air of great things accomplished and about to be accomplished; and it is not surprising that a school of thought, starting in such circumstances, should thrive and grow. (Heidbreder, 1933, p. 204)

John Dewey (1859–1952)

When functionalism is considered as a distinct school of psychology, rather than as an orientation or attitude, John Dewey is usually credited with sparking its development. An 1896 paper by Dewey is generally cited as a landmark in the formal establishment of functionalism, and Dewey exerted a great influence on this school of thought, though his years of active contribution to psychology were few.

Dewey had an undistinguished early life and showed no great intellectual promise until his junior year at the University of Vermont. After graduation he taught high school for a few years and studied philosophy on his own, publishing several scholarly articles. He went to graduate school at Johns Hopkins and received his doctorate in philosophy in 1884, after which he taught at the University of Michigan and the University of Minnesota. In 1886 he published the first American textbook in psychology (called, appropriately, *Psychology*), which was popular until it was eclipsed by James's *Principles*.

Functionalism:
Formal Development

In 1894 Dewey was invited to the University of Chicago, where he remained for ten years, during which time he became a moving force in psychology. He began an experimental or laboratory school, which at the time was a radical innovation in education. It served as the cornerstone for the modern progressive education movement, which made him famous and controversial. He spent the years 1904–1930 at Columbia University, working on the application of psychology to educational and philosophical problems.

Dewey's 1896 paper, "The Reflex Arc Concept in Psychology," published in *Psychological Review,* was the point of departure for the new movement. In this his most important and, unfortunately, last contribution to psychology proper, Dewey attacked the psychological molecularism, elementism, and reductionism of the reflex arc with its distinction between stimulus and response. He argued that the behavior involved in a reflex response cannot be meaningfully reduced to its basic sensory–motor elements any more than consciousness can be meaningfully analyzed into its elementary components.

When this form of artificial analysis and reduction of behavior is undertaken, Dewey believed, behavior loses all meaning and only abstractions in the minds of the psychologists performing the dissection are left. Dewey wrote that behavior should be treated not as an artificial scientific construct, but rather in terms of its significance to the organism in adapting to the environment. He argued that the proper subject matter for psychology is the study of the total organism functioning in its environment.

Dewey was strongly influenced by the theory of evolution and his philosophy was based on the notion of social change. He was against the idea of things remaining static, and was in favor of progress achieved through the struggle of the human intellect with reality. In this struggle for survival, both consciousness and behavior function for the organism, with consciousness bringing about the appropriate behavior that enables the organism to survive and to progress. A function is a total coordination of an organism toward the accomplishment of a goal—survival. Thus, functional psychology is the study of the organism in use.

Dewey's philosophical position brought him more acclaim than his psychological studies. As a social philosopher, he was concerned with human welfare and physical, social, and moral adjustment. He considered psychological processes such as thinking and learning to be vital to our adjustment to life. Thinking, he said, was a tool applied to meet the exigencies of life: We think so that we may live.

The human effort to survive results in knowledge, and knowledge is a weapon in the fight for survival, a tool in the adjustment process. Because life is learning, the problem of learning is an important issue for psychology.

The time Dewey spent in psychology was all too short. In keeping with his functional orientation, he devoted most of his efforts to education. His program for the progressive education movement is spelled out in "Psychology and Social Practice," a lecture given in 1899 on his retirement as president of the American Psychological Association (Dewey, 1900). He remained titular head of the progressive education movement for the rest of his life. More than anyone else, Dewey is responsible for the pragmatic spirit of American education. He believed that teaching should be oriented toward the student rather than toward the subject matter.

Dewey's significance for psychology lies in his influence on psychologists and other scholars and his development of the philosophical framework for functionalism. When he left Chicago, the leadership of functionalism passed to James Rowland Angell.

James Rowland Angell
(1869–1949)

Angell molded the functionalist movement into a working school. In the process he made the psychology department at Chicago the most influential of the day, the major training ground for functional psychologists.

Angell was born into an academic family in Vermont. His grandfather had been president of Brown University and his father president of the University of Vermont, and later of the University of Michigan. Angell did his undergraduate work at Michigan, where he studied under Dewey, and then he worked under James for a year at Harvard, receiving his M.A. in 1892. He continued his graduate studies at the University of Halle, in Germany, but did not obtain his Ph.D. His thesis was accepted subject to revision (rendering it into better German), but to undertake this task he would have had to remain at Halle without remuneration. He chose instead to accept an appointment at the University of Minnesota, where the salary, though low, was sufficient. Although he did not earn his Ph.D., he was instrumental in the granting of many doctorates to others, and in the course of his career was awarded 23 honorary degrees.

After a year at Minnesota Angell went to Chicago, where he remained for 25 years. Following in the family tradition, he became president of Yale University and helped to develop the Institute of Human Relations there. In 1906 he was elected the fifteenth president of the American Psychological Association. After retiring from academic life, he served as an officer of the National Broadcasting Company.

In 1904 Angell published a textbook (*Psychology*) that embodied the functionalist approach to psychology. The book was so successful that it had appeared in four editions by 1908, indicating the appeal of the functionalist position by that time. He maintained that the function of consciousness is to improve the adaptive abilities of the organism, and that psychology must study how the mind aids this adjustment of the organism to its environment. A more important contribution to functional psychology is Angell's presidential address to the American Psychological Association in 1906, published in 1907 in *Psychological Review*. "The Province of Functional Psychology" clearly spells out the functionalist position.

By articulating functionalism's utilitarian, operational aims, James Rowland Angell (1869–1949) transformed the perspective into a school that flourished under his leadership at Chicago. *(Archives of the History of American Psychology)*

Angell began by noting that

> *functional psychology is at the present moment little more than a point of view, a program, an ambition. It gains its vitality primarily perhaps as a protest against the exclusive excellence of another starting point for the study of the mind, and it enjoys for the time being at least the peculiar vigor which commonly attaches to Protestantism of any sort in its early stages before it has become respectable and orthodox. (Angell, 1907, p. 61)*

We have seen that a new movement gains its vitality and momentum only with reference to, or in opposition to, the established position. Angell drew the battle lines from the beginning, but concluded his introductory remarks with a modest proposal: "I formally renounce any intention to strike out new plans; I am engaged in what is meant as a dispassionate summary of actual conditions."

Functional psychology, he argued, was not at all new but had been a significant part of psychology from the earliest times. It was structural psychology that had set itself apart from the older and more truly pervasive functional form of psychology.

Angell brought together three conceptions of functionalism that he considered the major themes of the movement.

1. Functional psychology is the psychology of *mental operations,* in contrast to the psychology of mental elements (structuralism). Wundtian and Titchenerian elementism was still strong and Angell promoted functionalism in direct opposition to it. The task of functionalism is to discover how a mental process operates, what it accomplishes, and under what conditions it occurs. Angell argued that a mental function, unlike a given moment of consciousness studied by the structuralists, is not a momentary or perishable thing. It persists and endures in the same manner as biological functions. A physiological function may operate through different structures, and a mental function may operate through ideas that are different in content.

2. Functionalism is the psychology of the *fundamental utilities of consciousness.* Consciousness, viewed in this utilitarian spirit, serves to mediate between the needs of the organism and the demands of its environment. Functionalism studies mental processes not as isolated and independent events, but as an active, ongoing part of biological activity, and as part of the larger movement of organic evolution. Structures and functions of the organism exist because by adapting the organism to the conditions of its environment they have enabled it to survive. Angell believed that because consciousness has survived, it, too, must perform an essential service for the organism. Functionalism had to discover precisely what this service was, not only for consciousness, but also for more specific mental processes such as judging and willing.

3. Functional psychology is the psychology of *psychophysical relations,* concerned with the total relationship of the organism to the environment. Functionalism encompasses all mind–body functions and leaves open the study of nonconscious or habitual behavior. It assumes a relationship between the mental and the physical, an interplay of the same sort that occurs between forces in the physical world. Functionalism holds that there is no real distinction between the mind and the body. It considers them not as different entities but as belonging to the same order, and assumes an easy transfer from one to the other.

Angell's 1906 presidential address was given at a time when the spirit of functionalism was already an established and influential force. Angell shaped this force into an active, prominent enterprise with a laboratory, a body of research data, a vital and enthusiastic staff of teachers, and a core of graduate students. In guiding functionalism to the status of a formal school, he gave it the focus and stature necessary to make it effective.

Angell insisted, however, that functionalism did not really constitute a school and should not be identified exclusively with the psychology taught at Chicago. He believed that the movement was too broad to be encompassed within the framework of a single school. The school of functionalism flourished despite Angell's protestations, and was definitely associated with the kind of psychology practiced at the University of Chicago.

Harvey A. Carr
(1873–1954)

Carr, who majored in mathematics at DePauw University and the University of Colorado, switched to psychology as a result of the friendliness and interest of a professor who was a disciple of Hall. Because there was no laboratory at Colorado, Carr transferred to the University of Chicago, where his first course in experimental psychology was taught by a young assistant professor, Angell, who influenced Carr considerably. In his second year, in which he served as a "handy man" in the laboratory, Carr worked with John B. Watson, who was then an instructor. It was Watson who introduced Carr to animal psychology.

Carr received his Ph.D. in 1905 and after much difficulty obtained jobs first at a high school in Texas and then at a state normal school in Michigan. In 1908 he returned to Chicago to replace Watson, who had left for Johns Hopkins University. Later Carr succeeded Angell as chairman of the psychology department and went on to develop and extend Angell's position on functionalism. During Carr's tenure as chairman, from 1919 to 1938, the psychology department awarded 150 doctoral degrees.

The work of Carr represents functionalism when it ceased to be a crusade against structuralism and became a recognized system in its own right. Under Carr, Chicago functionalism reached its peak as a formally defined system. Carr took the position that functional psychology was *the* American psychology. The work being done at Chicago was the psychology of the time, and as such, it did not need a highly developed systematic formulation.

Other approaches to psychology, such as behaviorism, Gestalt psychology, and psychoanalysis, were regarded as needlessly exaggerated developments, operating on more limited aspects of psychology. It was thought that these schools had little to add to the all-encompassing functionalist psychology.

Because Carr's *Psychology* (1925) is an expression of the finished form of functionalism, it is instructive to consider two of its major points. Carr defined the subject matter of psychology as mental activity—processes such as memory, perception, feeling, imagination, judgment, and will. The function of mental activity is to acquire, fixate, retain, organize, and evaluate experiences, and to use these experiences in the determination of action. Carr called the specific form of action in which mental activities appear *adaptive* or *adjustive* behavior.

We see here the familiar emphasis on mental processes rather than on the elements and content of consciousness. And we see also a description of mental activity in terms of what it accomplishes in enabling the organism to adapt or adjust to its environment. It is significant that by 1925 these points were discussed dispassionately as fact, no longer as matters for argument.

In discussing the methods of studying mental activity, Carr recognized the validity of both introspective and objective observation. He noted that the experimental method is the more desirable, but admitted that adequate experimental investigation of the mind is difficult, if not impossible. Carr believed that the study of cultural products, such as literature, art, language, or social and political institutions, could provide information on the kinds of mental activities that produced them. He also recognized the value of knowledge of the physiological processes involved in mental activity.

Functionalism did not adhere to any one method of study, as did structuralism. In practice, however, there was a marked emphasis on objectivity in the functionalists' research. A great deal of the research undertaken at Chicago did not use introspection, and in those cases where it was used, it was checked as much as possible by objective controls. It is important to note that animal as well as human studies were carried out at Chicago.

The Chicago school of functionalism started the shift away from the exclusive study of the subjective (mind or consciousness) toward the inclusion of the study of the objective (overt behavior). Functionalism helped to move American psychology to the opposite extreme from structuralism, eventually to the point where it focused only on behavior, dropping the study of the mind altogether. Thus, the functionalists provided a bridge between structuralism and behaviorism.

ORIGINAL SOURCE MATERIAL ON FUNCTIONALISM: FROM *PSYCHOLOGY* BY H. A. CARR

The following discussion is reprinted from the first chapter of Carr's *Psychology* of 1925.[1] It indicates the finished form of functionalism and covers subject matter and methodology, as well as the psychophysical nature

[1] Harvey A. Carr, *Psychology* (New York: Longmans, Green, 1925), pp. 1–14.

Under Harvey A. Carr (1873–1954), Angell's successor at Chicago, functionalism ceased to be a protest against structuralism and assumed final systematic form. *(Archives of the History of American Psychology)*

of mental activity and the relationship between functional psychology and the other sciences.

THE SUBJECT MATTER OF PSYCHOLOGY.   Psychology is primarily concerned with the study of mental activity. This term is the generic name for such activities as perception, memory, imagination, reasoning, feeling, judgment, and will. The essential features of these various activities can hardly be characterized by a single term, for the mind does various things from time to time. Stated in comprehensive terms, we may say that mental activity is concerned with the acquisition, fixation, retention, organization, and evaluation of experiences, and their subsequent utilization in the guidance of conduct. The type of conduct that reflects mental activity may be termed adaptive or adjustive behavior. . . . An adaptive act is a response on the part of an organism in reference to its physical or social environment of such a character as to satisfy its motivating conditions. Illustrations of these mental operations may be drawn from the professional education of a physician. At times his mind is mainly engaged in the task of acquisition from lectures, books, and clinics, or from his experiences as a practitioner. At other moments his mind is primarily engaged in the attempt to memorize certain important data. Again, the reflective activities may predominate, and his mind is concerned with the task of analyzing, comparing, classifying, and relating the data in hand to other aspects of his medical knowledge. Finally comes the aspect of adaptive conduct—the use of this knowledge and skill in diagnosis, treatment, or surgical operation.

Every mental act is thus more or less directly concerned with the manipulation of experience as a means of attaining a more effective adjustment to the world. Every mental act can thus be studied from three aspects—its adaptive significance, its dependence upon previous experience, and its potential influence upon the future activity of the organism. For example, perception is a constituent part of a larger act; it is a process of cognizing objects on the basis of what we are doing, or in terms of their relation to some contemplated mode of behavior. Perception also involves the use of past experience, for the significance of any object can be appreciated only in terms of our previous experiences connected with that object. Likewise every experience with an object is likely to exert some effect upon the way in which that object is apprehended on subsequent occasions.

The importance of these various aspects of mental activity is apparent on a moment's reflection. Retention is essential to all learning, mental development, and social progress. The acquisition of an act of skill involves a series of successive trials or practice periods during which the act is gradually perfected and established. Each step of progress is a result of the preceding trials. The effects of each practice period are retained and it is these accumulated effects that render the succeeding attempts more facile. Without retention there could be no mind. If any individual should suddenly lose all his past experiences, he would become almost as helpless as an infant.

Our experiences must be properly organized and systematized in order to be utilized effectively. In popular speech, we often say that an insane person has lost his mind. As a matter of fact these people do have minds. They accumulate, organize, and evaluate their experiences in some sort of fashion, and they react to the world on the basis of these experiences. These people have disordered minds. Their experiences are improperly organized and evaluated. Theoretically, any group of experiences can be organized in various ways. An individual's manner of thinking and the character of his conduct are functions to a large extent of his previous organization. Certain types of organization are conducive to irrational modes of thought and to anti-social forms of behavior. Experiences must not only be organized, but they must be properly organized in order to be utilized effectively in reacting to the world in an intelligent and rational fashion.

The mind is also continuously evaluating the various aspects of experience. The mind not only labels things as good, bad, and indifferent, but it also arranges the good things of life in a crude scale of relative worth. Aesthetic appreciation in the realms of literature, music, and the graphic arts illustrates this function. Ethical values may also be cited. We label social conduct as right and wrong and develop concepts of such virtues as charity, chastity, honesty, sobriety, and punctuality. An individual's system of values constitutes perhaps the most important aspect of his personality. Some students overemphasize the relative value of study and become bookworms and grinds. Some boys attach too great an importance to the value of financial independence, and leave school to seek a job. Some people under-estimate the importance of neatness of dress, correct habits of speech, courtesy, kindliness, and many other traits that make for an effective personality in social relations. Some individuals take their politics, their religion, or their science too seriously, and over-estimate the relative importance of those aspects of life. . . . The mind does evaluate its experiences, and . . . an individual's conduct is to a large extent a function of his ideals and system of values.

All experiences of an individual during life are thus organized into a complex but unitary system of reaction tendencies that determine to a large extent the nature of his subsequent activity. The reactive disposition of an individual, i.e., what he does and what he can and can not do, is a function of his native equipment, of the nature of his previous experiences, and of the way in which these have been organized and evaluated. The term "self" is generally employed to characterize an individual from the standpoint of his reactive disposition. We also speak of an individual's personality when we wish to refer to all those traits and characteristics of his self that make or mar his efficiency in dealing with other individuals, while the term "mind" is used when we wish to characterize an individual from the standpoint of his intellectual characteristics and potentialities. . . . Psychology is thus concerned with the study of personality, mind, and the self, but these are conceptual objects that can be studied only indirectly through their manifestations—only insofar as they express themselves in the reactions of the individual. The various concrete activities involved in an act of adjustment are the observable data and the subject matter of psychology.

THE PSYCHO-PHYSICAL NATURE OF MENTAL ACTIVITY. These various mental operations that are involved in the performance of an adjustive response are usually termed psycho-physical processes. By their psychical character, we mean that they are acts of which the individual has some knowledge. For example, an individual not only perceives and reacts to an object, but he is at least aware of the fact and he may have some knowledge of the nature and significance of those acts. Individuals are not accustomed to reason, make decisions and react on the basis of those decisions and be wholly oblivious of the fact. The performance of any mental act on the part of an individual implies some sort of experiential contact with that act. For this reason we shall refer to these mental acts from time to time as experiences or as experiential activities. These acts are not only experienced, but they are also the reactions of a physical organism. They are acts that directly involve such structures as the sense organs, muscles, and nerves. The participation of sense organs and muscles in such activities as perception and voluntary acts is obvious. The nervous system is also concerned in every mental act. While this fact is not one of the obvious sort, yet the truth of the doctrine has been thoroughly established. The integrity of these structures is essential to normal mental activity. An excision or lesion in any part of the brain is usually correlated with some sort of a mental disturbance. All conditions that affect the metabolism of these structures also influence the character of the mental operations. We shall make no attempt to explain the nature of this psycho-physical relationship. We merely note the fact that these mental acts are psycho-physical events and insist that they must be studied as such.

In contrast with our conception, mental acts are often identified with the psychical aspects of these adjustive activities. This doctrine assumes that these psycho-physical activities are composed of two parallel series of processes that belong to different orders of reality. There are the "conscious" or immaterial processes on the one hand, and the organic or material processes on the other. The conscious processes constitute the subject matter of psychology, while the latter belong to the domain of physiology. Mind is thus defined in purely psychical or immaterial terms. Mental acts are regarded as a series of immaterial or psychical events that can occur only in conjunction with a series of physiological processes.

Two objections may be urged against this doctrine. 1. When we speak of the psychical or conscious characteristic of an act, we are dealing with an abstract or conceptual object that has no independent existential reality. This doctrine thus involves the logical fallacy of assuming that these conceptual objects are independent entities. Consciousness is an abstraction that has no more independent existence than the grin of a Cheshire cat. 2. By identifying mental acts with the psychical aspects of these adaptive activities, the exponents of this doctrine are logically confronted with the problem of explaining how these mental processes can exert any effect upon conduct. In other words, this conception necessarily raises the problem of the nature of the psycho-physical relation. We do not deny the validity of this problem, but we do assert that it is a metaphysical or philosophical problem that does not belong to the domain of an empirical or natural science.

Functionalism:
Formal Development

According to our conception, psychology can not be differentiated from physiology in terms of the metaphysical character of its subject matter. Both psychology and physiology are concerned with the study of the functional activities of organisms. Psychology is concerned with all those processes that are directly involved in the adjustment of the organism to its environment, while physiology is engaged in the study of the vital activities such as circulation, digestion, and metabolism that are primarily concerned with the maintenance of the structural integrity of the organism. Psychology and physiology are thus concerned with two mutually related and interactive groups of organic processes. . . .

METHODS OF APPROACH.   Mental acts can be studied from several avenues of approach. Mental acts can be directly observed, they can be studied indirectly through their creations and products, and finally they can be studied in terms of their relation to the structure of the organism.

Mental acts may be subjectively or objectively observed. Objective observation refers to the apprehension of the mental operations of another individual insofar as these are reflected in his behavior. Subjective observation refers to the apprehension of one's own mental operations. Subjective observation is often termed introspection, and in times past it was regarded as an unique mode of apprehension different in kind from that involved in perceiving an external event. As a matter of fact, the two processes are essentially alike in nature and they can be differentiated only in terms of the objects cognized. Each mode of observation possesses certain advantages and limitations.

1. Introspection gives us a more intimate and comprehensive knowledge of mental events. Some mental events can not be objectively apprehended. For example, we might know from an individual's behavior that he is engaged in thought without being able to tell what he is thinking about. The individual himself not only knows that he is thinking but is keenly aware of the topic under consideration. Neither will objective observation give us any clue as to whether these thoughts are mediated in terms of words or visual imagery. Introspection often reveals the motives and considerations derived from past experience that influence us in any particular act. It would be very difficult to obtain knowledge of this character by the exclusive use of the objective method.

2. Subjective observations are rather difficult. Many mental operations consist of a series of complex and rapidly shifting events that are difficult to analyze and apprehend in a comprehensive manner. Inasmuch as our minds are usually engaged in dealing with objective situations, many people encounter a considerable amount of difficulty in the attempt to break this habit and become introspective.

3. The validity of a subjective observation can not always be tested. Given a report by a subject that he thinks by means of visual imagery,

Original Source Material on
Functionalism

any verification or disproof of this statement is practically impossible inasmuch as this particular mental event can be observed only by that individual. Neither can we decide that the statement is untrue because other people assert that they think in verbal terms, for it is possible that individuals may differ in their manner of thinking. On the other hand, any objective act can be observed by several people and their reports compared.

4. Naturally the use of the subjective method must be confined to subjects of training and ability. Psychology must thus rely upon the objective method in the study of animals, children, primitive peoples, and many cases of insanity.

5. Instruments may be used to record and measure any of the objective manifestations of mind. These records can then be analyzed at leisure. Acts can be detected in this manner that would otherwise escape our notice. For example, photography has been utilized as a means of studying the finer eye movements that are involved in an act of perception. This method has been extensively employed in the study of the perceptual activities involved in reading and in certain visual illusions.

Subsidiary to observation is the method of experimentation. In an experiment, the mental operations are observed under certain prescribed and defined conditions. An experiment is often called a controlled observation. An experiment may be relatively simple or quite complex according to the degree of control that is exercised. As an illustration of a simple type of experiment, we may cite the case of memorizing a list of words for the purpose of analyzing this process and discovering some of the conditions that influence our ability to recall this material on some subsequent occasion. In general, the performance of any mental act for the purpose of studying that act may be termed an experiment. A psychological experiment does not necessarily involve the employment of an elaborate technique and complicated forms of apparatus. The character of the apparatus is a function of the problem. Instruments are employed as a means of controlling the experimental conditions, or as a means of measuring and recording any feature of the experimental situation. The primary value of an experiment depends upon the fact that the observations are made under certain prescribed and specified conditions. An experiment is thus a means of discovering facts and relations that would escape detection during the ordinary course of experience. Furthermore the results of any experiment can be tested by other investigators. The experimental method has its limitations in the field of psychology. Not all aspects of the human mind are subject to control. An individual's mental reactions are to a very large extent a function of his previous experiences. A complete experimental control of a human mind implies a freedom in manipulating its development throughout life in ways that are both impossible and socially undesirable.

The nature of mind may also be studied indirectly through its creations and products—industrial inventions, literature, art, religious customs and beliefs, ethical systems, political institutions, etc. This method might well be termed the social avenue of approach. Naturally this method will not be used when the mental operations themselves can be studied. Consequently the method is mainly utilized in the study of primitive races or of past civilizations. The method in practice is essentially historical or anthropological. Obviously our knowledge of the human mind would be exceedingly limited if we were forced to rely exclusively upon such data. Facts of this character, however, are significant for an understanding of the developmental aspects of mind.

Mental acts can also be studied from the standpoint of anatomy and physiology. The structure of any organ and its functional possibilities are intimately related. The neurologist attempts to conceive of the structural arrangements of the nervous system in terms of their relation to the various activities in which they are involved. A study of the mutual relations between mental acts and the architectural features of the nervous system will obviously clarify the conceptions of both psychology and neurology. We know that the character of mental acts is influenced by the metabolic conditions of the nervous system. Neural defects are frequently correlated with disturbances of perception, memory, recall, and voluntary activity. A considerable portion of our accurate and detailed knowledge of the relation of mental operations to the nervous structures has been gained in this way. Certain parts of the nervous structures are excised in animals and the effect of this loss of nerve tissue upon the subsequent ability of the organism is noted. Many features of mind must be explained in terms of the physiological peculiarities of the nervous system. The fact of retention, certain temperamental peculiarities of mind, and some aspects of the process of forgetting must be explained in this manner.

It is thus apparent that any fact is a psychological datum whenever it can be utilized in comprehending the nature and significance of the mental operations. The same fact may be significant to several sciences such as neurology, psychology, and physiology, and such a fact will constitute a part of the data of each of these branches of knowledge. Psychology like the other sciences utilizes any fact that is significant for its purposes irrespective of how or where or by whom it was obtained. No single avenue of approach can give a complete knowledge of a mental act. The various sources of knowledge supplement each other and psychology is concerned with the task of systematizing and harmonizing the various data in order to form an adequate conception of all that is involved in the operations of mind.

Facts of common observation constitute perhaps the major portion of the factual data upon which the present conceptions of psychology are based. Psychology differs from most of the natural sciences in that it deals to a considerable extent with the obvious facts of everyday life. Mental acts are experienced events, and naturally everyone must acquire a certain amount of knowledge concerning his own mental operations during the course of life. A considerable portion of our time and energy is also devoted to the task of dealing with other minds. Everyone thus acquires a certain amount of psychological knowledge of a practical sort. Psychology as a science differs from the common sense variety in several respects. It observes and analyzes mental operations more carefully and systematically, it employs the experimental method whenever possible, it gathers its factual data from a greater variety of sources, and it attempts to construct a more adequate system of conceptions for comprehending these data. Any such system of conceptions is valuable only insofar as the student utilizes them in comprehending his own mental operations or in understanding the actions of others. To a large extent a student must regard a textbook of psychology merely as a guide to the study of his own mind. . . .

RELATION TO OTHER SCIENCES.   So far as its systematic relations are concerned, psychology must be classed with the biological group of sciences which deal with the phenomena of living organisms. Psychology finds its closest kinship with physiology in that both are engaged in studying the reactions of animal organisms. There are no fixed lines of demarcation between the two fields. Psychology is interested in the adaptive reactions of organisms in reference to their environmental conditions insofar as those reactions are dependent upon their previous experiences. Physiologists have evinced but little systematic interest in this topic. They have been concerned for the most part with the study of the vital activities. If physiology be arbitrarily defined as the study of organic functions, psychology must naturally be regarded as a special branch of physiology. However, it is wholly immaterial whether psychology be regarded as subordinate to or coördinate with physiology. As a matter of fact, the two sciences do study different aspects of organic activity.

Psychology gathers materials from a great many fields of human endeavor. Psychology appropriates any facts that are significant for an understanding of mind. A professional psychologist naturally encounters a very limited range of mental phenomena and hence must gather his materials from a great variety of sources. Psychology takes facts from sociology, education, neurology, physiology, biology, and anthropology, and hopes in time to be able to borrow from biochemistry. Most of our factual knowledge concerning the great variety of mental disorders has been contributed by physicians and psychiatrists. Peculiar facts of mind and personality are frequently contributed by the legal profession. The various practices of business and industry contribute many suggestive data. In fact, psychological materials can be gathered from any line of human endeavor.

Psychology in turn is interested in making whatever contributions it can to all allied fields of thought and endeavor such as philosophy, sociology, education, medicine, law, business, and industry. Naturally, any knowledge of human nature will be extremely serviceable to any field of endeavor that is in any way concerned with human thought and action. While psychology has exerted a considerable amount of influence upon certain of these fields, yet this practical program must be regarded as somewhat of an ideal, for psychology has not as yet attained any very adequate or complete knowledge of human nature.

FUNCTIONALISM AT COLUMBIA

We have discussed the work of James McKeen Cattell (Chapter 7) and its functionalist orientation. Two of Cattell's students at Columbia University are also of importance because of the functionalist cast of their work. They are E. L. Thorndike (Chapter 9) and Robert S. Woodworth.

Robert Sessions Woodworth (1869–1962)

Woodworth did not belong formally to the functionalist school in the tradition of Angell and Carr. Indeed, he expressed dislike for the constraints imposed by membership in any school of thought. He wrote in 1930 that the kind of psychology he was developing "does not aspire to be a school. That is the very thing it does not wish to be. Personally, I have always balked on being told, as we have been told at intervals for as long as I can remember, what our marching orders are—what as psychologists we ought to be doing, and what in the divine order of the sciences psychology must be doing" (p. 327). Although we cannot label Woodworth a functionalist, his work is an appropriate subject in a chapter on American functionalism because he did express and reflect a free form of functionalism that still characterizes American psychology. Much of what Woodworth said about psychology is in the functionalist spirit of the Chicago school, but he added an important new ingredient.

Woodworth was active in psychology for more than 70 years as a researcher, beloved teacher, writer, and editor. After receiving his B.A. from Amherst College, he taught high school science for two years, and then mathematics in a small college for two years before beginning his graduate work. He received his M.A. from Harvard, and his Ph.D. from Columbia under Cattell in 1899. He taught physiology in New York City hospitals for three years, and spent a year with the physiologist Sir Charles Scott Sherrington in England. In 1903 he returned to Columbia, where he remained until his first retirement in 1945. In 1958, at the age of 89, he retired from Columbia a second time; he had continued to lecture to large classes after his first retirement.

Woodworth's list of publications is lengthy and his work has influenced several generations of students. His position is put forth in a number of journal articles and in *Dynamic Psychology* (1918) and *Dynamics of Behavior* (1958). In 1911 he revised George Trumbull Ladd's *Physiological Psychology,* and wrote an introductory text, *Psychology,* that first appeared in 1921 and had appeared in five editions by 1947. The book is said to have outsold every other psychology text for 25 years. His *Experimental Psychology,* written in 1938 and revised in 1954 with Harold Schlosberg, is a classic in that area. In 1931 he wrote *Contemporary Schools of Psychology,* which was revised in 1948 and again in 1964 with Mary Sheehan (appearing posthumously). In 1956 Woodworth received the first Gold Medal Award of the American Psychological Foundation and was cited as having made "unequaled contributions to shaping the destiny of scientific psychology," and as an "integrator and organizer of psychological knowledge" (American Psychological Association, 1956, pp. 587, 588).

Woodworth maintained that his approach was not really new, but was the one followed by "good" psychologists even in the days before psychology became a science. Psychological knowledge must begin, he wrote, with an investigation of the nature of the stimulus and the response, that is, with objective external events. When psychology considers only the stimulus and the response in attempting to explain behavior, however, it misses perhaps the most important element—the living organism itself. The stimulus is not the complete cause of a particular response. The organism, with its varying energy levels and its current and past experiences, also acts to determine the response.

> Even in a machine like a loaded gun, the action is not determined solely by the stimulus (the blow of the trigger); the structure of the gun and its stored energy (the gunpowder) must also be taken into account. In the human organism, as in the loaded gun, a stimulus, corresponding to the blow of the trigger, is necessary to start action; but the nature of the action is determined quite as much by the structure and condition of the organism itself as by the stimulus that initiates it. (Heidbreder, 1933, p. 300)

Thus, according to Woodworth, psychology must consider the organism as interpolated between the stimulus and response. It follows that the subject matter for psychology must be both consciousness and behavior, a position taken by contemporary humanistic psychology (Chapter 15). The external stimulus as well as the overt response may be discovered by the objective observation of behavior, but what happens inside the organism can be known only through introspection. Woodworth therefore accepted introspection as a useful method for psychology, but he also made full use of observation and experimentation.

Woodworth introduced into functionalism a dynamic psychology that seemed, in a way, to be a continuation of the teachings of Dewey and James. The word "dynamic" had been used as early as 1884 by Dewey and in 1908

Functionalism:
Formal Development

by James. A dynamic psychology—a psychology concerned with change and with the interpretation of the causal factors in change—represented an interest in motivation. Woodworth had said in 1897 that he wanted to develop a "motivology."

The first expression of Woodworth's systematic position is *Dynamic Psychology* (1918), a plea for a functional kind of psychology that included the topic of motivation. Although there are similarities between Woodworth's position and that of the Chicago functionalists, Woodworth stressed more heavily the physiological events underlying behavior. His dynamic psychology or motivology is concerned with cause-and-effect relationships, though his interest was not in the ultimate causes of human conduct, but rather in more immediate causes. He believed that psychology's goal should be to determine why people behave as they do, why they feel and act in certain ways, and his primary concern was the so-called driving forces that activate the human organism.

In discussing causal sequences in behavior, Woodworth distinguished between two kinds of events—mechanisms and drives. A *mechanism* is concerned with how a task is performed, such as the mechanical aspects of a physical movement. A *drive* is concerned with why the task is performed. However, mechanisms and drives are essentially alike in that both are responses of the organism. Mechanisms may become drives and vice versa.

Woodworth's position was essentially eclectic. He did not wish to adhere to a single system, nor did he want to develop a school of his own. His viewpoint was built not from protest but from growth, elaboration, and synthesis. He sought the best features of each system of thought.

CRITICISMS OF FUNCTIONALISM

Attacks on the functionalist movement came quickly and vehemently from the structuralist camp. For the first time, at least in America, the new psychology—so recently independent of philosophy—was divided into warring factions. Some saw this division as an indication that the new field was resisting pressures to become solidified within the confines of a single point of view. Opposition within the field meant vitality and flexibility, receptivity to the exploration of new concepts, goals, and approaches. To others, the division was disturbing because it seemed to indicate a lack of maturity relative to the natural sciences. The older sciences were no longer divided into differing camps or espousing varying approaches.

Cornell and Chicago became the respective headquarters of the structuralist and functionalist enemy camps. Accusations, charges, and counter-charges were flung back and forth between the universities with all the righteousness characteristic of those who believe they possess the truth.

One criticism directed against functionalism was that the term itself was not clearly defined. In 1913 C. A. Ruckmick, a student of Titchener's, examined 15 general psychology textbooks to determine how "function" was defined by the various writers. The two most common usages were an activity or process, and a service to other processes or to the whole organism. In the first usage, function is essentially the same as activity; for example, remembering and perceiving are functions. In the second case, function is defined in reference to the utility of some activity to the organism, such as the function of digestion or breathing. Ruckmick suggested that the functionalists sometimes used the word "function" to describe an activity, and sometimes to refer to its utility. He argued that this ambiguity created a tautology—one could speak of the function of an activity, or the function of a function.

It was some years before this charge of inconsistent and ambiguous usage was answered. Carr (1930) argued that the two definitions were not inconsistent because both referred to the same processes. Functionalism was interested in a particular activity both for its own sake (the first definition) and for its relationship to other conditions or activities (the second definition). A similar practice was followed in biology.

Carr's answer to this criticism came 17 years after it was first made. Heidbreder noted that "Functionalism used the concept first and defined it later; and this sequence of events is characteristic of the movement. . . . functionalism has never been disposed to place definition and systematization in the foreground" (1933, p. 228).

Another criticism, particularly from Titchener, related to the definition of psychology itself. The structuralists charged that functionalism was not psychology at all, because it was not restricted to the subject matter and methodology of structuralism. In Titchener's view, any approach other than the introspective analysis of the mind into elements was not psychology. Of course, it was just this definition of psychology that the functionalists were questioning and trying to replace.

Other critics found fault with the functionalists' interest in activities of a practical or applied nature, a manifestation of the long-standing controversy between pure and applied science. The structuralists did not look favorably on applied psychology. The functionalists, however, were unconcerned with maintaining psychology as a pure science and never apologized for their practical interests. Carr suggested that rigorous scientific procedures can be adhered to in both pure and applied psychology, and equally valid research can be performed in an industrial setting and in a university laboratory. In the final analysis, Carr noted, it is the method and not the subject matter that determines how scientific a field of inquiry is. The controversy between pure and applied science does not exist in such an extreme form in contemporary American psychology, and this may be seen as a contribution of functionalism, not as a fault.

Functionalists were also criticized for their eclecticism. Unlike the more dogmatic structuralists, they consistently made use of any theoretical or methodological approach that seemed appropriate to the solution of the problem at hand. Many see virtue in this more flexible approach to psychology, particularly because it coexisted with a tough-minded insistence on proper scientific control and methodology.

CONTRIBUTIONS OF FUNCTIONALISM

As an attitude or general viewpoint, functionalism became part of the mainstream of American psychology. Its early and vigorous opposition to structuralism was of immense value to the development of psychology in the United States. The long-range consequences of the shift in emphasis from structure to function were also significant. One result was that the rapidly increasing research on animal behavior became an important part of psychology. It was not a part of structural psychology, though Wundt did favor the interpretation of animal consciousness through the technique of introspection by analogy. Indeed, he once wrote about abstract reasoning in spiders (Mackenzie, 1977).

The functionalists' broadly defined psychology also incorporated studies of children, the mentally retarded, and the insane. In addition, it allowed psychologists to supplement the method of introspection with other ways of securing data, such as physiological research, mental tests, questionnaires, and objective descriptions of behavior. All these methods, which were anathema to the structuralists, became respectable sources of information for psychology.

By the time of Wundt's death in 1920, his structural form of psychology had been overshadowed in the United States by the broader, more practical approach of the functionalists. The functionalist victory was complete by 1930, and in the United States today psychology is, to some extent, functional in its orientation, though functionalism as a separate school of thought no longer exists. Because of its success, there was no longer any need for it to retain the characteristics of a school.

SUGGESTED READINGS

GENERAL

Angell, J. R. *Psychology: An introductory study of the structure and function of the human consciousness.* New York: Holt, 1904.

Carr, H. A. Functionalism. In C. Murchison (Ed.), *Psychologies of 1930.* Worcester, Mass.: Clark University Press, 1930. Pp. 59–78.

Harrison, R. Functionalism and its historical significance. *Genetic Psychology Monographs,* 1963, *68,* 387–423.

Heidbreder, E. Functionalism. In D. L. Krantz (Ed.), *Schools of psychology.* New York: Appleton, 1969. Pp. 35–50.

James, W. The Chicago school. *Psychological Bulletin,* 1904, *1,* 1–5.

McKinney, F. Functionalism at Chicago—memories of a graduate student: 1929–1931. *Journal of the History of the Behavioral Sciences,* 1978, *14,* 142–148.

Thorne, F. C. Reflections on the golden age of Columbia psychology. *Journal of the History of the Behavioral Sciences,* 1976, *12,* 159–165.

Whitely, P. L. A new name for an old idea? A student of Harvey Carr reflects. *Journal of the History of the Behavioral Sciences,* 1976, *12,* 260–274.

DEWEY

Boring, E. G. John Dewey: 1859–1952. *American Journal of Psychology,* 1953, *66,* 145–147.

Dewey, J. The reflex arc concept in psychology. *Psychological Review,* 1896, *3,* 357–370.

Dewey, J. Psychology and social practice. *Psychological Review,* 1900, *7,* 105–124.

ANGELL

Angell, J. R. The province of functional psychology. *Psychological Review,* 1907, *14,* 61–91.

Miles, W. James Rowland Angell, 1869–1949, psychologist–educator. *Science,* 1949, *110,* 1–4.

WOODWORTH

Poffenberger, A. T. Robert Sessions Woodworth: 1869–1962. *American Journal of Psychology,* 1962, *75,* 677–692.

9
BEHAVIORISM: ANTECEDENT INFLUENCES

INTRODUCTION

By the second decade of the twentieth century, less than 40 years after Wundt formally launched psychology, the science had undergone drastic revisions. Although structuralism was still a vital and strong position in Germany, attracting its share of loyal adherents, the new movement of functionalism had seriously eroded the earlier school's position in America.

No longer did all psychologists agree on the value of introspection, on the existence of elements of the mind, or on the necessity of psychology's remaining "pure." The functionalists were rewriting the rules of psychology, experimenting with and applying psychology in ways that could not be admitted into Leipzig or Cornell.

The movement from structuralism to functionalism was less revolutionary than evolutionary. The functionalists did not set out to destroy the establishment of Wundt and Titchener; rather, they modified it, adding a bit here, changing there, so that slowly, over a number of years, a new psychology emerged. It was more a chipping away from within than a deliberate attack from without.

The leaders of the functionalist movement did not even feel the need to solidify or formalize their position into a school. After all, it was, as they saw it, not a break with the past but a building upon it.

The change from structuralism to functionalism was, therefore, not all that noticeable at the time it was taking place. There is no particular day or year that we can point to as the start of functionalism, a time when psychology changed overnight. Indeed, it is difficult, as we have noted, to point to a particular individual as the founder of functionalism. This was the situation in the second decade of the twentieth century: Functionalism was maturing and structuralism still held a strong but no longer exclusive position.

In 1913 a revolution against both of these positions erupted. This was truly a revolt, an open break, a total war against the establishment, intent on shattering both points of view. Nothing about this event was gradual or smooth. It was sudden, traumatic, and dramatic, no modification of the past, no compromise, but a complete change.

The new movement was called *behaviorism* and its leader was the 35-year-old psychologist John Broadus Watson. Just ten years earlier Watson had

183
Introduction

received his Ph.D. under Angell at the University of Chicago, the center of one of the two movements Watson was out to smash.

Watson inaugurated his revolution with an article in the *Psychological Review.* The manifesto he wrote was a broad, slashing attack on the existing systems of psychology. The old order, he stated, was a failure and would have to give way to behaviorism if psychology were to advance. In relatively little time these older schools of thought were largely abandoned and behaviorism became the most important and controversial American system of psychology, a position it continues to enjoy today. Moreover, it assumed a prominent role in the cultural and social life of the times.

The basic tenets of Watson's behaviorism were simple, direct, and bold. He called for an objective psychology, a *science of behavior* dealing only with observable behavioral acts that could be objectively described in terms such as *stimulus* and *response*. He wanted to apply to human beings the experimental procedures and principles of animal psychology, a field in which he had been active.

Watson's interests shed light on what he wanted to discard. To be an objective science, behavioristic psychology had to reject all mentalistic concepts and terms. Such words as "image," "mind," and "consciousness"—carry-overs from mentalist philosophy—were meaningless for a science of behavior, and the technique of introspection, which assumed the existence of conscious processes, was irrelevant.

These basic points were forcefully propounded by the founder of behaviorism. Of course, as we have seen, founding is different from originating. The tenets of the behaviorist revolution that was soon to overtake psychology were not original with Watson. They had been developing in psychology and biology for several years.

It is no criticism of Watson to note that he, like all founders, promoted, organized, and integrated ideas and schemas already in existence. From this amalgamation he constructed his new system of psychology. The point is worth reiterating. "Creations absolutely *de novo* are very rare, if they occur at all; most novelties are only novel combinations of old elements, and the degree of novelty is thus a matter of interpretation" (Sarton, 1936, p. 36).

This chapter examines behaviorism's antecedent influences, the "old elements" Watson so effectively brought together to form his new psychology. At least three major trends affected his work: the philosophical tradition of objectivism and mechanism, animal psychology, and functionalism. Animal psychology and functionalism exerted the most direct and obvious impact. The philosophical traditions of objectivism and mechanism had been developing for quite some time and they favored and reinforced the growth of both functionalism and animal psychology.

Watson's insistence on the need for increased objectivity in psychology was not unusual by 1913. The movement has a long history, beginning perhaps with Descartes, whose attempts at mechanistic explanations of the body were among the first steps in the direction of greater objectivity.

More important in the history of objectivism is Auguste Comte (1798–1857), founder of the movement called *positivism*, which emphasized positive knowledge—facts—the truth of which is not debatable (see Chapter 2). According to Comte, the only valid knowledge is that which is social in nature and objectively observable. These criteria rule out introspection, which depends on a private consciousness that cannot be objectively observed. Comte vigorously protested against mentalism and subjective methodology.

By the beginning of the twentieth century objectivism, mechanism, and materialism had grown strong. Their influence was so pervasive that they led inexorably to a new kind of psychology, one without "consciousness" or "mind" or "soul," one that focused on only what could be seen and heard and touched. The science of behavior—viewing the human being as a machine—was the inescapable result.

We now turn to a discussion of the influence of animal psychology and functionalism on the founding of behaviorism, as both movements were infused by the mechanistic, materialistic, and positivistic climate of the times.

THE INFLUENCE OF ANIMAL PSYCHOLOGY ON BEHAVIORISM

Watson stated succinctly the relationship between animal psychology and behaviorism: "Behaviorism is a direct outgrowth of studies in animal behavior during the first decade of the twentieth century" (1929, p. 327). Clearly, then, the most important single antecedent of the development of Watson's program was animal psychology, which grew out of evolutionary theory. It led to attempts to demonstrate the existence of mind in lower organisms and the continuity between human and animal minds.

We have discussed the work of two pioneer animal psychologists, George Romanes and C. Lloyd Morgan (Chapter 6). With Morgan's law of parsimony and greater reliance on experimental instead of anecdotal techniques, the new field of animal psychology was becoming more objective. Consciousness was still its concern, however, and information about an animal's level of consciousness was inferred from observations of its behavior. Thus, while the methodology was becoming more objective, the subject matter was not.

In the early years of animal psychology in the United States, we find, not surprisingly, a continuing interest in animal consciousness. The founders of animal, or comparative, psychology, Romanes and Morgan, exerted a strong influence on the field for some time.

A significant step toward greater objectivity in animal psychology was taken by Jacques Loeb (1859–1924), a German physiologist and zoologist who worked mainly in the United States. Reacting against the anthropomorphic tradition of Romanes and the method of introspection by analogy, Loeb developed a new theory of animal behavior.

His approach was based on the concept of *tropism* or forced movement. In this view, an animal's response is a direct function of or reaction to a stimulus. The behavior is said to be forced by the stimulus, and thus it does not require any explanation in terms of consciousness. Loeb's theory was influential for a time in the biological sciences. It represented a great change from the earlier work of Romanes and Morgan, and was the most mechanistic and objective animal psychology to have developed.

However, Loeb had not completely thrown off the past. He did not reject consciousness, particularly in animals high on the evolutionary scale (such as humans). Loeb argued that consciousness among animals was revealed by *associative memory,* that is, by their learning to react in a desired way to certain stimuli or signs. For example, when an animal responds to the calling of its name, or when it reacts to a certain sound by going repeatedly to the place where it is fed, this is evidence of associative memory. Even in this otherwise highly mechanistic system, the mind or consciousness (specifically, the association of ideas) was still being invoked.

Watson took several courses with Loeb at the University of Chicago and expressed the desire to do research under his tutelage. This indicates Watson's sympathy with, or at least a curiosity about, Loeb's mechanistic views.[1]

By the beginning of the twentieth century the study of animal behavior within a biological framework had become widespread. At the same time experimental animal psychology—notably the work of Thorndike—was developing rapidly. Robert Yerkes began animal studies in 1900 and his work, using a wide range of animals, greatly strengthened the position and influence of comparative psychology. Also in 1900 the rat maze was introduced by W. S. Small, and the white rat and maze became a standard method of studying learning. Yet the problem of consciousness persisted in animal psychology, even with the white rat in the maze. In interpreting the rat's behavior, Small wrote in mentalistic terms:

> It is also clear, I think, that what properly may be called ideas, find slight place in the associative process. Cross images—visual, olfactory, motor—organic conditions, and instinctive activities are assuredly the main elements. That these elements may bleach out and attenuate into ideas is not impossible. Analogy with human experience would indeed point to that conclusion. (Mackenzie, 1977, p. 85)

Although this comment of Small's is more restricted than Romanes's brand of anthropomorphizing, it nevertheless represents a concern with

---

[1] Angell and another faculty member, the neurologist H. H. Donaldson, talked Watson out of this desire, arguing that Loeb was "unsafe," a word open to interpretation, but perhaps indicating objection to Loeb's uncompromising objectivism.

Behaviorism:
Antecedent Influences

mental processes, even with mental elements. Watson, in the early years of his career, came under the same influence. His doctoral dissertation, completed in 1903, was entitled "Animal Education: The Psychical Development of the White Rat." As late as 1907 Watson was discussing the conscious experience of sensation in his rats.

In general, however, the field of animal psychology was becoming increasingly objective in its methods and even in its subject matter. The kinds of conscious experiences being invoked were growing narrower and in a short time would disappear altogether.

Laboratories of comparative psychology were being established and many universities offered courses in the subject. Margaret Floy Washburn, Titchener's first doctoral student, wrote a major textbook in comparative psychology, *The Animal Mind* (1908), and taught animal psychology at Cornell. In 1911 the *Journal of Animal Behavior* (later the *Journal of Comparative Psychology*) was begun. In 1909 Pavlov's work, which greatly supported an objective psychology and Watson's behaviorism in particular, became known in the United States through an article written by Yerkes and a Russian student, S. Morgulis. Because their influence was so important in the development of behaviorism, we shall consider in detail the works of Thorndike and Pavlov.

Edward Lee Thorndike
(1874–1949)

Thorndike is one of the most important researchers in the development of animal psychology. He worked out an objective and mechanistic theory of learning that focused on overt behavior. He believed that psychology must study behavior, not mental elements or conscious experience in any form. Thus, he reinforced the trend toward greater objectivity that had been begun by the functionalists, and interpreted learning not in terms of subjective ideas, but rather in terms of concrete connections between stimuli and responses. However, as we shall see, there was still some reference to consciousness and mental processes in his system.

The work of Thorndike and Pavlov is another example of simultaneous independent discovery. Thorndike's *law of effect* was developed in 1898 and Pavlov's similar *law of reinforcement* in 1902, though it was many years before the resemblance between the two was recognized.

Thorndike was one of the first American psychologists to receive all of his education in the United States. It is significant that this was possible just two decades after psychology was founded.

The Life of Thorndike

Thorndike's interest in psychology was awakened (as it was for many others) when he read William James's *Principles* while an undergraduate at

Wesleyan University. He later studied under James at Harvard, where he began his investigation of animal learning, apparently inspired by a series of lectures given by C. Lloyd Morgan (Mackenzie, 1977). Thorndike's initial research was with chicks, which he trained to run through mazes improvised by placing books on end. The story is told of Thorndike's difficulties in finding room for his chicks. His landlady took a dim view of his raising them in his bedroom, so he turned to James for help. James was unsuccessful in finding space in either the laboratory or the museum, so he took Thorndike and chicks into the basement of his home, apparently to the delight of the James children.

For personal reasons Thorndike did not complete his education at Harvard. Believing that a certain young lady did not return his affections, he applied to Cattell at Columbia to get away from the Boston area. It was not what he really wanted to do; rather, it was "a move born of youthful despair and deeply felt frustration" (Jonçich, 1968, p. 103). He later married the woman in question.

Offered a fellowship by Cattell, Thorndike went to New York, taking his two best-trained chicks with him. He continued his animal research at Columbia, working with cats and dogs and using puzzle boxes of his own design. He was awarded his doctorate in 1898. His thesis, "Animal Intelligence: An Experimental Study of the Associative Processes in Animals," was subsequently published, along with other research on associative learning in chicks, fish, and monkeys.

Thorndike became an instructor in psychology at Teachers College, Columbia, in 1899, and remained there for the rest of his career. At Cattell's suggestion, he applied his animal research techniques to children and young people, and thereafter worked more with human subjects. The rest of his career was spent largely in the areas of human learning, education, and mental testing, and he is considered a leader in the mental testing movement.

Thorndike's 50 years at Columbia are among the most productive ever recorded. His bibliography includes 507 items, many of which are lengthy books and monographs. He retired in 1939, but continued to work actively until his death ten years later.

Thorndike's Connectionism

Thorndike created *connectionism*, an experimental approach to associationism that included several important departures from traditional views. He wrote that if he were to analyze the human mind he would:

> *find connections of varying strength between (a) situations, elements of situations, and compounds of situations and (b) responses, readinesses to respond, facilitations, inhibitions, and directions of responses. If all these could be completely inventoried, telling what the man would think and do and what would satisfy and annoy him, in every conceivable*

Behaviorism:
Antecedent Influences

Edward Lee Thorndike
(1874–1949) pioneered the field
of learning with
connectionism, his theoretical
attempt to explain how the
organism associates stimuli
with responses.
*(Office of Public Information,
Columbia University)*

*situation, it seems to me that nothing would be left out. . . . Learning is
connecting. The mind is man's connection-system. (Thorndike, 1931, p.
122)*

This associationist position was a direct descendant of the older philosophical associationism, with one significant difference. Instead of talking about
associations or connections between ideas, Thorndike talked about connections between situations and responses. He incorporated a more objective
frame of reference into his psychological theory.

His study of learning also differed from classical associationism in that the subjects were animals rather than humans. This method had become acceptable as a result of the Darwinian notion of continuity of species.

Although Thorndike focused on connections between situations and responses and argued that learning does not involve conscious reflection, he nevertheless was concerned with mental or subjective processes. In the quotation above (and in the one below) he spoke about "satisfaction," "annoyance," and "discomfort." These terms are more mentalistic than behavioristic. In other writings he also used mentalistic terms when discussing the behavior of his experimental animals.

Thorndike was still under the influence of the framework established by Romanes and Morgan. "For Thorndike, as for Morgan, detailed analyses of an animal's mental operations on the basis of objective inference was followed by descriptions of the animal's private experience on the basis of subjective inference" (Mackenzie, 1977, p. 70).

It must be noted, however, that like Loeb, Thorndike was not granting high levels of consciousness and intelligence to animals as freely and as wildly as Romanes had. We can see a steady diminution of the role of consciousness in animal psychology from its beginnings to the time of Thorndike, and a greater focus on the use of the experimental method to study more objective behavior.

Therefore, in spite of the mentalistic tinge to Thorndike's work, we must not lose sight of the mechanistic nature of his approach. He argued that to study behavior, it must be broken down or reduced to its simplest elements: stimulus–response units. He shared with the structuralists an analytic and atomistic point of view. The stimulus–response units are the elements of behavior (not of consciousness), the building blocks from which more complex behaviors are compounded.

Thorndike's conclusions were derived through the use of a new research apparatus, the puzzle box. An animal placed in the box was required to learn to operate a latch in order to escape. Thorndike's extensive research with cats involved placing a cat that had been deprived of food in the slatted puzzle box. Food was placed outside the box as a reward for escaping. The door of the box was fastened by several latches. The cat had to pull on a lever or a chain, and sometimes engage in several such acts in succession, to open the door.

At first, the cat displayed random, rather chaotic behaviors as it poked and sniffed and clawed in every direction to get to the food. Eventually the cat hit upon the correct behavior and the door opened. During the first trial the correct behavior occurred by accident. On subsequent trials the random behaviors were displayed less frequently until learning was complete and the cat would display the correct behavior as soon as it was placed in the box.

Thorndike used quantitative measures of learning. One technique was to record the number of "wrong" behaviors, behaviors that did not lead to escaping from the box. Over a series of trials, these became less frequent. Another technique was to record the time that had elapsed from the moment the cat was placed in the box until it succeeded in escaping. As learning took place, this time period decreased.

Thorndike wrote of the "stamping in" or "stamping out" of a response tendency by its favorable or unfavorable results. Unsuccessful response tendencies (those that do nothing to get the cat out of the box) are stamped out over a number of trials. Response tendencies that lead to success are stamped in after a number of trials. This kind of learning has been called "trial and error learning," though Thorndike preferred to call it "trial and accidental success" (Jonçich, 1968, p. 266).

The stamping in or out of a response tendency was formalized in 1905 as Thorndike's *law of effect*.

> *Any act which in a given situation produces satisfaction becomes associated with that situation, so that when the situation recurs the act is more likely than before to recur also. Conversely, any act which in a given situation produces discomfort becomes disassociated from that situation, so that when the situation recurs the act is less likely than before to recur. (Thorndike, 1905, p. 203)*

A companion law is the law of exercise or the law of use or disuse, which stated that any response made in a particular situation becomes associated with the situation. The more the response is used in the situation, the more strongly it becomes associated with it. Conversely, prolonged disuse of the response tends to weaken the association. In other words, repetition of any response in the situation tends to strengthen that response. Thorndike's later research convinced him that repetition of a response is relatively ineffective compared to the reward consequences of the response.

In the early 1930s Thorndike reexamined the law of effect in an extensive program of research using human subjects. The results revealed that rewarding a response did indeed strengthen that response, but punishment of a response did not produce a comparable negative effect. He therefore revised the law of effect to place greater emphasis on reward than on punishment.

Comment

Thorndike's pioneer investigations into the fields of human and animal learning are among the greatest in the history of psychology. His theory of association or learning heralded the rapid rise of learning theory to its present prominent position in American psychology. Although new learning theories and models have appeared since Thorndike's work, the significance of his contributions remains secure. His influence declined with the advent of more sophisticated learning systems, but his work remains a cornerstone of associationism, and the objective spirit in which he conducted his research is an important antecedent of behaviorism.

Pavlov paid tribute to Thorndike's work in the following manner:

> Some years after the beginning of the work with our new method I learned that somewhat similar experiments had been performed in America, and indeed not by physiologists but by psychologists. Thereupon I studied in more detail the American publications, and now I must acknowledge that the honour of having made the first steps along this path belongs to E. L. Thorndike. By two or three years his experiments preceded ours and his book [Animal Intelligence] must be considered a classic, both for its bold outlook on an immense task and for the accuracy of its results. (Pavlov, 1928; cited by Jonçich, 1968, pp. 415–416)

Ivan Petrovitch Pavlov
(1849–1936)

The influence of Ivan Pavlov is felt keenly in many areas of contemporary psychology. His work in the area of association or learning helped to cause associationism to shift from its traditional application to subjective ideas, to completely objective and quantifiable glandular secretions and muscular movements. As a result, Pavlov's work provided John B. Watson with a new way of investigating behavior and a means of attempting to control and modify it.

The Life of Pavlov

Pavlov was born in a provincial town in central Russia, the eldest of 11 children of a village priest. His position in such a large family brought him responsibility and hard work at an early age, characteristics he retained all his life. He was unable to attend school until the age of 11 because of an accident involving a severe blow to the head four years earlier.

His father had tutored him at home, and in 1860 he entered the local theological seminary, intending to prepare for the priesthood. He eventually changed his mind, and in 1870 went to the University of St. Petersburg, where he specialized in animal physiology. Miller (1962) commented that with this university training, Pavlov joined the emerging third class in Russian society—the intelligentsia:

> too well-educated and too intelligent for the peasantry from which he came, but too common and too poor for the aristocracy into which he could never rise. These social conditions often produced an especially dedicated intellectual, one whose entire life was centered on the intellectual pursuits that justified his existence. And so it was with Pavlov, whose almost fanatic devotion to pure science and to experimental research was supported by the energy and simplicity of a Russian peasant. (p. 177)

Pavlov obtained his degree in 1875 and began medical training, not to practice medicine, but in the hope of pursuing a career in physiological research. He studied in Germany for two years, and returned to St. Petersburg for several hard years as a laboratory research assistant.

Pavlov's dedication to research was of paramount importance in his life. His single-mindedness was not distracted by practical issues such as salary, clothing, or living conditions. Luckily, his wife, whom he married in 1881, devoted her life to protecting him from mundane matters. Characteristic of his indifference to everyday affairs is the story that she often had to remind him when it was time to collect his salary. She once said of him that "he shouldn't be trusted to buy a suit of clothes by himself." Nothing mattered to him except his research. When he was 73 and riding the streetcar to his laboratory, he jumped off before it stopped and broke his leg. "He was impetuous—he wouldn't wait for it to stop. A woman standing near him saw it and said, 'My, here is a man of genius, but he doesn't know how to get off a streetcar without breaking his leg.'" (Gantt, 1979, p. 28).

Pavlov lived in poverty until 1890 when, at the age of 41, he finally obtained the post of professor of pharmacology at the Military Medical Academy in St. Petersburg. For a time after his marriage he had slept on a cot in his laboratory while his wife lived with a relative; they could not afford an apartment. In 1883, when Pavlov was preparing his doctoral thesis, their first child was born. Frail and sickly, the infant would not live, said the doctor, unless both mother and child could rest in the country. After a great struggle they were able to borrow enough money for the journey to the home of a relative, but it was too late and the child died. Six years later they were still so destitute that his wife and second son again had to board with relatives. A group of Pavlov's students, knowing of his financial problems, gave him money on the pretext of covering the expenses of lectures they had asked him to give. Pavlov spent the money on laboratory animals and kept none for himself. So strong were his dedication and commitment to his work that he was not particularly bothered by financial hardships. He said that they never caused him "any undue worry."

Pavlov was given to explosive emotional tirades, often directed at his research assistants. The anecdote is told that during the Bolshevik Revolution (1917) Pavlov bitterly chastised one of his assistants for being ten minutes late for an experiment; pitched battles in the streets were not to interfere with research. "What the hell difference does the revolution make," he would shout, "when you've got work to do in the laboratory" (Gantt, 1979, p. 28). Usually these outbursts were quickly forgotten. His students knew exactly what was expected of them; Pavlov never hesitated to tell them. He was honest and direct, if not always considerate, in his dealings with other people.

Pavlov was known as an excellent teacher with a good sense of humor, capable of enthralling an audience of students or peers. Merciless in an argument, he was nevertheless willing to admit he had been in error, though this was a rare occurrence.

His relations with the Soviet regime were complicated and difficult; he was openly critical of the revolution and the Soviet government. He wrote dangerously strong, angry letters of protest to Stalin and boycotted Russian scientific meetings to demonstrate his disapproval of the government. Not until 1933 did he finally accept the government and acknowledge that it had achieved some success in uniting the Russian people. For the last three years of his life he lived in peace with the authorities of whom he had been so critical for 16 years. Despite his attitude, Pavlov received generous government support for his research throughout his career and was largely free of government pressure.

The following passage from Pavlov's autobiography sums up his attitude toward his life:

> *Looking back on my life I would describe it as being happy and successful. I have received all that can be demanded of life: the complete realization of the principles with which I began life. I dreamed of finding happiness in intellectual work, in science—and I found it. I wanted to have a kind person as a companion in life and I found this companion in my wife . . . who patiently endured all the hardships of our existence before my professorship, always encouraged my scientific aspirations and who devoted herself to our family just as I devoted myself to the laboratory. I have renounced practicality in life with its cunning and not always irreproachable ways, and I see no reason for regretting this; on the contrary, precisely in this I find now certain consolation. (1955, p. 46)*

Pavlov's Research

During his distinguished and productive career Pavlov worked on three research problems. The first concerned the function of the nerves of the heart and the second the primary digestive glands. His brilliant research on digestion won him worldwide recognition and in 1904 the Nobel Prize. His third research area, for which he occupies a vital place in the history of psychology, was the study of the higher nervous centers in the brain. He pursued this work with characteristic energetic determination and devotion from 1902 until his death in 1936. In his attack on this problem he made use of *conditioning*, his greatest scientific achievement. It is instructive to consider how Pavlov developed this technique, which changed the direction of his own career and profoundly influenced the development of psychology.

The notion of conditioned reflexes originated (as so many scientific breakthroughs) in an accidental discovery. In his work on digestive glands, Pavlov used the method of surgical exposure of the subjects (dogs) to permit the collection of the digestive secretions outside the body where they could be observed, measured, and recorded. The surgical operations necessary to divert the secretions of a particular gland through a tube to the outside of the body, without damaging the nerves and blood supply, were difficult.

194

Behaviorism:
Antecedent Influences

Awarded the Nobel Prize for his work on digestion, Ivan Petrovitch Pavlov (1849–1936) advanced the cause of objectivity in psychology through his precise research on the physiology of the conditioned reflex.
(National Library of Medicine)

Pavlov displayed considerable ingenuity and technical skill in performing these operations.

One aspect of his work dealt with the function of saliva, which would be involuntarily secreted whenever food was placed in the dog's mouth. Pavlov observed that sometimes saliva would be secreted before the food was given to the animal; there was an anticipatory saliva flow. The dogs salivated when they saw the food or the man who regularly fed them, and even when they heard his footsteps. The reflex of secretion, with its unlearned response of salivation, had somehow become attached or conditioned to stimuli that had previously been associated with feeding. These "psychic" reflexes (as Pavlov originally called them) were aroused in the animal by stimuli other than the original one (food), and Pavlov realized that this happened because these other stimuli (such as the sight and sounds of the attendant) had so often been associated with the ingestion of food. The associationists called this phenomenon "association by frequency of occurrence."

After a long period of doubting whether he should follow up this observation because of its psychical nature, Pavlov decided in 1902 to investigate these psychic reflexes. He soon became absorbed in the new research.

Pavlov (like Thorndike, Loeb, and others before him), in accordance with the prevailing *Zeitgeist* in animal psychology, initially focused on the mentalistic experiences of his laboratory animals; this can be seen in his original term for conditioned reflexes—psychic reflexes. In his early research he wrote about his animals' desires, judgment, and will. "In short, he interpreted animal psychic stimulation in terms of the subjective life of man" (Wells, 1956, p. 22). After a time, however, Pavlov decided to drop all mentalistic references in favor of a straightforward, objective approach. Pavlov described it as follows:

> At first in our psychical experiments with the psychical glands . . . we conscientiously endeavored to explain our results by imagining the subjective state of the animal. But nothing came of this except sterile controversy and individual views that could not be reconciled. And so we could do nothing but conduct the research on a purely objective basis. (Cuny, 1965, p. 65)

Pavlov's research became a model of objectivity and precision. His first experiments were simple. He showed a dog a piece of bread in his hand before giving it to the dog to eat. In time, salivation began as soon as the dog saw the bread. The dog's response of salivating when the bread was placed in its mouth is a natural reflexive response of the digestive system; no learning is necessary for it to occur. Accordingly, Pavlov called this an innate or *unconditioned* reflex. Salivation at the sight of food, however, is not a reflexive response but one that must be learned. This response Pavlov called a *conditional* reflex (having dropped the mentalistic term "psychic reflex"), because it was conditional upon the formation of an association between the sight of food and the subsequent eating of it.

Pavlov soon discovered that any stimulus could produce the conditioned salivary response so long as it was capable of attracting the animal's attention without arousing fear or anger. He used such stimuli as a bell, buzzer, light, and the tick of a metronome.

*Behaviorism:
Antecedent Influences*

His typical thoroughness and precision are evidenced by the elaborate and sophisticated technique he used to collect the saliva. A rubber tube was connected to the fistula; saliva flowed through this tube and onto a delicate platform resting on a sensitive spring. As each drop struck the platform, it caused a movement that was recorded by a marker on a revolving drum. This arrangement, which made possible the recording of the precise number of drops as well as the exact moment at which each fell, is but one example of Pavlov's painstaking efforts to standardize experimental conditions, use rigid controls, and eliminate sources of error.

He was so concerned about preventing intrusions from the environment that he designed special cubicles for his research. The experimental animal was placed in a harness in one cubicle while the experimenter occupied the other. The experimenter could then operate the various conditioning stimuli, collect the saliva, and present the food without being seen by the animal.

These precautions did not completely satisfy Pavlov. He believed that extraneous stimuli could still reach the animals. He designed a three-story research building, later known as the Tower of Silence, in which the windows were covered with extra-thick sheets of glass, the rooms had double steel doors that sealed hermetically when closed, and the steel girders that supported the floors were embedded in sand. A deep moat filled with straw encircled the building. Vibration, noise, temperature extremes, odors, and even drafts had been eliminated. Nothing could influence the experimental animals except the conditioning stimuli to which they were exposed (Cuny, 1965, p. 67).

A typical conditioning experiment runs as follows. The conditioned stimulus—a light, let us say—is turned on. Immediately, the unconditioned stimulus—the food—is presented. After a number of pairings of the light and the food, the animal salivates at the sight of the light. The animal has become conditioned to respond to the conditioned stimulus. An association or bond has been formed between the light and the food. Learning or conditioning will not occur unless the light is followed by the food a number of times. Thus, reinforcement (being fed) is necessary for learning to take place.

In addition to studying the formation of conditioned responses, Pavlov and his associates investigated other phenomena—reinforcement, extinction, spontaneous recovery, generalization, discrimination, and higher-order conditioning (all well-known words in the language of psychology today). Some 200 collaborators came to work with Pavlov, and the experimental program extended over a longer period of time and involved more people than any research effort since Wundt's. As noted, the conditioning situation itself was simple, but it generated many specific questions that required years of patient and thorough experimentation to answer.

Pavlov presented a preliminary report on his findings in 1923, after 20 years of research. In 1927 he published a more systematic account of his work. This long interval between the beginning of his research and the reports of his findings testifies not only to the enormous scope of the problem, but also to Pavlov's scientific integrity. He wanted to be certain of the accuracy and validity of his findings before making them widely known.

Comment

With Pavlov's work, more precise and objective measures and terminology were introduced into the study of association or learning. Also, Pavlov demonstrated that higher mental processes could be effectively studied in physiological terms with the use of animal subjects and without any reference to consciousness. He greatly influenced psychology's shift toward objectivity in subject matter and methodology. The effects of this trend are seen most strikingly in the development of behaviorism, in which the conditioned reflex plays a central part. This concept provided the science of psychology with a basic element or atom of behavior, a workable, concrete unit to which highly complex human behavior could be reduced and experimented upon under laboratory conditions. As we shall see, Watson seized upon this unit of behavior and made it the core of his program.

It is ironic that Pavlov's greatest influence has been in psychology, a field toward which he was not altogether favorable for some time. He believed that psychology would never achieve the status of an independent science and so he excluded it from his own work; he fined workers in his laboratory who used psychological rather than physiological terminology. Woodworth noted that in his lectures Pavlov frequently made such remarks as the following:

> In conclusion we must count it an uncontested fact that the physiology of the highest part of the nervous system of higher animals cannot be successfully studied, unless we utterly renounce the untenable pretensions of psychology. (1948, p. 60)

Toward the end of his life, however, Pavlov changed his attitude and even called himself an experimental psychologist (Wells, 1956). Pavlov's initially negative view did not, of course, prevent psychologists from making effective use of his work. At first, they used the conditioned response to measure sensory discrimination in animals; it is still used for that purpose today. During the 1920s it began to be used, primarily in America, as the foundation for learning theories. Since then, it has generated considerable research and theory as well as controversy.

Pavlov's immense contributions to science are widely recognized and respected, but the social and philosophical implications of his research and the resulting conception of human nature have been criticized. Many find the idea of conditioning people to respond to various stimuli offensive to their vision of human beings as far removed from animals and possessing free will.

198

Vladimir M. Bekhterev
(1857–1927)

Another important figure in the movement of animal psychology and associationism from subjective ideas toward objectively observed overt behavior is Vladimir Bekhterev. Although less well known than Pavlov, this Russian physiologist, neurologist, and psychiatrist was a pioneer in a number of research areas. He was a contemporary and rival of Pavlov in the opening years of the twentieth century, and independently of Pavlov became interested in conditioning.

Bekhterev received his degree from the Military Medical Academy in St. Petersburg in 1881. He studied in Leipzig, Berlin, and Paris, and returned to Russia to take the chair of mental diseases at the University of Kazan. In 1893 he accepted the chair of mental and nervous diseases at the Military Medical Academy, where he also organized a mental hospital. In 1907 he founded the Psychoneurological Institute and began a program of neurological research.

Whereas Pavlov's conditioning research had been conducted almost exclusively on glandular secretions, Bekhterev was interested in the motor conditioning response, a concern that extended the Pavlovian conditioning principle to striped muscles. His basic discovery was the *associated* reflex as revealed through the study of motor responses. He found that reflexive movements, such as withdrawing a finger from an electric shock, could be elicited not only by the unconditioned stimulus (the electric shock), but also by stimuli that had become associated with the original response-eliciting stimulus. For example, the visual and auditory cues present at the time the reflex occurred soon elicited the response by themselves.

The associationists had explained such connections in terms of the operation of some sort of mental process. Bekhterev, however, considered the reactions to be totally reflexive. He believed that higher-level behaviors of greater complexity could be explained in the same way—as a compounding of the low-level motor reflexes. Thought processes were of the same character in that they depended on inner activities of the speech musculature. Bekhterev argued for a completely objective approach to psychological phenomena and against the use of mentalistic terms and concepts. His stand was expressed in *Objective Psychology,* published in 1907 and translated into German and French in 1913. A third edition was published in English in 1932 (*General Principles of Human Reflexology*).

Comment

From the beginnings of animal psychology in the work of Romanes and Morgan we can see a steady and rapid movement toward greater objectivity in both subject matter and methodology. The early work in the field invoked the concepts of consciousness and mental processes and used research methods that were equally subjective.

By the beginning of the twentieth century, however, animal psychology was completely objective in subject matter and methodology. Glandular secretions, conditioned reflexes, responses, acts, behavior—such terms left no doubt that animal psychology had finally discarded its subjective past.

Animal psychology was shortly to serve as a model for behaviorism, whose leader much preferred animal to human subjects for psychological research. John B. Watson used the findings and methods of the animal psychologists as a foundation for the development of a science of behavior that was applicable to both humans and animals.

THE INFLUENCE OF FUNCTIONALISM ON BEHAVIORISM

Another direct antecedent of behaviorism was functionalism. Although not totally objective, functional psychology in Watson's day did represent greater objectivity than its predecessors. Cattell and other functionalists, who were emphasizing behavior and more objective methodology, had expressed dissatisfaction with introspection. The various areas of applied interest to the functionalists had little use for consciousness and introspection, and essentially constituted an objective functional psychology. Thus, the functional psychologists had moved away from the pure psychology of content of Wundt and Titchener before Watson came on the scene. In their writings and lectures some functional psychologists were quite specific in arguing for an objective psychology, a psychology that would focus on behavior instead of consciousness.

Cattell, speaking at the 1904 World's Fair in St. Louis, Missouri, commented:

> I am not convinced that psychology should be limited to the study of consciousness as such. . . . the rather wide-spread notion that there is no psychology apart from introspection is refuted by the brute argument of accomplished fact. It seems to me that most of the research work that has been done by me or in my laboratory is nearly as independent of introspection as work in physics or in zoology. . . . I see no reason why the application of systematized knowledge to the control of human nature may not in the course of the present century accomplish results commensurate with the nineteenth century applications of physical science to the material world. (1904, pp. 179–180, 186)

Watson heard this address and the similarity between his later position and Cattell's statement is so striking that it has been suggested that Cattell could be called the "grandfather of Watson's behaviorism" (J. Burnham, 1968, p. 149).

*Behaviorism:
Antecedent Influences*

In the decade before Watson formally founded behaviorism, the *Zeitgeist* was obviously favoring and reinforcing the idea of a totally objective psychology and the overall movement of American psychology was in a behavioristic direction. In 1911 Walter Pillsbury, in his textbook, *Essentials of Psychology,* defined psychology as the "science of human behavior" and argued that it was possible to treat human beings as objectively as any other aspect of the physical universe. Angell, perhaps the most forward-looking functionalist, predicted that American psychology was ready to move toward greater objectivity. In 1910 he commented that it seemed possible that the term *consciousness* would disappear from psychology, much as had the term *soul.* In 1913, shortly before Watson's manifesto, Angell elaborated on this point, suggesting that it would be profitable if the "possible existence" of consciousness were forgotten and animal and human behavior were described objectively instead. Yet Watson foresaw, perhaps more clearly than anyone else, what the times were calling for, and he responded vigorously and articulately as the agent of a revolution whose inevitability and success were already ensured.

SUGGESTED READINGS

ANTECEDENTS OF BEHAVIORISM

Diserens, C. M. Psychological objectivism. *Psychological Review,* 1925, *32,* 121–152.

Mackenzie, B. D. *Behaviourism and the limits of scientific method.* Atlantic Highlands, N.J.: Humanities Press, 1977. (See especially Chapter III, "Behaviourism's Background: The Instigation to Behaviourism in Studies in Animal Behaviour.")

EARLY ANIMAL PSYCHOLOGY

Warden, C. J., & Warner, L. H. The development of animal psychology in the U.S. during the past three decades. *Psychological Review,* 1927, *34,* 196–205.

PAVLOV

Babkin, B. P. *Pavlov: A biography.* Chicago, Ill.: University of Chicago Press, 1949.

Cuny, H. *Ivan Pavlov: The man and his theories.* New York: Paul S. Eriksson, 1965.

Gantt, H. Interview. *Johns Hopkins Magazine,* 1979, *30*(1), 26–32.

Pavlov, I. P. *Conditioned reflexes.* (G. Anrep, Trans.). London & New York: Oxford University Press, 1927.

Pavlov, I. P. *Lectures on conditioned reflexes.* (W. H. Gantt, Trans.). New York: Liveright, 1928.

Pavlov, I. P. *Selected works.* (S. Belsky, Trans.). Moscow: Foreign Languages Publishing House, 1955.

Wells, H. K. *Ivan P. Pavlov: Toward a scientific psychology and psychiatry.* New York: International Publishers, 1956.

THORNDIKE

Burnham, J. C. Thorndike's puzzle boxes. *Journal of the History of the Behavioral Sciences*, 1972, *8*, 159–167.

Jonçich, G. *The sane positivist: A biography of Edward L. Thorndike*. Middletown, Conn.: Wesleyan University Press, 1968.

Postman, L. The history and present status of the Law of Effect. *Psychological Bulletin*, 1947, *44*, 489–563.

BEHAVIORISM: THE BEGINNING

10

INTRODUCTION

We discussed several antecedents of the behaviorist movement that influenced John B. Watson in his attempt to construct a new school of thought for psychology. Watson recognized that founding was not the same as originating, and he described his efforts as a "crystallization" of current trends in psychology. Like Wilhelm Wundt, psychology's first promoter–founder, Watson set out deliberately to found a new school. This intent clearly sets him apart from others whom history now labels precursors of behaviorism.

JOHN B. WATSON
(1878–1958)

Watson was born on a farm near Greenville, South Carolina, where his early education was conducted in a one-room schoolhouse. The family later moved into Greenville and the 12-year-old Watson attended public schools. He described himself as lazy and insubordinate, and never earned more than passing grades. His teachers remember him as indolent, argumentative, and not easily controlled. He grew up in what Bakan (1966) described as a state of semidelinquency. Watson got into fights and was arrested twice, once for shooting firearms within the city limits. It was not a promising beginning.

Nevertheless, he entered Furman University in Greenville at the age of 16 with a firm plan for his future—he was going to become a minister. Many years earlier he had promised his mother, a devout Baptist, that he would follow the life of a clergyman. At Baptist-affiliated Furman Watson studied philosophy, mathematics, Latin, and Greek, and was expected to graduate in 1899 and enter Princeton Theological Seminary the following fall.

A curious thing happened during Watson's senior year. One of his professors warned the students (perhaps jokingly, but that is not known for sure) that anyone who handed in a paper backward would fail the course. Watson took the professor up on the challenge, turned in his paper backward, and failed. The stunt prevented him from graduating, which meant that he could not attend the seminary as planned.

203

John B. Watson

He stayed at Furman for another year and received an M.A. in 1900, but during that year his mother died, freeing him from the promise to undertake religious training. It is interesting to speculate whether Watson's deliberate failure to graduate on time was an attempt to escape the life of a minister to which he was committed (Creelan, 1974).

Instead of Princeton Theological Seminary, Watson went to the University of Chicago to pursue graduate work in philosophy under John Dewey. He reported that he found Dewey "incomprehensible." ("I never knew what he was talking about then, and unfortunately for me, I still don't know" [J. B. Watson, 1936, p. 274].) His enthusiasm for philosophy quickly diminished, though he did continue with it as a minor.

Watson became attracted to psychology under the influence of James Rowland Angell, and he took a second minor in neurology. He also studied biology and physiology with Jacques Loeb. He worked at several jobs—he was at various times a waiter in a fraternity house, a rat caretaker, and an assistant janitor. Toward the end of his graduate studies he suffered a breakdown, experiencing acute attacks of anxiety and an inability to sleep without a light on.

In 1903 Watson received his Ph.D., married, and accepted a position as an instructor at the University of Chicago, where he remained until 1908. He conducted much research there and demonstrated early his preference for animal subjects. In his autobiographical sketch he wrote:

> I never wanted to use human subjects. I hated to serve as a subject. I didn't like the stuffy, artificial instructions given to subjects. I always was uncomfortable and acted unnaturally. With animals I was at home. I felt that, in studying them, I was keeping close to biology with my feet on the ground. More and more the thought presented itself: Can't I find out by watching their behavior everything that the other students are finding out by using O's [observers]? (J. B. Watson, 1936, p. 276)

Watson's colleagues in graduate school and some of his professors reported that he was not a very good introspector. Whatever special talent or temperament was needed for introspection, Watson did not have it. Bingham (1930) asked "whether this fact may not have supplied part of the urge which eventually drove him toward a purely objective behavioristic system" (p. 7). After all, if one were not good at practicing the primary technique in one's field, prospects would appear to be dim, unless one can develop another approach.

In 1908, when Watson had become eligible for an assistant professorship at Chicago, he was offered a full professorship at Johns Hopkins University in Baltimore. He was reluctant to leave Chicago, but the opportunity to direct the laboratory, the higher position, and the substantial salary increase offered by Hopkins left him little choice. He remained at Hopkins until 1920, and those 12 years were to be his most productive for psychology.

Behaviorism: The Beginning

At Hopkins Watson was extremely popular with the students. The year after his arrival the students dedicated their yearbook to him, and in 1919 the senior class voted him the handsomest professor, certainly a unique accolade in the history of psychology.

Watson said that he began thinking about a more objective approach to psychology around 1903. His thoughts on the subject were expressed publicly for the first time in 1908, in a lecture at Yale University. In 1912, at the invitation of James McKeen Cattell, he spoke again on the subject in a series of lectures at Columbia University. The following year Watson's famous position paper was published and behaviorism was officially launched.

Watson's first book, *Behavior: An Introduction to Comparative Psychology*, appeared in 1914. In it he argued for the acceptance of animal psychology and stressed the advantages of animals as subjects in psychological research. Watsonian behaviorism appealed to many younger psychologists who believed that Watson was cleansing the muddled atmosphere of psychology by casting off long-standing mysteries and uncertainties carried over from philosophy. Mary Cover Jones, a graduate student during those years, wrote 55 years later that she could still remember the excitement that greeted the publication of one of Watson's books. "It shook the foundations of traditional European-bred psychology, and we welcomed it. . . . it pointed the way from armchair psychology to action and reform and was therefore hailed as a panacea" (1974, p. 582).

The rapid acceptance of Watson's position was evidenced by his election to the presidency of the American Psychological Association in 1915, just two years after his influential paper appeared. He was then 37 years of age.

Watson's professional activities were interrupted by a tour in the Army Aviation Service as a major during World War I. After the war, in 1918, he began his research on children, one of the earliest attempts at experimental work on human infants.

His second book, *Psychology from the Standpoint of a Behaviorist*, appeared in 1919, and presented a more complete statement of his position. He argued that the methods and principles he had earlier recommended for animal psychology were equally applicable and legitimate for the study of humans.

Around this time Watson became the first psychologist (indeed, the first scientist in any discipline) to study the physiological aspects of the human sexual response. Forty years before the research of Masters and Johnson, Watson studied the physiological changes that occurred during intercourse. He accomplished this in the most direct way possible, by attaching electrodes to the bodies of the man and woman who served as subjects and recording various measurements while they engaged in sexual intercourse. With a commitment to research worthy of any scientist, Watson himself served as one of the subjects.

The shattering consequences of this investigation have been described by McConnell.

Unfortunately for all concerned, his wife (who had refused to participate in such an outrageous undertaking) eventually discovered why her husband was spending so much time with his female assistant in the laboratory. Watson's wife not only sued him for divorce, she also confiscated the scientific records! (1974, p. 345)

Thus ended Watson's highly promising academic career. Because he was such a prominent figure, the divorce proceedings received sensational, nationwide publicity and he was forced to resign from Johns Hopkins University. Shortly thereafter he married his former laboratory assistant, Rosalie Rayner, who had worked with him on studies of infant behavior. He never returned to a full-time university position.

Many academic colleagues—including his former mentor, Angell—publicly criticized Watson on personal grounds during this difficult time and, understandably, he became embittered toward them. Strangely, considering his radically different personal temperament and theoretical position, E. B. Titchener was of great help to Watson during this crisis. "You have done more for me than all the rest of my colleagues put together," Watson wrote to Titchener in 1922 (Larson & Sullivan, 1965, p. 346).

In 1921 Watson began a second professional career, in the field of advertising. He joined the J. Walter Thompson agency, worked in every department, and made house-to-house surveys, sold coffee, and clerked in Macy's department store to learn about the business world. With characteristic enterprise and success, Watson became a vice president within three years. In 1936 he joined another advertising agency where he remained as vice president until his retirement in 1945.

After 1920 Watson's contact with academic psychology became less direct. Instead, he spent a great deal of time presenting his case for behaviorism to the general public. He lectured, gave radio talks, and wrote articles for such popular magazines as *Harper's, Cosmopolitan, McCall's, Collier's,* and *The Nation.* The fact that editors of these publications urged him to write for them attests to the great public interest in behaviorism. His second wife wrote an article for *Parent's Magazine* entitled "I Am the Mother of a Behaviorist's Sons."

In his articles Watson embarked on a crusade to sell the message of behaviorism to a wide audience. He wrote in a clear, readable style and he was paid well for his efforts. In his autobiography Watson pointed out that as long as he could no longer publish in the professional journals, he saw no reason why he should not go public and, in the language of his new field of advertising, sell his wares. These magazine articles have been described as

interesting, forceful, and assertive, but they are also propagandistic, sometimes simplistic, and occasionally unscholarly. They seem to betray a mischievous pleasure in shocking their audience—the educated, conventional American middle-class—by questioning cherished beliefs. (Herrnstein, 1973, pp. 111–112)

Watson lectured at the New School for Social Research in New York for a while, and out of these lectures came his semipopular book, *Behaviorism* (1925), which described a program for the improvement of society. This book attracted considerable attention, both favorable and unfavorable, from the public.

In 1928 Watson published a work on child care *(Psychological Care of the Infant and Child)*, in which he presented a regulatory as opposed to a permissive system of child rearing, in keeping with his strong environmentalist position. The book was full of stern, puritanical advice—the behaviorist way to bring up children. Watson suggested to parents that they should

> *Never hug and kiss them, never let them sit on your lap. If you must, kiss them once on the forehead when they say good night. Shake hands with them in the morning. Give them a pat on the head if they have made an extraordinarily good job of a difficult task. Try it out. In a week's time you will find how easy it is to be perfectly objective with your child and at the same time kindly. You will be utterly ashamed at the mawkish, sentimental way you have been handling it. (Watson, 1928, pp. 81–82)*

The book transformed American child-rearing practices, and a generation of children was raised in line with Watson's prescriptions. Skinner reported, however, that Watson "later publicly regretted" the book (1959, p. 198). In 1930 Watson revised *Behaviorism*—his last professional activity in psychology.

Watson possessed an attractive combination of personal characteristics and abilities. He was intelligent and articulate, and his handsome appearance and legendary charm would probably have made him a charismatic figure in today's media-oriented culture. He was very much in the public eye—a celebrity—throughout most of his life, and he courted and relished publicity. Larson and Sullivan noted that "In Watson's later life he did things in great style and loved to show a display of power" (1965, p. 352).

In 1935 his second wife died of a tropical fever contracted on a trip to the West Indies. "In a way the light seemed to go out of Watson's life at this time. He ceased to be a man-about-town and more and more spent time on his estate with his two boys" (Larson, 1979a, p. 5).

In 1957, a year before he died, the American Psychological Association honored Watson with a citation, lauding his work as "one of the vital determinants of the form and substance of modern psychology . . . the point of departure for continuing lines of fruitful research." Although his health was poor (he was 79 years old), and he was unable to receive the award in person, he was said to be pleased by this official professional recognition.

It is tragic that Watson was forced to leave the academic world at the age of 42. From around 1920 on, he made no major contributions to psychology, and by 1930 had completely abandoned the science of psychology for his business career.

ORIGINAL SOURCE
MATERIAL ON
BEHAVIORISM: FROM
*PSYCHOLOGY AS THE
BEHAVIORIST VIEWS IT*
BY J. B. WATSON

There is probably no better starting point for a discussion of Watson's behaviorism than the article that began the movement—"Psychology as the Behaviorist Views It"[1]—from the *Psychological Review* of 1913.

Psychology as the behaviorist views it is a purely objective experimental branch of natural science. Its theoretical goal is the prediction and control of behavior. Introspection forms no essential part of its methods, nor is the scientific value of its data dependent upon the readiness with which they lend themselves to interpretation in terms of consciousness. The behaviorist, in his efforts to get a unitary scheme of animal response, recognizes no dividing line between man and brute. The behavior of man, with all of its refinement and complexity, forms only a part of the behaviorist's total scheme of investigation.

It has been maintained by its followers generally that psychology is a study of the science of the phenomena of consciousness. It has taken as its problem, on the one hand, the analysis of complex mental states (or processes) into simple elementary constituents, and on the other the construction of complex states when the elementary constituents are given. The world of the physical objects (stimuli, including here anything which may excite activity in a receptor), which forms the total phenomena of the natural scientist, is looked upon merely as means to an end. That end is the production of mental states that may be "inspected" or "observed." The psychological object of observation in the case of an emotion, for example, is the mental state itself. The problem in emotion is the determination of the number and kind of

Behaviorism: The Beginning

elementary constituents present, their loci, intensity, order of appearance, etc. It is agreed that introspection is the method *par excellence* by means of which mental states may be manipulated for purposes of psychology. On this assumption, behavior data (including under this term everything which goes under the name of comparative psychology) have no value *per se*. They possess significance only in so far as they may throw light upon conscious states. Such data must have at least an analogical or indirect reference to belong to the realm of psychology. . . .

I do not wish unduly to criticize psychology. It has failed signally, I believe, during the fifty-odd years of its existence as an experimental discipline to make its place in the world as an undisputed natural science. Psychology, as it is generally thought of, has something esoteric in its methods. If you fail to reproduce my findings, it is not due to some fault in your apparatus or in the control of your stimulus, but it is due to the fact that your introspection is untrained. The attack is made upon the observer and not upon the experimental setting. In physics and in chemistry the attack is made upon the experimental conditions. The apparatus was not sensitive enough, impure chemicals were used, etc. In these sciences a better technique will give reproducible results. Psychology is otherwise. If you can't observe 3–9 states of clearness in attention, your introspection is poor. If, on the other hand, a feeling seems reasonably clear to you, your introspection is again faulty. You are seeing too much. Feelings are never clear.

The time seems to have come when psychology must discard all reference to consciousness; when it need no longer delude itself into thinking that it is making mental states the object of observation. We have become so enmeshed in speculative questions concerning the elements of mind, the nature of conscious content (for example, imageless thought, attitudes, . . . etc.) that I, as an experimental student, feel that something is wrong with our premises and the types of problems which develop from them. There is no longer any guarantee that we all mean the same thing when we use the terms now current in psychology. Take the case of sensation. A sensation is defined in terms of its attributes. One psychologist will state with readiness that the attributes of a visual sensation are *quality, extension, duration,* and *intensity.* Another will add *clearness.* Still another that of *order.* I doubt if any one psychologist can draw up a set of statements describing what he means by sensation which will be agreed to by three other psychologists of different training. Turn for a moment to the question of the number of isolable sensations. Is there an extremely large number of color sensations—or only four, red, green, yellow and blue? Again, yellow, while psychologically simple, can be obtained by superimposing red and green spectral rays upon the same diffusing surface! If, on the other hand, we say that every just noticeable difference in the spectrum is a simple sensation, and that

Original Source Material on Behaviorism

every just noticeable increase in the white value of a given color gives simple sensations, we are forced to admit that the number is so large and the conditions for obtaining them so complex that the concept of sensation is unusable, either for the purpose of analysis or that of synthesis. Titchener, who has fought the most valiant fight in this country for a psychology based upon introspection, feels that these differences of opinion as to the number of sensations and their attributes; as to whether there are relations (in the sense of elements) and on the many others which seem to be fundamental in every attempt at analysis, are perfectly natural in the present undeveloped state of psychology. While it is admitted that every growing science is full of unanswered questions, surely only those who are wedded to the system as we now have it, who have fought and suffered for it, can confidently believe that there will ever be any greater uniformity than there is now in the answers we have to such questions. I firmly believe that two hundred years from now, unless the introspective method is discarded, psychology will still be divided on the question as to whether auditory sensations have the quality of "extension," whether intensity is an attribute which can be applied to color, whether there is a difference in "texture" between image and sensation and upon many hundreds of others of like character.

The condition in regard to other mental processes is just as chaotic. Can image type be experimentally tested and verified? Are recondite thought processes dependent mechanically upon imagery at all? Are psychologists agreed upon what feeling is? One states that feelings are attitudes. Another finds them to be groups of organic sensations possessing a certain solidarity. Still another and larger group finds them to be new elements correlative with and ranking equally with sensations.

My psychological quarrel is not with the systematic and structural psychologist alone. The last fifteen years have seen the growth of what is called functional psychology. This type of psychology decries the use of elements in the static sense of the structuralists. It throws emphasis upon the biological significance of conscious processes instead of upon the analysis of conscious states into introspectively isolable elements. I have done my best to understand the difference between functional psychology and structural psychology. Instead of clarity, confusion grows upon me. The terms sensation, perception, affection, emotion, volition are used as much by the functionalist as by the structuralist. The addition of the word "process" ("mental act as a whole," and like terms are frequently met) after each serves in some way to remove the corpse of "content" and to leave "function" in its stead. Surely if these concepts are elusive when looked at from a content standpoint, they are still more deceptive when viewed from the angle of function, and especially so when function is obtained by the introspection method. It is rather interesting that no functional psychologist has carefully distinguished between "perception" (and

Behaviorism: The Beginning

this is true of the other psychological terms as well) as employed by the systematist, and "perceptual process" as used in functional psychology. It seems illogical and hardly fair to criticize the psychology which the systematist gives us, and then to utilize his terms without carefully showing the changes in meaning which are to be attached to them. I was greatly surprised some time ago when I opened Pillsbury's book and saw psychology defined as the "science of behavior." A still more recent text states that psychology is the "science of mental behavior." When I saw these promising statements I thought, now surely we will have texts based upon different lines. After a few pages the science of behavior is dropped and one finds the conventional treatment of sensation, perception, imagery, etc., along with certain shifts in emphasis and additional facts which serve to give the author's personal imprint.

I believe we can write a psychology, define it as Pillsbury, and never go back upon our definition: never use the terms consciousness, mental states, mind, content, introspectively verifiable, imagery, and the like. . . . It can be done in terms of stimulus and response, in terms of habit formation, habit integrations and the like. Furthermore, I believe that it is really worth while to make this attempt now.

The psychology which I should attempt to build up would take as a starting point, first, the observable fact that organisms, man and animal alike, do adjust themselves to their environment by means of hereditary and habit equipments. These adjustments may be very adequate or they may be so inadequate that the organism barely maintains its existence; secondly, that certain stimuli lead the organisms to make the responses. In a system of psychology completely worked out, given the response the stimuli can be predicted; given the stimuli the response can be predicted. Such a set of statements is crass and raw in the extreme, as all such generalizations must be. Yet they are hardly more raw and less realizable than the ones which appear in the psychology texts of the day. I possibly might illustrate my point better by choosing an everyday problem which anyone is likely to meet in the course of his work. Some time ago I was called upon to make a study of certain species of birds. Until I went to Tortugas I had never seen these birds alive. When I reached there I found the animals doing certain things: some of the acts seemed to work peculiarly well in such an environment, while others seemed to be unsuited to their type of life. I first studied the responses of the group as a whole and later those of individuals. In order to understand more thoroughly the relation between what was habit and what was hereditary in these responses, I took the young birds and reared them. In this way I was able to study the order of appearance of hereditary adjustments and their complexity, and later the beginnings of habit formation. My efforts in determining the stimuli which called forth such adjustments were crude indeed. Consequently my attempts to control behavior and to produce responses at will did not meet with much success. Their food and water, sex and other social relations, light and temperature conditions were all beyond control in a field study. I did find it possible to control their reactions in a measure by using the nest and egg (or young) as stimuli. It is not necessary in this paper to develop further how such a study should be carried out and how work of this kind must be supplemented by carefully controlled laboratory experiments. Had I been called upon to examine the natives of some of the Australian tribes, I should have gone about my task in the same way. I should have found the problem more difficult: the types of responses called forth by physical stimuli would have been more varied, and the number of effective stimuli larger. I should have had to determine the social setting of their lives in a far more careful way. These savages would be more influenced by the responses of each other than was the case with the birds. Furthermore, habits would have been more complex and the influences of past habits upon the present responses would have appeared more clearly. Finally, if I had been called upon to work out the psychology of the educated European, my problem would have required several lifetimes. But in the one I have at my disposal I should have followed the same general line of attack. In the main, my desire in all such work is to gain an accurate knowledge of adjustments and the stimuli calling them forth. My final reason for this is to learn general and particular methods by which I may control behavior. My goal is not "the description and explanation of states of consciousness as such," nor that of obtaining such proficiency in mental gymnastics that I can immediately lay hold of a state of consciousness and say, "this, as a whole, consists of gray sensation number 350, of such and such extent, occurring in conjunction with the sensation of cold of a certain intensity; one of pressure of a certain intensity and extent," and so on *ad infinitum*. If psychology would follow the plan I suggest, the educator, the physician, the jurist and the business man could utilize our data in a practical way, as soon as we are able, experimentally, to obtain them. Those who have occasion to apply psychological principles practically would find no need to complain as they do at the present time. Ask any physician or jurist today whether scientific psychology plays a practical part in his daily routine and you will hear him deny that the psychology of the laboratories finds a place in his scheme of work. I think the criticism is extremely just. One of the earliest conditions which made me dissatisfied with psychology was the feeling that there was no realm of application for the principles which were being worked out in content terms.

What gives me hope that the behaviorist's position is a defensible one is the fact that those branches of psychology which have already partially withdrawn from the parent, experimental psychology, and which are consequently less dependent upon introspection are today in a most flourishing condition. Experimental pedagogy, the psychology of drugs, the psychology of advertising, legal psychology, the psychology of tests, and psychopathology are all vigorous growths.

These are sometimes wrongly called "practical" or "applied" psychology. Surely there was never a worse misnomer. In the future there may grow up vocational bureaus which really apply psychology. At present these fields are truly scientific and are in search of broad generalizations which will lead to the control of human behavior. For example, we find out by experimentation whether a series of stanzas may be acquired more readily if the whole is learned at once, or whether it is more advantageous to learn each stanza separately and then pass to the succeeding. We do not attempt to apply our findings. The application of this principle is purely voluntary on the part of the teacher. In the psychology of drugs we may show the effect upon behavior of certain doses of caffeine. We may reach the conclusion that caffeine has a good effect upon the speed and accuracy of work. But these are general principles. We leave it to the individual as to whether the results of our tests shall be applied or not. Again, in legal testimony, we test the effects of recency upon the reliability of a witness's report. We test the accuracy of the report with respect to moving objects, stationary objects, color, etc. It depends upon the judicial machinery of the country to decide whether these facts are ever to be applied. For a "pure" psychologist to say that he is not interested in the questions raised in these divisions of the science because they relate indirectly to the application of psychology shows, in the first place, that he fails to understand the scientific aim in such problems, and secondly, that he is not interested in a psychology which concerns itself with human life. The only fault I have to find with these disciplines is that much of their material is stated in terms of introspection, whereas a statement in terms of objective results would be far more valuable. There is no reason why appeal should ever be made to consciousness in any of them. Or why introspective data should ever be sought during the experimentation, or published in the results. In experimental pedagogy especially one can see the desirability of keeping all of the results on a purely objective plane. If this is done, work there on the human being will be comparable directly with the work upon animals. For example, at Hopkins, Mr. Ulrich has obtained certain results upon the distribution of effort in learning—using rats as subjects. He is prepared to give comparative results upon the effect of having an animal work at the problem once per day, three times per day, and five times per day. Whether it is advisable to have the animal learn only one problem at a time or to learn three abreast. We need to have similar experiments made upon man, but we care as little about his "conscious processes" during the conduct of the experiment as we care about such processes in the rats.

I am more interested at the present moment in trying to show the necessity for maintaining uniformity in experimental procedure and in the method of stating results in both human and animal work, than in developing any ideas I may have upon the changes which are certain to come in the scope of human psychology. Let us consider for a moment the subject of the range of stimuli to which animals respond. I shall speak first of the work upon vision in animals. We put our animal in a situation where he will respond (or learn to respond) to one of two monochromatic lights. We feed him at the one (positive) and punish him at the other (negative). In a short time the animal learns to go to the light at which he is fed. At this point questions arise which I may phrase in two ways: I may choose the psychological way and say "does the animal see these two lights as I do, i.e., as two distinct colors, or does he see them as two grays differing in brightness, as does the totally color blind?" Phrased by the behaviorist, it would read as follows: "Is my animal responding upon the basis of the difference in intensity between the two stimuli, or upon the difference in wave-lengths?" He nowhere thinks of the animal's response in terms of his own experiences of colors and grays. He wishes to establish the fact whether wave-length is a factor in that animal's adjustment. If so, what wave-lengths are effective and what differences in wave-length must be maintained in the different regions to afford bases for differential responses? If wave-length is not a factor in adjustment he wishes to know what difference in intensity will serve as a basis for response, and whether that same difference will suffice throughout the spectrum. Furthermore, he wishes to test whether the animal can respond to wave-lengths which do not affect the human eye. He is as much interested in comparing the rat's spectrum with that of the chick as in comparing it with man's. The point of view when the various sets of comparisons are made does not change in the slightest.

However we phrase the question to ourselves, we take our animal after the association has been formed and then introduce certain control experiments which enable us to return answers to the questions just raised. But there is just as keen a desire on our part to test man under the same conditions, and to state the results in both cases in common terms.

The man and the animal should be placed as nearly as possible under the same experimental conditions. Instead of feeding or punishing the human subject, we should ask him to respond by setting a second apparatus until standard and control offered no basis for a differential response. Do I lay myself open to the charge here that I am using introspection? My reply is not at all; that while I might very well feed my human subject for a right choice and punish him for a wrong one and thus produce the response if the subject could give it, there is no need of going to extremes even on the platform I suggest. But be it understood that I am merely using this second method as an abridged behavior method. We can go just as far and reach just as dependable results by the longer method as by the abridged. In many cases the direct and typically human method cannot be safely used. Suppose, for example, that I doubt the accuracy of the setting of the control instrument, in the above experiment, as I am very likely to do if I suspect a defect in vision? It is hopeless for me to get his introspective

Behaviorism: The Beginning

report. He will say: "There is no difference in sensation, both are reds, identical in quality." But suppose I confront him with the standard and the control and so arrange conditions that he is punished if he responds to the "control" but not with the standard. I interchange the positions of the standard and the control at will and force him to attempt to differentiate the one from the other. If he can learn to make the adjustment even after a large number of trials it is evident that the two stimuli do afford the basis for a differential response. Such a method may sound nonsensical, but I firmly believe we will have to resort increasingly to just such a method where we have reason to distrust the language method.

There is hardly a problem in human vision which is not also a problem in animal vision: I mention the limits of the spectrum, threshold values, absolute and relative, flicker, Talbot's law, Weber's law, field of vision, the Purkinje phenomenon, etc. Every one is capable of being worked out by behavior methods. Many of them are being worked out at the present time.

I feel that all the work upon the senses can be consistently carried forward along the lines I have suggested here for vision. Our results will, in the end, give an excellent picture of what each organ stands for in the way of function. The anatomist and the physiologist may take our data and show, on the one hand, the structures which are responsible for these responses, and, on the other, the physico-chemical relations which are necessarily involved (physiological chemistry of nerve and muscle) in these and other reactions.

The situation in regard to the study of memory is hardly different. Nearly all of the memory methods in actual use in the laboratory today yield the type of results I am arguing for. A certain series of nonsense syllables or other material is presented to the human subject. What should receive the emphasis are the rapidity of the habit formation, the errors, peculiarities in the form of the curve, the persistence of the habit so formed, the relation of such habits to those formed when more complex material is used, etc. Now such results are taken down with the subject's introspection. The experiments are made for the purpose of discussing the mental machinery involved in learning, in recall, recollection and forgetting, and not for the purpose of seeking the human being's way of shaping his responses to meet the problems in the terribly complex environment into which he is thrown, nor for that of showing the similarities and differences between man's methods and those of other animals.

The situation is somewhat different when we come to a study of the more complex forms of behavior, such as imagination, judgment, reasoning, and conception. At present the only statements we have of them are in content terms. Our minds have been so warped by the fifty-odd years which have been devoted to the study of states of consciousness that we can envisage these problems only in one way.

We should meet the situation squarely and say that we are not able to carry forward investigations along all of these lines by the behavior methods which are in use at the present time. In extenuation I should like to call attention to the paragraph above where I made the point that the introspective method itself has reached a *cul-de-sac* with respect to them. The topics have become so threadbare from much handling that they may well be put away for a time. As our methods become better developed it will be possible to undertake investigations of more and more complex forms of behavior. Problems which are now laid aside will again become imperative, but they can be viewed as they arise from a new angle and in more concrete settings.

Will there be left over in psychology a world of pure psychics, to use Yerkes' term? I confess I do not know. The plans which I most favor for psychology lead practically to the ignoring of consciousness in the sense that that term is used by psychologists today. I have virtually denied that this realm of psychics is open to experimental investigation. I don't wish to go further into the problem at present because it leads inevitably over into metaphysics. If you will grant the behaviorist the right to use consciousness in the same way that other natural scientists employ it—that is, without making consciousness a special object of observation—you have granted all that my thesis requires.

In concluding, I suppose I must confess to a deep bias on these questions. I have devoted nearly twelve years to experimentation on animals. It is natural that such a one should drift into a theoretical position which is in harmony with his experimental work. Possibly I have put up a straw man and have been fighting that. There may be no absolute lack of harmony between the position outlined here and that of functional psychology. I am inclined to think, however, that the two positions cannot be easily harmonized. Certainly the position I advocate is weak enough at present and can be attacked from many standpoints. Yet when all this is admitted I still feel that the considerations which I have urged should have a wide influence upon the type of psychology which is to be developed in the future. What we need to do is to start work upon psychology, making *behavior*, not *consciousness*, the objective point of our attack. Certainly there are enough problems in the control of behavior to keep us all working many lifetimes without ever allowing us time to think of consciousness *an sich*. Once launched in the undertaking, we will find ourselves in a short time as far divorced from an introspective psychology as the psychology of the present time is divorced from faculty psychology.

Comment

Watson's vigorous attack on the old psychology and his call for a new approach was a stirring appeal to many psychologists. Consider the major points. Psychology was to be the science of behavior, not the introspective study of consciousness—a purely objective experimental branch of natural science. Both human and animal behavior would be investigated. The new psychology would discard all mentalistic concepts and use only behavior concepts such as stimulus and response. The goal of psychology would be the prediction and control of behavior.

As we have discussed, these points did not originate with Watson. Objective experimental methods had been used for some time, and functional concepts had been influential, indeed dominant, in America. Research on animal learning had begun to yield data applicable to human learning, and objective tests had been developed and used with some success to predict and control behavior. Even Watson's definition of psychology as the science of behavior had been anticipated.

Thus, Watson's basic issues were not new. What was unique and provocative about his program was what he proposed to eliminate from psychology—the mind and consciousness, mentalistic concepts, speculation about what might be occurring in the brain, and the use of introspection. The ideas were "a breath of fresh air, clearing away the musty accumulation of the centuries" (R. I. Watson, 1978, p. 461).

THE METHODS OF BEHAVIORISM

We have seen that when scientific psychology began, it was eager to ally itself with the older, well-established natural science of physics. The new psychology consistently tried to adapt the methods of the natural sciences to its own needs. In no previous form of psychology, however, was this appeal to physics as strong as it was in Watsonian behaviorism. The distinction made by Wundt and Titchener between mediate and immediate experience—the first yielding the data of physics and the second the data of psychology—was abolished at one stroke.

Under Watson, the data of physics and of psychology were one and the same:

> bodies in motion. Applying this precept to psychology dictated a restriction of concern to publicly observable behaviours. Thus, that behaviour alone is the proper subject matter for psychology was indicated by the example of successful sciences as well as by the example of what was defined as an unsuccessful one, Wundtian introspective psychology. (Mackenzie, 1977, p. 14)

Hence, Watson argued that psychology must restrict itself to the data of the natural sciences, to what can be observed—behavior. Therefore, only the most truly objective methods of investigation were admissible in the behaviorist's laboratory. Watson stated explicitly the methods to be used in research: (a) observation, with and without the use of instruments, (b) testing methods, *(c)* the verbal report method, and *(d)* the conditioned reflex method.

The method of *observation*, self-explanatory and fundamental, is a necessary basis for the other methods. Objective *testing methods* were already in use, but Watson proposed that test results be treated as samples of behavior, not as measures of mental qualities. To Watson, a test did not measure intelligence or personality. Rather, it measured the responses the subject made to the stimulus situation of the test and nothing more.

The *verbal report* method is unique to Watson's system and deserves extra comment, indeed perhaps justification. Because Watson was so violently opposed to introspection, his use of verbal reporting in the laboratory has been regarded by some as a questionable compromise whereby he let introspection in the back door after having vigorously thrown it out the front. His system is particularly sensitive to this criticism.

Let us consider why Watson opposed introspection. In addition to the suggestion that he was not very good at it, there is the fact that introspection could not be used for animal research (unless one accepted Romanes's technique of introspection by analogy). Also, he distrusted the accuracy of introspection. If highly trained introspectionists could not agree on what they had observed, Watson asked, how was psychology to progress? More fundamental was the argument that a behaviorist could not tolerate in the laboratory anything that could not be objectively observed. Watson wanted to deal only with tangibles, and he disagreed with the introspectionists' pretensions of reporting on occurrences within an organism that could not be verified by observation.

In spite of his opposition to introspection, Watson could not ignore the work in psychophysics, which had made use of introspection. He suggested, therefore, that because speech reactions are objectively observable, they are as meaningful to the behaviorist as any other type of motor reaction.

> *Now what can we observe? We can observe* behavior—what the organism does or says. *And let us point out at once: that* saying *is* doing—that is, behaving. *Speaking overtly or to ourselves (thinking) is just as objective a type of behavior as baseball. (J. B. Watson, 1930, p. 6)*[2]

The use of the verbal report method in behaviorism was a concession widely debated by Watson's critics, who contended that Watson was proposing merely semantic changes, not a genuine alteration of research procedures. We note that Watson (1914) considered verbal report to be an

[2] This and all subsequent quotations credited to J. B. Watson, 1930 are from *Behaviorism* by John B. Watson, reprinted by permission of W. W. Norton & Company, Inc. Copyright 1924, 1925, 1930 by W. W. Norton & Company, Inc. Copyright renewed 1952, 1953, 1958, by John B. Watson.

Behaviorism: The Beginning

"inexact" method and not a satisfactory substitute for more objective methods of observation. He wanted to limit its use to those situations in which it was capable of verification, for example, in observing differences in tones. Unverifiable verbal reports, such as imageless thoughts or comments about feeling states, were ruled out. However, he never indicated precisely how he would restrict the use of verbal report.

The most important research method of the behaviorists—the *conditioned reflex* method—was not adopted until 1915, two years after behaviorism's formal beginning. Conditioning methods were being used before the advent of behaviorism, but their adoption by American psychologists had been limited. Watson was largely responsible for their subsequent widespread application in American psychological research. In later writings he acknowledged his debt to Pavlov and Bekhterev for the conditioning method.

Watson wrote of conditioning in terms of "stimulus substitution." A response, he said, is conditioned when it becomes attached or connected to a stimulus other than the one that originally aroused it. (The salivating of Pavlov's dogs to the sound of a bell instead of to the sight of food is a conditioned response.)

Watson seized upon this approach because it provided an objective method of analyzing behavior, that is, of reducing behavior to its most elementary units: the *stimulus–response* (S–R) bonds. All behavior, he argued, could be reduced to these elements, providing a method for laboratory investigation of complex human behavior.

Thus, Watson continued in the atomistic and mechanistic tradition established by the British empiricists and used by Wundt. Psychologists must study human behavior in the same way physical scientists study the universe, by breaking it down into the component elements or atoms.

This exclusive focus on the use of objective methods and the elimination of introspection meant a change in the nature and role of the human subject in the psychological laboratory. In Wundt's and Titchener's structuralist system subjects (reagents) were both observer and observed; they observed their own conscious experience. In behaviorism subjects assumed a less important role; they no longer observed, but instead were observed by the experimenter. The true observer (the experimenter) set up the conditions of the experiment and then observed how the subjects responded to these conditions. Thus, human subjects were demoted in status; they no longer observed but merely behaved. And almost anyone can behave—children, the mentally ill, animals. This viewpoint reinforced psychology's image or model of the human being as "a stimulus–response machine: you put a stimulus in one of the slots, and out comes a packet of reactions" (Burt, 1962, p. 232).

Initially, Watson's arguments for the use of only objective methods (the so-called methodological behaviorism) seemed to many to be a major advance. Retrospective analysis, however, suggests that the behaviorists contributed little because objective methodology had characterized psychology since its beginnings as a science. Studies in psychophysics, memory, and conditioning had applied objective methods. Therefore, the behaviorists' contributions consisted more of extending and refining existing methods than of developing new ones.

THE SUBJECT MATTER
OF BEHAVIORISM

Watson's "conceptual behaviorism" (the spirit or basic notion of behaviorism) has proved to be of greater importance for psychology than his methodological behaviorism. The primary subject matter or data must always be items of behavior: muscular movements or glandular secretions. Watson wrote that these responses constitute evidence of the organism's ability to react in discriminating fashion to its environment. Psychology, as the science of behavior, must deal only with acts that can be described objectively in terms such as stimulus and response, habit formation, and habit integration. All human and animal behavior can be reported in this way without resorting to mentalistic concepts and terminology. Through the objective study of behavior, behaviorist psychology can fulfill its aim of predicting the response given the stimulus, and predicting the antecedent stimulus given the response. Human and animal behavior can be effectively understood, predicted, and controlled by reducing behavior to the level of stimulus and response.

Despite the goal of reducing behavior to stimulus–response units, Watson argued that behaviorism deals with the overall behavior of the whole organism. Although a response can be something as simple as a knee jerk or other reflex, it can also be much more complex; in this case the term *act* is applied. Watson considered response acts to include such things as taking food, writing a book, playing baseball, or building a house. Thus, an act involves the organism's response through movement in space—talking, reaching, walking, and the like. Watson seems to have thought of response in terms of accomplishing some result in the environment rather than as an assemblage of muscular elements—that is, in more molar than molecular terms. Nevertheless, these behavioral acts, no matter how complex, can be reduced to lower-level motor or glandular responses.

Responses are classified in two ways: learned or unlearned, and explicit or implicit. Watson considered it important for behaviorism to distinguish between innate responses and those that are learned, and to discover for the latter the laws of learning.

Explicit responses are overt and therefore directly observable. Implicit responses, such as visceral movements, glandular secretions, and nerve impulses, take place inside the organism. Although such movements are not overt, they are nonetheless items of behavior. In introducing this notion of implicit behavior, Watson modified his initial requirement that the subject matter of psychology be *actually* observable and said instead that

220
Behaviorism: The Beginning

Though his academic career was brief, founder of behaviorism John B. Watson (1878–1958) remains influential for conceiving an objective psychology free of mentalism and as scientific as physics. *(Bachrach Studios)*

everything must be *potentially* observable (Woodworth, 1948, p. 75). The movements or responses occurring within the organism are theoretically observable through the use of instrumentation.

The exciting stimuli, like the responses with which the behaviorist deals, may be complex. A stimulus may be something relatively simple, such as light waves striking the retina, but it can also be a physical object in the environment, or a larger situation (a constellation of specific stimuli). Just as the constellation of responses involved in an act can be reduced to particular responses, so the *stimulus situation* can be resolved into its specific component stimuli.

Thus, behaviorism deals with the behavior of the whole organism in relation to its environment. Specific laws of behavior can be worked out through the analysis of the total stimulus and response complexes into their more elemental stimulus and response segments. This analysis was not to be as detailed as that performed by the physiologist in determining the structure and organization of the central nervous system. Because of the inaccessibility of the "mystery box" (Watson's term for the brain), Watson had little interest in cortical functioning. Behavior, he believed, concerned the total organism and could not be restricted to the nervous system alone. He focused on larger units of behavior—the whole response of the organism to a given situation.

In both subject matter and methodology the new psychology of John B. Watson was an attempt to construct a science that was free of mentalistic notions and subjective methods, a science as objective as physics.

SPECIFIC VIEWS AND CONCEPTS

We consider here Watson's treatment of some of the traditional topics in psychology—instinct, learning, emotion, and thought. Like all systematic theorists, Watson developed his psychology in accordance with his fundamental theses. All areas of behavior—emotions, feelings, thought—were to be treated in objective, stimulus–response terms.

Instinct

Initially, Watson accepted the role of instincts in behavior. In his first book, *Behavior: An Introduction to Comparative Psychology* (1914), he described in detail 11 instincts, including one dealing with random behaviors. Earlier, he had studied the instinctive behaviors of terns in the Dry Tortugas Islands off the Florida Keys with Karl Lashley, a student at Johns Hopkins University.[3]

By 1925, however, Watson had changed his position and ruled out the concept of instinct. All those aspects of human behavior that seem instinc-

---

[3] Harlow reported that Lashley later told him that the expedition to the Dry Tortugas was cut short when he and Watson ran out of cigarettes and whiskey. "Had Watson and Lashley only taken more cigarettes and whiskey to the Dry Tortugas, the history of psychology might have been very different" (Harlow, 1969, p. 26).

tive, he argued, are in reality socially conditioned responses. With the view that learning is the key to understanding the development of human behavior, Watson became an extreme environmentalist. He went beyond the denial of instincts and refused to admit that there were inherited capacities, temperaments, or talents of any kind. Those things that seemed inherited, he wrote:

> depend on training that goes on mainly in the cradle. The behaviorist would not say: "He inherits his father's capacity or talent for being a fine swordsman." He would say: "This child certainly has his father's slender build of body, the same type of eyes . . . ." And he would go on to say: "—and his father is very fond of him. He put a tiny sword into his hand when he was a year of age, and in all their walks he talks sword play, attack and defense, the code of duelling and the like." A certain type of structure, plus early training—slanting—accounts for adult performance. (J. B. Watson, 1930, p. 94)

This emphasis on the overwhelming influence of the environment, with its corollary that one can train children to be whatever one wants them to be, was one reason for Watson's large public following.

Learning

According to Watson, there are no instincts or inherited capacities; the adult is a product of childhood conditioning. Therefore, learning plays a major role in behaviorism.

Watson's views on learning progressed to incorporate conditioning. In his 1913 article there is no mention of conditioning, and *Behavior* (1914) gives but slight emphasis to Pavlov's conditioning experiments. Indeed, Watson expressed doubt that the method could be used with primates.

In his 1915 presidential address to the American Psychological Association, however, Watson suggested that the conditioned reflex method should displace introspection. From that time, conditioning became an important research method for the behaviorists. It is surprising that Watson never developed a satisfactory theory of learning, and conceptually seemed to belong with the antiquated pre-Thorndikian associationists. He rejected Thorndike's law of effect, in part because of its mentalistic terminology, and relied primarily on the older laws of contiguity, frequency, and recency. He maintained that the correct response was the most recent one and that it occurred more and more frequently during the process of learning.

In spite of his enthusiasm for classical conditioning, Watson failed to recognize the importance of Pavlov's law of reinforcement and its similarity to Thorndike's law of effect. Thus, although he accepted conditioning principles and used them in his research, he continued to cling to a law of exercise and to emphasize frequency and recency as primary factors in learning.

Emotion

Emotions, to Watson, were simply bodily responses to specific stimuli. The stimulus (the presence of danger, for instance) produces internal body changes and the appropriate learned overt responses. This notion implies no conscious perception of the emotion or mass of sensations from the internal organs. Each emotion involves its particular pattern of changes in the general body mechanism, particularly in the visceral and glandular systems. Although Watson recognized that all emotional responses involve overt bodily movements, the internal responses predominate in his conception. Emotion, then, is a form of implicit behavior in which the hidden visceral responses are evident, at least to some extent, as physical changes in, for example, pulse rate, breathing, or blushing.

Watson's theory of emotion is less complex than that of James, discussed in Chapter 7. In James's theory, the bodily changes immediately follow the perception of the exciting stimulus, and the feeling of these bodily changes is the emotion. Watson was critical of this position and wrote that "James gave to the psychology of the emotions a setback from which it has only recently begun to recover" (1930, p. 140). Discarding the conscious process of perception of the situation and the feeling state, he claimed that emotions can be understood in terms of the objective stimulus situation, the overt bodily response, and the internal visceral changes.

A famous study is the investigation of the stimuli that produce emotional responses in infants. Watson described what he believed to be the three fundamental emotions—fear, rage, and love. Fear is produced by loud sounds and sudden loss of support, rage by the hampering of body movement, and love by the stroking of the skin and by rocking and patting. Watson also found characteristic reaction patterns to these stimuli. He believed that fear, rage, and love are the only unlearned emotional responses. The remaining human emotional responses are built up from these three emotions through the process of conditioning. The basic emotional responses may become attached, through conditioning, to environmental stimuli that were not originally capable of eliciting them.

Watson experimentally demonstrated this theory in his study of an 11-month-old infant, Albert, who was conditioned to fear a white rat, something he had not feared before the conditioning trials (Watson & Rayner, 1920). The fear was established by making a loud noise (striking a steel bar with a hammer) behind Albert's head whenever the rat was presented to him. In a short time the mere sight of the rat produced signs of fear and discomfort in the child. Watson demonstrated that this conditioned fear could be generalized to similar stimuli, such as a rabbit, a white fur coat, and a set of Santa Claus whiskers. Watson believed that adult fears, aversions, and anxieties are likewise conditioned in early childhood.

Watson went on to demonstrate that these conditioned fears could be eliminated. Several common techniques, such as disuse, verbal appeal, and frequent application of the fear stimulus, proved unsuitable. Success was achieved in a study by Mary Cover Jones (1924) through the use of the unconditioning or reconditioning technique. The subject was another child (Peter), who already showed a fear of rabbits; his fear had not been conditioned in the laboratory. While the child was eating, the rabbit was brought into the room, but kept at a distance great enough so as not to elicit the fear response. The rabbit was brought progressively closer, always while the child was eating. Eventually the child could handle the rabbit without fear. Watson found that generalized fear responses to similar objects could also be eliminated by this procedure.

Watson's behaviorist approach to the emotions and his interest in the physiological changes that accompany emotional behavior stimulated research on emotional development in children and on the reaction patterns for the specific emotions.

Thought

Until the advent of behaviorism, the traditional view of the thought processes was the "centralist" theory of thinking, which held that thought processes occur in the brain "so faintly that no neural impulse passes out over the motor nerve to the muscle, hence no response takes place in the muscles and glands" (J. B. Watson, 1930, p. 239). According to this thesis, thought processes, because they occur in the absence of muscular movements, are not accessible to observation and experimentation. Thought is regarded as intangible, something exclusively mental with no physical referents. The concept of image used by the structuralists is an example of this viewpoint.

Watson's *peripheral theory of thinking*, perhaps his most widely known theory, takes issue with the older notion and attempts to reduce thinking to nothing more than implicit motor behavior. Watson argued that thinking, like all other aspects of human functioning, must be sensorimotor behavior of some sort. He reasoned that the behavior of thinking is implicit speech movements. Verbal thinking is reduced to subvocal talking that involves muscular habits learned in overt speech. These muscular habits become inaudible as the child grows up.

> The child talks incessantly when alone. At three he even plans the day aloud, *as my own ear placed outside the key hole of the nursery door has very often confirmed. Soon society in the form of nurse and parents steps in. "Don't talk aloud—daddy and mother are not always talking to themselves." Soon the overt speech dies down to whispered speech and a good lip reader can still read what the child thinks of the world and of himself. Some individuals never even make this concession to society. When alone they talk aloud to themselves. A still larger number never go*

beyond even the whispering stage when alone. Watch people reading on the street car; peep through the key hole sometime when individuals not too highly socialized are just sitting and thinking. But the great majority of people pass on to the third stage under the influence of social pressure constantly exerted. "Quit whispering to yourself," and "Can't you even read without moving your lips?" and the like are constant mandates. Soon the process is forced to take place behind the lips. Behind these walls you can call the biggest bully the worst name you can think of without even smiling. (J. B. Watson, 1930, pp. 240–241)

After we learn to talk (by conditioning), thought becomes simply talking silently to ourselves. Watson suggested that the focal points for much of this implicit behavior are the muscles of the larynx and the tongue. Watson's term for thinking was "laryngeal habits"; initially, the larynx was considered to be the "organ of thought." In addition to these laryngeal habits, language or thought is mediated by gestures, frowns, and shrugs, which symbolize more overt reactions to situations.

One obvious source of corroboration for Watson's hypothesis is that most of us are aware that we often talk to ourselves while thinking. This is inadmissible evidence, however, because it is purely introspective, and Watson could hardly use introspection to support a tenet of behaviorism. Behaviorism required objective evidence of these implicit speech movements, so attempts were made to record movement in the tongue and larynx during thought. Such measurements revealed slight movements some of the time that the subjects were thinking. Similarly, measurements taken from the hands and fingers of deaf-mutes revealed movement some of the time during thought. In spite of the inability to secure more supportive results in these studies, Watson was convinced that implicit speech movements existed and that their demonstration awaited only the development of more sophisticated instrumentation.

WATSON'S POPULAR APPEAL

Watson's bold pronouncements won him a large following not only among psychologists, but among the lay public as well. Why this public acclaim? Surely people were not fascinated because some psychologists practiced introspection and others refuted its use, or because some psychologists pretended to be conscious while others joyously proclaimed that psychology had finally lost its mind, or because there was dispute about whether thinking took place in the head or in the neck. These issues aroused comment among psychologists, but hardly concerned others.

What did stir the public was Watson's call for a world based on scientifically shaped and controlled behavior, free from myths, customs, and

Behaviorism: The Beginning

conventions. This idea offered hope to people who had become disenchanted with the older guiding creeds. In fervor and faith behaviorism had many of the aspects of a religion, and large numbers of people flocked to this new cult. One of the many articles and books about behaviorism of that time was entitled *The Religion Called Behaviorism* (1927), written by Louis Berman, an endocrinologist. A young man of 23 read Berman's book and became so excited that he wrote a review of it, which he sent to a popular literary magazine. That young man, B. F. Skinner, later wrote that "They did not publish [my review] but in writing it I was more or less defining myself for the first time as a behaviorist" (1976, p. 299).

Some of the ferment generated by Watson's ideas can be appreciated from newspaper reviews of *Behaviorism. The New York Times* said dramatically, "It marks an epoch in the intellectual history of man" (August 2, 1925); the *New York Herald Tribune* commented, "Perhaps this is the most important book ever written. One stands for an instant blinded with a great hope" (Woodworth, 1948, p. 93).

The hope stemmed in part from Watson's environmentalist position, as reflected in the following passage:

> *Give me a dozen healthy infants, well-formed, and my own specified world to bring them up in and I'll guarantee to take any one at random and train him to become any type of specialist I might select—doctor, lawyer, artist, merchant-chief and, yes, even beggarman and thief, regardless of his talents, penchants, tendencies, abilities, vocations, and race of his ancestors. (1930, p. 104)*

Watson's conditioning experiments, such as the study of Albert, persuaded him that emotional disturbances in adults cannot be traced to sex alone, as Freud held. Watson argued that adult problems can be traced instead to conditioned and transferred responses established in infancy and adolescence. If such disturbances were a function of faulty conditioning in childhood, a proper program of childhood conditioning should prevent their emergence. Watson believed that this sort of practical control of infant behavior (and hence of adult behavior) was not only possible but absolutely necessary. He developed a plan for social improvement, a program of "experimental ethics," based on the principles of behaviorism.

No one gave him "a dozen healthy infants" so that he might test his claim, and he admitted that in making it he was going beyond the facts. He noted, however, that those who believed in the predominance of heredity over environment had been arguing their case for thousands of years and still had no real supporting evidence.

The following paragraph from the end of *Behaviorism* (1930) reveals some of the fervor with which Watson described his program for living under the banner of behaviorism, and may help to explain why it became a new faith to so many people.

Behaviorism ought to be a science that prepares men and women for understanding the principles of their own behavior. It ought to make men and women eager to rearrange their own lives, and especially eager to prepare themselves to bring up their own children in a healthy way. I wish I could picture for you what a rich and wonderful individual we should make of every healthy child if only we could let it shape itself properly and then provide for it a universe in which it could exercise that organization—a universe unshackled by legendary folk-lore of happenings thousands of years ago; unhampered by disgraceful political history; free of foolish customs and conventions which have no significance in themselves, yet which hem the individual in like taut steel bands. I am not asking here for revolution; I am not asking people to go out to some God-forsaken place, form a colony, go naked and live a communal life, nor am I asking for a change to a diet of roots and herbs. I am not asking for "free love." I am trying to dangle a stimulus in front of you, a verbal stimulus which, if acted upon, will gradually change this universe. For the universe will change if you bring up your children, not in the freedom of the libertine, but in behavioristic freedom—a freedom which we cannot even picture in words, so little do we know of it. Will not these children in turn, with their better ways of living and thinking, replace us as society and in turn bring up their children in a still more scientific way, until the world finally becomes a place fit for human habitation? (pp. 303–304)

Watson's program of experimental ethics to replace the older speculative ethics based on religion remained only a hope; it was never carried out. He outlined his plan in brief terms and left it as a framework for future research. As we shall see in Chapter 11, a contemporary behaviorist, B. F. Skinner, formulated a more detailed program for a scientifically shaped utopia that seems to be in the spirit of the one Watson espoused.

A FINAL NOTE

Although Watson's productive career in psychology lasted less than 20 years, he profoundly influenced the course of psychology and his impact compels us to include him among psychology's leaders. Watson was an effective agent of the *Zeitgeist*, and the times were changing not only in psychology but in general scientific attitudes as well. The nineteenth century had witnessed magnificent advances in every branch of science. The twentieth century promised even more marvels. It was thought that science, if given enough time, was capable of finding answers to every problem. It was an era in which idealism was rapidly yielding to a spirit of tough-minded realism. Watson's behaviorist crusade helped American psychology in its transition from a focus on consciousness and subjectivism to materialism and objectivism in the study of behavior.

Although Watson's program did not realize its ambitious goals, the

Behaviorism: The Beginning

behavioristic orientation in general remains a strong and active force in modern psychology, and Watson is widely recognized for his founding role. The centennial of his birth was celebrated in April 1979, the same year as the centennial of the birth of psychology as a science. A symposium at Watson's alma mater, Furman University, whose psychology laboratory is named after him, drew psychologists and others from all over the country. The speakers included B. F. Skinner, whose talk was entitled "What J. B. Watson Meant to Me."[4]

CRITICISMS OF WATSONIAN BEHAVIORISM

Any systematic program that so blatantly attacks the existing order—indeed, suggests discarding the earlier version of the truth—and proposes radical and sweeping revisions is bound to receive criticism. We know that American psychology was already moving toward greater objectivity when Watsonian behaviorism was formally founded, but not all psychologists were pleased at the extreme form of objectivity Watson proposed. Many, including some who supported the objectivity movement, believed that Watson's system omitted important components of psychology, such as sensory and perceptual processes.

One of Watson's outstanding opponents was William McDougall (1871–1938), an English psychologist who came to the United States in 1920. McDougall is recognized for his instinct theory of behavior. He is also known for the impetus his book, *Introduction to Social Psychology*, gave to that area. This book, published in 1908, appeared in 14 editions by 1921. McDougall was an ardent supporter of a number of unpopular causes, including freedom of the will, Nordic superiority, and psychic research.

McDougall's instinct theory states that all human action results from innate tendencies to thought and action. It was well received initially by social scientists, but rapidly lost ground when behaviorism came to the fore. By 1925 Watson had rejected the notion of instincts, and on this issue the two men locked horns.

They met to debate their differences on February 5, 1924, at the Psychology Club in Washington, D.C. Washington was only a small city at that time— some described it as a sleepy Southern town—and the fact that it had a psychology club not affiliated with a university attests to the widespread popularity of psychology.

---

[4] Apparently, Watson is remembered less favorably by the residents of his home town, many of whom "regarded him as an upstart and an atheist who had turned his back on his Southern heritage and Baptist upbringing" (*Greenville South Carolina News*, April 5, 1979, p. D18). I am grateful to Cedric A. Larson for this information.

One thousand people attended the debate. Only a few were psychologists because there were only 464 members of the American Psychological Association nationwide. Thus, the size of the crowd also reflects the popularity of Watson's behaviorism. The judges of the debate, however, voted in McDougall's favor. Much of the argument was published by Watson and McDougall in 1929 in a book entitled *The Battle of Behaviorism*.

McDougall began the debate on a falsely optimistic note: "I have an initial advantage over Dr. Watson, an advantage which I feel to be so great as to be unfair; namely, all persons of common-sense will of necessity be on my side from the outset" (Watson & McDougall, 1929, p. 40).

McDougall agreed with Watson that the data of behavior are necessary to the science of psychology, but he argued forcefully that the data of consciousness are equally indispensable. He (and other critics as well) emphasized that psychology must use both kinds of data, a position taken in more recent times by humanistic psychologists.

Without the use of introspection, McDougall asked, how can psychology determine the meaning of a subject's response or the accuracy of speech behavior (verbal report)? How can we know anything of the world of daydreams and fantasies, or understand and appreciate esthetic experiences?

In an eloquent challenge to Watson McDougall asked how a strict behaviorist would account for the experience of enjoying a concert. McDougall said:

> I come into this hall and see a man on this platform scraping the guts of a cat with hairs from the tail of a horse; and, sitting silently in attitudes of rapt attention, are a thousand persons, who presently break into wild applause. How will the Behaviorist explain these strange incidents? How explain the fact that the vibrations emitted by the cat-gut stimulate all the thousands into absolute silence and quiescence; and the further fact that the cessation of the stimulus seems to be a stimulus to the most frantic activity? Common sense and psychology agree in accepting the explanation that the audience heard the music with keen pleasure, and vented their gratitude and admiration for the artist in shouts and handclappings. But the Behaviorist knows nothing of pleasure and pain, of admiration and gratitude. He has relegated all such "metaphysical entities" to the dust heap, and must seek some other explanation. Let us leave him seeking it. The search will keep him harmlessly occupied for some centuries to come. (Watson & McDougall, 1929, pp. 62–63)[5]

McDougall also questioned Watson's assumption that human behavior is fully determined, that everything we do is the direct result of past experience and can be predicted once the past events are known. Such a psychology leaves no room for free will or freedom of choice.

[5] From J. B. Watson and W. McDougall, *The Battle of Behaviorism* (New York: Norton, 1929). Reprinted by permission.

The issue of whether behavior is predetermined did not, of course, begin with Watson and McDougall. The opposition between advocates of determinism and those of free will is long-standing. Science accepts a determined natural world, whereas theology and some philosophies accept freedom of the will. Watson belongs in the determinist camp; if all behavior can be interpreted in physical terms, all acts of behavior must be physically predetermined. Watson thus believed that we are not personally responsible for our actions, and this belief has had important social consequences, particularly for the treatment of criminals. According to Watson, such persons should not be punished for their actions, they should be reconditioned.

McDougall and others argued that if the determinist position were true— that we have no free will and cannot be held responsible for our actions— then there would be no human striving, exertion, or desire to improve ourselves and our society. No one, he argued, would make any effort to prevent war, alleviate injustice, or achieve other personal or social ideals.

The free will–determinist controversy may never be resolved. A point worth noting is that many determinists, including Watson and B. F. Skinner, have made "determined" efforts to bring about improvements in the individual and in society.

Mention has already been made of the criticism directed at Watson's admission of verbal report as a method of research. Critics argued that its use was discriminatory, that Watson used it only when it could be verified and rejected it when it could not. But of course that was Watson's point and the point of the entire behaviorist movement: to use only verifiable data.

The attacks on Watsonian behaviorism were many and diverse and are still being voiced, in modified form, against the varieties of behaviorism that have derived from Watson's work.

The Watson–McDougall debates were held 11 years after behaviorism formally began. McDougall predicted that in a few years Watson's position would disappear without a trace. A few years later, in a postscript to the published version of the debate, McDougall wrote that his forecast had been "too optimistic; it was founded upon a too generous estimate of the intelligence of the American public. . . . Dr. Watson continues, as a prophet of much honor in his own country, to issue his pronouncements" (Watson & McDougall, 1929, pp. 86, 87).

CONTRIBUTIONS OF WATSONIAN BEHAVIORISM

Watson's primary contribution was his advocacy of a completely objective science of behavior. He exerted an enormous influence in rendering psychology more objective in both methods and terminology. Methodological behaviorism is so much a part of American psychology today that it "has conquered itself to death. It . . . has become a truism. Virtually every American psychologist, whether he knows it or not, is nowadays a methodological behaviorist" (Bergmann, 1956, p. 270).

Although his positions on specific topics have stimulated a great deal of research, Watson's original formulations are no longer useful. Watsonian behaviorism as a separate school has been replaced by newer forms of psychological objectivism that built upon it. Boring said in 1929 that behaviorism was already past its prime as a movement. Because movements depend on protest for their existence and strength, it is an effective tribute to Watsonian behaviorism that only 16 years after its inception, it no longer needed to protest. Watsonian behaviorism had certainly overcome the structuralist position. A graduate student at the University of Wisconsin in 1926, studying under Clark Hull, reported that few of his fellow students had ever heard of Wundt and Titchener (Gengerelli, 1976, p. 10).

Objective methodology and terminology have largely become the American psychology, and Watsonian behaviorism died, as have other successful movements, by being incorporated into the main body of thought, where it continues to reside today in modified form.

To some degree, the acceptance of Watsonian behaviorism was a function of the abilities and force of Watson himself. He was a charming and attractive man who expressed his ideas with great enthusiasm, optimism, self-confidence, and clarity. He was a bold and appealing revolutionary who scorned tradition and rejected the current version of psychology. These personal qualities, interacting with the spirit of the times which he reflected so ably, define J. B. Watson as one of psychology's great figures.

SUGGESTED READINGS

WATSON

Bergmann, G. The contributions of John B. Watson. *Psychological Review*, 1956, 63, 265–276.

Burnham, J. On the origins of behaviorism. *Journal of the History of the Behavioral Sciences*, 1968, 4, 143–151.

Creelan, P. G. Watsonian behaviorism and the Calvinist conscience. *Journal of the History of the Behavioral Sciences*, 1974, 10, 95–118. (An attempt to relate behaviorism to Watson's conflicts over his fundamentalist religious training.)

Jones, M. C. Albert, Peter, and John B. Watson. *American Psychologist*, 1974, 29, 581–583. (Reminiscences about Watson by a former student who conducted the "Peter" study.)

Skinner, B. F. John Broadus Watson, behaviorist. *Science*, 1959, 129, 197–198.

Watson, J. B. Autobiography. In C. Murchison (Ed.), *A history of psychology in autobiography* (Vol. 3). Worcester, Mass.: Clark University Press, 1936. Pp. 271–281.

Woodworth, R. S. John Broadus Watson: 1878–1958. *American Journal of Psychology*, 1959, 72, 301–310.

GENERAL

Bakan, D. Behaviorism and American urbanization. *Journal of the History of the Behavioral Sciences*, 1966, *2*, 5–28.

Harris, B. Whatever happened to little Albert? *American Psychologist*, 1979, *34*, 151–160. (Despite its title, the article does not solve one of psychology's great mysteries. It describes the distortions to be found in latter-day descriptions of a piece of research, and reinforces the rule that one should always go to the original source.)

Mackenzie, B. D. *Behaviourism and the limits of scientific method.* Atlantic Highlands, N.J.: Humanities Press, 1977. (An essay on the development of behaviorism from Watson to Skinner, arguing that the movement failed because it tried too hard to be scientific.)

Schultz, D. The human subject in psychological research. *Psychological Bulletin*, 1969, *72*, 214–228.

Watson, J. B., & McDougall, W. *The battle of behaviorism.* New York: Norton, 1929.

BEHAVIORISM: AFTER THE FOUNDING

EARLY BEHAVIORISTS

In the early 1920s behaviorism seemed to capture the attention and imagination of nearly all American psychologists, except those few who remained loyal to Titchener. However, not everyone in this new generation of behaviorists adopted Watsonian ideas. Some developed their own approaches and were more receptive to divergent views than Watson had been. Although Watson was the founder of behaviorism and its most effective leader for a time, other psychologists who embraced the same general point of view attempted to move in somewhat different directions. We will mention several of these psychologists and then consider the work of contemporary psychologists who might appropriately be called neobehaviorists.

Edwin B. Holt
(1873–1946)

Holt received his Ph.D. at Harvard in 1901 and spent his academic career there and at Princeton. His main influence was in terms of the philosophical framework he provided for behaviorism. His somewhat unorthodox view of behaviorism probably originated in his training as both an experimentalist and a philosopher. Holt did not agree with Watson's complete rejection of consciousness and mental phenomena. He suggested that consciousness be related to epistemological realism, according to which objects exist as perceived even when we are not perceiving them.

Holt believed that consciousness was simply a label given to the process of sensorimotor adjustment to physical objects. To be conscious of an object involved the relation of the sensorimotor aspects of the organism to that object, such as the oculomotor movements necessary to focus clearly on something. Physical objects in the environment have qualities similar to those within consciousness. There were, therefore, physical referents for what Holt called conscious experiencing.

Holt agreed with Watson on the relative unimportance of heredity in shaping human behavior. He believed that our behavior patterns are

234

developed in two ways. The primary way is through learning, which occurs in response to inner or outer motivation. Outer motivation, according to Holt, refers to external forms of stimulation; inner motivation refers to internal needs or drives, such as hunger and thirst. The latter conception anticipated the development of Hull's learning theory, with its emphasis on internal drive reduction as a necessary condition for learning. The second way in which behavior patterns are acquired is through the preservation in adulthood of childhood patterns of behavior.

Holt did not believe that psychology should attempt to reduce behavior to elemental units, whether stimulus–response connections or some other formulation. He wanted to deal with responses on a molar level, as wholes accomplishing some end. He was concerned with behavior on a larger scale, behavior that had both unity and purpose, concepts that Watson could not allow in his behaviorist system.

Holt's unique form of behaviorism enabled him to draw on a variety of sources and to take an interest in problems outside the mainstream of American behaviorism. In one of his books, *The Freudian Wish and Its Place in Ethics* (1915), he attempted to synthesize the major features of behaviorism and psychoanalysis. Perhaps his greatest contribution is his role as a stimulus for a later behaviorist, E. C. Tolman.

Albert P. Weiss
(1879–1931)

Weiss was born in Germany and came to the United States when he was very young. He received his Ph.D. in 1916 from the University of Missouri and pursued his career as a behaviorist, primarily studying child development, at Ohio State University. His book, *A Theoretical Basis of Human Behavior* (1925), outlines his program of unabashed behaviorism. He believed that psychology must operate as a natural science. All reference to conscious and mental phenomena had to be eliminated, along with the subjective method of introspection. Anything not accessible to a natural science approach had no place in psychology.

Weiss's behaviorism stressed an extreme form of reductionism that urged psychology to deal only with those elements of matter treated by physics. Thus, all behavior was seen as capable of analysis and reduction to physical–chemical entities. Weiss believed that psychology was actually a branch of physics and as such should not claim a nonphysical entity (consciousness) as its subject matter. We see in Weiss's system an emphasis on biological components of behavior, which are, in turn, reducible to physical elements. If this were his complete system, we might reasonably label him a physiologist and not a psychologist, but there was more. Humans are not only biological, but social as well. Weiss argued that we are a product of both forces, and he coined the term *biosocial* to denote this.

biological or social forces

Human organisms are solely biological entities only during infancy, according to Weiss. As we mature and develop, our behavior is shaped and modified by social forces encountered in interaction with other people. The importance of biological forces does not diminish, however; behavior can be reduced to physical–chemical units whether the individual is alone or is influenced by others. Weiss suggested that psychology must study both physiological and social processes, and that its primary task was to understand how the infant develops into a social adult. He outlined a program of research on child development and learning, but he died before it could be implemented.

Karl Lashley (1890–1958)

Lashley was a student of Watson's at Johns Hopkins University, where he received his Ph.D. in 1915. His productive career as a physiological psychologist took him to the universities of Minnesota and Chicago, to Harvard, and finally to the Yerkes Laboratory of Primate Biology. An ardent supporter of behaviorism, Lashley vigorously championed increased objectivism in psychology and opposed the study of consciousness through introspection.

His thorough research produced some results that differed from Watson's position on certain points. Specifically, he believed that S–R connections developed through conditioning were not the most effective approach to the analysis of behavior. However, his adherence to the basic tenets of behaviorist psychology never wavered; only his attitude toward some of Watson's secondary points changed.

Lashley is perhaps best known for his work involving the effect of brain extirpation on the learning abilities of rats. The results of this research were surprising, and disturbing, because they contradicted accepted views of localization of function within the cortex. Earlier investigators had demonstrated specific sensory and motor areas within the cortex. Lashley's research showed that even though destruction of large cortical areas resulted in slower learning, it seemed not to matter which specific cortical area was destroyed. Animals were able to learn just as well with one part of the cortex as with another. This perplexing finding seemed to indicate that other cortical centers were capable of taking over the functions performed by the destroyed centers, and Lashley concluded that the brain must function as a whole.

Lashley summarized his research findings in *Brain Mechanisms and Intelligence* (1929), in which he plotted errors in learning against the amount of cortical tissue destroyed and the difficulty of the learning task. His results led him to postulate two famous principles: mass action and equipotentiality.

The law of *mass action* states that the efficiency of learning is a function of the total mass of the cortex left intact. In other words, the more cortical tissue available, the better the learning.

Learning depends on the amount of cortex left functioning rather than on the integrity of a particular part; Lashley's principle of *equipotentiality* states that one part of the cortex is essentially equal to another in terms of its contribution to tasks such as maze learning. There are, however, some exceptions to this principle. Visual perception of a shape or pattern, for example, requires that a certain part of the cortex be intact, though within that specific cortical area the subparts are, to a large degree, equal in potential.

Lashley had expected to find in his research specific pathways and connections between sensory and motor apparatus, with definite points of localization in the cortex. Such findings would have supported the primacy of the reflex arc as an elemental unit of behavior. His results, however, challenged the Watsonian notion of a simple point-to-point connection in reflexes, according to which the brain serves merely to switch incoming sensory nerve impulses into outgoing motor impulses. Lashley's results suggested that the brain plays a more active role in learning and challenged Watson's assumption that behavior is compounded bit by bit through conditioned reflexes.

Although Lashley's work discredited a basic point of Watson's system, it did not weaken the behaviorists' fundamental contention that only completely objective methods should be used. Indeed, his research demonstrates the value of objective methods in psychological research.

THE INFLUENCE OF OPERATIONISM

The increasingly dominant behaviorist movement in American psychology was further strengthened by the development of the principle known as *operationism*. Actually, the relationship between this principle and behaviorism was somewhat circular. On the one hand, behaviorism was fortified by operationism; on the other, the increasingly objective framework of behaviorist psychology prepared the way for the acceptance of operationism.

Operationism is an attitude or general principle, not a formal school in the sense in which we have been using the term. Its purpose is to render the language and terminology of science more objective and precise and to rid science of those problems that are not actually observable or physically demonstrable (the so-called pseudo-problems). Briefly, operationism holds that the validity of a given scientific finding or theoretical construct is dependent on the validity of the operations used in arriving at that finding.

The operationist viewpoint was championed by the Harvard physicist Percy W. Bridgman in *The Logic of Modern Physics* (1927), which captured the attention of many psychologists. Bridgman proposed that physical concepts be defined in more precise and rigid terms and that all concepts lacking physical referents be promptly discarded.

The new attitude toward a concept is entirely different. We may illustrate by considering the concept of length: what do we mean by the length of an object? We evidently know what we mean by length if we can tell what the length of any and every object is, and for the physicist nothing more is required. To find the length of an object, we have to perform certain physical operations. The concept of length is therefore fixed when the operations by which length is measured are fixed: that is, the concept of length involves as much as and nothing more than a set of operations; the concept is synonymous with the corresponding set of operations. *(Bridgman, 1927, p. 5)*

Thus, a physical concept is the same as the set of operations or procedures by which it is determined. Many psychologists quickly found this principle to be of use in the science of psychology, and some applied it eagerly. But as promptly as it was accepted by some psychologists, it provoked opposition from others.

Bridgman's concern with pseudo-problems—the questions that defy answer by any known objective test—is noteworthy. Notions or propositions that cannot be put to experimental test are meaningless for science. An example of a pseudo-problem is the issue of the existence and nature of the soul. What is this thing "soul?" Can it be observed in the laboratory? Can it be measured and manipulated under controlled conditions to determine its effects on behavior? If something cannot be so observed, measured, and manipulated, it has no use, no meaning, and no relevance for science. It follows that the concept of an individual and private consciousness is a pseudo-problem for psychology; neither its existence nor its characteristics can be determined or even investigated through objective methods. Therefore, according to the operationist viewpoint, consciousness has no place in a scientific psychology.

It can be argued that operationism was not much more than a formal statement of principles already in use in psychology when the meanings of words and concepts were defined in terms of their physical referents. There is little in operationism that cannot be found in the works of the British empiricists (Turner, 1967). We have noted the long-term trend in American psychology toward an increasing objectification of methods and subject matter, so it can be said that operationism—as an attitude and a framework within which to conduct research and formulate theories—had already been accepted by a number of American psychologists for some years before the publication of Bridgman's 1927 book. Since the time of Wundt, however, physics had been the paragon of scientific respectability for the newer psychology, and when physics favored operationism as a formal doctrine, psychology followed suit. Indeed, psychology accepted and used operationism to a much greater degree than physics did.

As noted, operationism did not win universal recognition in psychology, nor is it universally accepted today. Controversy continues about the relative utility or futility of limiting psychology's subject matter to that which has

Behaviorism: After the Founding

empirical reference. Boring (1950b) pointed out that "The reduction of concepts to their operations turned out to be dull business. No one wants to trouble with it when there is no special need" (p. 658). Turner (1967) and others take the position that operationism is no longer the orthodoxy it was in the 1920s and 1930s. Even Bridgman had second thoughts about the use psychology made of the concept. Writing 27 years after proposing the operationist viewpoint, he said, "I feel that I have created a Frankenstein which has certainly gotten away from me. I abhor the word *operationalism* or *operationism*. . . . The thing I have envisaged is too simple to be so dignified by so pretentious a name" (1954, p. 224).

This appears to be another case in which the disciples became more fanatical than their leader. Nevertheless, the important point about operationism for our purpose is that the generation of behaviorists that came of age in the late 1920s and 1930s characteristically included operationism in their approach to psychology.

NEOBEHAVIORISTS

Segal and Lachman (1972) discuss a second stage in the evolution of behaviorism, which they call *neobehaviorism*. Lasting for some 30 years, from about 1930 to about 1960, this "period of relative stability" had as its most prominent representatives Edward Tolman, Edwin Guthrie, Clark Hull, and B. F. Skinner.

During this time large numbers of American experimental psychologists agreed on several points, despite their differing theoretical and methodological approaches to psychology. The first of these shared "dimensions," as Segal and Lachman called them, was a common data base derived from animal learning. Through conditioning and discrimination learning experiments, the neobehaviorists collected enormous numbers of facts, and, in general, they agreed on what the important facts or data were for psychology. The second dimension of the neobehaviorists involved the explanatory systems designed to account for their data. In Watsonian behaviorism there were many facts and findings but little in the way of useful explanatory and predictive principles "comparable to the crowning achievement of physics: its theories. Instead, experimentation seemed aimless, 'theoretical' hypotheses but loosely related to data, and debate idle" (Koch, 1964, p. 9).

In the neobehaviorist stage of development the explanatory systems were of several varieties, providing the psychologists of the day with different theoretical options. Hull offered a hypothetico–deductive approach, Skinner a radical empiricism demonstrating functional relations between variables, and Tolman the concept of intervening variables. The important point here is not so much the differences among the neobehaviorists as their shared concern with establishing some way to explain the behavior being observed.

Other dimensions that characterized the neobehaviorists include the acceptance of operationism and positivism, and the beliefs that the core of psychology is the study of learning, that association of a mechanical sort is the key concept of learning, and that all behavior, no matter how complex, can be described in terms of the laws of conditioning.

We shall discuss the work of the four leading neobehaviorists (Tolman, Guthrie, Hull, and Skinner), and then describe the third stage in behaviorism's evolution, neo-neobehaviorism, which is discussed more fully in Chapter 15.

Edward Chace Tolman
(1886–1959)

One of the early adherents of behaviorism, Tolman originally studied engineering at the Massachusetts Institute of Technology. He changed to psychology and studied under Holt at Harvard, where he received his Ph.D. in 1915. In the summer of 1912 he worked with one of the Gestalt psychologists, Kurt Koffka, in Germany. In his last year of graduate work, while being trained in the Wundt–Titchener tradition, Tolman became acquainted with Watsonian behaviorism. As a graduate student, he had already questioned the scientific usefulness of introspection, and he wrote in his *Autobiography* (1952) that Watson's behaviorism came as a "tremendous stimulus and relief."

After receiving his degree Tolman became an instructor at Northwestern University, and in 1918 went to the University of California at Berkeley. It was at Berkeley, where he taught comparative psychology and conducted research on learning with rats, that he definitely became a behaviorist, though of a different sort than Watson.

Tolman's career at Berkeley was interrupted twice. During World War II he served in the Office of Strategic Services (1944–1945), and from 1950 to 1953 he was a leader in the spirited and commendable faculty opposition to the California state loyalty oath. During this latter period he taught at Harvard and at the University of Chicago.

Tolman's Purposive
Behaviorism

The definitive statement of Tolman's position is presented in his first and most important book, *Purposive Behavior in Animals and Men* (1932). His system may appear at first glance to be a curious blend of two contradictory terms: *purpose* and *behavior*. Attributing purpose to an organism seems to imply consciousness. Surely such a mentalistic concept can have no place in a behaviorist system.

Tolman made it clear, however, both in this book and in his careful research that he was very much the behaviorist in subject matter and methodology, and that he was not urging psychology to return to conscious-

240

Employing some Gestalt concepts, Edward Chace Tolman (1886–1959) invoked purposive behaviorism to give empirical form to the unobservable processes prompting an organism's goal-directed behavior.
(Archives of the History of American Psychology)

ness. He vigorously rejected introspection of the structuralist sort. Like Watson, he had no interest in assumed internal experiences that were not accessible to objective observation. Any reference to conscious processes in Tolman's system was phrased in terms of cautious inference from observed behavior.

It is equally clear that Tolman was not a Watsonian behaviorist, for the two men differed in at least two important respects. First, Tolman was not interested in studying behavior at the molecular levels—in terms of stimulus–response connections. Unlike Watson, he was not concerned with elemental units of behavior, the activities of the nerves, muscles, and glands. His focus was molar behavior—the total response actions of the whole organism. In this respect, his system combines behaviorist and Gestalt concepts (see Chapter 12).

The second and more important difference between Watson and Tolman, and the major tenet of Tolman's system, is the notion of purposive behavior. Purposiveness in behavior, Tolman said, can be defined in objective behavioral terms without appeal to introspection or to how the organism might "feel" about an experience. It seemed obvious to him that all behavior is goal directed; the cat tries to get out of the puzzle box, the rat learns a difficult maze, the human studies music. Behavior, he said, "reeks of purpose." All behavior is oriented toward the achievement of some goal object, learning the means to an end. The rat persistently goes through a maze, making fewer errors, getting to the goal faster each time. In other words, the rat is learning, and the fact of learning, in a rat or a human, is highly objective behavioral evidence of purpose. Note that Tolman is dealing with the response of the organism, and that his measures are in terms of the response behavior changing as a function of learning; these are objective data.

Watsonian behaviorists were quick to criticize the attribution of purpose to behavior because, they argued, did this not rest on the assumption of consciousness in the organism? Tolman's answer was that it made no difference to him whether the animal was conscious or not. The conscious experience—if any—associated with purposing did not in any way influence the behavioral responses of the organism. Tolman was concerned only with the overt response behavior.

If there were a conscious awareness of the goal, Tolman said, this would be a private matter within each organism and not available to the objective tools of science. Anything that is internal and cannot be observed from outside the organism is not within the realm of science. Woodworth (1948) described Tolman's argument in the following fashion:

> If I try to describe to you my sensation of the color red, I find it cannot be done. I can point to a red object, I can say that red is somewhat like orange or purple, and very different from green and blue, quite a gay, stimulating color, very nice for a tie but a little too gay for a professor's overcoat—I can put red in many such relations but I cannot describe the sensation itself. I should have the same difficulty in trying to describe my feelings of pleasantness. Now what is essentially private cannot be made the subject matter of science . . . . Only to the extent that private experience can be reported, made public, can it have any place in science. (p. 106)

Intervening Variables

Tolman's unique and, in the long run, most useful contribution to psychology may be the concept of the *intervening variable.* As a behaviorist, Tolman believed that the initiating causes of behavior and the final resulting behavior must be capable of objective observation and operational definition. He suggested that the initiating causes of behavior consist of five independent variables: the environmental stimuli (S), physiological drive (P), heredity (H), previous training (T), and age (A). With animal subjects the experimenter can control these variables, but with humans there is obviously less control. Behavior, then, is a function of these independent variables:

$$B = f_x (S, P, H, T, A)$$

Between these observable independent variables and the final response measure (the observable dependent or behavior variable), Tolman postulated a set of inferred and unobserved factors, the intervening variables, which are the actual determinants of behavior. They are the internal processes that connect the antecedent stimulus situation with the observed response. The statement S–R must now read S–O–R. The intervening variable is what is going on within O (the organism) that brings about a given response to a given stimulus.

Because this intervening variable cannot be objectively observed, it is of no use to science unless it can be clearly related to both the experimental (independent) variable and the behavior (dependent) variable. The classic example is the intervening variable of hunger, which cannot be seen in a person or laboratory animal. Hunger can, however, be precisely and objectively related to an objective experimental variable—the length of time since the organism last had food. It can also be related to an objective response variable such as the amount of food eaten or how rapidly it is consumed. Thus, this unobservable inferred variable can be given precise empirical referents and is therefore amenable to quantification and experimental manipulation.

Tolman introduced the concept of intervening variable so that psychology would have a way of making precise and objective statements about inner states and processes that cannot be observed. In other words, intervening variables were a way of rendering these states useful to psychology. By specifying the independent and dependent variables (observable events), Tolman was, in effect, able to provide operational definitions of unobservable inner states. Before he chose the term *intervening variable,* he called his new approach "operational behaviorism" (Mackenzie, 1977).

Tolman originally proposed two kinds of intervening variables: demand variables and cognitive variables. The demand variables are essentially motives and include sex, hunger, and the demand for safety in the face of danger. The cognitive or "know-how" variables are abilities and include perception of objects, motor skills, and the like.

In 1951 Tolman revised his intervening variables and established three categories: *(1) need systems*—the physiological deprivation or drive situation at a given moment in time; *(2) belief–value motives*—to represent the intensity of preference for certain goal objects and the relative strength of these objects in satisfying needs; and *(3) behavior-spaces*—noting that behavior takes place within the behavior space of the individual. In the behavior-space some objects attract (have a positive valence), whereas others repel (have a negative valence).

Tolman's concept of the intervening variable has been useful to psychology, though it has not gone uncriticized. Intervening variables appear to be of value in developing an acceptable theory of behavior so long as they are empirically related to both experimental and behavior variables. Doing this comprehensively and completely, however, turned out to be such a monumental task that Tolman later came "to repudiate the hope of ever making a complete definition of any intervening variables and declared that, if they were not to be abandoned altogether, then at best all they could be considered was 'an aid to thinking' " (Mackenzie, 1977, p. 146).

Theory of Learning

Tolman's research on learning has proved stimulating to subsequent researchers and provides considerable support for his position. He believed that all animal and human behavior (with the exception of tropisms and simple reflexes) is capable of modification through experience. Thus, learning plays a major role in his system. He rejected Thorndike's law of effect, saying that reward or reinforcement has little, if any, role in learning. In its place he proposed a cognitive theory of learning in which the continued performance of a task builds up *sign Gestalts*, which are learned relationships between cues in the environment and the organism's expectations. The animal, Tolman said, gets to know some of its environment.

Let us follow Tolman's system as we watch a hungry rat placed in a maze. The animal moves about in the maze, sometimes in correct alleys and sometimes in blind alleys. Eventually, it discovers the food. In subsequent trials in the maze, Tolman argued, purpose and direction are given to the rat's behavior by the goal. At each choice point expectations are established. The rat comes to expect that certain cues associated with the choice point will lead on to food. When the rat's expectancy is confirmed (when it gets food), the sign Gestalt of cue expectancy associated with that choice point is strengthened. Over all the choice points in the maze there is established a pattern of sign Gestalts, which Tolman called a *cognitive map*. This pattern is what the animal learns—a cognitive map of the maze, not a set of motor habits. In a sense, then, the rat establishes a comprehensive "knowledge" of the maze or of any familiar environment. Something like a field map is developed in its brain, enabling it to go from one spot in the environment to another without being restricted to a fixed series of bodily movements.

More than 30 years of research was conducted in Tolman's laboratory, and it is important to consider the nature of the research that supports his theory of learning.

One classic experiment investigated the basic question whether the rat in the maze learns a set of motor responses or a cognitive map of the maze. A cross-shaped maze was used. One set of rats always found food at the same place, even though (using different starting points) the rats had sometimes to turn to the right and other times to the left to reach the food. Thus, the motor responses differed, but the location of the food remained the same.

The second group of rats always made the same response regardless of the starting point, but the food was found in different places. For example, starting from one end of the cross, the rats would find food only by turning to the right at the choice point; when starting from the other end of the cross, they also found food only by turning to the right.

The results showed that the "place learners" (the first group) performed significantly better than the "response learners." Tolman concluded that the same thing occurs with persons who are familiar with their town or neighborhood. They can go from one point to another by a number of different routes because of the cognitive map that they have developed of the area.

Another experiment involved *latent learning*—learning that cannot be observed at the time it is taking place. A hungry rat was placed in a maze and allowed to wander about freely. There was no food to be found. Was the rat learning anything in the absence of reinforcement? After a number of no-reinforcement trials, the rat found food. Its improvement thereafter in running the maze was extremely rapid, indicating that some learning had taken place during the period of no reinforcement. Its performance quickly equaled that of a control group, which had been reinforced with food on every trial.

Comment

Tolman's work had a great influence on psychology, particularly in the area of learning, for more than 40 years, and its impact is recognized today. Tolman has been criticized for his failure to develop a fully integrated theoretical system, and many psychologists believe that he never adequately related behavior to the more covert functioning, such as cognitive states. A more obvious point of attack relates to Tolman's language, which many find subjective and mentalistic.

On the positive side, Tolman initiated many important research topics in learning and introduced the concept of the intervening variable to psychology. Because intervening variables are a way of operationally defining unobservable states such as hunger, they have made these states scientifically respectable to some behaviorists. Intervening variables have become a necessary format for dealing with hypothetical constructs and have been widely used by other neobehaviorists, namely, Guthrie and Hull. For a time they were used by Skinner.

Another significant contribution is Tolman's support for the rat as an appropriate subject for psychological study. An essay written in 1945 clearly and delightfully states his position on this issue:

> What . . . can we now say as to the contributions of us rodent psychologists to human behavior? What is it that we rat runners still have to contribute to the understanding of the deeds and the misdeeds, the absurdities and the tragedies of our friend, and our enemy—homo sapiens? The answer is that, whereas man's successes, persistences, and socially unacceptable divagations . . . are all ultimately shaped and materialized by specific cultures, it is still true that most of the formal underlying laws of intelligence, motivation, and instability can still be studied in rats as well as, and more easily than, in men.
>
> And, as a final peroration, let it be noted that rats live in cages; they do not go on binges the night before one has planned an experiment; they do not kill each other off in wars; they do not invent engines of destruction, and, if they did, they would not be so inept about controlling such engines; they do not go in for either class conflicts or race conflicts; they avoid politics, economics, and papers on psychology. They are marvelous, pure, and delightful. And, as soon as I possibly can, I am going to climb back again out on that good old phylogenetic limb and sit there, this time right side up and unashamed, wiggling my whiskers at all the silly, yet at the same time far too complicated, specimens of homo sapiens, whom I shall see strutting and fighting and messing things up, down there on the ground below me. (p. 166)[1]

Edwin Ray Guthrie
(1886–1959)

Guthrie received his Ph.D. in 1912 from the University of Pennsylvania, and began his academic career in 1914 at the University of Washington, where he remained until his retirement in 1956. While in graduate school, he became an ardent convert to a behaviorist approach to psychology, an approach from which he never wavered. He believed that science must deal only with objectively observable conditions and events. So extreme an empiricist was Guthrie that he opposed the practice of attempting to relate behavioral events to what he considered the invisible brain and nervous system. Although his basic orientation is definitely behavioristic, he cannot be described as a Watsonian behaviorist.

---

[1] From E. C. Tolman, A stimulus–expectancy need–cathexis psychology. *Science*, 1945, *101*, 160–166. Reprinted by permission of the American Assocation for the Advancement of Science.

Guthrie's most important influence on psychology is his formulation of an extremely simple learning theory, set forth in *The Psychology of Learning* (1935). Variously described as the most persistent advocate of conditioning and the most radical of all those who dealt with association, Guthrie remained for several decades a forceful proponent of a theory of learning based on one principle—*contiguity*. To account for the strengthening of learned responses, he rejected Thorndike's laws of effect and frequency as well as Pavlovian reinforcement. He relied instead on what he called "simultaneous conditioning," which he considered the most general law for psychology.

To Guthrie, all learning depends on the contiguity of stimulus and response. When a stimulus just once elicits a response, then the S–R association is established. It is, in essence, a *one-trial learning* situation, which is Guthrie's most famous principle. Repetition and reinforcement form no essential part of his system. His only formal law of learning states: "A combination of stimuli which has accompanied a movement will on its recurrence tend to be followed by that movement" (1935, p. 26). Note that there is no mention of internal drive states, repetitions of the stimulus–response pairings, or any form of reinforcement. One pairing of the stimulus and the resulting movement serves to establish the association; thus, the behavior is learned.

Note also that the law refers to movements, which Guthrie carefully distinguished from acts. He defined a movement as a pattern of motor and glandular responses or actions. An act, on the other hand, is a movement or series of movements that brings about results. Although an act is a movement, a movement is not an act. An act is on a larger scale. For example, hitting a nail with a hammer is an act composed of a number of separate movements. Guthrie believed that in measuring learning, the performance of the complete act is usually taken as the criterion of learning, whereas it is the movements that are actually conditioned as responses.

He considered this focus on movements to be a distinguishing feature of his theory. He argued that Thorndike, for instance, was concerned with the total act, with the acquisition of a skill (such as a cat escaping from a puzzle box) that is a function of a number of individual muscular movements. These individual movements are developed or acquired in single trials, but learning of the total act calls for repeated practice. The movements, or individual parts of the learned act, are the raw data in Guthrie's system. Because they are smaller, these movements are more difficult to observe in a learning situation, which, Guthrie explained, is why they are often overlooked.

Just as the response of the organism is composed of a number of separate components, so too is the stimulation to which the organism is exposed. Because the stimulus and response are made up of many parts, it is necessary to have a large number of pairings of the total stimulus and response situations to achieve any consistency in the behavior under study. Therefore, practice is necessary to bring about improvement of the constellation of movements (the act), but each component movement is learned after a single pairing with the stimulus.

Comment

Guthrie seemed to prefer writing and anecdotal observation to experimentation. He believed in the importance of theory for the development of psychology, and commented that theories, not facts, endure. His several books contain evidence of an anecdotal nature and comparatively little experimental evidence. There is some empirical support for his theory, mainly his own research involving stereotypy in the behavior of the cat in a puzzle box. Compared to some other theoretical positions in neobehaviorist psychology, however, there is relatively little empirical support. Much of the appeal of Guthrie's system rests upon its simplicity and its consistency over the years. It is easy to understand when compared with more complex learning theories, particularly Hull's.

The inherent simplicity of Guthrie's system draws praise from some psychologists, but it provides a point of criticism for others. It has been suggested that Guthrie maintained this simplicity by failing to deal explicitly with major problems in learning that might defy explanation within his framework. Mueller and Schoenfeld (1954) noted that "It is undoubtedly true that many reviews of Guthrie in the literature have mistaken incompleteness for simplicity" (p. 368). Such critics suggest that additional constructs and assumptions are necessary to encompass the major problem areas of learning.

Nevertheless, Guthrie was able to maintain his theoretical position and stature as a leading learning theorist, and his system is given serious consideration in contemporary psychology. His contributions received formal recognition in 1958 when the American Psychological Foundation presented him with their Gold Medal Award. Statistical models of learning have grown largely out of the Guthrian scheme.

Clark Leonard Hull
(1884–1952)

First and foremost a behaviorist, Hull has achieved a highly respected position in contemporary psychology. Perhaps no previous psychologist was so consistently and keenly devoted to the problems inherent in scientific method. "Few psychologists have had such a mastery of mathematics and formal logic as Hull had. Hull applied the language of mathematics to psychological theory in a manner used by no other psychologist" (Wolman, 1960, p. 105).

The Life of Hull

For most of his childhood and young adult life, Hull was plagued by poor health. Illnesses struck him frequently, and poor eyesight affected him all his life. At the age of 24 he contracted polio, which left him crippled in one leg. His family had little income and he was forced to interrupt his education several times to take teaching jobs to earn money. Hull's greatest asset, however, was a driving motivation and aspiration to greatness, and he persevered in the face of many obstacles.

In 1918 he received his Ph.D. from the University of Wisconsin, where he had studied mining engineering before switching to psychology. He remained a member of the faculty at Wisconsin for ten years.

Hull's early research presaged his lifelong emphasis on objective methods and functional laws. He investigated concept formation and the effects of tobacco on behavioral efficiency, and surveyed the literature on tests and measurements, publishing an important early text in that area in 1928. He worked on the development of practical methods of statistical analysis, and invented a machine for calculating correlations.

Hull devoted ten years to the study of hypnosis and suggestibility, publishing 32 papers and a book, *Hypnosis and Suggestibility* (1933), that summarized the research. In 1929 he became a research professor at Yale, where he developed his final major research interest: a theory of behavior based on Pavlov's laws of conditioning. He had first read Pavlov in 1927 and become greatly interested in the problem of conditioned reflexes and learning.

In the 1930s Hull wrote articles on conditioning, arguing that complex higher-order behaviors could be explained in terms of the basic principles of conditioning. In 1940 he published, with five colleagues, *Mathematico–Deductive Theory of Rote Learning: A Study in Scientific Methodology*. Although the book was considered a notable achievement in the development of scientific psychology, it was difficult to understand and so was read by very few people.

Hull's next major publication, *Principles of Behavior* (1943), was considerably easier to read. In it he outlined, in great detail and with characteristic precision, a theoretical framework so comprehensive as to include all behavior. With the publication of this book, Hull's system assumed a position of importance in the area of learning in the United States. It stimulated a great deal of research, and Hull soon became the most frequently cited psychologist in the field. He revised the system in a number of journal articles, and the final statement appeared in *A Behavior System* (1952). Unfortunately, Hull had been ill for a number of years and he died before reading the galley proofs of this book.

*Hull's System: The Frame
of Reference*

Hull believed that human behavior involves a continuing interaction between the organism and the environment. The objective stimuli provided by the environment and the objective behavioral responses provided by the organism are, of course, observable facts. This interaction takes place,

The radical behaviorism of Clark Leonard Hull (1884–1952) saw all behavior as quantifiable and conditioned by the reinforcement an organism derives from reducing its biological needs. *(Archives of the History of American Psychology)*

however, within a larger context that cannot be totally defined in observable stimulus–response terms.

This broader context or *frame of reference* is the biological adaptation of the organism to its unique environment. The survival of the organism is aided by this biological adaptation. When survival is in jeopardy, the organism is in a state of need. Thus, to Hull, need involves a situation in which the biological requirements for survival are not being met. When in a state of need, the organism behaves in a manner designed to reduce that need. Its behavior serves to reinstate the optimal biological conditions necessary for survival.

Hull's concern with biological survival grew out of his interest in aspects of evolutionary theory. It is also consistent with the functionalist emphasis on adaptation to the environment.

Hull was committed to an objective behaviorist psychology; there was no place in his system for consciousness, purpose, or any other mentalistic notion. The system was an uncompromising radical behaviorism in which Hull attempted to reduce every concept to physical terms. Although his methodological behaviorism was perhaps more rigid than Watson's, he did allow for the notion of intervening variables. However, these variables were closely and concretely tied to objective stimulus and response conditions, which could be quantified and measured with precision.

Hull's system and his image of human nature were couched in mechanistic terms. He regarded human behavior as automatic and cyclical, capable of reduction to the terminology of physics, and warned against the intrusion of "anthropomorphic subjectivism"—giving subjective interpretations of the behavior being observed. The observation and interpretation of behavior must be uncompromisingly objective. One way of attaining this, Hull initially suggested, was to think in terms of the behavior of animals. Even this had its dangers, however.

> [*It*] *all too often breaks down when the theorist begins thinking what he would do if he were a rat, a cat, or a chimpanzee; when that happens, all his knowledge of his own behavior, born of years of self-observation, at once begins to function in place of the objectively stated general rules or principles which are the proper substance of science. (Hull, 1943, p. 27)*

There must be a more rigid safeguard against subjectivism, and Hull found it in an attitude that considers "the behaving organism as a completely self-maintaining robot, constructed of materials as unlike ourselves as may be" (Hull, 1943, p. 27).

Thus, behaviorists should take a "robot" view of their subject matter. The spirit of mechanism in the mechanical figures of European seventeenth-century gardens was faithfully followed and strengthened in Hull's work. One advantage of this robot approach, according to Hull, is that it prevents the reifying of behavior, that is, explaining behavior by attributing it to causes other than strictly mechanical ones.

Clearly, there is little, if any, difference between psychology and physics, as far as Hull is concerned. Any such difference is, he stated, only in degree, not in kind.

Methodology

Our discussion of Hull's mechanistic, reductionist, and objective behaviorism provides a clear view of what his methods of study must be. Obviously, they are characterized by as much objectivity as possible.

In addition, Hull's approach to psychology is distinguished by quantification. The laws of behavior must be stated or expressed in the precise language of mathematics, and quantification became a second cornerstone on which Hull erected his behaviorism.

Psychologists, he wrote, must not only develop a thorough understanding of mathematics, they must *think* mathematics. In *Principles of Behavior* (1943) Hull wrote how a mathematically defined psychology would proceed.

> *Progress . . . will consist in the laborious writing, one by one, of hundreds of equations; in the experimental determination, one by one, of hundreds of the empirical constants contained in the equations; in the devising of practically usable units in which to measure the quantities expressed by the equations; in the objective definition of hundreds of symbols appearing in the equations; in the rigorous deduction, one by one, of thousands of theorems and corollaries from the primary definitions and equations; in the meticulous performance of thousands of critical quantitative experiments. (pp. 400–401)*

This statement provides a good indication of the rigor—and patience—required of a follower of the Hullian system.

Hull described four specific methods that could be useful to science. Three of these were already in use: *(1)* simple observation, *(2)* systematic controlled observation, and *(3)* experimental testing of hypotheses. In addition, Hull argued for strict adherence to the *hypothetico–deductive method*, which utilizes rigorous deduction from a set of formulations that are determined *a priori*. The method involves establishing postulates from which experimentally testable conclusions can be deduced. These conclusions are then submitted to experimental test; failure results in revision and verification allows for their incorporation into the body of science. Hull believed that if psychology were to become an objective science on the order of other natural sciences (in accordance with the behaviorist program), the only appropriate approach would be the hypothetico–deductive one.

Drives

Hull considered bodily need arising from a deviation from optimal biological conditions to be the basis of motivation. However, rather than introducing the concept of biological need directly into his system, he postulated the intervening variable of *drive*, a term that had already come into use in psychology. Drive was posited as a stimulus (S_D), arising from a state of tissue need, that functions to arouse or activate behavior. The strength of the drive can be empirically determined in terms of the length of deprivation, or the intensity, strength, and energy expenditure of the resulting behavior. Hull considered the duration of deprivation to be a rather imperfect index, and he placed greater emphasis on behavior strength.

It is important to note that Hull considered drive to be nonspecific. In other words, any kind of deprivation—food, water, or sex, for example—contributed in the same way (though perhaps in differing degree) to the drive. This nonspecificity means that drive does not direct behavior, but functions solely to energize it. The steering or guiding of behavior is accomplished by environmental stimuli. Also, according to Hull, drive reduction is the sole basis for reinforcement.

Hull's system postulates two major kinds of drive: primary and secondary. *Primary* drives are associated with biological need states and are directly and intimately involved with the organism's survival. These drives, which arise from a state of tissue need, include the needs for food, water, air, temperature regulation, defecation, urination, sleep, activity, sexual intercourse, and relief from pain. These are basic, innate processes of the organism and vital to its survival.

Hull recognized that humans and animals are motivated by forces other than primary drives. Accordingly, he postulated the *secondary* or learned drives, which refer to situations or stimuli in the environment that are associated with the reduction of primary drives, and which may, as a result, become drives themselves. This means that previously neutral stimuli may assume drive characteristics because they are capable of eliciting responses that are similar to those aroused by the original need state or primary drive. A simple example involves being burned by touching a stove. The painful burn (tissue damage) produces a primary drive (relief from pain). Other stimuli associated with this primary drive, such as the sight of the stove, may lead to the withdrawing of the hand when this visual stimulus is perceived. Thus, the sight of the stove may become the stimulus for the learned drive of fear. These secondary drives or motivating forces develop on the basis of the primary drives. Because of this focus on learned drives, learning obviously plays a key role in Hull's system.

Learning

Hull's system is primarily concerned with motivation. This may surprise those who first heard of Hull in discussions of learning. Certainly he focused great attention on problems of learning, but "learning was, in the last analysis, only an instrumentality that permitted an organism to extend the range and variety of its efforts to satisfy its needs" (Cofer & Appley, 1964, p. 469). In the course of developing his system Hull became less concerned with learning and more concerned with other factors capable of influencing behavior, although he is most frequently studied in terms of his theory of learning.

A major part of Hull's theory is his attempt to integrate, or at least reconcile, Thorndike's law of effect with Pavlovian conditioning. He believed that learning could not be adequately explained by the principles of recency and frequency. His learning theory focuses mainly on the principle of reinforcement, which is essentially Thorndike's effect principle.

Hull's law of primary reinforcement states that when a stimulus–response relationship is followed by a reduction in need, the probability is increased that on subsequent occasions the same stimulus will evoke the same response. Note that reward or reinforcement is defined not in terms of Thorndike's notion of satisfaction, but rather in terms of reduction of a primary need. Thus, primary reinforcement, referring to the reduction of a primary drive, is the cornerstone of Hull's system of learning.

Just as his system contains secondary drives, it also deals with secondary reinforcement. If the intensity of the stimulus is reduced as the result of a secondary or learned drive, it will act as a secondary reinforcement.

> It follows that any stimulus consistently associated with a reinforcement situation will through that association acquire the power of evoking the conditioned inhibition, i.e., reduction in stimulus intensity, and so of itself producing the resulting reinforcement. Since this indirect power of reinforcement is acquired through learning, it is called secondary reinforcement. (1951, pp. 27–28)

Hull believed that the stimulus–response connection is strengthened by the number of reinforcements that have taken place. He called the strength of the S–R connection *habit strength*, which refers to the persistence of the conditioning and is a function of reinforcement.

Learning cannot take place in the absence of reinforcement that is necessary to bring about a reduction of the drive. Because of this emphasis on reinforcement, Hull's system is called a *need-reduction* theory, as opposed to Guthrie's contiguity theory and Tolman's cognitive theory.

Hull's system is presented in terms of specific and detailed postulates and corollaries expressed in verbal and mathematical form. In its last presentation (*A Behavior System*, 1952) there are 18 postulates and 12 corollaries. Although the system was based on conditioning principles, Hull believed that his fundamental position could be expanded to include complex processes such as problem solving, social behavior, and forms of learning other than conditioning. He lived to see only a portion of this ambition realized.

Comment

This overview of Hull's system is, of course, far too brief to encompass the scope of his work. Our purpose in dealing with later systems is to point out how they derive from older ways of thinking. There has been a continuity of development in psychology, and our descriptions of derivatives of past systems are intended to provide an appreciation of the relevance of the past for the present.

Hull's system has achieved such prominence that it has generated a great deal of criticism. A few general points are noted.

As a leading exponent of neobehaviorism, Hull is subject to the same attacks aimed at Watson and others who followed in the behaviorist tradition. Those who oppose a behaviorist approach to psychology on methodological and theoretical grounds will, of course, include Hull in the enemy camp.

Hull's system is faulted for its lack of generalizability. It has been asserted that in his attempt to define his variables so precisely in quantitative terms, he functioned at times on a narrow, miniature-system basis. In other words, his approach was extremely particularistic in that he often formulated postulates from results obtained in a single experimental situation. Opponents argue that generalization to all behavior on the basis of such specific experimental demonstrations is questionable.

> Surely a set of laws of mammalian behavior ought not reflect in the constants of its basic postulates such specialized information as the most favorable interval for human eyelid conditioning (Postulate 2) . . . the weight in grams of food needed to condition a rat (Postulate 7) . . . or the amplitude in millimeters of galvanometer deflection in human conditioning (Postulate 15). (Hilgard, 1956, p. 181)

Although precise quantification is necessary and commendable in a natural science approach to psychology, Hull's extreme approach does tend to reduce the range of applicability of the findings.

Thus, Hull's adherence to a mathematical and formal system of theory building is open to both praise and criticism at the same time. Wolman (1960) suggested that "Hull became, to a certain extent, a victim of his zest for mathematics. . . . Whenever the opportunity came, he quantified his statements, sometimes pursuing the issue *ad absurdum*" (p. 124). His system is so thoroughly and minutely developed in quantitative terms that incomplete or inaccurate formulations are relatively easy to spot. Gaps and inconsistencies in a theory expressed in ordinary verbal terms can be easily filled in with appropriate illustrative examples. Critics have found such gaps in Hull's system and argue that at least some of Hull's formulations are not so tightly constructed as was originally thought.

Damaging though these points are, Hull's influence on contemporary psychology cannot be minimized. We have already mentioned the great amount of research occasioned by his work, perhaps more than by any other theory; this alone constitutes a major contribution to psychology. He provided an objective terminology that was well accepted and represented a new approach to psychological data rather than a simple relabeling of older concepts.

Marx and Hillix (1979) suggested that no other psychologist has had such a pronounced and extensive effect on the professional motivation of so many other psychologists. Hull defended, extended, and expounded the objective behaviorist approach as had never been done before.

Perhaps it is true that Hull's contribution to systematic psychological theory building in general is greater than his own theory, but it is still too soon to determine this. Although psychologists question parts or all of Hull's theory, there is general respect and admiration for the rigorous methods used to develop it. Lowry (1971) noted that "It is not often in any field that a true theoretical genius comes along; of the very few to whom psychology can lay claim, Hull must surely rank among the foremost" (p. 183).[2]

Burrhus Frederick Skinner (1904–)

B.F. Skinner has become the most important and influential individual in psychology today. His areas of interest over his long career, and their implications for modern society, are diverse. The magazine *Psychology Today* called him "very much the man of today. . . . when history makes its judgment, he may well be known as the major contributor to psychology in this century" (M.H. Hall, 1967b, p. 21).

For many years Skinner has been America's leading behaviorist, with a large, loyal, and enthusiastic band of followers. He has developed a program for behavioral control of societies, invented an automatic crib for the care of infants, and more than anyone else is responsible for the large-scale use of both teaching machines and techniques of behavior modification. In addition, he wrote a novel (*Walden Two*) which continues to be popular more than 30 years after publication, and in 1971 his book, *Beyond Freedom and Dignity*, became a best seller nationwide. He has published many professional articles and books and has been compared to Sir Francis Galton in terms of diversity and scope of interests.

The Life of Skinner

Skinner was born and raised in a small town in northeastern Pennsylvania where he lived until he went away to college. By his own report, his

---

[2] It is also a tribute to the greatness of the man to note a few of the more contemporary psychologists who were his disciples and followers: John Dollard, Carl Hovland, Gregory Kimble, Neal Miller, Robert Sears, Hobart Mowrer, and Kenneth Spence.

childhood environment was "warm and stable." He attended the same high school from which his parents had graduated; there were only seven others in his graduating class.

He liked school and was always the first to arrive every morning. As a child and adolescent, he was interested in building things: sleds, wagons, rafts, merry-go-rounds, slingshots, model airplanes, and a steam cannon with which he shot potato and carrot plugs over the roofs of his neighbors' houses. He even spent years trying to develop a perpetual motion machine.

He was also interested in the behavior of animals. He read a great deal about animals and kept an assortment of pets: turtles, snakes, lizards, toads, and chipmunks. At a county fair he once observed a flock of performing pigeons; years later Skinner would train pigeons to perform a variety of amusing and amazing feats, from playing Ping-Pong to guiding a missile to its target.

On the advice of a family friend Skinner enrolled in Hamilton College where, he wrote:

> I never fitted into student life . . . I joined a fraternity without knowing what it was all about. I was not good at sports and suffered acutely as my shins were cracked in ice hockey or better players bounced basketballs off my cranium. . . . In a paper I wrote at the end of my freshman year, I complained that the college was pushing me around with unnecessary requirements (one of them daily chapel) and that almost no intellectual interest was shown by most of the students. By my senior year I was in open revolt. (1967, p. 392)

As part of his "open revolt," Skinner participated in hoaxes that disrupted the college community and indulged in verbal attacks on the faculty and administration. His revolt continued up to graduation day when, at commencement ceremonies, the college president warned Skinner and his friends that if they did not settle down they would not graduate.

Skinner did graduate with a degree in English, a Phi Beta Kappa key, and a desire to become a writer. As a child he had written poems and stories, and in 1925, at a summer writing school, Robert Frost had commented favorably on his work.

For two years after his graduation Skinner worked at writing, then decided that he had "nothing important to say." After reading about the works of Watson and Pavlov, he turned from a literary investigation of human behavior to a scientific one. He enrolled as a graduate student in psychology at Harvard, never having taken a psychology course before. There he developed the rigorous program of self-discipline that continues to characterize his life.

> I would rise at six, study until breakfast, go to classes, laboratories, and libraries with no more than fifteen minutes unscheduled during the day, study until exactly nine o'clock at night and go to bed. I saw no movies

or plays, seldom went to concerts, had scarcely any dates and read nothing but psychology and physiology. (Skinner, 1967, p. 398)[3]

He maintained this schedule for two years and in 1931 received his Ph.D. His dissertation topic provides an early glimpse of the position to which he has consistently adhered throughout his career. His major proposition was that a reflex is the correlation between a stimulus and a response, and nothing more.

Following several years of postdoctoral fellowships, Skinner taught at the University of Minnesota (1936–1945) and Indiana University (1945–1947). In 1947 he returned to Harvard, where he has remained. His 1938 book, *The Behavior of Organisms*, describes the basic points of his system. *Science and Human Behavior* (1953) was written as a textbook for his behaviorist psychology.

Skinner's System: General Approach

In a number of important respects Skinner's position represents a renewal of Watsonian behaviorism. As MacLeod stated, "Watson's spirit is indestructible. Cleaned and purified, it breathes through the writings of B. F. Skinner" (1959, p. 34).

Although Hull was also a behaviorist, there are marked differences between Hull's and Skinner's approaches to psychology. Whereas Hull stressed the importance of theory, Skinner advocates a strictly empirical system with no theoretical framework within which to conduct research. Where Hull's work consisted of postulating theory on an *a priori* basis, then checking the deduced conclusions against experimental evidence, Skinner avoids theory and practices a stringent brand of positivism. Skinner begins with empirical data and proceeds carefully and slowly (if at all) toward tentative generalizations. Hull represents the deductive method; Skinner represents the inductive method.

---

[3] Twelve years after writing that description of his schedule (and 51 years after the event itself) Skinner denied that his life as a graduate student had been as spartan as the passage suggests. "I was recalling a pose rather than the life I had actually led" (Skinner, 1979, p. 5). Although the event itself is of minor importance in the history of psychology, the two versions of it, both written by the person who experienced it, indicate something of the difficulty a historian faces. Which version of Skinner's time in graduate school is the more accurate description? Which is biased by the vagaries of memory or the attempt to appear in a different light? Or is neither a totally accurate description of the event? Wertheimer reminds us that "historical truth is much more elusive than scientific truth" (1979, p. 1). The scientific truth can be tested repeatedly, but not the historical truth; the event in history cannot be repeated. What this means is that history is highly subjective and can, therefore, only approximate the truth. History cannot provide a mirror image of the truth, just as a painting—another subjective process—cannot exactly duplicate an object.

All behavior is operant and subject to reinforcement contingencies, according to leading behaviorist B. F. Skinner (1904–), who has applied his laboratory data to problems of childrearing and education and proposed large-scale programs for behavior control.
(National Library of Medicine)

Skinner's point of view is summarized in this way:

> *I never attacked a problem by constructing a Hypothesis. I never deduced Theorems or submitted them to Experimental check. So far as I can see I had no preconceived Model of Behavior—certainly not a physiological or*

mentalistic one, and I believe not a conceptual one. (Skinner, 1956, p. 227)

Skinner's position is an exclusively descriptive kind of behaviorism devoted to the study of responses; it is atheoretical in nature. His concern is with describing behavior rather than explaining it. He deals only with observable behavior and believes that the task of scientific inquiry is to establish functional relations between the antecedent experimenter-controlled stimulus conditions and the organism's subsequent response.

In *Science and Human Behavior* (1953) Skinner wrote about the mechanical figures in the royal gardens of seventeenth-century Europe and the mechanical image of humans they portrayed. Under the heading "Man a Machine," he described how his view is compatible with that earlier mechanical image. The human organism, Skinner said flatly, is a machine. And, like any other machine, a human being behaves in lawful and predictable ways in response to external forces (stimuli) that impinge on it.

Thus, Skinner is not at all concerned with theorizing or speculating about what might be going on inside the organism. His program includes no reference to presumed internal entities, whether described as intervening variables or physiological processes. Whatever might occur between the stimulus and the response does not represent objective data for a Skinnerian behaviorist. This purely descriptive behaviorism has been called, with good reason, the "empty-organism" approach. There is nothing inside the organism that is useful, or even necessary, for explaining behavior. We are operated by forces in the environment, the external world, not by forces within ourselves.

It is important to note that although his system is atheoretical, Skinner is not totally opposed to theorizing. Rather, he is against premature theorizing in the absence of adequate supporting data. In an interview in 1968 Skinner said that he looks forward "to an overall theory of human behavior which will bring together a lot of facts and express them in a general way. That kind of theory I would be very much interested in prompting". (R.I. Evans, 1968, p. 88).

In contrast to many contemporary psychologists, Skinner does not believe in the use of large numbers of subjects and statistical comparisons between mean responses of groups. Instead, he has focused on the intense and thorough investigation of a single subject:

> *A prediction of what the* average *individual will do is often of little or no value in dealing with a particular individual. . . . a science is helpful in dealing with the individual only insofar as its laws refer to individuals. A science of behavior which concerns only the behavior of groups is not likely to be of help in our understanding of the particular case. (Skinner, 1953, p. 19)*

Skinner believes that truly valid replicable results can be obtained without the use of statistical analysis so long as sufficient data are collected from a single subject under well-controlled experimental conditions. He argues that the use of a large group of subjects forces the experimenter to attend to average behavior. As a result, individual response behavior and individual differences in behavior do not appear as part of the data of the experiment. In 1958 the Skinnerians established their *Journal for the Experimental Analysis of Behavior* because of the unwritten requirements of the current journals concerning subject sample size and statistical analysis.

Operant Conditioning

All psychology students are aware of the Skinner box and of Skinner's emphasis on operant as opposed to respondent behavior. In the Pavlovian conditioning situation a known stimulus is paired with a response under conditions of reinforcement. The behavioral response is elicited by a specific observable stimulus situation and is called, by Skinner, a respondent behavior.

Operant behavior, on the other hand, occurs without any observable external stimulus. The organism's response is seemingly spontaneous in that it is not related to any known observable stimulus. This is not to say that there is definitely no stimulus eliciting the response, but rather that no stimulus is detected when the response occurs. As far as the experimenters are concerned, there is no stimulus because they have not applied any and cannot see any.

Another difference between the two kinds of response behavior is that operant behavior operates on the organism's environment and respondent behavior does not. The harnessed dog in Pavlov's laboratory can do nothing but respond when the experimenter presents the stimulus. The dog cannot act on its own to secure the stimulus. The operant behavior of the rat in the Skinner box, however, is instrumental in securing the stimulus (food); when the rat presses the bar, it receives food, and it does not get any food until it does press the bar.

Skinner believes that operant behavior is much more representative of the real-life human learning situation. Because behavior is mostly of the operant variety, the most effective approach to a science of behavior, according to Skinner, is to study the conditioning and extinguishing of operant behaviors.

Skinner's classic experimental demonstration involved bar pressing in a Skinner box constructed to eliminate extraneous stimuli. In this experiment a rat that had been deprived of food was placed in the box and allowed to explore. In the course of this general exploratory behavior the rat sooner or later accidentally depressed a lever activating a food magazine that released a food pellet into a tray. After a few reinforcements, conditioning was usually rapid. Note that the rat's behavior operated on the environment (pressed the lever) and was instrumental in securing food. The dependent variable in this kind of experiment is simple and direct: the rate of the response. A cumulative recorder attached to the Skinner box keeps a moment-by-moment record of the rate of bar pressing.

From this basic experiment Skinner derived his law of acquisition, which states that the strength of an operant is increased when that operant is followed by presentation of a reinforcing stimulus. Although practice is important in the establishment of high rates of bar pressing, the key variable is *reinforcement*. Practice by itself will not increase the rate; all it does is provide the opportunity for additional reinforcement to occur.

Skinner's law of acquisition differs from the positions of Thorndike and Hull on learning. Skinner does not speak in terms of pleasure–pain consequences of reinforcement, as did Thorndike. In opposition to Hull, Skinner makes no attempt to interpret reinforcement in terms of drive reduction. Whereas the systems of Thorndike and Hull are explanatory, Skinner's is descriptive. Skinner does not view drive as a stimulus or a physiological state; he considers drive as simply a set of operations that influence response behavior in a certain way. He defines drive objectively in terms of number of hours of deprivation.

Skinner and his followers have conducted a great deal of research on various problems in learning. Their topics include the role of punishment in the acquisition of responses, the effect of different schedules of reinforcement, the extinction of operant response, secondary reinforcement, and generalization.

Skinner has also worked with other animals and with human subjects, using the same basic approach as the Skinner box. With pigeons, the operant behavior involves pecking at a spot, with food as a reinforcement. The operant behavior for human subjects involves problem solving reinforced by verbal approval or by knowledge of having given the correct answer.

Schedules of Reinforcement

To many psychologists, Skinner's most notable research is that devoted to the determination of the effects of different schedules of reinforcement. The initial research on bar pressing in the Skinner box demonstrated the necessary role of reinforcement in operant behavior. In that situation the rat's behavior was reinforced for every bar press; that is, it received food every time it made the correct response.

However, as Skinner points out, reinforcement in the real world is not always so consistent or continuous, yet learning occurs and behaviors continue even when reinforced only intermittently. There are many examples.

> *We do not always find good ice or snow when we go skating or skiing. . . . We do not always get a good meal in a particular restaurant because cooks are not always predictable. We do not always get an answer when we telephone a friend because the friend is not always at home. . . . The reinforcements characteristic of industry and education are almost always intermittent because it is not feasible to control behavior by reinforcing every response. (Skinner, 1953, p. 99)*

Even though you may study consistently, you may not get an A on every examination or term paper. If you had a job, you would not receive praise or a pay increase every day. In a football pool or at a slot machine you do not win every time. How is behavior affected by such intermittent reinforcement? Are different schedules of reinforcement optimal in terms of influencing behavior? Skinner and his colleagues devoted years of research to these questions.

The impetus for this research came not from intellectual curiosity but from expediency, and it demonstrates how science sometimes operates—a manner which is different from the idealized picture presented in some textbooks. One Saturday afternoon Skinner found that his supply of food pellets was running low. At that time (the 1930s) food pellets could not be purchased from a laboratory supply company. They had to be made by the experimenter, through a time-consuming and laborious process. So rather than spend the weekend making more pellets, Skinner asked himself what would happen if he reinforced his rats only once a minute regardless of how many responses they were making. That way, of course, many fewer food pellets would be needed. Skinner went on to conduct a lengthy series of experiments.

One set of studies compared the response rates of animals reinforced for every response versus those reinforced only after a certain time interval. The latter is known as *fixed-interval reinforcement*. A reinforcement could be given, for instance, once per minute or once every four minutes. The point is that the reinforcement does not in any way depend on the animal's making a certain number of responses. It depends solely on the passage of a fixed interval of time. A job in which a salary is paid once a week or once a month provides reinforcement on a fixed-interval schedule. Workers in such systems are paid not for the number of items they produce (the number of responses made), but for the number of days or weeks that elapse.

The research has shown that the shorter the interval between reinforcements, the more rapidly the animal will respond. Conversely, as the interval between reinforcements gets longer, the rate of responding falls off.

The frequency of reinforcement also affects the extinguishing of a response. Behaviors are extinguished more quickly when they have been reinforced continuously and the reinforcement is then stopped than when they have been reinforced intermittently. Some pigeons have responded as many as 10,000 times in the absence of reinforcement when they had been conditioned on a schedule of intermittent reinforcement.

Skinner also investigated a *fixed-ratio reinforcement* schedule. In this case, reinforcement is presented not after a certain time interval, but after a predetermined number of responses. The animal determines how often it will be reinforced; it must respond, for example, ten times or 20 times after the last reinforcement to get another.

Not surprisingly, animals on a fixed-ratio schedule respond much faster than those on a fixed-interval schedule. Responding faster on fixed-interval reinforcement will not make any difference; the animal may press the bar five times or 50 times and it will still be reinforced only when the predetermined time interval has passed.

The higher rate of responding on the fixed-ratio schedule has been found to hold for rats and pigeons as well as humans. A fixed-ratio schedule of payment is used in industry and business in situations where a worker's pay depends on the number of units produced, or a sales commission on the number of items sold. This reinforcement schedule is effective as long as the ratio is not set too high (that is, an impossible amount of work required for each unit of pay or reinforcement) and the reinforcement is worth the effort.

Other reinforcement schedules include variable ratios, variable intervals, and mixed schedules. The research is discussed in *Schedules of Reinforcement* (1957) by C. B. Ferster and Skinner, and *Contingencies of Reinforcement* (Skinner, 1969).

Verbal Behavior

Skinner has long had an interest in verbal behavior, the only area in which he admits that there is any difference between rat and human. The sounds the human organism makes in speech, Skinner argues, are responses that can be reinforced (by other speech sounds or gestures) in the same way a rat's bar-pressing behavior can be reinforced by food. For the infant, the sounds that will be reinforced depend on the culture in which it is being raised, but the "mechanics" of verbal behavior apply independently of culture.

Verbal behavior, Skinner said, requires two people in interaction—one speaking and one listening. The speaker makes a response, that is, utters a sound. The listener, by his or her behavior in reinforcing, not reinforcing, or punishing the speaker for what has been said, can control the speaker's subsequent behavior. For example, if every time the speaker used a certain word or phrase, the listener smiled or said, "That's nice," the listener would increase the probability that the speaker would use that word or phrase again. If the listener responded by frowning, making hostile gestures, or commenting unfavorably on certain words, he or she would increase the likelihood that the speaker would avoid using those words in the future.

One can see this situation in the behavior of parents when their children are learning to speak. "Naughty" words, incorrect usage, or poor pronunciation elicit different reactions from correct usage and pronunciation. In this way the child is taught the proper use of speech, at least as its parents understand it.

These simple examples do not, of course, reflect the complexity of Skinner's work in this field. The point to be remembered is that, to Skinner, speech is behavior and is therefore subject to contingencies of reinforcement and prediction and control. His work in this area is summarized in *Verbal Behavior* (1957).

The Machines of Skinner's Behaviorism

We have discussed the Skinner box and its use in operant conditioning, but that was not the only machine Skinner developed.[4] The Skinner box brought him prominence in psychology, but it was another invention that first gained him notice (or at least notoriety) among the general public. In 1945, in an article in the *Ladies Home Journal*, Skinner described his "aircrib"—a device to mechanize the care of an infant.

When Skinner and his wife decided they wanted another child, she protested that caring for a baby through the first two years required too much attention and menial labor, so Skinner invented a way of relieving parents of that task. The aircribs were made available commercially but never became a big success. The aircrib

> *is a large, air-conditioned, temperature controlled, germ free, soundproof compartment in which a baby can sleep and play without blankets or clothing other than a diaper. It allows complete freedom of movement, and relative safety from the usual colds and heat rashes. (Rice, 1968, p. 98)*

Skinner and his wife raised their second child in an aircrib. Except for a broken leg the child suffered in a skiing accident while out of the box, she apparently bore no ill effects and even learned to beat Skinner at chess.

Skinner's best-known apparatus is the teaching machine, invented by Sidney Pressey. Skinner popularized the machine after a visit to his daughter's fourth-grade class, about which he commented, "It's absolutely horrible. They're ruining minds over there. I can do something much better" (Rice, 1968, p. 98). Whether or not he did is controversial, but there is no denying that teaching machines (programmed learning) have been put to

---

[4] Skinner is reported to deplore the use of "Skinner box" as a label for his "operant conditioning apparatus" (M.H. Hall, 1967b, p. 22).

use in a great many areas, from elementary mathematics to music. In 1968 Skinner wrote *The Technology of Teaching*.

Walden Two—A Behaviorist Society

More than any other behaviorist Skinner has mapped out a program of behavioral control in which he attempts to transpose the findings from his laboratory to society at large. What he has tried to develop is a "technology of behavior." Whereas Watson talked in general terms about a "foundation for saner living" through the principles of conditioning, Skinner has outlined in detail the operation of such a society.

In 1948 he published a novel, *Walden Two*, which describes a 1000-member rural community in which every aspect of life is controlled by positive reinforcement. The book was both hailed and reviled in reviews, and never sold more than a few thousand copies a year until the early 1960s when, for some reason, sales increased sharply. The book continues to be popular and is required reading in many college courses.

A national Walden Two conference was held in 1966 and small Walden Two communities have been reported in several parts of the United States. One such community, Twin Oaks (Louisa, Virginia 23093), publishes a newsletter for those interested in how the experiment is working.[5]

The long line of thought from Galileo and Newton, through the British empiricists, to Wundt and Watson reaches its culmination in Skinner's designed society and his basic assumption about the nature of the human being as a machine.

> *If we are to use the methods of science in the field of human affairs, we must assume that behavior is lawful and determined. . . . that what a man does is the result of specifiable conditions and that once these conditions have been discovered, we can anticipate and to some extent determine his actions. (Skinner, 1953, p. 6)*

The mechanistic, analytic, and deterministic approach of natural science, reinforced by Skinner's conditioning experiments, has persuaded the behaviorists that human behavior can be controlled, guided, modified, and shaped by the proper use of positive reinforcement.

In the free will–determinism controversy it is easy to see on which side of the fence the Skinnerians sit. Skinner repeatedly makes the point that

> *the issue of personal freedom must not be allowed to interfere with a scientific analysis of human behavior. . . . We cannot expect to profit*

[5] See also K. Kinkade, *A Walden Two Experiment: The First Five Years of Twin Oaks Community* (New York, Morrow, 1973). Foreword by B. F. Skinner.

from applying the methods of science to human behavior if for some extraneous reason we refuse to admit that our subject matter can be controlled. (1953, p. 322)

This position is discussed in *Beyond Freedom and Dignity* (1971), a book that generated a great deal of publicity, brought about Skinner's appearance on several television talk shows, and became a best-seller. As with *Walden Two*, the work was praised by some and derided by others. But the fact that it was read by so many people demonstrates public curiosity about—if not acceptance of—the Skinnerian position.

Behavior Modification

Skinner's program for society based on positive reinforcement exists only in fictional terms (so far), but the control or modification of behavior at the level of individuals and small groups is widespread. Behavior modification through positive reinforcement has become immensely popular and has been used with great success in mental hospitals, prisons, and schools to change abnormal or undesirable behaviors to more desirable ones. In essence, the technique of behavior modification works with people in the same way the Skinner box works to change the behavior of rats, through reinforcing the desired behavior and not reinforcing undesired behavior.

Consider the child who throws temper tantrums to get its own way. By giving in to the child, the parents are reinforcing the undesirable temper tantrums. In behavior modification such behavior would never be reinforced. Instead, more desirable and pleasant bebaviors would be reinforced. After a time the child's behavior will be modified because the temper tantrums no longer work to bring attention and rewards, whereas more pleasant behaviors do.

These principles have been applied to groups of mental patients. By rewarding these people with tokens (which can be exchanged for possessions or privileges) when they behave in the desired ways, and by not reinforcing negative or disruptive behavior, positive changes in behavior are induced. Note that unlike traditional clinical techniques, there is no concern with what might be going on in the minds of the patients, no more than there is for what might be going on inside the rats in the Skinner box. The focus is exclusively on overt behavior and positive reinforcement.

Note also that punishment is not used. The subjects are not punished for failing to behave in desirable ways. Instead, they are reinforced only when their behavior changes in positive ways. Skinner's research has demonstrated (as Thorndike's did earlier) that positive reinforcement is much more effective than punishment in getting people or animals to alter their behavior.

Comment

However one might view Skinner's intentions—as a savior or enslaver of human beings (and it is difficult to take a neutral position)—there is no denying the extent of his influence on contemporary psychology. Even more so than Hull's system, Skinner's work is not yet history and so the judgment that the perspective of time allows cannot be made.

Skinner has received much criticism, both from inside and outside the psychological establishment. His attitude toward his critics is to ignore them. Discussing a particularly scathing review of one of his books, he said, "I read a bit of it and saw that he missed the point, so I never read the rest. I never answer any of my critics. I generally don't even read them. here are better things to do with my time than clear up their misunderstanding" (Rice, 1968, p. 90).

Perhaps the most frequent criticism is directed at Skinner's extreme brand of positivism and its accompanying opposition to theory. Opponents argue that it is impossible to eliminate all theorizing, as Skinner would have it. Because the details of an experiment must be planned in advance of the actual situation, this in itself is evidence of theorizing, however simple. It has been noted that Skinner's acceptance of the basic principles of conditioning as the framework for his research constitutes some degree of theorizing. Further, Skinner has made confident assertions about economic, social, political, and religious affairs that apparently are derived from his system. This willingness to extrapolate beyond the data, particularly in regard to proposals about complex human problems, is inconsistent with an antitheory stand. Certainly, critics argue, Skinner has gone beyond the observable data in presenting blueprints for the redesign of society; this seems contrary to the principles of his system.

The narrow range of behavior studied in Skinnerian laboratories (bar pressing and key pecking, for example) has also been attacked. Critics argue that numerous aspects or examples of behavior have been largely ignored.

No one can say whether the criticism or the praise will prevail in the long run, but it can be said that Skinner is the incontestable leader and champion of behaviorist psychology. Most of his critics would be forced to agree that contemporary American psychology is molded more by his work than by the work of any other psychologist.

The American Psychological Association recognized the magnitude of Skinner's contribution when in 1958 it granted him the Distinguished Scientific Contribution Award, with the following citation:

> *An imaginative and creative scientist, characterized by great objectivity in scientific matters and by warmth and enthusiasm in personal contacts. Choosing simple operant behavior as subject matter, he has challenged alternative analyses of behavior, insisting that description take precedence over hypotheses. By careful control of experimental conditions, he has produced data which are relatively free from fortuitous variation. Despite his antitheoretical position, he is considered an*

important systematist and has developed a self-consistent description of behavior which has greatly increased our ability to predict and control the behavior of organisms from rat to man. Few American psychologists have had so profound an impact on the development of psychology and on promising younger psychologists. (APA, Committee on Distinguished Scientific Contribution Awards, 1958, p. 735)

In 1968 Skinner was awarded the National Medal of Science, the highest accolade given by the United States government for distinguished contributions to science. In 1971 the American Psychological Foundation presented him with its gold medal.

There is no question that Skinner's radical behaviorism is a strong position in contemporary psychology. The Skinnerian *Journal of the Experimental Analysis of Behavior* continues to flourish, as does the Division for the Experimental Analysis of Behavior (Division 25) of the American Psychological Association. Behavior modification is gaining in popularity and its results provide additional support for Skinner's approach. The term "Skinner box" is listed in *Webster's Third New International Dictionary.* "By any measure of public recognition, Skinnerian psychology has flourished, crowding out of the American public eye other varieties of behaviorism" (Herrnstein, 1977, p. 593).

CHALLENGES TO BEHAVIORISM

Behaviorism, like the other systematic positions, has a long history, as we have seen in these three chapters. Watson gave voice to the changing climate of the times in American psychology, revolted against its mentalistic background, and formally established an objective science of behavior. This vigorous Watsonian revolt marked the beginning of the positivist era in American psychology, which seems to have grown stronger with each passing year. There followed, immediately and up to the present day, enthusiastic formulations of different kinds of behaviorism. To the extent that American experimental psychology is today objective, empirical, reductionist and, to some degree, environmentalist, the spirit, if not the letter, of Watsonian behaviorism lives on. Fifty years after the publication of Watson's article, which formally began behaviorism, Skinner celebrated the anniversary with his article, "Behaviorism at Fifty" (1963), in which he noted that the tremendous progress in experimental psychology in America has been due primarily to the influence of behaviorism.

However, for all its popularity and influence, behaviorism is being attacked from two directions. One source of unrest is within the behaviorist camp. Increasing numbers of psychologists who consider themselves behaviorists in the large are questioning behaviorism's total denial of mentalistic or cognitive processes. This movement, which has been labeled the "cognitive revolution," marks the third stage in the development of behaviorism: *neo-neobehaviorism*. Koch (1964) described this emphasis on cognitive variables as the *"Return of the repressed . . . the massive return to a concern with empirical problem areas long bypassed or only glancingly acknowledged because of their subjectivistic 'odor' "* (p. 19).

The other source of dissatisfaction comes from outside the behaviorist circle and includes psychologists who are disinclined to view psychology wholly as a science of behavior. Although they generally agree on the value of studying behavior, they argue that psychology should not be so limited or restrictive. These "humanistic" psychologists call for a return to consciousness even more directly and boldly than do the cognitive psychologists, and advocate methods other than strictly experimental ones.

Both of these movements have been documented for a quarter of a century, a significant period in a discipline only 100 years old. Therefore, they deserve consideration as part of the development of modern psychology. The cognitive revolution and humanistic psychology will be discussed in Chapter 15.

SUGGESTED READINGS

LASHLEY

Beach, F. A., Hebb, D. O., Morgan, C. T., & Nissen, H. W. (Eds.). *The neuropsychology of Lashley.* New York: McGraw-Hill, 1960.

Carmichael, L. Karl Spencer Lashley, experimental psychologist. *Science*, 1959, *129*, 1409–1412.

OPERATIONISM

Bergmann, G. Sense and nonsense in operationism. *Scientific Monthly*, 1954, *79*, 210–214.

Bridgman, P. W. Remarks on the present state of operationism. *Scientific Monthly*, 1954, *79*, 224–226.

Margenau, H. On interpretations and misinterpretations of operationalism. *Scientific Monthly*, 1954, *79*, 209–210.

Stevens, S. S. The operational basis of psychology. *American Journal of Psychology*, 1935, *47*, 323–330.

TOLMAN

MacCorquodale, K., & Meehl, P. E. Edward C. Tolman. In W. Estes, S. Koch, K. MacCorquodale, P. E. Meehl, C. G. Mueller, Jr., W. N. Schoenfeld, & W. Verplanck (Eds.), *Modern learning theory*. New York: Appleton, 1954. Pp. 177–266.

Tolman, E. C. Principles of purposive behavior. In S. Koch (Ed.), *Psychology: A study of a science* (Vol. 2). New York: McGraw-Hill, 1959. Pp. 92–157.

GUTHRIE

Guthrie, E. R. *The psychology of learning*. New York: Harper, 1935.

Guthrie, E. R. Association by contiguity. In S. Koch (Ed.), *Psychology: A study of a science* (Vol. 2). New York: McGraw-Hill, 1959. Pp. 158–195.

Mueller, C. G., Jr., & Schoenfeld, W. N. Edwin R. Guthrie. In W. Estes, S. Koch, K. MacCorquodale, P. E. Meehl, C. G. Mueller, Jr., W. N. Schoenfeld, & W. Verplanck (Eds.), *Modern learning theory*. New York: Appleton, 1954. Pp. 345–379.

HULL

Hull, C. L. Mind, mechanism and adaptive behavior. *Psychological Review*, 1937, *44*, 1–32.

Koch, S. Clark L. Hull. In W. Estes, S. Koch, K. MacCorquodale, P. E. Meehl, C. G. Mueller, Jr., W. N. Schoenfeld, & W. Verplanck (Eds.), *Modern learning theory*. New York: Appleton, 1954. Pp. 1–176.

SKINNER

Bixenstine, V. E. Empiricism in latter-day behavioral science. *Science*, 1964, *145*, 464–467.

Evans, R. *B. F. Skinner: The man and his ideas*. New York: Dutton, 1968.

Krantz, D. L. Schools and systems: The mutual isolation of operant and non-operant psychology as a case study. *Journal of the History of the Behavioral Sciences*, 1972, *8*, 86–102.

Skinner, B. F. A case history in scientific method. In S. Koch (Ed.), *Psychology: A study of a science* (Vol. 2). New York: McGraw-Hill, 1959. Pp. 359–379.

Skinner, B. F. *Beyond freedom and dignity*. New York: Knopf, 1971.

Skinner, B. F. *Cumulative record* (3rd ed.). New York: Appleton, 1972.

Skinner, B. F. *About behaviorism*. New York: Knopf, 1974.

Skinner, B. F. *Particulars of my life*. New York: Knopf, 1976. (Skinner's autobiography through the age of 24 when he began graduate study in psychology.)

Skinner, B. F. *The shaping of a behaviorist*. New York: Knopf, 1979. (Vol. 2 of the autobiography, to 1948.)

CONTEMPORARY LEARNING
THEORY

Deese, J., & Hulse, S. *The psychology of learning* (2nd ed.). New York: McGraw-Hill, 1967.

Hilgard, E. R., & Bower, G. *Theories of learning* (4th ed.). Englewood Cliffs, NJ: Prentice-Hall, 1974.

GENERAL

Blanshard, B. Critical reflections on behaviorism. *Proceedings of the American Philosophical Society*, 1965, *109*, 22–28.

Boring, E. G. The trend toward mechanism. *Proceedings of the American Philosophical Society*, 1964, *108*, 451–454.

Hebb, D. O. The American revolution. *American Psychologist*, 1960, *15*, 735–745.

Herrnstein, R. J. The evolution of behaviorism. *American Psychologist*, 1977, 32, 593–603.

Matson, F. (Ed.). *Without/within: Behaviorism and humanism*. Monterey, CA: Brooks/Cole, 1973.

Rachlin, H. *Introduction to modern behaviorism*. San Francisco, CA: Freeman, 1976.

Skinner, B. F. Behaviorism at fifty. *Science*, 1963, 140, 951–958.

Wann, T. W. (Ed.). *Behaviorism and phenomenology: Contrasting bases for modern psychology*. Chicago: University of Chicago Press, 1964.

12
GESTALT
PSYCHOLOGY[1]

INTRODUCTION

We have traced the development of psychology from the beginning psychology of Wilhelm Wundt to the contemporary psychology of B. F. Skinner. We have seen how functionalism followed structuralism, and how behaviorism developed in opposition to both of these schools.

While these major movements were forming and growing in the United States, another movement—a revolution—was taking hold in Germany. It was yet an additional protest against structuralism, further testimony to the importance of that initial school of thought as an inspiration for opposing points of view and an effective base from which to launch new systems of psychology.

To understand this revolution, Gestalt psychology, we must go back to around 1912, the year described by Woodworth and Sheehan (1964) as a "time of troubles" for the old approach to psychology, the time when behaviorism was beginning its violent attack against both the Wundtian order of things and the newer functionalism. The animal research of Thorndike and Pavlov had been on the rise for a decade. Thorndike's first full statement of his position was made in 1911–1913, and the significance for psychology of Pavlov's conditioned reflex was soon to be acknowledged. Another fresh approach, psychoanalysis, was also more than a decade old.

The Gestalt psychologists' attack on structuralism in Germany was simultaneous with, although independent of, the American behaviorist movement. Both movements started by opposing Wundtian structuralism, and later they came to oppose each other. There were sharp differences between the Gestaltists and the behaviorists. Gestalt psychology accepted the value of consciousness, but criticized the attempt to analyze it into elements. Behaviorism refused even to acknowledge consciousness.

---

[1] Gestalt psychology should not be confused or linked with Fritz Perls's Gestalt therapy, although increasing numbers of people have come to make this linkage. Henle (1978a) pointed out that many students and psychologists "believe that Gestalt therapy *is* Gestalt psychology or, more moderately, that it is an extension of Gestalt psychology" (pp. 23–24). There is no relationship between these two approaches other than their common use of the word *Gestalt*. Perls wrote that he had never read any of the Gestalt psychologists' books and that he was not a "pure Gestaltist."

Gestalt psychologists referred to the Wundtian approach (with a sneer) as "brick-and-mortar psychology," implying that the elements (the bricks) were held together by the mortar of the process of association. They argued that when one looks out a window one immediately sees the trees and the sky, not the alleged sensory elements such as brightnesses and hues that, according to the structuralists, constitute the perception of the trees and the sky. Wundtians claimed that perception of objects consists of the accumulation of elements into groups or collections; Gestaltists called this the "bundle hypothesis." The Gestalt psychologists maintained that when sensory elements are combined, something new is formed. Put together a number of musical notes and something new—a melody—emerges from their combination, something that did not exist in any of the individual notes. Put simply and succinctly: the whole is different from the sum of its parts. This was the keynote of the Gestalt opposition to Wundtian structuralism.

Miller (1962)[2] described an imaginary visit to a psychological laboratory in Germany around 1912, which points out the basic difference between the Gestalt and structural approaches to perception. As you walk into the laboratory, a psychologist asks you what you see on the table:

> "A book."
>
> "Yes, of course, it is a book," he agrees, "but what do you really see?"
>
> "What do you mean, 'What do I really see'?" you ask, puzzled. "I told you that I see a book. It is a small book with a red cover."
>
> The psychologist is persistent. "What is your perception really?" he insists. "Describe it to me as precisely as you can."
>
> "You mean it isn't a book? What is this, some kind of trick?"
>
> There is a hint of impatience. "Yes, it is a book. There is no trickery involved. I just want you to describe to me exactly what you can see, no more and no less."
>
> You are growing very suspicious now. "Well," you say, "from this angle the cover of the book looks like a dark red parallelogram."
>
> "Yes," he says, pleased. "Yes, you see a patch of dark red in the shape of a parallelogram. What else?"
>
> "There is a grayish white edge below it and another thin line of the same dark red below that. Under it I see the table—" He winces. "Around it I see a somewhat mottled brown with wavering streaks of lighter brown running roughly parallel to one another."
>
> "Fine, fine." He thanks you for your cooperation.

[2] From pp. 103–105 in *Psychology* by George A. Miller. Copyright 1962 by George A. Miller. Reprinted by permission of Harper & Row, Publishers, Inc.

As you stand there looking at the book on the table you are a little embarrassed that this persistent fellow was able to drive you to such an analysis. He made you so cautious that you were not sure any longer what you really saw and what you only thought you saw. You were, in fact, as suspicious as the New England farmer who would admit only that, "It looks like a cow on this side." In your caution you began talking about what you saw in terms of sensations, where just a moment earlier you were quite certain that you perceived a book on a table.

Your reverie is interrupted suddenly by the appearance of a psychologist who looks vaguely like Wilhelm Wundt. "Thank you, for helping to confirm once more my theory of perception. You have proved," he says, "that the book you see is nothing but a compound of elementary sensations. When you were trying to be precise and say accurately what it was you really saw, you had to speak in terms of color patches, not objects. It is the color sensations that are primary, and every visual object is reducible to them. Your perception of the book is constructed from sensations just as a molecule is constructed from atoms."

This little speech is apparently a signal for battle to begin. "Nonsense!" shouts a voice from the opposite end of the hall. "Nonsense! Any fool knows that the book is the primary, immediate, direct, compelling, perceptual fact!" The psychologist who charges down upon you now bears a faint resemblance to William James, but he seems to have a German accent, and his face is so flushed with anger that you cannot be sure. "This reduction of a perception into sensations that you keep talking about is nothing but an intellectual game. An object is not just a bundle of sensations. Any man who goes about seeing patches of dark redness where he ought to see books is sick!"

As the fight begins to gather momentum you close the door softly and slip away. You have what you came for, an illustration that there are two different attitudes, two different ways to talk about the information that our senses provide.

The Gestalt psychologists believe there is more to perception than meets the eye, so to speak—that our perception somehow goes beyond the basic physical data provided to the sense organs. As with other movements, the basic ideas of the Gestalt protest have their historical antecedents. After examining these early influences, we shall discuss the three key figures in the formal founding of the Gestalt movement and the basic principles of the Gestalt school.

ANTECEDENT INFLUENCES

The basis of the Gestalt position—the focus on the unity of perception—can be found in the work of the German philosopher Immanuel Kant (1724–1804). This eminent man, who never ventured more than 60 miles from his place of birth, dominated philosophical thinking for more than a generation. Although his contribution to psychology is less extensive than his contribution to philosophy, it is important nonetheless.

Kant influenced psychology through his stress on the unity of a perceptual act. He argued that when we perceive objects (or what we call objects), we encounter mental states that might seem to be composed of bits and pieces (the sensory elements of which the empiricists and associationists spoke). However, these elements are meaningfully organized in *a priori* fashion and not through the mechanical process of association. The mind, in the process of perception, forms or creates a unitary experience. According to Kant, perception is not a passive impression and combination of sensory elements, but an active organization of these elements into a unitary and coherent experience. Thus, the raw material of perception is given form and organization by the mind. This position is contrary to the very heart of associationism.

To Kant, some of the forms that the mind imposes on experience are innate, such as space, time, and causality. That is, time and space are not derived from experience, but exist innately in the mind as *a priori* forms of perception; they are intuitively knowable.

As he was for functionalism and behaviorism, Wundt, in his role as a target for criticism, was a precursor of Gestalt psychology. He was also a more direct influence in that his principle of creative synthesis recognized that new characteristics might emerge when elements are combined into wholes. Wundt made little of this notion, however.

Franz Brentano anticipated the formal Gestalt movement through his insistence that psychology study the process or act of experiencing rather than the content of experience (elementary sensations). He considered Wundtian introspection to be artificial and favored a less rigid and more direct observation of experience as it occurs, much like the later Gestalt method.

Ernst Mach (1838–1916), a physicist, exerted more direct influence on the Gestalt revolution. In his book, *The Analysis of Sensations* (1885), Mach wrote about sensations of space-form and time-form. He considered spatial patterns such as geometric figures and temporal patterns such as melodies to be sensations. These space-form and time-form sensations were independent of their elements. For example, a circle might be white or black, large or small, and lose nothing of its elemental quality of circularity.

Mach argued that our visual or aural perception of an object does not change, even though we may change our spatial orientation with regard to the object. For example, a table remains a table in our perception whether looked at from the side or the top or from an angle. Similarly, a series of sounds, as in a melody, remains the same in our perception even though the tempo may be altered.

Mach's work was expanded by Christian von Ehrenfels (1859–1932), who many consider the most important forebear of Gestalt psychology. Von Ehrenfels suggested that there are qualities of experience that cannot be

276

Gestalt Psychology

explained in terms of combinations of the traditional kinds of sensations. He called these qualities *Gestalt qualitäten* or form qualities, perceptions based on something beyond the individual sensations. A melody, for example, is a form quality because it sounds the same even when transposed to different keys. The melody is independent of the particular sensations of which it is composed. To von Ehrenfels, and the Austrian school of *Gestalt qualität* founded at Graz, form itself was an element (though not a sensation), a new element created by the action of the mind operating on the sensory elements. Thus, the mind creates form out of elementary sensations.

Although Mach and von Ehrenfels thought along the lines that came to be known as Gestalt psychology, they deviated little from the older elementist position of the structuralists. Rather than opposing the notion of elementism, as the Gestalt psychologists later did, they simply added a new element, that of form. Although they attacked the same position as the Gestalt psychologists, they offered a quite different solution. Gestalt psychologists deny any relationship with them.

In the United States William James, by opposing psychological elementism, served as a precursor of Gestalt psychology. James regarded elements of consciousness as artificial abstractions and noted that we see objects, not bundles of sensations.

Another early influence is the phenomenological movement in German philosophy and psychology. Methodologically, phenomenology refers to a free and unbiased description of immediate experience exactly as it occurs. It is "uncorrected" observation in which an experience is not analyzed into elements or otherwise artificially abstracted. It involves the almost naïve experience of common sense rather than experience as reported by a trained introspector with a special systematic orientation, as was the case with structuralism.

The phenomenological tradition in psychology is generally assumed to have begun with Goethe, and its active use can be traced to a number of scholars in psychology and other disciplines. An active group of phenomenological psychologists was at G. E. Müller's laboratory at Göttingen in the years 1909–1915. There, Erich R. Jaensch, David Katz, and Edgar Rubin conducted extensive phenomenological research that was supportive of, indeed anticipated, the formal Gestalt school, which was later to use the phenomenological approach.

Not to be neglected among antecedent influences of Gestalt psychology is the *Zeitgeist*, particularly with regard to physics. In the closing decades of the nineteenth century physics was becoming less atomistic as it came to recognize and accept the notion of fields of force.

The classic example of this new force in physics is magnetism, a property or quality that seemed difficult to define or understand in traditional Galilean–Newtonian terms. For example, when iron filings are shaken onto a sheet of paper that is resting on top of a magnet, the filings become arranged in a characteristic pattern. The filings do not touch the magnet, yet they are obviously affected by the force, the field of force, around the magnet. At the time, light and electricity were considered to operate similarly. These fields of force were thought to possess both spatial extension and configuration or pattern. They were, in other words, believed to be new structural entities, not summations of effects of individual elements or particles.

Thus, the notion of atomism, which had been so important for Wundt, was under serious attack in physics. Physicists were beginning to think in terms of organic wholes, a concept congruent with the new Gestalt psychology. The changes offered by Gestalt psychologists paralleled the changes in the physics of the time. Psychology still desired to emulate the natural sciences.

The impact on psychology of this changing emphasis in physics came about in a personal way. Wolfgang Köhler, one of the founders of Gestalt psychology, had a strong background in physics and had studied for a time under Max Planck, one of the greatest physicists of the twentieth century. Köhler wrote that it was because of Planck's influence that he began to sense a connection between field physics and the Gestalt emphasis on wholes. Everywhere he looked in physics Köhler saw an increasing reluctance to continue to deal with elements and a focus instead on larger systems or fields. He later wrote that "Gestalt psychology has since become a kind of application of field physics to essential parts of psychology" (Köhler, 1969, p. 77).

Watson, by contrast, seems to have had no training in the new physics and so could continue to develop a reductionist approach to psychology, focusing on elements of behavior, a view compatible with the principles of the older atomistic physics.

THE FOUNDING OF GESTALT PSYCHOLOGY

The formal movement known as Gestalt psychology grew out of a research study conducted in 1910 by the German psychologist Max Wertheimer, the primary founder of the new school. While riding on a train during his vacation, Wertheimer had an idea for an experiment on the seeing of motion when no actual motion had taken place. Promptly forgetting his vacation, he left the train at Frankfurt am Main, purchased a toy stroboscope,[3] and verified his insight in a preliminary way in his hotel room. He later carried out more formal research at the University of Frankfurt, which provided a

---

[3] The stroboscope, invented about 80 years earlier by J. Plateau, was a forerunner of the motion picture camera. It is an instrument that rapidly projects a series of different pictures on the eye, producing apparent motion.

tachistoscope for his use. In Frankfurt were two other young German psychologists who, some years earlier, had been students with Wertheimer at the University of Berlin—Kurt Koffka and Wolfgang Köhler. Each had been working productively in psychology. Shortly they all embarked on a joint crusade against Wundtian elementism.

Wertheimer's research problem, on which Koffka and Köhler served as subjects, involved the perception of apparent movement, that is, the perception of motion when no actual physical movement has taken place. Using the tachistoscope, Wertheimer projected light through two slits, one vertical and the other 20 or 30 degrees from the vertical. If light was shown through one slit and then the other, with a long interval in between (over 200 milliseconds), the subjects saw two successive lights, first at one slit and then at the other. When the interval between the lights was very short, the subjects saw both lights on continuously. With an optimal interval (about 60 milliseconds) between the lights, however, the subjects saw a single line of light move from one place to the other and back again.

These findings may seem straightforward; the phenomenon had been known for many years and may even be considered a matter of common sense. But according to the prevailing psychological position, the structuralist viewpoint, all conscious experience could be analyzed into its sensory elements. Yet how could this perception of apparent movement be explained in terms of a summation of individual sensory elements? Could one stationary stimulus be added to another to produce a sensation of movement? It could not, and this was precisely the point of Wertheimer's brilliantly simple demonstration: it defied explanation by the prevailing Wundtian system!

Wertheimer believed that the phenomenon verified in his laboratory was, in its own way, as elementary as a sensation, yet it obviously differed from a sensation or even a succession of sensations. Wertheimer gave the occurrence a name befitting its unique status: the *phi phenomenon*.

We may ask how Wertheimer explained the phi phenomenon when the traditional introspective structuralism could not. His answer was as simple and ingenious as the verifying experiment itself: apparent movement did not need explaining. It existed as perceived and could not be reduced to anything simpler.

According to Wundt, introspection of the stimulus would produce two successive lines and nothing else, but no matter how rigorously one might try to introspect the two exposures, the experience of a single line in motion persisted. Any further attempt at analysis was a failure. The whole (the movement) was indeed different from the sum of its parts (the two stationary lines). The traditional associationist–structuralist psychology, dominant for so many years, had been challenged, and it was a challenge it could not meet. Wertheimer's results were published in 1912 in an article, "Experimental Studies of the Perception of Movement," that is often considered to mark the beginning of the new school.

Max Wertheimer
(1880–1943)

Born in Prague, Max Wertheimer attended the local *Gymnasium* until the age of 18 and studied law for 2½ years at the university. He shifted to philosophy and attended the lectures of von Ehrenfels, among others. He later studied philosophy and psychology at Berlin and took his degree in 1904 at Würzburg under Oswald Külpe, at the height of the imageless thought controversy. Between 1904 and 1912 he spent his time variously at Prague, Vienna, and Berlin before settling in Frankfurt. He lectured at Frankfurt from 1912 until 1916 and in 1929 was granted a professorship

From his study of the perception of apparent motion, Max Wertheimer (1880–1943) started the formal movement of Gestalt psychology. (*The Bettmann Archive*)

there. During World War I he conducted research of military value on listening devices for submarines and harbor fortifications.

Wertheimer was the oldest of the three original Gestalt psychologists and the intellectual leader of the movement. Koffka and Köhler served to promote Wertheimer's prominent position, though each was influential in his own right. Though he did not publish as much as Koffka and Köhler, Wertheimer produced important papers on creative thinking (1920) and perceptual grouping (1923).

In 1921 Wertheimer, Koffka, and Köhler, assisted by K. Goldstein and H. Gruhle, founded the journal *Psychologische Forschung (Psychological Research)*, which became the official organ of the Gestalt school. Twenty-two volumes were published before it was suspended in 1938 under the Hitler regime.

Wertheimer was among the first group of refugee scholars from Germany to arrive in New York in 1933. In 1934 he became associated with the New School for Social Research, where he remained until his death in 1943. His years in the United States were busy, but he became increasingly exhausted by the burdens of adapting to a new language and culture. His research was conducted rather informally and was communicated personally to his friends and at meetings of psychologists.[4]

Kurt Koffka (1886–1941)

Koffka is considered the most productive of the three primary Gestaltists.[5] He received his education at Berlin, his place of birth, and during his youth developed an interest in science and philosophy that was strengthened at Edinburgh in 1903–1904. After returning to Berlin he studied psychology and received his degree in 1909 under Carl Stumpf. He took a number of research positions and in 1910 began his long and productive association with Wertheimer and Köhler in Frankfurt. In 1911 he went to the University of Giessen, some 40 miles from Frankfurt, and remained there until 1924. At Giessen he conducted a good deal of research, and during World War I worked with brain-damaged and aphasic patients at the psychiatric clinic.

After the war, when American psychology was becoming vaguely aware of the school developing in Germany, Koffka was persuaded to write an article on the new movement for the *Psychological Bulletin*. This article, "Perception: An Introduction to Gestalt-Theorie" (1922), presented the basic

[4] During his last years in New York Wertheimer made a strong impression on a young American psychologist, Abraham Maslow. Maslow was so in awe of Wertheimer that he began to study the man's personal qualities and characteristics. It was from these initial observations of Wertheimer (and of Ruth Benedict, an anthropologist) that Maslow developed his concept of self-actualization (see Chapter 15).

[5] Boring (1950b) has suggested that "the originality of these three men varied inversely with their productivity" (p. 594).

concepts of Gestalt psychology and the results and implications of much research.

Although the article was important as the first formal exposition of the Gestalt revolution to many American psychologists, it may have done a disservice to the spread of Gestalt psychology. As Michael Wertheimer (1979) pointed out, the title of the article, with "perception" its first word, started a misunderstanding that lingers today: the idea that Gestalt psy-

Kurt Koffka (1886–1941) is often considered the most productive of the early Gestalt psychologists.
(*Archives of the History of American Psychology*)

chology deals exclusively (or nearly so) with perception, and therefore has no relevance for other areas of psychology.

In reality Gestalt psychology was "primarily concerned with thinking, with philosophical questions, and with learning; the main reason why the early Gestalt psychologists concentrated their systematic publications on perception was because of the *Zeitgeist:* Wundt's psychology, against which the Gestaltists rebelled, had obtained most of its support from studies of sensation and perception, so the Gestalt psychologists chose perception as the arena in order to attack Wundt in his own stronghold" (Wertheimer, 1979, p. 134).

In 1921 Koffka published *The Growth of the Mind,* a book on developmental child psychology that became a great success in Germany and America. He was a visiting professor at Cornell and the University of Wisconsin in 1924, and in 1927 was appointed a professor at Smith College, where he remained until his death in 1941. In 1932 Koffka accompanied an expedition to study the people of Central Asia. While recovering from recurrent fever contracted on this expedition, he began work on his *Principles of Gestalt Psychology,* published in 1935. It was a difficult book to read and did not become the definitive treatment of Gestalt psychology he intended it to be.

Wolfgang Köhler
(1887–1967)

Köhler, the youngest of the three, was the spokesman for the Gestalt movement. His books, written with great care and precision, became the definitive works on certain aspects of Gestalt psychology. Köhler's considerable training in physics under the eminent Max Planck convinced him that psychology must ally itself with physics. Born in the Baltic provinces, Köhler was 5 years old when his family moved to northern Germany. His university education was at Tübingen, Bonn, and Berlin; he received his degree from Berlin in 1909 under Stumpf. He went on to Frankfurt, arriving just before Wertheimer and his stroboscope.

In 1913, at the invitation of the Prussian Academy of Science, Köhler went to the Spanish island of Tenerife in the Canary Islands to study chimpanzees. Six months after his arrival World War I began and he was unable to leave. For the next seven years he studied learning in chimpanzees and produced the classic volume *Mentality of Apes* (1917). The book appeared in a second edition in 1924, and was translated into English (1927) and French (1928).

In 1920 Köhler returned to Germany, and in 1922 succeeded Stumpf at Berlin, where he remained until 1935. The apparent reason for his appointment to this coveted position was the publication of *Static and Stationary Physical Gestalts* (1920), which won critical acclaim for its high level of scholarship.

Köhler lectured at Clark University and Harvard in 1925–1926, and in 1929 published, in English, *Gestalt Psychology,* the most comprehensive argument

Wolfgang Köhler (1887–1967) was originally trained in physics and became one of the most prominent spokesmen for the Gestalt movement. *(Swarthmore College)*

for the Gestalt movement. In 1934–1935 Köhler gave the William James lectures at Harvard, and in 1935 left Germany because of his continual conflicts with the Nazi regime; he had written a courageous anti-Nazi letter to a Berlin newspaper. Köhler's letter was "the last anti-Nazi article to be published openly in Germany under the Nazi regime" (Henle, 1978c, p. 940). Köhler, who was not Jewish, was incensed at the Nazi dismissals of all Jewish professors from German universities, and he spoke openly in his classes against the new government. A gang of Nazis once invaded his classroom. On the evening his article appeared in the newspaper he and a few friends sat quietly in his home playing chamber music, waiting for the Gestapo to arrest him. The dreaded knock on the door never came.

He emigrated to the United States where he taught at Swarthmore College. His later books include *The Place of Value in a World of Facts* (1938), *Dynamics in Psychology* (1940), and *Figural After-Effects* (1944), the last with Hans Wallach. In 1956 he received the Distinguished Scientific Contribution Award from the American Psychological Association, and in 1959 was elected its president.

THE NATURE OF THE
GESTALT REVOLT

The Gestalt principles were in direct opposition to much of the academic tradition of psychology in Germany. Behaviorism was less an immediate revolution against structuralism because functionalism had already brought about some changes in American psychology. No such tempering paved the way for the Gestalt revolt in Germany; the pronouncements of the Gestaltists were nothing short of heresy to the German structuralist tradition. Consider the basic points of Gestalt psychology in the light of Wundt's brand of psychology: *(a)* complex mental experience can have an existence of its own, *(b)* the primary data of perception are not elements but significantly structured forms, and *(c)* it is acceptable when introspecting to use simple descriptive words, that is, one may say, "I see a book"!

The initiators of the Gestalt movement realized that they were taking on a powerful and rigid tradition, that they were striking at the foundation of psychology as it was then defined. Like most revolutionary movements, the Gestalt school demanded a complete revision of the old order. After the study of apparent movement, they were quick to seize upon other perceptual phenomena to support their position. The experience of perceptual constancies afforded ample corroboration. For example, when one stands directly in front of a window, a rectangular image is projected onto the retina. But when one stands off to one side and looks at the window, the retinal image becomes a trapezoid, though the window is still perceived as rectangular. Our perception of the window remains unchanged even though the sensory datum (the image projected on the retina) has changed.

The same thing occurs with brightness and size constancy; the actual sensory elements can change radically, yet our perception does not. There are many similar examples in everyday experience. In these cases, as with apparent movement, the perceptual experience as a quality of wholeness that is not found in any of the parts. There can exist, then, a difference between the character of the actual perception and the character of the sensory stimulation. The perception cannot be explained as a collection of sensory elements or as the mere sum of the parts.

The perception itself shows a character of totality, a form, a Gestalt, which in the very attempt at analysis is destroyed; and this experience, as directly given, sets the problem for psychology. It is this experience that presents the raw data which psychology must explain, and which it must never be content to explain away. To begin with elements is to begin at the wrong end; for elements are products of reflection and abstraction, remotely derived from the immediate experience they are invoked to explain. Gestalt psychology attempts to get back to naïve perception, to immediate experience "undebauched by learning"; and it insists that it finds there not assemblages of elements, but unified wholes; not masses of sensations, but trees, clouds, and sky. And this assertion it invites any one to verify simply by opening his eyes and looking at the world about him in his ordinary everyday way. (Heidbreder, 1933, p. 331)

Boring (1950b) commented that the word "Gestalt" has caused some difficulty because it does not clearly indicate—as does "functionalism" or "behaviorism"—what the movement stands for. Also, it has no exact English counterpart. Several equivalents are in common use (form, shape, configuration, for example), and in modern usage "Gestalt" has become part of the English language.

In *Gestalt Psychology* (1929) Köhler noted that the word was used in two ways in German. One usage denoted shape or form as a property of objects. In this sense, "Gestalt" refers to general properties that could be expressed in such terms as "angular" or "symmetrical." It describes characteristics such as triangularity (in geometrical figures) or temporal sequences (in a melody). The second usage denoted an entity that is concrete and has as one of its attributes a specific shape or form. In this sense, the word may refer, say, to triangles, rather than, as in the first usage, the notion of triangularity. Thus, the word is used for reference to objects rather than to the characteristic forms of these objects. In this sense, "Gestalt" refers to any segregated whole.

Finally, the use of the term is not restricted to the visual field or even to the total sensory field.

In fact, the concept "Gestalt" may be applied far beyond the limits of sensory experience. According to the most general functional definition of the term, the processes of learning, of recall, of striving, of emotional attitude, of thinking, acting, and so forth, may have to be included . . . . "Gestalt" in the meaning of shape is no longer the center of the Gestalt Psychologist's attention. (Köhler, 1947, pp. 178–179)

It is in this larger sense of the word that the Gestalt psychologists wanted to deal with the whole province of psychology, in terms of *Gestalten*.

ORIGINAL SOURCE MATERIAL ON GESTALT PSYCHOLOGY: FROM *GESTALT THEORY* BY MAX WERTHEIMER

The following article is a lecture presented by Max Wertheimer to the Kant Society in Berlin on December 17, 1924.[6] Ranging from psychology and mathematics to philosophy and the social sciences, Wertheimer pointed out the differences between a Gestalt (whole) approach and an approach involving the reduction of the subject matter to elements. The lecture demonstrates the basic conflict between these two divergent views of the world, as represented in psychology by Wertheimer and by Wundt.

What is Gestalt theory and what does it intend? . . .

The fundamental "formula" of Gestalt theory might be expressed in this way: There are wholes, the behaviour of which is not determined by that of their individual elements, but where the part-processes are themselves determined by the intrinsic nature of the whole. It is the hope of Gestalt theory to determine the nature of such wholes.

With a formula such as this, one might close, for Gestalt theory is neither more nor less than this. It is not interested in puzzling out philosophic questions which such a formula might suggest. Gestalt theory has to do with concrete research; it is not only an *outcome* but a *device*: not only a theory *about* results but a means toward further discoveries. This is not merely the proposal of one or more problems but an attempt to see what is really taking place in science. This problem cannot be solved by listing possibilities for systematization, classification, and arrangement. If it is to be attacked at all, we must be guided by the spirit of the new method and by the concrete nature of the things themselves which we are studying, and set ourselves to penetrate to that which is really given by nature.

There is another difficulty that may be illustrated by the following example. Suppose a mathematician shows you a proposition and you begin to "classify" it. This proposition, you say, is of such and such type, belongs in this or that historical category, and so on. Is that how the mathematician works?

"Why, you haven't grasped the thing at all," the mathematician will exclaim. "See here, this formula is not an independent, closed fact that can be dealt with for itself alone. You must see its dynamic *functional* relationship to the whole from which it was lifted or you will never understand it."

[6] From M. Wertheimer, "Gestalt Theory." In W. D. Ellis (Ed.), *A Source Book of Gestalt Psychology.* (London: Routledge & Kegan Paul, 1938; New York: Humanities Press, Inc., 1967), pp. 1–11. (Footnotes omitted.)

What holds for the mathematical formula applies also to the "formula" of Gestalt theory. The attempt of Gestalt theory to disclose the functional meaning of its own formula is no less strict than is the mathematician's. The attempt to explain Gestalt theory in a short essay is the more difficult because of the terms which are used: part, whole, intrinsic determination. All of them have in the past been the topic of endless discussions where each disputant has understood them differently. And even worse has been the cataloguing attitude adopted toward them. What they *lacked* has been actual research. Like many another "philosophic" problem they have been withheld from contact with reality and scientific work.

About all I can hope for in so short a discussion is to suggest a few of the problems which at present occupy the attention of Gestalt theory and something of the way they are being attacked.

To repeat: the *problem* has not merely to do with scientific work—it is a fundamental problem of our times. Gestalt theory is not something suddenly and unexpectedly dropped upon us from above; it is, rather, a palpable convergence of problems ranging throughout the sciences and the various philosophic standpoints of modern times.

Let us take, for example, an event in the history of psychology. One turned from a living experience to science and asked what it had to say about this experience, and one found an assortment of elements, sensations, images, feelings, acts of will and laws governing these elements—and was told, "Take your choice, reconstruct from them the experience you had." Such procedure led to difficulties in concrete psychological research and to the emergence of problems which defied solution by the traditional analytic methods. Historically the most important impulse came from v. Ehrenfels who raised the following problem. Psychology had said that experience is a compound of elements: we hear a melody and then, upon hearing it again, memory enables us to recognize it. But what is it that enables us to recognize the melody when it is played in a new key? The sum of the elements is different, yet the melody is the same; indeed, one is often not even aware that a transposition has been made.

When in retrospect we consider the prevailing situation we are struck by two aspects of v. Ehrenfels's thesis; on the one hand one is surprised at the essentially summative character of his theory, on the other one admires his courage in propounding and defending his proposition. Strictly interpreted v. Ehrenfels's position was this: I play a familiar melody of six tones and employ six *new* tones, yet you recognize the melody despite the change. There must be a something *more* than the sum of six tones, viz. a seventh something, which is the form-quality, the *Gestaltqualität*, of the original six. It is this *seventh* factor or element which enabled you to recognize the melody despite its transposition.

However strange this view may seem, it shares with many another subsequently abandoned hypothesis the honour of having clearly seen and emphasized a fundamental problem

But other explanations were also proposed. One maintained that in addition to the six tones there were intervals—relations—and that *these* were what remained constant. In other words we are asked to assume not only elements but "relations-between-elements" as additional components of the total complex. But this view failed to account for the phenomenon because in some cases the relations *too* may be altered without destroying the original melody.

Another type of explanation, also designed to bolster the elementaristic hypothesis, was that *to* this total of six or more tones there come certain "higher processes" which operate upon the given material to "*produce*" unity.

This was the situation until Gestalt theory raised the radical question: Is it really true that when I hear a melody I have a *sum* of individual tones (pieces) which constitute the primary foundation of my experience? Is not perhaps the reverse of this true? What I really have, what I hear of each individual note, what I experience at each place in the melody is a *part* which is itself determined by the character of the whole. What is given me by the melody does not arise (through the agency of any auxiliary factor) as a *secondary* process from the sum of the pieces as such. Instead, what takes place in each single part already depends upon what the whole is. The flesh and blood of a tone depends from the start upon its role in the melody. . . . It belongs to the flesh and blood of the things given in experience (*Gegebenheiten*), how, in what role, in what function they are in their whole.

Let us leave the melody example and turn to another field. Take the case of threshold phenomena. It has long been held that a certain stimulus necessarily produces a certain sensation. Thus, when two stimuli are sufficiently different, the sensations also will be different. Psychology is filled with careful inquiries regarding threshold phenomena. To account for the difficulties constantly being encountered it was assumed that these phenomena must be influenced by higher mental functions, judgments, illusions, attention, etc. And this continued until the radical question was raised: Is it really true that a specific stimulus *always* gives rise to the same sensation? Perhaps the prevailing whole-conditions will themselves determine the effect of stimulation? This kind of formulation leads to experimentation, and experiments show, for example, that when I see two colours the sensations I have are determined by the whole-conditions of the entire stimulus situation. Thus, also, the same local *physical* stimulus pattern can give rise to either a unitary and homogeneous figure, or to an articulated figure with different parts, all depending upon the whole-conditions which may favour either unity or articulation.

Obviously the task, then, is to investigate these "whole-conditions" and discover what influences they exert upon experience. . . .

Our next point is that my field comprises also my Ego. There is not from the beginning an Ego over-against others, but the genesis of an Ego offers one of the most fascinating problems, the solution of which seems to lie in Gestalt principles. However, once constituted, the Ego is a functional part of the total field. Proceeding as before we may therefore ask: What happens to the Ego as a part of the field? Is the resulting behaviour the piecewise sort of thing associationism, experience theory, and the like, would have us believe? Experimental results contradict this interpretation and again we often find that the laws of whole-processes operative in such a field tend toward a meaningful behaviour of its parts.

This field is not a summation of sense data and no description of it which considers such separate pieces to be *primary* will be correct. If it were, then for children, primitive peoples and animals experience would be nothing but piece-sensations. The next most developed creatures would have, in addition to independent sensations, something higher, and so on. But this whole picture is the opposite of what actual inquiry has disclosed. We have learned to recognize the "sensations" of our textbooks as products of a late culture utterly different from the experiences of more primitive stages. Who experiences the sensation of a specific red in that sense? What the man of the streets, children, or primitive men normally react to is something coloured but at the same time exciting, gay, strong, or affecting—*not* "sensations."

The programme to treat the organism as a part in a larger field necessitates the reformulation of the problem as to the relation between organism and environment. The stimulus–sensation connection must be replaced by a connection between alteration in the field conditions, the vital situation, and the total reaction of the organism by a change in its attitude, striving, and feeling.

There is, however, another step to be considered. A man is not only a part of his field, he is also one among other men. When a group of people work together it rarely occurs, and then only under very special conditions, that they constitute a mere sum of independent Egos. Instead the common enterprise often becomes their mutual concern and each works *as* a meaningfully functioning part of the whole. Consider a group of South Sea Islanders engaged in some community occupation, or a group of children playing together. Only under very special circumstances does an "I" stand out alone. Then the balance which obtained during harmonious and systematic occupation may be upset and give way to a surrogate (under certain conditions, pathological) *new* balance. . . .

The fundamental question can be very simply stated: Are the parts of a given whole determined by the inner structure of that whole, or are the events such that, as independent, piecemeal, fortuitous and blind the total activity is a sum of the part-activities? Human beings can, of course, *devise* a kind of physics of their own—e.g., a sequence of machines—exemplifying the latter half of our question, but this does not signify that *all natural* phenomena are of this type. Here is a place where Gestalt theory is least easily understood and this because of the great number of prejudices about nature which have accumulated during the centuries. Nature is thought of as something essentially blind in its laws, where whatever takes place in the whole is purely a sum of individual occurrences. This view was the natural result of the struggle which physics has always had to purge itself of teleology. Today it can be seen that we are obliged to traverse other routes than those suggested by this kind of purposivism.

Let us proceed another step and ask: How does all this stand with regard to the problem of body and mind? What does my knowledge of another's mental experiences amount to and how do I obtain it? There are, of course, old and established dogmas on these points: The mental and physical are wholly heterogeneous: there obtains between them an absolute dichotomy. (From this point of departure philosophers have drawn an array of metaphysical deductions so as to attribute all the good qualities to mind while reserving for nature the odious.) As regards the second question, my discerning mental phenomena in others is traditionally explained as inference by analogy. Strictly interpreted the principle here is that something mental is meaninglessly coupled with something physical. I observe the physical and infer the mental from it more or less according to the following scheme: I see someone press a button on the wall and infer that he wants the light to go on. There *may be* couplings of this sort. However, many scientists have been disturbed by this dualism and have tried to save themselves by recourse to very curious hypotheses. Indeed, the ordinary person would violently refuse to believe that when he sees his companion startled, frightened, or angry he is seeing only certain physical occurrences which themselves have nothing to do (in their inner nature) with the mental, being only superficially coupled with it: you have frequently seen this and this combined . . . etc. There have been many attempts to surmount this problem. One speaks, for example, of *intuition* and says there can be no other possibility, for I *see* my companion's fear. It is not true, argue the intuitionists, that I see only the bare bodily activities meaninglessly coupled with other and invisible activities. However inadmissible it may otherwise be, an intuition theory does have at least this in its favour, it shows a suspicion that the traditional procedure might be successfully reversed. But the word intuition is at best only a *naming* of that which we must strive to lay hold of.

This and other hypotheses, apprehended as they now are, will not advance scientific pursuit, for science demands fruitful penetration, not mere cataloguing and systematization. But the question is, How does the matter really stand? Looking more closely we find a third

Original Source Material on Gestalt Psychology

assumption, namely that a process such as fear is a matter of consciousness. Is this true? Suppose you see a person who is kindly or benevolent. Does anyone suppose that this person is feeling mawkish? No one could possibly believe that. The characteristic feature of such behaviour has very little to do with consciousness. It has been one of the easiest contrivances of philosophy to identify a man's real behaviour and the direction of his mind with his consciousness. Parenthetically, in the opinion of many people the distinction between idealism and materialism implies that between the noble and the ignoble. Yet does one really mean by this to contrast consciousness with the blithesome budding of trees? Indeed, what is there so repugnant about the materialistic and mechanical? What is so attractive about the idealistic? Does it come from the *material* qualities of the connected pieces? Broadly speaking most psychological theories and textbooks, despite their continued emphasis upon consciousness, are far more "materialistic," arid, and spiritless than a living tree—which probably has no consciousness at all. The point is not what the material pieces are, but what *kind* of whole it is. Proceeding in terms of specific problems one soon realizes how many bodily activities there are which give no hint of a separation between body and mind. Imagine a dance, a dance full of grace and joy. What is the situation in such a dance? Do we have a summation of *physical* limb movements and a *psychical* consciousness? No. Obviously this answer does not solve the problem; we have to start anew—and it seems to me that a proper and fruitful point of attack has been discovered. One finds many processes which, in their dynamical form, are identical regardless of variations in the material character of their elements. When a man is timid, afraid or energetic, happy or sad, it can often be shown that the course of his physical processes is Gestalt-identical with the course pursued by the mental processes.

Again I can only indicate the direction of thought. I have touched on the question of body and mind merely to show that the problem we are discussing also has its philosophic aspects. . . .

This brings us to the close of an attempt to present a view of the problem as illustrated by its specific appearances in various fields. In concluding I may suggest a certain unification of these illustrations somewhat as follows. I consider the situation from the point of view of a theory of aggregates and say: How should a world be where science, concepts, inquiry, investigation, and comprehension of inner unities were impossible? The answer is obvious. This world would be a manifold of disparate pieces. Secondly, what kind of world would there have to be in which a piecewise science would apply? The answer is again quite simple, for here one needs only a system of recurrent couplings that are blind and piecewise in character, whereupon everything is available for a pursuit of the traditional piecewise methods of logic, mathematics, and science generally in so far as these presuppose this kind of world. But there is a third kind of aggregate which has been but cursorily investigated. These are the aggregates in which a manifold is not compounded from adjacently situated pieces but rather such that a term at its place in that aggregate is determined by the whole-laws of the aggregate itself.

Pictorially: suppose the world were a vast plateau upon which were many musicians. I walk about listening and watching the players. First suppose that the world is a meaningless plurality. Everyone does as he will, each for himself. What happens together when I hear ten players might be the basis for my guessing as to what they all are doing, but this is merely a matter of chance and probability much as in the kinetics of gas molecules.—A second possibility would be that each time one musician played c, another played f so and so many seconds later. I work out a theory of blind couplings but the playing as a whole remains meaningless. This is what many people think physics does, but the real work of physics belies this.—The third possibility is, say, a Beethoven symphony where it would be possible for one to select one part of the whole and work from that towards an idea of the structural principle motivating and determining the whole. Here the fundamental laws are not those of fortuitous pieces, but concern the very character of the event.

MAJOR PRINCIPLES OF GESTALT PSYCHOLOGY

Principles of Organization

Wertheimer's principles of perceptual organization were presented in a paper in 1923. Wertheimer took the position that we perceive objects in the same immediate and unified manner in which we perceive apparent motion—as unified wholes, not as clusters of individual sensations. His principles of organization, which are described in most modern psychology texts, are essentially rules or laws by which our perceptual world is organized.

A basic premise of Wertheimer's principles is that in perception, organization occurs instantly whenever we see or hear different shapes or patterns. Parts of the perceptual field become connected, and these groups or collections of parts unite to form structures that are distinct from the background. This perceptual organization is spontaneous and inevitable whenever we look around our environment. We do not have to learn to so organize, as the structuralists and associationists claimed, although higher-level perception, such as labeling an object by name, is, of course, more dependent on learning.

According to Gestalt theory, the primary brain process in visual perception is not a collection of small, separate activities but a dynamic system. The visual area of the brain does not respond in terms of separate elements of visual input, with these elements connected by a principle of association.

Rather, the brain is a dynamic system in which all elements active at a given time interact. Elements that are similar or close together tend to combine; elements that are dissimilar or far apart do not tend to combine.

Several of the principles of organization are listed here, and examples are given in Figure 12.1.

1. *Proximity:* Parts that are close together in time or space tend to be perceived together. For example, in Figure 12.1(a) the circles are seen in three columns rather than as one large collection.

2. *Similarity:* Similar parts tend to be seen together as forming a group (Figure 12.1(b)). Because the circles and the dots each appear to belong together, we tend to perceive rows instead of columns.

3. *Closure:* There is a tendency in our perception to complete incomplete figures, to fill in gaps. In Figure 12.1(c) we perceive three squares even though the figures are incomplete.

4. *Prägnanz:* There is a tendency to see a figure as being as "good" as possible under the stimulus conditions. A "good" figure is one that is symmetrical, simple, and stable, and that cannot be made simpler or more orderly.

Figure 12.1
Examples of perceptual organization.

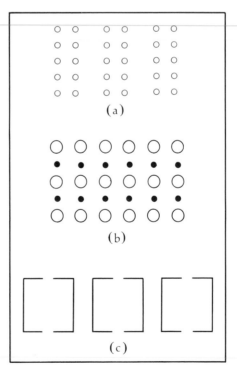

These organizing factors do not depend on the higher mental processes of the individual or on past experience. They are present in the stimuli themselves. Wertheimer stressed these "peripheral" factors, but also recognized that "central" factors (factors within the organism) can influence perception. For example, the factors of familiarity and set or attitude (higher mental processes) can influence perception. In general, however, the Gestaltists tended to concentrate on the more direct and primitive peripheral factors of perceptual organization rather than on the role of learning or experience.

Principles of Learning

Perception was an early focus of the Gestalt psychologists, and they took the position that learning plays only a small role in perceptual processes. It is not correct, however, to conclude that the topic of learning, considered independently of perception, received no attention from the Gestalt psychologists. Some of the most significant experiments in the history of psychology, experiments still cited in contemporary psychology books, are those devised by Köhler to study problem solving in apes.

From its beginning, Gestalt psychology opposed Thorndikian trial-and-error learning, and later, Watsonian stimulus–response learning. Members of the Gestalt school believed that one of their most important contributions to psychology was their consistent criticism of associationist and S–R theories of learning. The Gestalt view of learning is expressed in Köhler's work on apes and Wertheimer's work on productive thinking in humans.

The Mentality of Apes

We mentioned Köhler's confinement on the island of Tenerife during World War I, during which time he investigated the intelligence of chimpanzees as shown in their solving of problems. These studies were conducted in and around the animals' cages and involved simple props, such as the bars of the cages themselves (to block access), bananas, sticks for drawing the bananas into the cages, and boxes for climbing.

Congruent with the Gestalt view of perception, Köhler interpreted the results of his animal studies in terms of the whole situation and the relations between the various stimuli found therein. He considered problem solving a matter of restructuring the perceptual field.

In one of his studies a banana was placed outside the cage, and a string attached to the banana led into the cage. The apes pulled the banana into the cage with little hesitation. Köhler said that in this situation the problem was easily grasped as a whole by the animal. However, if several strings led from the cage in the general direction of the banana, the ape would not clearly recognize at first which string to pull. To Köhler, this indicated that the problem could not be envisioned clearly all at once.

A more explicit example involved placing a banana outside the cage just beyond the ape's reach. If a stick were placed near the bars of the cage (facing the banana), the stick and the banana would be seen as parts of the same situation and the ape would readily use the stick to pull in the banana. If the stick were placed at the back of the cage, the two objects would be less readily perceived as parts of the same situation. In this case, a restructuring of the perceptual field was necessary to solve the problem.

Another experiment involved positioning a banana outside the cage, beyond reach, and placing several hollow bamboo sticks inside the cage. Each stick by itself was too short to reach the banana. To solve this problem, the animal would have to push two sticks together (inserting the end of one into the end of the other) to produce a stick of sufficient length to reach the banana. Thus, the animal had to perceive a new relationship between the sticks.

Sultan, Köhler's brightest ape, failed when initially confronted with this problem. He first tried to get the banana with one stick. Next, he pushed a stick out as far as he could, then pushed it farther with a second stick until the first one touched the banana. Sultan did not succeed during a one-hour trial. Immediately after this trial, however, while playing with the sticks, Sultan solved the problem, as reported by his keeper.

> Sultan first of all squats indifferently on the box, which has been left standing a little back from the railings; then he gets up, picks up the two sticks, sits down again on the box and plays carelessly with them. While doing this, it happens that he finds himself holding one rod in either hand in such a way that they lie in a straight line; he pushes the thinner one a little way into the opening of the thicker, jumps up and is already on the run toward the railings, to which he has up to now half turned his back, and begins to draw a banana towards him with the double stick. I call the master: meanwhile, one of the animal's rods has fallen out of the other, as he has pushed one of them only a little way into the other; whereupon he connects them again. (Köhler, 1927, p. 127)

In later trials Sultan solved the problem without any difficulty, even when some of the sticks provided would not fit together. Köhler reported that Sultan did not even attempt to join these unsuitable sticks.

Studies such as these were interpreted by Köhler as evidence of *insight*— the apparently spontaneous seeing of relations.

> The solutions of such problems, when they came, appeared to come suddenly, as though a new "configuration," embracing the whole complicated means to the desired end, had suddenly sprung up in the animal's consciousness; it was exactly as though the appropriate action followed on a "flash of insight," and, as in the case of all insightful behavior, the insight remained a permanent possession, enabling its possessor to act at once appropriately on a subsequent occasion. (Flugel & West, 1964, p. 206)

This viewpoint differed dramatically from the trial-and-error learning described by Thorndike and others. Köhler was a vocal critic of Thorndike's work, arguing that his experimental arrangements were artificial and allowed for nothing but blind, random, trial-and-error behavior on the part of the animal. Köhler suggested that the cats in Thorndike's puzzle box, for instance, could not survey the entire release mechanism (all the elements pertaining to the whole), and thus could only engage in trial-and-error behavior. Similarly, an animal in a maze could not see the overall pattern or design. It could see nothing but each alley as it came to it, and so could do nothing but try each of these new paths. In the Gestalt view, the organism must be able to see the relationship among the various parts of the problem before insight can occur.

These studies of insight were used to support the Gestalt molar conception of behavior—as opposed to the molecular view of the associationists and behaviorists—and the Gestalt notion that learning involves a reorganization or restructuring of the psychological environment.

Productive Thinking

Wertheimer's book, *Productive Thinking* (1945), published posthumously, applied the Gestalt learning principles to human creative thinking and suggested that such thinking should be done in terms of wholes. Not only must the learner regard the situation as a whole, but the teacher must also present the situation as a whole, not, like Thorndike, hiding the solution and thus, in a sense, requiring the person to make errors.

The case material in this book ranged from the study of children solving geometrical problems to the study of Einstein's thought processes that led to the theory of relativity. (Wertheimer and Einstein were close friends for a number of years.) At all ages and levels of problem difficulty Wertheimer found evidence to support the notion that the whole problem must dominate the parts. He believed that the detailed aspects of a problem should be considered only in relation to the structure of the total situation, and that problem solving should proceed from the whole problem downward to the parts, not the reverse.

Wertheimer believed that if a teacher arranged problems so that elements of classroom exercises were organized into meaningful wholes, then insight could occur. He also demonstrated that once the principle of a problem's solution had been grasped, it was readily transferred to other situations.

Wertheimer attacked the traditional educational practice of mechanical drills and rote learning, which derived from the associationist theory of learning. Blind repetition is rarely productive, he argued, and he cited as evidence the student's inability to solve a variation of a problem when the solution had been learned by rote rather than by insight. He did agree, however, that some material, such as names and dates, should be learned in rote fashion through association strengthened by repetition. He believed that repetition was useful to a point, but that its habitual use could produce mechanical performance rather than truly creative or productive thinking.

The Principle of Isomorphism

Having established that perceptions are organized wholes, the Gestalt psychologists turned to the problem of the cortical mechanisms involved in perception and attempted to develop a theory of the underlying neurological correlates of perceived *Gestalten*. The Gestalt view of the cortex as a dynamic system, in which the elements active at a given time interact, contrasts with the so-called machine conception of the nervous system, which likens nervous activity to a telephone switchboard that mechanically links the sensory elements received via associationist principles. In the latter view, the brain functions passively and is not capable of actively organizing or modifying the sensory elements received. Also, this view of the brain implies a one-to-one correspondence between the perception and its neurological counterpart.

In his original research on apparent movement Wertheimer suggested that cortical activity is a configural whole process. Because apparent and actual motion are experienced identically, he argued, the cortical processes for actual and apparent motion must be similar. On the assumption that these two kinds of movement are identical, there must be corresponding brain processes. To account for the phi phenomenon, there must be a correspondence between the psychological or conscious experience and the underlying "brain experience."

This point of view has been called isomorphism: *"Experienced order in space is always structurally identical with a functional order in the distribution of underlying brain processes"* (Köhler, 1947, p. 61). According to the principle of isomorphism, there is no one-to-one correspondence between the stimulus and the perception. It is the form of the perceptual experience that corresponds to the form of the stimulus. Thus, *Gestalten* are indeed representations of the real world, but not perfect reproductions of it. A percept is not a literal copy of the stimulus, just as a map is not a literal copy of the terrain it represents. The percept, however, like the map, is identical (*iso*) in form or shape (*morphic*) to that which it represents, so that it does serve as a reliable guide to the perceived real world. This view was supported by the three principal Gestaltists and is associated with the Gestalt school.

The position was extended by Köhler in his 1920 book, *Static and Stationary Physical Gestalts*. He considered that cortical processes behave in a manner similar to fields of electrical force, and suggested that like the behavior of an electromagnetic field of force around a magnet, fields of neuronal activity may be established by electromechanical processes in the brain in response to sensory impulses. He conducted an extensive research program to investigate various aspects of the concept of isomorphism and cortical brain fields. To Köhler, the notion of isomorphism was but one phase of an ambitious undertaking to demonstrate that physics, chemistry, and biology, as well as psychology, all involve *Gestalten*.

POSTFOUNDING DEVELOPMENTS

The Spread of Gestalt Psychology

By the mid-1920s the Gestalt movement was a strongly united, coherent, and forceful school in Germany. It was centered at the Psychological Institute of the University of Berlin, where it attracted large numbers of students from many countries. The Gestalt journal *Psychologische Forschung* was very active, and researchers were investigating various psychological problems.

After 1933 and the rise to power of the Nazis, the rampant anti-intellectualism and repression in Germany caused the leaders of Gestalt psychology to leave the country. The movement was reduced to a minor position in the German academic system of the day. Some work in the Gestalt tradition went on, but it had been diluted. Several areas of applied psychology using theories of wholeness (such as graphology, the study of handwriting), did play a role in clinical assessment, and personality testing based on derivatives of Gestalt theory was used extensively in German psychological warfare. On the whole, however, the years of Nazi domination were sterile for German psychology in general. Gestalt psychology has shown a renewed vitality since the 1950s as part of the vigorous resurgence of interest in psychology in West Germany.

When Gestalt psychology migrated to the United States, it first met with a less than enthusiastic response. Its progress was comparatively slow for several reasons. Behaviorism was at the peak of its popularity in American psychology and was difficult, if not impossible, to overcome. Another problem was the language barrier, which delayed dissemination of the Gestalt principles. And, as noted, many American psychologists believed (incorrectly, as it turned out) that Gestalt psychology dealt only with perception. Also, Wertheimer, Koffka, and Köhler all taught at American colleges that lacked graduate programs, so it was difficult for them to attract disciples (Henle, 1977).

The most important reason, however, for the relatively slow initial acceptance of Gestalt psychology in the United States was that American psychology had already advanced far beyond structuralism; behaviorism was already the second phase of American opposition to structuralism. Hence, American psychology was much further removed from Wundtian elementism than was European psychology at that time. As far as American psychologists were concerned, the Gestaltists had come to America protesting something that was a dead issue. This is a dangerous situation; recall that movements need something to oppose, something to push against, if they are to survive.

When the Gestaltists became familiar with the trend in the United States, they readily perceived a new target, behaviorism, with its reductionist and atomistic tendencies. The Gestaltists argued that behaviorism, like structuralism, dealt with artificial abstractions. It made little difference, they said, whether analysis was in terms of introspective reduction to elements (Wundt) or objective reduction to conditioned reflexes (Watson). The result is the same—a molecular instead of a molar approach.

The Gestalt psychologists also took issue with the behaviorists' denial of the validity of introspection and their elimination of consciousness. Although the Gestaltists did not use Wundtian introspection, they favored the study of direct conscious experience.

Gradually, in spite of these many obstacles, the doctrines and principles of Gestalt psychology came to be used in child psychology, applied psychology, psychiatry, education, anthropology, and sociology. In addition, certain clinical psychologists began to combine the Gestalt approach with that of psychoanalysis.

According to Murphy and Kovach (1972), the general tendency in the United States has been to consider the principles of Gestalt psychology interesting and potentially useful additions to other systems, but not as the basis of an all-encompassing system. American psychology has attempted to demonstrate that both elemental and organized responses occur, and that both are useful.

For many psychologists, the Gestalt view is still an ongoing concern, and it continues to promote substantial research. It no longer enjoys the combative spirit of a revolution, but many of its adherents are working to elaborate and refine its basic points. This activity indicates that Gestalt psychology has not been totally accepted into the mainstream of American psychology. "In America, Gestalt psychology has always been a minority movement." (Henle, 1977, p. 3) Although Gestalt psychology retains much of its separateness, it has exerted a visible influence on many areas of psychology, including work in perception, thinking, learning, personality, social psychology, and motivation.

Field Theory: Kurt Lewin
(1890–1947)

The trend in nineteenth-century science was to think in terms of field relationships and to move away from an atomistic and elementistic framework. As we have seen, Wertheimer and Gestalt psychology reflected this trend. The concept of field theory arose within psychology as an analogy to the concept of fields of force in physics.

In psychology the term *field theory* has come to refer almost exclusively to the work of Kurt Lewin, an active disciple of Gestalt psychology.[7] Lewin's position in relation to Gestalt psychology, however, is not clear-cut. Although he is sometimes classed as a member of the Gestalt school, he is equally regarded as the developer of a separate but related system. He began work independently, but was later associated with Köhler and Wertheimer at the center of the Gestalt movement at Berlin. In his career he went well beyond the framework of the orthodox Gestalt position.

Lewin's work is Gestalt in orientation, but it centers on needs, personality, and social factors, whereas the Gestaltists emphasized perception and learning. Whereas the Gestaltists stressed physiological constructs to attempt to explain behavior, Lewin considered psychology as more of a social science. It is simplest to consider Lewin's system as an elaboration or outgrowth of the Gestalt movement for two reasons: (a) he was closely associated with the Gestaltists at Berlin for a time, and (b) his position fits the Gestalt system more readily than any other system.

Lewin was born in Mogilno, Germany, undertook his university education at Freiburg, Munich, and Berlin, and received his Ph.D. from Berlin in psychology in 1914. He also studied mathematics and physics. After a period of military service, for which he was awarded the Iron Cross, he returned to the University of Berlin, where he became such a productive and creative member of the Gestalt group that he was considered a colleague of the three senior Gestaltists. He performed important research on association and motivation and began to develop his field theory.

He was already well known in the United States when, in 1932, he spent six months as visiting professor at Stanford. In 1933 he decided to leave Germany permanently because of the Nazi menace. He spent two years at Cornell and in 1935 went to the University of Iowa, where he conducted a series of studies in the experimental social psychology of the child. As a result of his research efforts in social psychology, he was invited to develop and head the new Research Center for Group Dynamics at the Massachusetts Institute of Technology in 1944. Although he died shortly after (in 1947), his program was so effective that the research center remains active, now located at the University of Michigan.

Throughout his 30 years of professional activity Lewin devoted himself consistently to the broadly defined area of human motivation. His research emphasized the study of human behavior in its total physical and social context.

Field theory in physics led Lewin to consider that the psychological activities of a person occur in a kind of psychological field or *life space*. The life space comprises all the events that may possibly influence a person—past, present and future. From a psychological standpoint, each of these three aspects of life can determine behavior in any single situation. The life

---

[7] Tolman's system (Chapter 11) is often considered a field theory. We noted his attempt to combine parts of behaviorism and Gestalt psychology.

space consists of the needs of the individual as they interact with the psychological environment.

The life space may show varying degrees of differentiation as a function of the amount and kind of experience the individual has accumulated. Because it lacks experiences, an infant has few, if any, differentiated regions in its life space. A highly educated, sophisticated adult shows a complex and well-differentiated life space as a function of his or her past experiences.

Lewin wanted to use a mathematical model to represent his theoretical concept of psychological processes. Because he was concerned with the single case, statistics were not useful for his purpose. He chose a form of geometry—topology—that he felt was adequate to the task of mapping the life space to show at any given moment all possible goals of an individual and all the routes to these goals. Topology treats transformations in space by representing spatial relationships in nonquantitative fashion. It is a conception of space that deals with the order of relationships, but not with their direction or distance. It can show connections among regions within the life space and their spatial relationships to one another. To represent direction, Lewin developed a new form of qualitative geometry called *hodological space*, in which he used vectors to represent directions of movement toward a goal. To complete the schematic representation of his system, Lewin introduced the notion of *valences* to refer to the positive or negative value of objects within the life space. Objects that are attractive to the individual or that satisfy needs have positive valence; objects that are threatening have negative valence.

Lewin postulated a state of equilibrium between the person and the environment. When this equilibrium is disturbed, a tension (Lewin's concept of motivation or need) arises that leads to locomotion in the attempt to restore the equilibrium. Lewin believed that human behavior involves the continual appearance of tensions, locomotions, and reliefs. This sequence of tension–locomotion–equilibrium is akin to need–activity–relief. Whenever a need is felt, a state of tension exists, and the organism acts to release the tension by restoring the equilibrium.

Lewin's "blackboard psychology" included complex diagrams representing all manner of psychological phenomena. In field theory all forms of behavior can be represented schematically. A simple example of a bit of behavior as it would be represented in Lewin's system is shown in Figure 12.2, which illustrates a situation in which a child wants to go to the movies but is forbidden to do so by his or her parents. The ellipse represents the life space and C represents the child. The arrow is a vector indicating that C is motivated to go to the movie, which, as indicated, has positive valence. The vertical line is the barrier (the parents) to the goal and is shown to have negative valence. (This is a simplified example and is not typical of the highly complex psychological phenomena that Lewin was able to represent through his topological and hodological space.)

Lewin's theoretical system generated a great deal of important research.

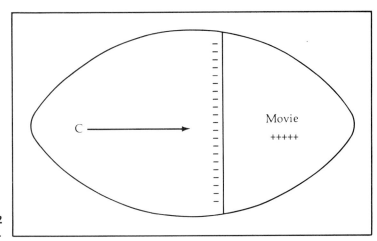

Figure 12.2
Example of a life space.

One series of studies involved his assumption of a *tension-system*. Tension means motivation or need, and Lewin believed that when a goal is reached, the tension is discharged. The first experimental attempt to test this tension-system proposition was performed, under Lewin's supervision, by Bluma Zeigarnik in 1927. Subjects were given a series of tasks and allowed to complete some of them, but were interrupted before they could complete others. From Lewin's system it could be predicted that: (1) a tension-system develops in a subject when he or she is given a task to perform, (2) when the task is completed, the tension is dissipated, (3) when the task is not completed, the persistence of the tension results in greater likelihood of recall of the task. Zeigarnik's results confirmed the predictions in that the subjects recalled the uncompleted tasks more easily than they recalled the completed ones. Much subsequent research has been performed on this phenomenon, which has come to be known as the *Zeigarnik effect*.

The Influence of Lewin on Social Psychology

In the early years of his career Lewin was chiefly concerned with theoretical problems and issues. By the late 1930s, however, he became interested in social psychology, and his pioneering efforts in this field alone are sufficient to justify his position in the history of psychology. It is probably no exaggeration to state that social psychology in America is "a Lewinian development" (Marx & Hillix, 1979, p. 322). Some of today's prominent social psychologists were associated with Lewin, either as students or as colleagues at the Research Center for Group Dynamics at MIT—for example, Dorwin Cartwright, Leon Festinger, J. P. French, Harold H. Kelley, Rensis Likert, Stanley Schacter, and Alvin Zander.

Perhaps the outstanding feature of Lewin's social psychology is *group dynamics*, the application of concepts dealing with the individual and group behavior. Just as the individual and his or her environment form a psychological field, the group and its environment form a social field. Social behaviors are seen as occurring in and resulting from simultaneously existing social entities, such as subgroups, members, barriers, and channels of communication. Thus, group behavior is a function of the total field situation at any given time.

Lewin's early social-psychological research was concerned with behavior in various social climates. A classic experiment in social psychology involves democratic and authoritarian leadership and its effects on the productiveness and general behavior of groups of boys (Lewin, Lippitt, & White, 1939). Studies such as this opened up important new areas of social research and contributed to the rapid growth of social psychology.

Lewin stressed the importance of "social action" research—the study of relevant social problems with a view to introducing change. He was greatly concerned with racial conflicts, and conducted studies in the community on the effects of integrated housing on prejudice, on equalizing opportunity for employment, and on the development and prevention of prejudice in children. His interest was the realities of everyday life, and his social action research transformed real-world problems such as prejudice into controlled experiments so as to benefit from the rigor of the experimental approach without the artificiality and sterility of the academic laboratory.

A year before his death Lewin was instrumental in developing what is now called *sensitivity training*. The T-groups (training groups) set up in his National Training Laboratories were the beginning of a movement later characterized by encounter groups. Sensitivity training has been applied with great zeal in many situations from industry to education, from reducing intergroup conflict to developing individual potential.

In general, Lewin's experimental programs and research findings are more acceptable to psychologists than are his theoretical views. In spite of this, his influence in social and child psychology—and, to some degree, in experimental psychology—is considerable. Many of his concepts and experimental techniques are widely used in the areas of personality and motivation. Lewin's influence did not end with his death. His concerns are being actively extended and elaborated upon in psychology today.

CRITICISMS OF GESTALT PSYCHOLOGY[8]

Criticisms of the Gestalt position appeared promptly. They included the major charge that the Gestaltists were trying to solve problems simply by

[8] The comments in this section refer only to the original Gestalt formulations, not to derivatives such as Lewinian field theory.

changing them into postulates. For example, organization of conscious perception was not treated as a problem requiring resolution, but as a "given," a phenomenon that exists in its own right. Critics argued that this is tantamount to solving a problem by denying its existence.

Many tough-minded scientists have asserted that the Gestalt position is vague. They have charged that some basic concepts and many terms (organization, for example) are not defined with sufficient rigor to be scientifically meaningful. If it were true that they used vague and ambiguous terms, the Gestaltists might not differ greatly in this respect from psychologists of other theoretical persuasions, including many behaviorists. The Gestalt psychologists countered these charges by insisting that in a young science attempts at explanations and definitions must necessarily be incomplete, but that being incomplete is not the same as being vague.

It was also claimed that the basic tenets of Gestalt psychology were not really new, which is, of course, true. The Gestalt movement, like the others we have discussed, had its anticipators. This issue, however, has no bearing on the relative merits of the Gestalt position.

Some critics allege that Gestalt psychology is too occupied with theory at the expense of experimental research and empirical supporting data. The Gestalt school has been heavily oriented toward theory, but since the time of its founders it has also stressed experimentation and has been both directly and indirectly responsible for a great deal of research.

Related to this point is the suggestion that the experimental work of the Gestaltists is inferior to that of S–R theorists in that it lacks adequate control of variables. The same critics argue that the Gestaltists' nonquantified data are not amenable to statistical analysis. The Gestaltists take the position that qualitative results must come first in the investigation of a problem area, so much of their research has deliberately been less quantitative than psychologists of other orientations consider necessary. Much Gestalt research has been preliminary and exploratory, investigating new problem areas or older areas from a different point of view.

A final criticism relates to what some consider the poorly supported and defined physiological assumptions of the system. The Gestaltists admit that their theorizing in this area is tentative, but they add that such speculation is a useful adjunct to any system. In this case, it has generated a great deal of research, and the validity of the results has not been lessened by the speculative framework within which the research was conducted.

CONTRIBUTIONS OF GESTALT PSYCHOLOGY

The Gestalt movement has unquestionably left an indelible imprint on psychology. Like other movements that challenged traditional views, it had a refreshing and stimulating effect on psychology as a whole.

The Gestalt point of view has greatly influenced the area of perception and, to some extent, learning. Its impact on the study of perception is evident in contemporary psychology textbooks. More recent work deriving from the Gestalt school strongly suggests that the movement is still vital.

Unlike its chief temporal competitor, behaviorism, Gestalt psychology remains a separate entity in that its major tenets have not been fully absorbed into the mainstream of psychological thought. It continues to foster interest in conscious experience as a legitimate problem for at least part of psychology. This focus on conscious experience is not of the Wundt–Titchener introspective variety, but centers on a modern version of phenomenology. Contemporary adherents of the Gestalt position are convinced that conscious experience does occur and must be studied. They recognize, however, that it cannot be investigated with the same precision and objectivity as overt behavior. Contemporary proponents of a phenomenological psychology are numerous in Europe and the point of view seems to be gaining support in the United States. Although phenomenology is not yet widely accepted in America, psychologists are becoming more familiar with it, and its influence can be seen in the humanistic psychology movement (see Chapter 15).

Finally, the pointed and consistent criticisms of current systems offered by Gestalt psychology have been influential by demanding a thorough reexamination of opposing positions.

SUGGESTED READINGS

WERTHEIMER

Asch, S. E. Max Wertheimer's contribution to modern psychology. *Social Research*, 1946, *13*, 81–102.

Köhler, W. Max Wertheimer, 1880–1943. *Psychological Review*, 1944, *51*, 143–146.

KOFFKA

Köhler, W. Kurt Koffka. *Psychological Review*, 1942, *49*, 97–101.

KÖHLER

Crannell, C. W. Wolfgang Köhler. *Journal of the History of the Behavioral Sciences*, 1970, *6*, 267–268.

Henle, M. (Ed.). *The selected papers of Wolfgang Köhler.* New York: Liveright, 1971.

Henle, M. One man against the Nazis—Wolfgang Köhler. *American Psychologist*, 1978, *33*, 939–944.

Köhler, W. Gestalt psychology. In D. Krantz (Ed.), *Schools of psychology.* New York: Appleton, 1969. Pp. 69–85.

Prentice, W. C. H. The systematic psychology of Wolfgang Köhler. In S. Koch (Ed.), *Psychology: A study of a science* (Vol. 1). New York: McGraw-Hill, 1959. Pp. 427–455.

LEWIN

Eng, E. Looking back on Kurt Lewin: From field theory to action research. *Journal of the History of the Behavioral Sciences*, 1978, *14*, 228–232.

Frank, J. D. Kurt Lewin in retrospect—a psychiatrist's view. *Journal of the History of the Behavioral Sciences*, 1978, *14*, 223–227.

Lewin, K. *Field theory in social science.* New York: Harper, 1951.

Marrow, A. *The practical theorist: The life and work of Kurt Lewin.* New York: Basic Books, 1969.

PHENOMENOLOGY

Combs, A. W., & Snygg, D. *Individual behavior: A perceptual approach to behavior* (Rev. ed.). New York: Harper, 1959.

Wann, T. W. (Ed.). *Behaviorism and phenomenology: Contrasting bases for modern psychology.* Chicago: University of Chicago Press, 1964.

GENERAL

Ellis, W. D. *A source book of Gestalt psychology.* New York: Humanities Press, 1967.

Heider, F. Gestalt theory: Early history and reminiscences. *Journal of the History of the Behavioral Sciences*, 1970, *6*, 131–139.

Helson, H. Why did their precursors fail and the Gestalt Psychologists succeed? *American Psychologist*, 1969, *24*, 1006–1011.

Henle, M. (Ed.). *Documents of Gestalt psychology.* Berkeley: University of California Press, 1961.

Henle, M. The influence of Gestalt psychology in America. *Annals of the New York Academy of Sciences*, 1977, *291*, 3–12.

Henle, M. Gestalt psychology and Gestalt therapy. *Journal of the History of the Behavioral Sciences*, 1978, *14*, 23–32. (Argues that Perls's Gestalt therapy "has *no* substantive relation to scientific Gestalt psychology.")

Hochberg, J. Effects of the Gestalt revolution: The Cornell symposium on perception. *Psychological Review*, 1957, *64*, 73–84.

Katz, D. *Gestalt psychology.* New York: Ronald Press, 1950.

Köhler, W. Gestalt psychology today. In E. Hilgard (Ed.), *American psychology in historical perspective: Addresses of the presidents of the American Psychological Association.* Washington, D.C.: APA, 1978. Pp. 251–263.

Mandler, J. M., & Mandler, G. The diaspora of experimental psychology: The Gestaltists and others. In D. Fleming & B. Bailyn (Eds.), *The intellectual migration: Europe and America, 1930–1960.* Cambridge, MA: Harvard University Press, 1969. Pp. 371–419.

PSYCHOANALYSIS: THE BEGINNINGS

INTRODUCTION

The term *psychoanalysis* and the name Sigmund Freud are familiar to most literate people. Although other prominent figures in the history of psychology—Fechner, Wundt, or Titchener, for example—are little known outside professional psychology, Freud enjoys phenomenal popularity, although his system may be known to the lay public only superficially and inaccurately. It is often a source of disappointment to teachers of psychology to find that so many beginning students believe that Freud *is* psychology, and that psychology deals only with the treatment of the mentally disturbed.

Chronologically, psychoanalysis overlapped to a considerable degree the other schools of psychology with which we have dealt. Consider the situation in 1895, the year in which Freud published his first book, marking the formal beginning of his new movement. In that year Wundt was 63 years old and Titchener, just 28, had been at Cornell only two years; structuralism was still a vital system. The spirit of functionalism was beginning to grow in the United States, but it had not yet been formalized into a school. Neither behaviorism nor Gestalt psychology had begun; Watson was then 17 and Wertheimer 15.

Yet by the time of Freud's death in 1939, the entire psychological outlook had changed. Structuralism and functionalism were history, Gestalt psychology was being vigorously transplanted to the United States, and behaviorism had become the dominant American form of psychology. Not only had Freud achieved prominence, but his position had already splintered into subschools and derivative movements.

The relationship between psychoanalysis and the other schools of psychology we have discussed was only temporal. There was no substantive link, either through assent or dissent, between Freud and the other founders in psychology.

The other schools owed their impetus and form to structuralism, either evolving from it, as was the case with functionalism, or revolting against it, as with behaviorism and Gestalt psychology. In contrast, psychoanalysis was not directly related to these evolutionary and revolutionary movements because psychoanalysis did not originate within academic psychology.

Freud's study of personality and its disturbances was far removed from the psychology of the university laboratory.

Regardless of their fundamental disagreements, the other systems shared an academic heritage; all of these schools formed their basic concepts and approaches in a milieu of laboratories, libraries, and lecture halls. Their traditional concerns were topics such as perception, sensation, and learning. They were, or strove to be, pure science. Psychoanalysis was neither a product of academe nor a pure science. Further, it was not (and is not) a school or systematic theory of psychology directly comparable to the others.

Psychoanalysis has not been concerned with traditional areas of psychology primarily because its goal is to provide therapy for emotionally disturbed persons. In aim, subject matter, and method, psychoanalysis diverged from the mainstream of psychological thought from the beginning. Its subject matter is abnormal behavior, which had been relatively neglected by the other schools, and its method is clinical observation instead of controlled laboratory experimentation. Also, psychoanalysis deals with the unconscious, a topic virtually ignored by the other schools of thought in psychology.

Despite its radically different nature, psychoanalysis has exerted an undeniable influence on contemporary psychology. Other areas—the social sciences, literature, language, religion, philosophy, ethics, and the arts—have also felt its impact. We shall see, however, that its acceptance by academic psychology has been, for the most part, less than enthusiastic.

ANTECEDENT INFLUENCES

Despite the claims of some of his followers, Freud's insights were not without anticipators. The psychoanalytic movement had definite intellectual and cultural antecedents. Two major sources of influence led to the formal founding of psychoanalysis. One was the early philosophical speculation on the nature of unconscious psychological phenomena, and the other was the work in psychopathology.

Early Theories of the Unconscious

We have noted that most of the early history of scientific psychology was concerned with consciousness. The experimental psychologists of the late nineteenth century were convinced that the only proper field of study was the content of consciousness, and thus the main focus of work in these early years of psychology was the analysis of conscious experience. There was little consideration of unconscious determinants of behavior. As well, the empirical philosophers provided for the new psychology a background oriented toward conscious experience. However, not everyone who pioneered the new psychology or its antecedent philosophy agreed with this exclusive focus on conscious mental content. Some did believe in the importance of nonconscious processes. Although the influence of the unconscious can be traced to Plato, we will consider more recent thought.

In the early eighteenth century the German mathematician and philosopher Gottfried Wilhelm Leibnitz (1646–1716) developed his theory of *mon-*

The theory of monadology proposed by Gottfried Wilhelm Leibnitz (1646–1716) was an early attempt to explain unconscious processes.
(National Library of Medicine)

adology. Monads, which Leibnitz considered the individual elements of all reality, were not physical atoms; they were not even material in the usual sense of the word. Each monad was an unextended psychic entity. Leibnitz insisted that although each monad was mental in nature, it had some of the properties of physical matter; when enough of them were collected into an aggregate, they created an extension.

Monads were centers of activity and energy. In general terms, they could be likened to perception and are similar to consciousness. Leibnitz believed that mental events (the activity of monads) had differing degrees of clearness or consciousness, which could range from the completely unconscious to the most clear or definitely conscious. Thus, there were lesser degrees of consciousness, called *petites perceptions*. The conscious actualization of these was called *apperception*.

For example, the sound of waves breaking on the shore is an apperception. This apperception is composed of all the falling drops of water. The individual drop of water, like the monad, is the *petite perception* and is not consciously perceived by itself. When sufficient numbers of them congregate, however, they summate to produce an apperception.

A century later Johann Friedrich Herbart (1776–1841) developed the Leibnitzian notion of the unconscious into the concept of threshold or limen of consciousness. Those ideas below the limen are unconscious. When an idea rises to a conscious level of awareness, it is apperceived, in Leibnitz's terms, but Herbart went beyond this. For an idea to rise into consciousness, it must be compatible and congruent with the ideas in consciousness. Incongruous ideas cannot exist in consciousness at the same time, and ideas that are irrelevant are forced out of consciousness to become what Herbart called *inhibited ideas*. Inhibited ideas existed below the threshold of consciousness and were akin to Leibnitz's *petites perceptions*. According to Herbart, there is a conflict among ideas in which they actively struggle for realization in consciousness. Boring (1950b) suggested that Leibnitz foreshadowed the doctrine of the unconscious, but that Herbart actually began it.

Fechner also contributed to the development of theories about the unconscious. He used the notion of limen or threshold, but his suggestion that the mind is analogous to an iceberg, in that a considerable portion of it is hidden below the surface where it is influenced by unobservable forces, had a greater influence on Freud.

It is interesting that Fechner, to whom experimental psychology owes so much, was also a precursor of psychoanalysis. Freud quoted from Fechner's *Elements of Psychophysics* in several of his books and derived some major concepts from his work, including the pleasure principle, the notion of psychic or mental energy, the topographical concept of mind, and the importance of the destructive instinct. Jones noted that "Fechner was the only psychologist from whom Freud ever borrowed any idea" (1957, p. 268).

Shakow (1969) pointed out that the notion of the unconscious was very much part of the *Zeitgeist* of the 1880s in Europe. Not only was the idea of interest to professionals, but it was also considered by the lay public to be a fashionable topic of conversation. A book entitled *The Philosophy of the Unconscious* (Von Hartmann) was so popular that it appeared in nine editions between 1868 and 1882, and in the decade 1870–1880 at least a half dozen other books were published in Germany that contained the word "unconscious" in their titles. "At the time Freud started his clinical practice every educated person must have become familiar with the idea of the unconscious" (Jahoda, 1977, p. 132).

Freud, therefore, was not the first to discover or even to discuss seriously the unconscious. Although some early thinkers had merely mentioned the unconscious, others had attributed great importance to it. No one before Freud, however, had fully realized the significance of unconscious motivation or found a way to study it. Freud thought that in exploring the unconscious he would be able to explain what had previously been considered inexplicable. He believed that unconscious feelings and thoughts directly or indirectly influence behavior.

Psychopathology

We have observed that a new movement always requires something to revolt against, something to push away from in order to gain momentum. Because psychoanalysis did not develop within academic psychology, the existing order that it opposed was not Wundtian structuralism or any other school of psychological thought. To discover what Freud opposed, we must look at the prevailing thought in the area in which he worked—the understanding and treatment of mental disorders.

The history of the treatment of the mentally ill is itself both fascinating and depressing and presents a striking picture of inhumanity. In the Middle Ages the disturbed individual received almost no understanding and very little treatment. The mind was alleged to be a free agent and responsible for its own condition. The "treatment" for the mentally disturbed consisted primarily of blame and punishment, because the causes of emotional disturbance were believed to be wickedness, witchcraft, and possession by demons.

Conditions did not improve during the Renaissance. A passage from Boring (1950b) recounts events and attitudes characteristic of that period.

> The great changes in the social structure at the time of the Renaissance created a general feeling of uncertainty and insecurity . . . . Insecure men, uncertain of the future, frustrated by change, stand ready to exorcise the threat of evil by an uncritical distribution of blame and punishment. Then, as now, they were ready to go witch hunting because they were afraid, and in the fifteenth century the Church did it for them. In 1489 Jacob Sprenger and Heinrich Kraemer, two Dominican brothers, taking advantage of the recent invention of the printing press, published the Malleus maleficarum, a title which perhaps can best be

translated as the Witch Hammer, *since the book was designed to be a tool for hammering at the witches. The* Malleus maleficarum *is a cruel encyclopedia on witchcraft, the detection of witches and the procedures for examining them by torture and for sentencing them. . . . It identified witchcraft with heresy and for us it identifies witchcraft with the mental disorders, many of whose symptoms it describes with care. For three hundred years in nineteen editions this malevolent compendium remained the authority and guide of the Inquisition as it sought out heresy and demoniacal possession among the people. (pp. 694–695)*

The Inquisition continued through the eighteenth century, but in the nineteenth century a more humane and rational attitude toward the mentally ill took hold. In Europe and America the chains were struck (literally) from the insane as a decline in the influence of religious superstition paved the way for scientific investigation of the causes of mental illness.

During the nineteenth century there were two main schools of thought in psychiatry, the somatic and the psychic. The *somatic* school held that organic disturbances of the brain account for abnormalities of behavior; the *psychic* school sought causes in the mental or psychological sphere. Physical disturbances of the brain had been found in certain kinds of mental illness but not in others. On the whole, however, nineteenth-century psychiatry was dominated by the somatic school. Psychoanalysis developed as one aspect of a revolt against this somatic orientation. As work with the mentally ill continued, some scientists became convinced that emotional stress was of greater importance than brain lesions in the etiology of abnormal behavior.

Hypnosis played an important role in fostering interest in the psychic causes of abnormal behavior. In the latter part of the eighteenth century hypnosis was brought to the attention of the medical world by Franz Anton Mesmer. For a century *mesmerism* was almost universally rejected by the medical profession, which regarded it as quackery. In England James Braid (1795–1860) called the phenomena characteristic of the hypnotic state "neurypnology," from which the term hypnosis was later derived. His careful work and disdain for exaggerated claims earned some scientific respectability for hypnosis.

Hypnosis achieved greater prominence with the work of Jean Martin Charcot (1825–1893), who was a physician and head of a neurological clinic at Salpêtrière, the Parisian hospital for insane women. Charcot treated hysterical patients by means of hypnosis with some degree of success. More important, he described the symptoms of both hysteria and hypnosis in medical terms, making the latter phenomenon more readily acceptable to medicine and to the French Academy of Science (which had rejected mesmerism three times). Approval by the Academy was vital because it made it possible for neurologists to begin to investigate the psychological aspects of mental illness.

Charcot's work remained primarily neurological, emphasizing physical disturbances, paralysis, and the like. Hysteria continued to be ascribed to somatic causes until Charcot's pupil and successor, Pierre Janet (1859–1947), accepted Charcot's invitation in 1889 to become director of the psychological laboratory at Salpêtrière. Janet rejected the opinion that hysteria was a physiological disturbance and saw it instead as a mental disorder. Accordingly, he emphasized mental phenomena, particularly impairments of memory and fixed ideas, and stressed hypnosis as a method of treatment. Thus, in the early years of Freud's career the published literature on hypnosis was growing rapidly.

This overview, of course, barely indicates the important work of Charcot and Janet in the treatment of the mentally disturbed. The relevant point here is the change in beliefs about the cause of mental illness from the somatic to the psychic or mental. More and more people were beginning to think in terms of curing emotional disturbances through the mind instead of through the body, and the term *psychotherapy* was widely accepted before Freud started to publish his ideas.

Other Sources of Influence

Several other influences on Freud deserve mention. The intellectual climate of the eighteenth and nineteenth centuries included the motivational doctrine of *hedonism*, which states, in essence, that we strive to gain pleasure and to avoid pain. Associated primarily with Jeremy Bentham and his notion of utilitarianism, hedonism was also supported by some of the British associationists. One of Freud's concepts, the pleasure principle, was strongly supported by hedonism.

During Freud's university training he came in contact with the mechanistic school of thought, as represented by the physiologists mentioned in Chapter 3, Carl Ludwig, Emil du Bois-Reymond, Ernst Brücke, and Hermann von Helmholtz. These students of the great Johannes Müller had united to take the position that no forces are to be found in living things that do not exist in inanimate objects. They argued that there are no forces active within the organism other than the common physical and chemical ones. Freud was a student of Brücke's, and this mechanistic orientation influenced him in the formulation of his notion of the determined nature of human behavior, a concept he called "psychic determinism."

Freud's deterministic orientation was also supported by his interest in Darwinian evolution. Like Darwin, Freud tended to take a biological view of human nature. (Freud acknowledged that Darwin's work, along with an essay on nature by Goethe, influenced his choice of medicine as a profession.)

Another aspect of the *Zeitgeist* that influenced and reinforced Freud's work was the sexual climate in Vienna in the late nineteenth century. It has often been alleged that because society in Freud's day was repressive and puritanical, he was far ahead of his time in discussing sexual matters so frankly and openly. Although such inhibitions may have characterized the upper-middle-class neurotic women who were Freud's patients (as well as Freud himself), it certainly did not characterize the culture as a whole. Unlike Victorian England or the United States at that time, turn-of-the-century Vienna was "sexually permissive and sex flourished openly and everywhere" (Drucker, 1978, p. 92). Further, the widespread sensuality was not accompanied by guilt feelings or repression.

Interest in sexual matters was visible in everyday life and in the scientific literature. In the years before Freud advanced his sex-based theory, a large number of studies had been published on sexual pathologies, infantile sexuality, and the suppression of sexual impulses and its effects on mental and physical health. Even the word "libido," which was to assume such prominence in psychoanalysis, was already in use and had the same meaning Freud later gave it. With regard to the sexual component of Freud's work, then, "there is hardly anything . . . that had not been anticipated in one way or another" (Ellenberger, 1970, p. 792). Because both public and professional interest in sex was strong, Freud's ideas received a great deal of attention.

The concept of *catharsis,* of central importance in Freud's theory, was also popular before Freud published any of his work. In 1880, a year before Freud received his M.D., an uncle of his future wife wrote a book on Aristotle's concept of catharsis. There ensued "a craze for the topic of catharsis. . . . For a time catharsis was one of the most discussed subjects among scholars and one of the topics of conversation in sophisticated Viennese salons" (Ellenberger, 1972, p. 272).

Thus, there were many diverse sources of influence on Freud's thinking. It has been said that no small part of Freud's genius was the ability to draw on these various ideas to develop his system, a characteristic possessed by all the founders we have discussed.

THE DEVELOPMENT OF PSYCHOANALYSIS: SIGMUND FREUD (1856–1939)

The psychoanalytic movement is a highly personal school centered primarily on Freud and secondarily on his disciples. The system Freud developed is intimately related to his own life and is, to a large degree, autobiographical; consequently, the story of his life is vital to an understanding of his system.

Freud was born on May 6, 1856, in Freiberg, Moravia (now Pribor, Czechoslovakia). His father was a relatively unsuccessful Jewish wool merchant who, when his business failed in Moravia, moved his family first to Leipzig and then (when Freud was 4 years old) to Vienna. Freud remained in Vienna for nearly 80 years.

Freud's father was 20 years older than his mother and was somewhat strict and authoritarian. As a young boy, Freud apparently felt both fear and love toward him. His mother was protective and loving, and he felt a passionate attachment to her. This fear of the father and sexual attraction to the mother is, of course, what Freud later called the *Oedipus complex*, and it seems to have been derived from his boyhood experiences and recollections.

One of eight children, Freud early demonstrated great intellectual ability, which his family did everything possible to encourage. His bedroom was the only room in the house to have an oil lamp, providing better light for study; other family members used candles. The other children, toward whom he displayed much rivalry and resentment, were not allowed to study music, lest their practicing disturb the young scholar.

Freud entered *Gymnasium* a year earlier than normal and was a brilliant student, graduating with distinction at the age of 17. He was undecided about his career; his interests included civilization, human culture, human relationships, and even military history. Darwin's theory of evolution awakened in him an interest in a scientific approach to an understanding of life, and with some hesitation Freud decided on medicine. He had no real desire to be a practicing physician, but selected medicine in the hope that it would lead to a career in scientific research.

Freud began his studies at the University of Vienna in 1873. Because of his interests in several fields not directly connected with medical training, he spent eight years completing his studies. At first he concentrated on biology and dissected more than 400 male eels in search of the precise structure of the testes. His results were not conclusive, but it is noteworthy that his first attempt at research concerned sex.

He moved on to physiology and work on the spinal cord of the fish. Apparently he enjoyed physiology because he worked for six years over a microscope in Brücke's physiological institute.

During his medical training Freud began experimenting with the drug cocaine. He used it himself, made it available to his fiancée, his sisters, and his friends, and was responsible for introducing cocaine into medical practice. He was enthusiastic about the substance and found that it cured his depression and helped his almost chronic indigestion. He was convinced that he had discovered a wonder drug that would cure everything from sciatica to seasickness and win for him the fame and recognition he sought so eagerly.

But this was not to be. One of Freud's medical colleagues, after hearing his casual conversation about cocaine, found that the drug could be used to anesthetize the human eye, thus making eye surgery possible for the first time. Although the colleague became famous, Freud was criticized severely for advocating the use of cocaine for purposes other than eye surgery. (Freud was never a cocaine addict, as is sometimes alleged today, and he did not use the drug after leaving medical school.)

316

Freud wanted to remain in scientific work within a university setting, but Brücke discouraged this inclination because of Freud's financial circumstances. He was too poor to support himself during the many years one had to wait to secure one of the few available professorships. Freud reluctantly agreed that it would be too long a time before he could earn a livelihood in the Austrian university system, so he decided to take his medical examinations and enter private practice as a physician. This meant that he had to undertake work in clinics and hospitals, because he had neglected the clinical aspect of his medical education to pursue his research in physiology. During his hospital training he specialized as much as possible in the anatomy and organic diseases of the nervous system, particularly paralysis, aphasia, brain injuries in children, and speech pathology.

Freud received his M.D. in 1881 and the following year began private practice as a clinical neurologist. It was a difficult step; although he had become well known for his research in neurology, he was not greatly attracted to private practice in the field. The most compelling reason for beginning a practice was his engagement in 1882 to Martha Bernays, who was as poor as he. Their marriage was postponed several times for financial reasons but finally, after a frustrating four-year engagement, they were married. During the first few months of marriage Freud had to borrow money and even pawn their watches. The situation eventually improved, but they never forgot those early years of poverty.

Freud's long working hours prevented his spending a great deal of time with his wife and children (of whom there were eventually six). He also vacationed alone, because his wife could not maintain the pace of hiking and sightseeing he set for himself.

During these years a friendship of utmost importance to Freud developed with Josef Breuer (1842–1925), a physician who had gained renown for his study of respiration and the discovery of the functioning of the semicircular canals. A successful and sophisticated general practitioner, Breuer gave the impoverished young Freud advice and friendship, and even loaned him money. They frequently discussed some of Breuer's patients, including Anna O.,[1] whose case is pivotal in the development of psychoanalysis.

An intelligent and attractive 21-year-old woman, Anna showed a wide range of severe hysterical symptoms including paralysis, memory losses, mental deterioration, nausea, and disturbances of vision and speech. Breuer began treating her by using hypnosis. He found that while she was under hypnosis, she would remember specific experiences that seemed to have given rise to certain symptoms, and talking about the experiences while in a hypnotic state seemed to relieve the symptoms.

For example, Anna went through a period when she could not drink water, despite feelings of thirst. Under hypnosis, she related that she had

---

[1] Anna O.'s real name was Bertha Pappenheim, and she later became a social worker in West Germany. See L. Freeman, *The Story of Anna O.* (New York: Walker, 1972).

The psychoanalytic movement began with Sigmund Freud (1856–1939) and grew to become one of the most important forces of the time. His work has had a profound influence on the development of modern psychology and on many aspects of western culture.
(*National Library of Medicine*)

had a similar aversion to water in childhood; she recalled seeing a dog she disliked drinking from a glass. After relating this incident to Breuer, she found that she could drink water again with no difficulty and the symptom never recurred.

Breuer saw Anna every day for more than a year. During their meetings Anna would recount the disturbing incidents of the day, after which she often experienced some relief from her symptoms. She referred to her talks with Breuer as "chimney sweeping" and the "talking cure."

As the treatment continued, Breuer realized (and described to Freud) that the incidents Anna recalled under hypnosis involved some thought or experience that was repulsive to her. When she was able to relive these experiences under hypnosis, her symptoms either became less severe or disappeared altogether.

Breuer's wife grew jealous of the close emotional relationship that arose between Anna and Breuer. Anna exhibited what was later called a "positive transference" to Breuer, that is, she transferred her feelings for her father to Breuer. Later in the development of psychoanalysis transference was considered a necessary part of the therapeutic process. Breuer, however, saw the situation as a threat and stopped Anna's treatment. A few hours after he told Anna that he could not continue to see her, she experienced the symptoms of hysterical childbirth. Breuer terminated this event through hypnosis and, according to legend, left with his wife the next day for a second honeymoon in Venice, at which time his wife became pregnant.

This tale seems to have been a myth perpetuated by several generations of psychoanalysts and historians. Breuer and his wife may have gone to Venice for a second honeymoon, but the dates of birth of their children reveal that none could have been conceived at that time (Ellenberger, 1972).

Indeed, much of the story of Anna O. seems to be more fiction than fact, particularly with regard to her cure by Breuer's cathartic treatments. Research by Ellenberger has disclosed that "the famed 'prototype of a cathartic cure' was neither a cure nor a catharsis" (1972, p. 279), and that Anna O. was institutionalized for a period of time after Breuer stopped treating her. The case provides an instructive example of myth-making in history; in this instance, the myth endured for almost 100 years.

Breuer's treatment of Anna O. is, however, important in the development of psychoanalysis because it did introduce Freud to the "talking cure" that figures so prominently in his work.

In 1885 a small postgraduate grant enabled Freud to spend 4½ months studying in France under Charcot. A significant incident took place during this stay in Paris. At a reception one evening, Freud heard Charcot assert that a certain patient's difficulties had a sexual basis. "But in this sort of case it's always a question of the genitals—always, always, always" (Freud, 1914). To Freud, this assessment was an illuminating and exciting insight; thereafter, he was alert to the suggestion of sexual problems in his patients.

He also had an opportunity to observe Charcot's use of hypnosis in the treatment of hysterics. The French physician had shown that the traditional view of hysteria as an exclusively female malady (the word is derived from the Greek *hystera*, meaning womb) was incorrect; he had demonstrated the existence of hysterical symptoms in some of his male patients.

A year after his return from Paris Freud was once again reminded of the possible sexual basis of a patient's disturbance. A noted gynecologist asked Freud if he would take the case of a woman who suffered strong anxiety attacks that were relieved only when she knew where her doctor was at every moment. The physician told Freud that the woman's anxieties were caused by her impotent husband; the woman was still a virgin after 18 years of marriage. "The sole prescription for such a malady," the doctor told Freud, "is familiar enough to us, but we cannot order it. It runs: R_x *Penis normalis dosim repetatur!*" (Freud, 1914).

Freud had adopted Breuer's methods of hypnosis and catharsis in dealing with his patients. He gradually became less satisfied with hypnosis; although it was apparently successful in removing symptoms, it did not seem able to effect a complete cure. Many patients returned with a different set of symptoms. Furthermore, some neurotic patients could not be easily or deeply hypnotized.

These and other problems induced Freud to abandon the hypnotic portion of the treatment, but he retained catharsis. Gradually he developed what has been called the most important step in the evolution of the psychoanalytic method: the technique of *free association*. In this procedure the patient lies on a couch and is encouraged to talk freely and spontaneously, giving complete expression to every idea, no matter how embarrassing, unimportant, or foolish it may seem. The aim of Freud's developing method of psychoanalysis was to bring into conscious awareness repressed memories or thoughts, presumably the source of the patient's abnormal behavior. Through the technique of free association, Freud found that his patients' memories invariably went far back into their childhood experiences, and that many of these repressed memories concerned sexual matters. Already alert to the possible role of sexual factors in the etiology of his patients' illnesses, and certainly aware of the current literature on sexual pathology, Freud became more attuned to the occurrence of sexual material in the narratives of his patients.

In 1895 Breuer and Freud published *Studies on Hysteria*, often considered the formal starting point of psychoanalysis. The book contained a joint paper that had been published previously; five case histories, including that of Anna O.; a theoretical paper by Breuer; and a chapter by Freud on psychotherapy. Although the book received some negative reviews, it also received positive ones in scientific and literary journals, not only in Austria but in other countries as well. It was a definite, if modest, beginning of the recognition Freud wanted. Breuer had been reluctant to publish the book, and this decision may mark the beginning of the end of his personal relationship with Freud. The split was apparently caused by Freud's emphasis in his theories on sex. By around 1898 the break between the two was complete and never healed.

By the mid-1890s Freud was convinced that sex played the dominant role in neurosis. He observed that most of his patients reported traumatic sexual experiences in their childhoods, often involving members of their own families. He came to believe that neurosis was not possible in a person who led a normal sex life.

In a paper presented to the Society of Psychiatry and Neurology in Vienna in 1896, Freud reported that his patients had revealed experiences resembling seduction in childhood, with the seducer usually being an older relative, most often the father. These seduction traumas, Freud believed, caused the adult neurotic behavior. He further reported that his patients were hesitant when describing the seduction experience in detail and that the entire situation seemed somewhat unreal. Patients recounted the events in a manner suggesting that they were not fully remembered; it was as though they had never happened. The paper was received with skepticism, and the president of the Society, the neurologist Richard von Krafft-Ebing, commented that "It sounds like a scientific fairy tale" (Jones, 1953, p. 263).

About a year after the presentation of this paper Freud experienced the sudden revelation of a "great secret": In most cases, the childhood seduction experiences his patients had described had never actually occurred! This realization marks a turning point in the history of psychoanalysis. At first, the awareness that his patients were reporting fantasies was a stunning blow to Freud, whose theory of hysteria was based on the reality of these childhood sexual traumas. On reflection, however, he concluded that his patients' fantasies were quite real to them. Also, because their fantasies centered on sexual matters, sex still had to be the root of their problems. Thus, Freud's basic thesis of sex as a causative factor in neurosis remained intact.

It is interesting that Freud, who so strongly stressed the role of sex in our emotional lives, held an extremely negative personal attitude toward sex. He consistently wrote of the dangers of sexuality, even for non-neurotics, and argued that people should strive to rise above that "common animal need." The sex act, he wrote, is degrading; it contaminates both the mind and the body. In 1897, when he was 41 years old, he reported that he had personally given up sex altogether.

Also in 1897 Freud began the monumental task of self-analysis. He had experienced a number of neurotic difficulties for several years. He diagnosed his condition as anxiety neurosis, which he said was caused by the accumulation of sexual tension. This was a time of intense inner turmoil for Freud, yet it was also one of the most creative periods of his life. He undertook self-analysis as a means toward better understanding of himself and his patients, and the method he used was *dream analysis*.

In the course of his work Freud had discovered that a patient's dreams could be a rich source of significant emotional material. Dreams often contained valuable clues to the underlying causes of a disturbance. Because of his positivist belief that everything had a cause, he thought that events in a dream could not be completely without meaning; they must result from something in the person's unconscious. (This notion that dream images are symbolic is not unique to Freud; it is actually an ancient theory.)

Realizing that he could not analyze himself by the technique of free association (it is difficult to assume the roles of patient and therapist at the same time), Freud decided to investigate his dreams. Upon waking each morning, he recorded his dream material of the night before and then free-associated to this material. His self-analysis continued for about two years, culminating in the publication of *The Interpretation of Dreams* (1900), a book that is now considered his major work. In it he outlined for the first time the nature of the Oedipus complex, drawing largely on his own childhood experiences. The work was not universally praised, but it nevertheless achieved far-ranging recognition and much favorable comment. Professional journals in fields as diverse as philosophy and neuropsychiatry reviewed it, as did popular magazines and newspapers in Vienna, Berlin, and other major European cities (Ellenberger, 1970). In Zurich a young man by the name of Carl Jung read the book and quickly became a convert to the new psychoanalysis, at least for a time.

The Interpretation of Dreams was eventually so successful that it appeared in eight editions during Freud's lifetime. He incorporated dream analysis into the body of techniques used in psychoanalysis, and for the remainder of his life devoted the last half hour of each day to self-analysis.

In the very productive years after 1900 Freud developed and expanded his new ideas. In 1901 he published *The Psychopathology of Everyday Life*, which contained the description of the now famous Freudian slip. He suggested that in the everyday behavior of the normal person as well as in neurotic symptoms unconscious ideas are struggling for expression and thus are capable of modifying thought and action. What might seem to be casual slips of the tongue or "forgetting," Freud suggested, are actually reflections of real, though unacknowledged, motives.

His next book, *Three Essays on the Theory of Sexuality*, appeared in 1905. Three years earlier some students had urged him to conduct a weekly discussion group so that they might learn about his psychoanalysis, as he had then begun to call his work. These early disciples, including Alfred Adler and Carl Jung, later achieved fame through their opposition to Freud (see Chapter 14), who tolerated no dissent from his emphasis on the role of sexuality. Anyone who did not accept this tenet was promptly excommunicated, and this happened to several of his major disciples. Later Freud wrote: "psycho-analysis is my creation; for ten years I was the only person who concerned himself with it . . . no one can know better than I do what psycho-analysis is" (Freud, 1914).

During the first decade of the twentieth century Freud's personal and professional positions improved. His practice increased and a growing number of people took his pronouncements seriously. In 1909 he received the first sign of international recognition when he was invited by G. Stanley Hall to speak at the twentieth anniversary celebration of Clark University in Massachusetts. He was awarded an honorary doctorate, which moved him deeply, and he met many prominent psychologists of the day, including William James, James McKeen Cattell, and E. B. Titchener. The five lectures that he gave at Clark were published the following year in the *American Journal of Psychology,* and were later translated into several languages.

Freud was well received and honored on this visit to the United States, yet he left with an unfavorable impression of America, which he harbored for many years. He complained of the quality of American cooking, the scarcity of bathrooms, difficulties with the language, and the informality in manners, which seemed shockingly free to a cultured European. He was offended by a guide at Niagara Falls who referred to him as "the old fellow."

He never returned to America, and commented to his biographer, Ernest Jones, that "America is a mistake; a gigantic mistake, it is true, but none the less a mistake" (Jones, 1955, p. 60). In the interest of fairness, it should be noted that Freud also disliked Vienna, the city in which he lived for so many years (Jones, 1953, pp. 293–294).

During the first two decades of this century the official psychoanalytic family was torn by discord, dissent, and defections. The break with Adler came in 1911, and with Jung, whom Freud had considered his spiritual son and the heir to psychoanalysis, in 1914. By World War I three rival groups existed, but Freud managed to keep the name "psychoanalysis" for his group. The war years impeded his intellectual advancement and reduced the number of his patients and hence his income. With a wife, six children,

Freud, surrounded by members of the American psychological community, at Clark University in 1909. The lectures he gave here were later published in the *American* (*Archives of the History of American Psychology*)

The Development of Psychoanalysis: Sigmund Freud

and a sister-in-law to support, Freud had to be continually concerned with financial matters.

He reached the pinnacle of his fame in the period from 1919 to 1939, the year of his death. He continued to work hard and saw patients for several hours each day, but was able to take three months' vacation every summer. During the 1920s psychoanalysis developed as a theoretical system for the understanding of all human motivation and personality, rather than solely as a method of treatment for the disturbed. (This conceptual system is discussed later in this chapter.)

In 1923 it was discovered that Freud suffered from cancer of the mouth. The last 16 years of his life were marked by almost continuous pain. He underwent 33 operations, and portions of his palate and upper jaw were removed. The prosthetic device that this surgery made necessary hampered his speech, and it became increasingly difficult to understand him. Although he continued to see patients and disciples, he shunned other personal contact. He had typically smoked 20 cigars a day, and he continued to smoke after his illness was diagnosed.

When Hitler came to power in 1933, the official Nazi position on psychoanalysis was made clear when Freud's books were publicly burned in May 1933 at a rally in Berlin. As the volumes were flung onto the fire, a Nazi speaker shouted, "Against the soul-destroying overestimation of the sex life—and on behalf of the nobility of the human soul—I offer to the flames the writings of one Sigmund Freud!" (Schur, 1972, p. 446). Freud commented, "What progress we are making. In the Middle Ages they would have burnt me; nowadays they are content with burning my books" (Jones, 1957, p. 182). By 1934 the more farsighted Jewish psychoanalysts had left Germany. The vigorous Nazi campaign to eradicate psychoanalysis in Germany was so effective that knowledge of Freud, once so widespread, was almost completely obliterated.

Against the advice of his friends, Freud insisted on remaining in Vienna. In March 1938 the Nazis invaded Austria, and on March 15 his home was overrun by a gang of Nazis. A week later his daughter Anna was arrested and detained for a day. Freud was finally convinced that he should flee, but he was not permitted to go until his unsold books had been brought back from Switzerland to be burned. Partly because of the intervention of the American ambassador to France, the Nazis agreed to let Freud go to England. Four of Freud's sisters were later killed in Nazi concentration camps.

A wry note attended Freud's departure from Vienna. To secure an exit visa, he had to sign a document attesting to his "respectful and considerate" treatment by the Gestapo, and noting that he had no reason to complain. He signed the form and asked if he might add, "I can heartily recommend the Gestapo to anyone" (Jones, 1957, p. 226).

Although Freud was received well in England, he was unable to enjoy the last year of his life because his health was failing rapidly. He remained mentally alert, however, and worked almost to the very end. Years before, when he selected the young Max Schur to be his personal physician, Freud made him promise that he would not let him suffer unnecessarily. On September 21, 1939, he reminded Schur of their earlier talk. "You promised me then not to forsake me when my time comes. Now it's nothing but torture and makes no sense any more" (Schur, 1972, p. 529). The doctor gave Freud two centigrams of morphine and repeated the dose 12 hours later. Freud went into a coma, his years of suffering finally at an end, and died on September 23, 1939.

PSYCHOANALYSIS AS
A METHOD OF
TREATMENT

Freud found that the method of free association did not always operate so freely; sooner or later the patients reached a point in their narrative where they were unable or unwilling to continue. Freud believed that these *resistances* indicated that the patients had called up memories or ideas that were too horrible, shameful, or repulsive to be faced. He saw the resistance as a form of protection from emotional pain, and the presence of the pain itself as an indication that the analysis was getting close to the source of the difficulty.

Thus, resistance indicated that treatment was proceeding in the right direction and must continue to probe in that area. Freud placed great stress on helping patients to overcome their resistances. He insisted that they face the hidden experiences, no matter how disturbing, and see them in the light of reality. In the course of a complete analysis it was expected that resistance would be encountered and overcome a number of times.

Freud's notion of resistance led to the formulation of the fundamental psychoanalytic principle of *repression*, which involved the ejecting of painful ideas or memories from conscious awareness. Freud regarded repression as the only adequate explanation for the occurrence of resistance. Unpleasant ideas are pushed out of consciousness and forcefully kept out. The therapist must help patients bring this repressed material back into conscious awareness so that they can face it and learn to live with it. (It has been suggested that Freud developed the concepts of resistance and repression from Schopenhauer. In 1938 Freud noted that he had arrived at these ideas without having read Schopenhauer, to whom, however, he did yield precedence.)

Freud recognized that effective work with neurotic patients depends on the development of a personal, intimate relationship between patient and therapist. We noted earlier how the *transference* that Anna O. developed toward Breuer so disturbed him that he felt compelled to end the treatment. Freud viewed the transference of a patient's emotional attitudes from parent to therapist as vital and necessary. The therapist had to wean the patient from childish dependence and help him or her to assume a more adult role in life.

Freud's recognition of the importance of dream material has already been described. He believed that dreams represent a disguised satisfaction of repressed desires and wishes, and therefore the dream story is much more meaningful and complex than it might otherwise seem.

As an aside, let us note that on Wednesday evening, July 24, 1895, at a table in the northeast corner of the terrace of the Bellevue Restaurant in Vienna, Freud realized that the essence of a dream is wish fulfillment. In accordance with Boring's later notion that genius often flatters itself by dating its own inspirations, Freud quipped that a tablet should be erected at that spot noting that "Here the secret of dreams was revealed to Dr. Sigm. Freud on July 24, 1895" (Jones, 1953, p. 354).

Dreams, according to Freud, have both a manifest and a latent content. The *manifest* content is the actual story told in recalling the events that occurred in the dream. The true significance of the dream, however, lies in the *latent* content, which is its hidden or symbolic meaning. To interpret this hidden meaning, the therapist must proceed from manifest to latent content, that is, interpret the symbolic meaning of the events that are related in the manifest content.

This is a complex task. Freud believed that the forbidden desires in the latent dream content are expressed in symbolic form in the manifest content. Although many symbols that crop up in dreams are relevant only to experiences of the particular dreamer, others are common to all persons, and hence always have the same meaning. According to Freud, these universal symbols include gardens, balconies, and doors to signify the female body, and church spires, candles, and serpents to signify the male genitals. Dreams of falling represent giving in to erotic wishes, and dreams of flying represent a desire for sexual achievement. Freud warned that despite the universality of these common symbols, interpretation of a patient's dreams requires knowledge of the patient's specific conflicts.

Freud also wrote that not all dreams are caused by emotional conflicts. Some dreams are caused by such mundane stimuli as the room temperature, contact with one's partner, or overeating before bedtime. Therefore, not all dreams contain hidden, symbolic material.

Freud believed that a long and intensive course of therapy was required to effect a cure. With his own patients, he found that no fewer than five sessions a week, for months or even years, were necessary. With such extensive care, an analyst could handle only a few patients in the course of a year.

Freud also had definite ideas about the training of analysts. He thought that each should be analyzed and work for at least two years under supervision before treating patients. He also believed strongly that the practice of psychoanalysis should be a profession independent from medicine.

It should be noted that despite the widespread use of psychoanalysis as a method of treatment, Freud had little interest in its potential therapeutic value. He was not primarily concerned with curing people, but rather with understanding the dynamics underlying human behavior. He saw himself much more as a scientist than a therapist, and considered his techniques of free association and dream analysis to be research tools for collecting data. That these techniques also had therapeutic use was, to Freud, secondary to their scientific value.

Perhaps because of his relative lack of interest in the therapeutic aspect of psychoanalysis, Freud has been described as impersonal and brisk in dealing with patients (Roazen, 1975). He deliberately placed his chair at the head of the psychoanalytic couch because he could not bear to be stared at by patients for long hours. He noted that he had become a therapist with great reluctance and felt indifferent toward his patients. "I lack that passion for helping," he wrote to a friend (Jones, 1955, p. 446). Freud's passion was his research and the data that formed the basis of his system of personality.

FREUD'S METHOD OF RESEARCH

Because Freud's system differed greatly in content and methodology from traditional experimental psychology, examining his method of research is instructive. It is difficult at times to reconcile some of Freud's theories with his thorough training as a scientist, especially his years of physiological research. Despite his background, Freud did not use customary experimental methods of research. Although he was undoubtedly familiar with experimental psychology, he did not collect data from controlled experiments or analyze his results quantitatively. The data he collected and the ways in which he interpreted them were totally at variance with the ideas of experimental psychology. They had to be different because of the subject matter Freud chose to study.

Freud derived his theories from observations of the narratives and behavior of his patients who were undergoing analysis, primarily through the free association and dream analysis techniques. Because psychoanalysis was such a lengthy process, Freud accumulated a mass of such data, which he tested for internal consistency. Assumptions and interpretations derived from the data were then carefully cross-checked to make sure they were well grounded.

Freud found no inherent obstacles to making relevant and meaningful observations from this material.

> When I set myself the task of bringing to light what human beings keep hidden within them, not by the compelling power of hypnosis, but by observing what they say and what they show, I thought the task was a harder one than it really is. He that has eyes to see and ears to hear may convince himself that no mortal can keep a secret. If the lips are silent, he chatters with his finger-tips; betrayal oozes out of him at every pore. And thus the task of making conscious the most hidden recesses of the

mind is one which it is quite possible to accomplish. (Freud, 1905b, pp. 77–78)

Freud's theories were formulated, revised, and extended in terms of the evidence as he alone interpreted it. Thus, his own critical abilities were the predominant, indeed the only, guide in his theory building. He ignored criticism from others, particularly from those who were not sympathetic to psychoanalysis, and even the wide-ranging criticism from close friends and colleagues throughout his life had little influence on his thinking. Only rarely did he bother to reply to critics. Psychoanalysis was his system, and his alone.

PSYCHOANALYSIS AS A SYSTEM OF PERSONALITY

Freud's theoretical system did not cover the topics that were usually included in psychology textbooks of the day. He explored areas that traditional psychology tended to ignore. His theoretical formulations dealt with unconscious motivating forces, the conflicts among these forces, and the effects of these conflicts on human behavior.

Instincts

Instincts are the propelling or locomotive factors in the dynamics of personality, the biological forces of the individual that release mental energy. Although the word "instinct" has come to be the accepted usage in English, it does not convey the meaning Freud intended. Freud's term in German, *Trieb*, is best translated as driving force or urge. The Freudian instincts are not inherited predispositions (the usual meaning of "instinct"), but rather refer to sources of stimulation within the body, and their aim is to remove or reduce the stimulation through some activity such as sexual relations, eating, or drinking.

Freud did not attempt to delimit the number of instincts, but he classified them in two distinct categories: the life instincts and the death instinct. The *life instincts,* including hunger, sex, and thirst, are concerned with self-preservation and survival of the species. They consist of the creative forces that sustain life itself. The form of energy through which the life instincts are manifested is called *libido.*

In addition to the creative force of the life instincts, there is the destructive force of the *death instinct.* This can be directed inward as in suicide or masochism, or outward as in aggression and hatred. Freud believed that we are irresistibly drawn toward death, that "The goal of all life is death" (1920, p. 160).

Thus, Freud gradually acknowledged that aggression and hostility as well as sex are important forces in personality. As he grew older, he became more convinced that aggression was as powerful as sex in motivating human behavior. He even became more conscious of an aggressive tendency within himself. Some of his closest colleagues described him as a "good hater," and some of his writings, as well as the sharpness and finality of his breaks with dissenters, suggest a high level of aggressiveness.

Unconscious and Conscious Aspects of Personality

In his early work Freud expressed the belief that psychic life consists of two parts—the conscious and the unconscious. The *conscious* part, like the visible portion of an iceberg, is small and insignificant, presenting but a superficial aspect of total personality. The vast and powerful *unconscious* contains the instincts that are the driving power behind all human behavior. Freud also postulated the existence of the *preconscious*, or foreconscious. Unlike the material in the unconscious, that in the preconscious has not been actively repressed and can be easily summoned into conscious awareness. For example, if your mind strayed from the words on this page and you began thinking about something you did last night, you would be summoning material from the preconscious to your conscious awareness.

Freud later revised this simple conscious–unconscious distinction and introduced the id, ego, and superego constructs of the mental apparatus. The *id*, corresponding somewhat to Freud's previous notion of the unconscious, is the most primitive and least accessible part of the personality. The powerful forces of the id include sexual and aggressive instincts: "We call it a chaos, a cauldron full of seething excitations." Freud further noted that "The id of course knows no judgements of value: no good and evil, no morality" (Freud, 1933, p. 74). The id seeks immediate satisfaction without regard for the circumstances of objective reality, and thus operates according to what Freud called the *pleasure principle*, which is concerned with the reduction of tension.

Our basic psychic energy, or libido, is contained in the id and is expressed through tension reduction. Increases in libidinal energy result in increased tension that we attempt to reduce to a more tolerable level. To satisfy our needs and maintain a comfortable tension level, we must interact with the real world. For example, the person who is hungry must make appropriate movements in the environment to find food, thus discharging the tension induced by hunger. An effective and appropriate liaison between the demands of the id and the circumstances of reality must be effected. The *ego*, which serves as a mediating agent between the id and the external world, develops to facilitate this interaction. The ego represents what is commonly known as reason or rationality, in contrast to the passions of the id.

The id craves blindly, unaware of reality; the ego is aware of reality, perceives and manipulates it, and regulates the id with reference to it. The ego operates in accordance with what Freud called the *reality principle*, holding in abeyance the pleasure-seeking demands of the id until an appropriate object has been found with which to satisfy the need and reduce or discharge the tension. The ego does not exist independently of the id; indeed, it derives its power from the id. It serves to help and not to hinder the id, and is constantly striving to bring about id satisfaction. Freud compared the relationship of the ego and the id to a rider on a horse. The horse supplies the energy that is directed along the path the rider wants to travel. However, the power of the horse must be constantly guided or checked, or the horse may throw the rider to the ground. Similarly, the id must be constantly guided and checked, or it will overthrow the rational ego.

The third part of Freud's structure of personality, the *superego*, develops early in childhood, when rules of conduct taught by parents through a system of rewards and punishments are assimilated. Behaviors that are wrong (that bring punishment) become part of the child's *conscience*, which is one part of the superego. Behaviors that are right (that are rewarded) become part of the child's *ego-ideal*, the other part of the superego. Thus, childhood behavior is initially governed by parental control, but once the superego has formed a pattern for conduct, behavior is determined by self-control. The behavior-guiding rewards and punishments are then administered by the individual.

Freud wrote that the superego represents "every moral restriction, the advocate of a striving towards perfection—it is, in short, as much as we have been able to grasp psychologically of what is described as the higher side of human life" (1933, p. 67). Obviously, the superego is in conflict with the id. Unlike the ego, the superego does not merely attempt to postpone id satisfaction; it tries to inhibit it completely.

The ego is in a difficult position, pressured on three sides by insistent and opposing forces. It must try to delay the relentless urgings of the id, perceive and manipulate reality to relieve the tensions of the id impulses, and deal with the superego's striving for perfection. Whenever the ego is too sorely pressed, the inevitable result is the development of *anxiety*.

Anxiety

An important concept in psychoanalysis, particularly when dealing with neurotic and psychotic behavior, is anxiety, which functions as a warning that the ego is being threatened. Freud described three kinds of anxiety: objective, neurotic, and moral. *Objective* anxiety is occasioned by fear of real dangers from the objective world; from this are derived the other two types of anxiety.

Neurotic anxiety arises from recognition of the potential danger inherent in instinctual gratification. It is a fear not of the instincts, but of the punishment likely to follow indiscriminate id-dominated behavior. Neurotic anxiety is a fear of being punished for expressing impulsive desires. *Moral* anxiety arises out of a fear of the conscience. When a person performs or thinks of performing some act that is contrary to the set of moral values composing the conscience, he or she may experience guilt or shame. Moral anxiety, then, is a function of how well developed one's conscience is. The less virtuous individual is less likely to develop moral anxiety.

Regardless of type, anxiety is a tension-inducing force in human behavior, motivating an individual to reduce this state of tension. Freud believed that the ego develops a number of protective defenses against anxiety, the so-called *defense mechanisms,* which are unconscious denials or distortions of reality. In the mechanism of *identification,* a person identifies with (for example, takes on the manner, dress, or speech of) someone who seems admirable and less vulnerable to the danger giving rise to the anxiety. Another defense mechanism, *repression,* is the barring from conscious awareness of an anxiety-provoking stimulus. *Sublimation* involves substituting a socially acceptable goal for one that cannot be directly satisfied. In *projection,* the source of anxiety is attributed to someone else, for example, by saying "He hates me" instead of "I hate him." In *reaction formation,* a person conceals a disturbing impulse by converting it into its opposite, for instance, by replacing hate with love. With the mechanism of *fixation,* a person's development becomes arrested at an early stage because the next stage is too fraught with anxiety. The defense mechanism of *regression* involves behavior that indicates a reversion to an earlier developmental stage, one at which there was greater security and the current source of anxiety was not operative. Freud believed that anxiety with which an individual could not adequately cope became traumatic, reducing the person to a state of infantile helplessness.

Stages of Personality Development

Freud was convinced that the neurotic disturbances manifested by his patients had originated in childhood experiences. Consequently he became one of the first theorists to place great stress on the development of the child. He believed that the adult personality pattern was established early in life and was almost completely formed by the age of 5.

In the psychoanalytic theory of development, the child passes through a series of *psychosexual stages of development.* During these stages the child is considered "autoerotic," that is, he or she derives sensual or erotic pleasure by stimulating the various erogenous zones of the body or being stimulated by the parents in their handling. Each stage during this period tends to be localized in specific bodily erogenous zones.

The first, or *oral*, stage lasts from birth into the second year. During this stage stimulation of the mouth, such as sucking, biting, and swallowing, is the primary source of erotic satisfaction. Inadequate satisfaction (too much or too little) at this stage may produce an oral personality, whereby the person becomes preoccupied with mouth habits, such as smoking, kissing, and eating. Freud believed that a wide range of adult behaviors, from excessive optimism to sarcasm and cynicism, were attributable to incidents occurring during this stage of development.

In the *anal* phase sexual gratification shifts from the mouth to the anus and the child derives pleasure from the anal zone. R. I. Watson imagined this situation as a child might see it:

> There is nothing about the odor, texture, or appearance of the feces that is inherently unpleasant. The infant has no innate repulsion. He has created it, and the mother seems to prize it, since she is pleased when he has a movement and concerned when he does not. According to Freudian thinking, defecation is "perceived" by the infant as the giving of a gift. What happens to his gift? The mother flushes it down the toilet! Often he acts out his puzzlement about this strange behavior by toilet play, throwing toys in the toilet, only to retrieve them again. (1978, p. 516)

During this stage (which coincides with the period of toilet training) the child may either expel or withhold, and may in either case defy its parents. Conflict during this period can result in an anal-expulsive adult, who is dirty, wasteful, and extravagant, or an anal-retentive adult, who is excessively neat, clean, and compulsive.

During the *phallic* stage, which occurs at about the end of the third or fourth year, erotic gratification shifts to the genital region. There is much fondling and exhibiting of the genitals, and sexual fantasizing. Freud posited the development at this stage of the *Oedipus complex* (named after the Greek legend in which Oedipus unknowingly killed his father and married his mother). The child becomes at this time sexually attracted to the parent of the opposite sex and fearful of the parent of the same sex, who is now perceived as a rival. Ordinarily, the child overcomes this complex by identifying with the parent of the same sex and substituting affection for sexual longing for the parent of the opposite sex. However, the attitudes toward the opposite sex that develop during this stage persist and influence adult relations with members of the opposite sex.

Children who are able to outlast the many struggles of these early stages enter a period of *latency* lasting from about the fifth to the twelfth year. At the start of adolescence (with the onset of puberty) the final, *genital* stage begins. Heterosexual behavior is evident and various activities by which the individual prepares for marriage and family are undertaken.

MECHANISM AND DETERMINISM IN FREUD'S SYSTEM

During Freud's university training he was influenced by the mechanistic school of thought in German physiology. At first glance, the notion of mechanism, which infuses so much of academic psychology, would seem to be irrelevant to Freud's work on the hidden motives of behavior. To the structuralists, and then the behaviorists, humans were considered machine-like in their processes and functions. First the human mind and then human behavior were reduced to their most elemental components, analyzed, and studied in positivist and material terms.

It is surprising to many readers of Freud to learn that he too was influenced by this same mechanistic tradition. No less than experimental psychologists, Freud believed that all mental events, even mistakes and dreams, were determined. No bit of behavior or thought can occur by chance or by free will. There is always a cause for each act, a motive, if not conscious, then unconscious.

But there is more to this general mechanistic spirit than determinism. In Chapter 3 we discussed the solemn pledge taken by Brücke, Ludwig, du Bois-Reymond, and Helmholtz: "No other forces than the common physical–chemical ones are active within the organism." Freud, at least early in his career, subscribed to this physicalism, the notion that all phenomena of life could be reduced to the principles of physics.

In 1895 Freud worked feverishly on his "Project for a Scientific Psychology," in which he attempted to show that psychology must have a physical basis and that purely mental phenomena exhibit many of the same patterns and characteristics as the neurophysiological processes on which they are based. Psychology, in Freud's view, must be a natural science whose aim is "to represent psychical processes as quantitatively determined states of specifiable material particles" (Freud, 1895, p. 359). His "Project" was never completed, but one can discern throughout his later writings the physicalist principles with which he grappled, along with terminology from mechanics, electricity, and hydraulics. Even though he modified his original intent to model his psychology after physics, finding that his subject matter was not amenable to physical and chemical techniques, he remained true to the abiding positivist philosophy—particularly to determinism—that nurtured academic psychology.

It must be said, however, that although he was influenced by this model, he was not constrained by it. When and where he saw that it would not fit, he modified or discarded it. In the end he demonstrated how restrictive the mechanistic conception of humans was. Freud used this tradition where appropriate, but was also an effective critic of mechanism when the doctrine was not appropriate.

CONFLICTS BETWEEN PSYCHOANALYSIS AND PSYCHOLOGY

Psychoanalysis, as we noted earlier, developed outside the mainstream of academic psychology. The fact that both the system and its originator were outsiders complicated and delayed their acceptance. Indeed, this was even a barrier to serious consideration of psychoanalysis for a time. Shakow (1969) commented that "Freudian ideas had more obstacles to overcome before being accepted in psychology than had other revolutionary ideas" (p. 100).

A number of points of conflict, discussed by Shakow (1969) and Jahoda (1963), functioned to keep psychoanalysis and academic psychology apart. The first point involves the absence of a sense of continuity in Freud's work relative to advances in psychology. There were no parallels, no overlapping efforts, because Freud's work had no precedent in the development of psychology. Psychologists could not find a meaningful way of connecting Freud's efforts with their own, or those of their predecessors.

Wundt, for example, was never moved to admit the unconscious into psychology because it did not relate to his own efforts to investigate the structural elements of consciousness. In talking about structuralism, Freud said, "We cannot help thinking that the old psychology has been killed by my . . . doctrine; but the old psychology is quite unaware of the fact, and goes on teaching as usual" (Wittels, 1924, p. 130).

A second point of conflict is that Freud and most of his disciples were trained in medicine, not in psychology; they were M.D.s, not Ph.D.s. Not only did this mean that they spoke and thought in different terms, but also it reinforced the psychologists' notion that psychoanalysts were alien because they had a different kind of training. According to Barber (1961), one source of resistance to a new discovery or theory in science is any difference in professional specialization between an innovator and the discipline to which he or she offers new work.

This difference in training points up a third reason for opposition. Psychology, in its early attempts to become or remain a pure science, was method centered; psychoanalysis was problem centered. The aim of psychoanalysis—attempting to help neurotic patients—was at sharp variance with psychology's aim of finding laws of human behavior through the methods of natural science.

These different goals and subject matter necessitated different methods. Freud's concern was more molar or global than that of psychology—the total human personality as opposed to specific functions such as perception or learning. Psychology, trying to be a natural science, used the experimental

Psychoanalysis: The Beginnings

method in which each variable (usually a minute aspect of behavior) was isolated for study. Psychoanalysis was concerned with the total human being, not for a short period in the laboratory, but over a long period of time, and used data covering all aspects of the person's past and present experiences.

Finally, academic psychologists, steeped in the rigor of science, seeking precision and operational definitions of concepts, distrusted and disliked many of the Freudian concepts and terms that could not be quantified or related precisely to concrete empirical variables. Terms such as *ego, id,* and *repression* were anathema to psychologists who were trying to work with only specific stimulus–response terms.

There were, then, several reasons for the antipathy shown by psychologists toward psychoanalysis. In spite of these differences, however, the barriers between the two disciplines, at first so rigid and absolute, have been breached here and there.

CRITICISMS OF PSYCHOANALYSIS

The amount of criticism directed against Freud and his theories, much of which has come from the lay public, is enormous, but we shall restrict our discussion to criticisms from psychologists. Some of these criticisms were noted in the preceding section.

Particularly vulnerable to attack by experimental psychologists are Freud's methods of data collection. He drew his insights and conclusions from his patients' responses while they were undergoing psychoanalysis. Consider some of the deficiencies of such an approach in the light of the experimental method of systematically collecting objective data under controlled conditions of observation.

First, the conditions under which Freud collected his data seem to be unsystematic and uncontrolled. He did not make a verbatim transcript of each patient's words, but preferred to work from notes made several hours after seeing a patient. Some of the original data (the patient's words) must surely have been lost in the interim as a result of the vagaries of recall and the well-documented possibility of distortion and omission. Data consisted only of what Freud remembered.

Also, it is possible that in the course of recollection Freud reinterpreted the raw data. His reconstruction of the data may not have accurately reflected the data as they occurred. In drawing his inferences, he may have been guided by his desire to find material supportive of his hypotheses. In other words, he may have remembered and recorded only what he wanted to hear. Of course, we must consider the possibility that Freud's notes were accurate, but it is impossible to know this with any degree of certainty; the original data do not survive.

There is a more basic criticism of the raw data. Even if a complete, verbatim record had been kept, it would not always have been possible to determine the validity of what the patients reported. Freud made few attempts to verify his patients' stories. Critics argue that he should have tried to check the accuracy of the patients' reports, for example, by questioning relatives and friends about the events described. Thus, it can be suggested that the first step in Freud's theory building—data collection—may be characterized as incomplete, imperfect, and inaccurate.

As for the next step—drawing inferences and generalizations from the data—no one knows exactly how this was done because Freud never explained the process fully. This is, of course, another major point of criticism. In addition, because Freud's data were not amenable to quantification, it is impossible to determine the reliability or statistical significance of his findings.

These are serious charges from the standpoint of scientific methodology and theory building. The reader of Freud must, in a sense, accept on faith the validity of his operations and conclusions. Freud wrote in 1938 that his work was "based on an incalculable number of observations and experiences, and only someone who has repeated those observations on himself and on others is in a position to arrive at a judgement of his own upon it" (p. 144). But, of course, Freud's observations cannot be repeated because it is not known exactly what he did in collecting data and translating observations into generalizations and hypotheses. The language of science is precise and orderly, leaving no room for ambiguities, distortions, and vagaries. It seems that Freud did not speak that language and it is difficult to translate from one to the other.

Another point of attack concerns the difficulty of deriving empirically testable propositions from many of Freud's hypotheses. How, for instance, would we test the notion of a death wish? It is used to explain behavior such as suicide, after the fact. How can we use it empirically to predict behavior?

Adherents of operationism argue that Freud's concepts are not operationally defined. (Part of Bridgman's discussion of operationism in Chapter 11 included a description of so-called pseudo-problems, or questions that defy answer by any known experimental test.) By this criterion, many of Freud's concepts cannot be experimentally tested, and some critics believe that they are pseudo-problems, meaningless, indeed useless, for science. Recently, however, this objection has been questioned. Some of Freud's ideas have been submitted to scientific test (see the following section).

In addition to these points of methodology, Freud's major theories and assumptions about human behavior have been criticized. Even some supporters of Freud agree that he often contradicted himself and that his definitions of key concepts are ambiguous (Jahoda, 1977). There is confusion in the definitions of basic concepts, such as the id, ego, and superego, making it difficult to know precisely what they are. In his later writings

Psychoanalysis: The Beginnings

Freud himself noted the difficulties and ambiguities in defining these and other ideas.

In Chapters 14 and 15 we shall examine the work of several theorists who broke with Freud and describe additional criticisms, which these dissidents attempted to meet in their modifications of Freud's position. Briefly, they argued that Freud placed too much emphasis on biological forces, particularly on sex, as the primary shapers of personality. These critics believe that personality is influenced more by social forces. Others criticized Freud's extreme determinism, which denies free will, and his exclusive emphasis on past behavior and consequent denial of the role of future hopes, goals, and dreams in influencing personality. Some have attacked Freud for developing a theory of human personality based only on observations of neurotics, ignoring the characteristics of those persons who are emotionally healthy. All these points were used to construct competing views of personality, which quickly led to divisiveness in the psychoanalytic camp and the formation of derivative schools of Freudian psychoanalysis.

THE SCIENTIFIC CREDIBILITY OF PSYCHOANALYSIS

We have seen that psychoanalysis is weak from the standpoint of scientific methodology and theory building, and that many of Freud's concepts cannot be submitted to experimental test. However, some of his ideas can be tested scientifically, provided the term "science" is broadened to include techniques other than the experimental method of the psychological laboratory. In an exhaustive analysis of some 2000 studies in psychiatry, psychology, anthropology, and other disciplines, Fisher and Greenberg (1977) evaluated the scientific credibility of some of Freud's theories. Case histories, the standard method of reporting data in the psychoanalytic literature, were not used, for some of the reasons listed in the preceding section. Instead, the authors accepted only those data that had been "secured through procedures that are repeatable and involve techniques that make it possible to check on the objectivity of the reporting observer" (p. 15).

Though some large-scale Freudian concepts continue to resist attempts at scientific validation—there are no conclusions in the Fisher–Greenberg study about the id, ego, superego, death wish, libido, or anxiety—other concepts were amenable to scientific validation. Those that appear to be supported by the published data include aspects of the oral and anal personality types; causative factors of homosexuality; the notion that dreams can serve as an outlet for tension; and parts of the Oedipus complex as it applies to males—for example, the notion of rivalry with the father, sexual fantasy about the mother, and castration anxiety.

Freudian concepts not supported by the data include the notion that dreams represent a disguised satisfaction of repressed wishes and desires; aspects of the Oedipus complex in males—for example, the theory that the male resolves the complex, identifies with the father, and accepts the father's superego standards out of fear of the father; and certain theories about women—for example, that women have an inferior concept of their bodies, that they have a less severe set of superego standards than men, and that it is more difficult for women to achieve identity.

Fisher and Greenberg concluded that, in general, those of Freud's concepts that were amenable to validation fared well, though far from perfectly. A more important conclusion is the demonstration, after so many years, that at least some of Freud's ideas can be reduced to propositions that are scientifically testable. It must be remembered, however, that major portions of Freudian psychoanalysis defy testing by the methods of science.

CONTRIBUTIONS OF PSYCHOANALYSIS

Having noted important and damaging criticisms of psychoanalysis, offered primarily by experimentally oriented psychologists, we must ask why psychoanalysis has not only survived, but prospered. All theories of behavior can be criticized as lacking in scientific validity to some degree. As a result, a psychologist in search of a theory must choose on the basis of criteria other than formal scientific rigidity and precision. One who selects psychoanalysis does not do so in the absence of evidence, however; psychoanalysis does offer evidence, although not of the variety traditionally accepted by science. The psychoanalysts' evidence is based on the observation of experience as it occurs.

That psychoanalytic evidence is not the strictly scientific sort does not necessarily mean that the theory is incorrect or misleading. However, belief in psychoanalysis is often based on the intuitive grounds of an appearance of plausibility in Freud's system.

> Any one who accepts or rejects the psychoanalytic theories does so by means of the same kind of reasoning that gives him the thousand and one judgments he is forced to make in everyday life on the basis of insufficient or inadequate evidence—the kind of judgments, in fact, that he is forced to live by, but which have no standing in science. Such estimates, growing out of a multitude of impressions and interpretations, guesses and insights, often result in unshakable convictions, convictions which may be right or wrong but which, from the standpoint of science, cannot be recognized as either proved or disproved. (Heidbreder, 1933, pp. 403–404)

Freud's influence on psychiatry and clinical psychology has been profound, and his theories are of considerable significance in American academic psychology. Certain Freudian concepts have gained wide acceptance and been assimilated into the mainstream of contemporary psychology. These include the role of unconscious motivation, the importance of childhood experiences in shaping adult behavior, and the operation of the defense mechanisms. Interest in these areas has generated much research.

Freud's influence on the general culture has, of course, been enormous. The impact of his system was felt immediately after his visit to Clark University. Bakan (1966) noted that newspapers in the United States were full of articles about Freud after 1910, and by 1920 over 200 books had been published in America on Freudian analysis. Thus, his acceptance by the lay public came much earlier and with greater force than his acceptance by academic psychology.

One general impact is Freud's contribution to the radical change that has taken place in sexual mores. The twentieth century has seen a gradual loosening of sexual restraint in behavior as well as in art, literature, and the entertainment media. The culture seems to have adopted the view that it is harmful to inhibit or repress sexual satisfaction. It is ironic that Freud's message with regard to sex has been subject to such misinterpretation. He was not arguing for a weakening of sexual codes of conduct or for greater sexual freedom. His consistent position was that inhibition of sex was necessary for the survival of civilization. Despite his intention, the greater sexual freedom of the twentieth century is partly a result of Freud's work. It also seems that the emphasis on sex helped to popularize his views. Even in scientific writing, sex has a sensational appeal (witness the sales of the highly technical volumes by sex researchers Masters and Johnson).

Despite criticism of his lack of scientific rigor and methodology, Freud's psychoanalysis has become an important force in modern psychology. Boring, in the 1929 edition of his *History of Experimental Psychology*, expressed regret that psychology had no truly great exponent of the stature of a Darwin or a Helmholtz. Only 21 years later, in the second edition of his text, Boring changed his opinion. Reflecting the development of psychology during those two decades, Boring spoke of Freud as psychology's "great man." "Now he is seen as the greatest originator of all, the agent of the *Zeitgeist* who accomplished the invasion of psychology by the principle of the unconscious process" (Boring, 1950b, p. 743).

It must be stressed that despite Freud's recognized genius and the acceptance, or at least consideration, of some parts of his system, psychoanalysis retains a separate identity today, and, in general, has not been absorbed by the mainstream of psychological thought. However, no matter what one's evaluation of psychoanalysis and whatever the eventual status of the system, there is no denying that Freud possessed the attributes of greatness.

He was a pioneer in a field of thought, in a new technique for the understanding of human nature. He was also an originator, even though he picked his conceptions out of the stream of the culture—an originator who remained true to his fundamental intent for fifty years of hard work, while he altered and brought to maturity the system of ideas that was his contribution to knowledge. . . . It is not likely that the history of psychology can be written in the next three centuries without mention of Freud's name and still claim to be a general history of psychology. And there you have the best criterion of greatness: posthumous fame. (Boring, 1950b, pp. 706–707)

SUGGESTED READINGS

HYPNOTISM

Shor, R. E., & Orne, M. T. (Eds.). *The nature of hypnosis: Selected basic writings.* New York: Holt, 1965.

FREUD

Choisy, M. *Sigmund Freud: A new appraisal.* New York: Philosophical Library, 1963.

Decker, H. S. *The Interpretation of Dreams:* Early reception by the educated German public. *Journal of the History of the Behavioral Sciences,* 1975, *11,* 129–141.

Decker, H. S. *Freud in Germany: Revolution and reaction in science, 1893–1907.* New York: International Universities Press, 1978.

Fisher, S., & Greenberg, R. P. *The scientific credibility of Freud's theories and therapy.* New York: Basic Books, 1977.

Freud, S. *An autobiographical study* (J. Strachey, Trans.). New York: Norton, 1963. (Originally published, 1925.)

Hale, N. *Freud and the Americans: The beginnings of psychoanalysis in the United States, 1876–1917.* London & New York: Oxford University Press, 1971.

Jahoda, M. *Freud and the dilemmas of psychology.* New York: Basic Books, 1977.

Jones, E. *The life and work of Sigmund Freud* (3 vols.). New York: Basic Books, 1953–1957.

Nelson, B. (Ed.). *Freud and the 20th century.* New York: Meridian, 1957.

Roazen, P. *Freud and his followers.* New York: Knopf, 1974. (A study of Freud and those who formed his circle, including Jung, Adler, and Rank.)

Ruitenbeek, H. M. *Freud and America.* New York: Macmillan, 1966.

Schur, M. *Freud: Living and dying.* New York: International Universities Press, 1972.

Sulloway, F. J. *Freud: Biologist of the mind.* New York: Basic Books, 1979.

Whyte, L. *The unconscious before Freud.* New York: Doubleday, 1962.

Wollheim, R. *Sigmund Freud.* New York: Viking Press, 1971.

GENERAL

Ellenberger, H. F. *The discovery of the unconscious: The history and evolution of dynamic psychiatry.* New York: Basic Books, 1970.

Ellenberger, H. F. The story of "Anna O": A critical review with new data. *Journal of the History of the Behavioral Sciences,* 1972, *8,* 267–279. (Reports that Anna O. underwent neither a cure nor a catharsis as a result of her treatment by Breuer.)

Freeman, L. *The story of Anna O.* New York: Walker, 1972.

Psychoanalysis: The Beginnings

Hale, N. G. From Berggasse XIX to Central Park West: The Americanization of psychoanalysis, 1919–1940. *Journal of the History of the Behavioral Sciences*, 1978, *14*, 299–315.

Jahoda, M. Some notes on the influence of psychoanalytic ideas on American psychology. *Human Relations*, 1963, *16*, 111–129.

Powell, R. C. The "subliminal" versus the "subconscious" in the American acceptance of psychoanalysis, 1906–1910. *Journal of the History of the Behavioral Sciences*, 1979, *15*, 155–165.

Shakow, D., & Rapaport, D. *The influence of Freud on American psychology.* New York: International Universities Press, 1964.

Skinner, B. F. Critique of psychoanalytic concepts and theories. *Scientific Monthly*, 1954, *79*, 300–305.

PSYCHOANALYSIS: AFTER THE FOUNDING

14

INTRODUCTION

After its formal founding, psychoanalysis proceeded in two directions. One group of analysts more or less adhered to the central tenets of Freudian thought, although they modified and elaborated certain ideas after Freud's death. A second group disagreed completely with some of Freud's major points, and among themselves.

The first group, the neo-Freudians, used Freud's system as a base from which to extend or amplify psychoanalytic concepts, while remaining in the Freudian tradition. Some of these modifications of Freudian theory are described in Chapter 15, where we consider recent developments in personality theory. For example, an increased emphasis on the autonomy of the ego, and less of a focus on instinctual determinants of personality, can be seen in the work of Allport and Erikson. Greater interest in the formation of personality from early experiences is reflected in the studies of Anna Freud and others, reported since 1945 in annual volumes of *The Psychoanalytic Study of the Child.* Another extension of Freud's system relates to the experimental testing of psychoanalytic propositions, discussed in Chapter 13.

The second group of analysts, the dissenters, although they did not disavow their basic psychoanalytic orientation, devised new theories to correct what were considered to be deficiencies and inadequacies in Freud's formulations. Freud, we noted, did not tolerate dissension, and those who espoused these new positions "left the movement not at all with the tacit agreement to differ but rather in an aura of heavy disapproval and the sort of invective that was once heaped upon the heads of heretics" (Brown, 1963, p. 37). We shall discuss four psychoanalysts in this second category: Jung, Adler, Horney, and Fromm.

CARL GUSTAV JUNG
(1875–1961)

Jung was once regarded by Freud as heir apparent of the psychoanalytic movement. Freud had even referred to him as the "crown prince." When

Psychoanalysis: After the Founding

his close friendship with Freud disintegrated in 1914, Jung began what he called *analytical psychology*.

The Life of Jung

Jung was raised in a small village in northern Switzerland near the famous Rhine Falls. By his own account, his childhood was lonely, isolated, and unhappy. His father was a clergyman who had apparently lost his faith and was often moody and irritable. His mother suffered from several emotional disorders and her behavior was erratic, changing in an instant from that of a happy housewife to that of a "witch-like demon" who mumbled incoherently.

The marriage was an unhappy one. Jung learned at an early age not to trust or confide in his parents and, by extension, in the external world. As a result, he turned inward to the world of his dreams, visions, and fantasies—the world of his unconscious. Dreams and the unconscious, not the conscious world of reason, became his guides in childhood and for the rest of his life.

At crucial times in his life Jung resolved problems and made decisions on the basis of what his unconscious told him through his dreams. When he was ready to begin his university studies, the solution to the problem of what to major in was revealed to him in a dream in which he found himself unearthing bones of prehistoric animals. He interpreted this to mean that he should study nature and science. That dream of digging beneath the surface, plus a dream he had had at the age of 3 in which he was in an underground cavern, may have determined the direction of his future study of personality: the unconscious forces that lie beneath the mind's surface.

In 1900 Jung graduated with a medical degree from the University of Basel. He became attracted to psychiatry and his first professional appointment was at the psychiatric clinic at the University of Zurich, which was directed by Eugen Bleuler, a psychiatrist noted for his work on schizophrenia. In 1905 Jung was appointed lecturer in psychiatry at the university, but after several years he resigned to devote his efforts to private practice, research, and writing.

Jung became interested in Freud's work in 1900 after reading *The Interpretation of Dreams*, which he described as a "masterpiece." By 1906 the two men had begun to correspond, and a year later Jung went to Vienna to meet Freud. At their initial meeting they talked with great animation for 13 hours, an exciting beginning for their close but short-lived friendship. In 1909 Jung accompanied Freud to the United States for the Clark University commemorative ceremonies, at which they both delivered lectures.

It is important to note that unlike some of Freud's disciples, Jung had already established his professional reputation at the time he began his association with Freud. He was one of the best known of the early converts to psychoanalysis. Thus, he was perhaps less malleable, less suggestible, than younger persons who became Freud's early followers; many of these were still students, unsure of their professional identities.

Although he did become a disciple of Freud's, Jung was never—even at the beginning of the relationship—a totally uncritical one, although he did suppress his criticisms early in their affiliation. Later, while writing *The Psychology of the Unconscious* (1912), he was troubled because he realized that this public statement of his position, which was at variance with Freud's, would damage their relationship. For two months he was unable to proceed with the book, so disturbed was he at Freud's possible reaction. Of course, he did publish, and the inevitable occurred.

In 1911, at Freud's insistence, and in spite of opposition from its Viennese members, Jung became the first president of the International Psychoanalytic Association. Freud believed that anti-Semitism might impede the psychoanalytic movement if a Jew headed the group. The Viennese members, almost all of whom were Jewish, distrusted and resented Jung, who was clearly Freud's favorite. They not only had seniority in the movement, but also believed Jung himself to be anti-Semitic.

Shortly after Jung was elected, his friendship with Freud showed signs of strain. Jung had begun to deemphasize the role of sex in his system and expressed a different concept of the libido in his 1912 book and in lectures at Fordham University. Friction grew, and in 1912 the two men agreed to terminate their personal correspondence. Relations were severed in 1914 when Jung resigned his presidency and withdrew from the association.

Beginning in 1913, when Jung was 38, he underwent a period of intense inner turmoil lasting three years, just as Freud had suffered at the same time of life. Believing that he was going insane, Jung was unable to carry on any intellectual work or even read a scientific book. (It is interesting, however, that he continued to treat his patients.) Jung resolved his emotional suffering in essentially the same way Freud had, by confronting his unconscious. Although he did not analyze his dreams systematically, as Freud had, he nonetheless listened to and followed the impulses of his unconscious as they were revealed in his dreams and fantasies. As with Freud, this emotional crisis of Jung's was a time of immense creativity, and it led to the formulation of his unusual approach to personality.

In line with his interest in the relevance of myths for the individual, Jung made a number of field expeditions to Africa and the southwestern United States in the 1920s to study the mental processes of preliterate peoples. In 1932 he was appointed professor at the Federal Polytechnical University in Zurich, a position he occupied until poor health forced him to resign in 1942. In 1944 a chair of medical psychology was founded for him at the University of Basel, but again illness prevented his keeping the position for more than a year. He remained active in research and writing for most of

An early Freudian, Carl Gustav Jung (1875–1961) came to disagree with Freud over the issues of the unconscious mind and the importance of sex, and developed his analytical psychology.
(*National Library of Medicine*)

his 86 years, publishing an astonishing array of books. His many awards include honorary degrees from Harvard and Oxford universities. He is read and respected throughout the world and known to people in all walks of life.

Jung's System: Analytical Psychology

Perhaps the basic point of difference between the views of Jung and Freud concerns the nature of libido. Whereas Freud defined libido in predominantly sexual terms, Jung regarded it as a generalized life energy, of which sex was only one part. For Jung, this libidinal life energy expressed itself in growth and reproduction, as well as in other kinds of activity, depending on what was most important for an individual at a given time.

Jung's refusal to regard the basic life energy as exclusively sexual left him free to give different interpretations to behavior that Freud could define only in sexual terms. For instance, during the first three to five years of life (which Jung called the *presexual* phase), the Jungian view is that libidinal energy serves the functions of nutrition and growth, with none of the sexual overtones of Freud's conception of these early years. Jung rejected the Freudian Oedipus complex and explained the child's attachment to its mother in terms of a dependency need, with satisfactions and rivalries associated with the mother's food-providing function. As the child matures and develops sexual functioning, Jung maintained, these nutritive functions become overlaid with sexual feelings. To Jung, libidinal energy took a heterosexual form only after puberty. Jung did not altogether deny the existence of sexual factors, but he reduced the role of sex to one of several drives that compose libido.

The second major difference between Jung and Freud is in the direction of the forces that influence the human personality. Whereas Freud viewed people as victims of childhood events, Jung believed that we are shaped by our future goals, hopes, and aspirations as well as by our past. Our behavior is not fully determined by childhood experiences but is subject to change later in life.

The Structure of Personality

Jung used the term *psyche* to refer to the mind, which he said consisted of three levels: the conscious, the personal unconscious, and the collective unconscious. At the center of consciousness is the *ego*, which is generally akin to our conception of ourselves. *Consciousness* includes perceptions, memories, and the like, and is the avenue of contact with reality that enables us to adapt to our environment.

Jung believed that too much emphasis had been given to the conscious; he considered it second in importance to the *unconscious*. The conscious aspect of the psyche is like the visible portion of an island. A larger, unknown part exists beneath the small part that can be seen above the waterline, and Jung focused on this mysterious, hidden base.

He postulated two levels or parts of the unconscious. Just beneath consciousness is the *personal unconscious*, which belongs to the individual.

It consists of all the impulses and wishes, the faint perceptions, and numerous other experiences in an individual's life that have been suppressed or forgotten. Incidents from the personal unconscious can easily be recalled to conscious awareness, indicating that this level of unconsciousness is not very deep.

The experiences in the personal unconscious are grouped into clusters called *complexes*. These are patterns of emotions, memories, and wishes with common themes that are characterized by a preoccupation with some idea, such as power or inferiority. A person may be preoccupied with power, for example, and this will influence his or her behavior. A complex is essentially a smaller personality that forms within the total personality.

Below the personal unconscious is the third and deepest level, the *collective unconscious*, which contains, unknown to the individual, the cumulative experiences of all previous generations, including our animal ancestors. The collective unconscious consists of universal evolutionary experiences and forms the basis of personality. It directs all present behavior and is therefore the most powerful force in the personality. It bears repeating that these evolutionary experiences are unconscious. We do not remember them or have images of them, as we do of the experiences that are found in the personal unconscious. Indeed, we are not at all aware of them. Jung believed that the universality of the collective unconscious could be accounted for by evolutionary theory, through the similarity of brain structure evident in all human races.

Viewed in terms of our island analogy, a number of small islands rising above the surface of the water represent the individual conscious awarenesses of a number of people. Land areas just beneath the water, which are exposed by the action of the tides, represent each individual's personal unconscious. The ocean floor, on which all the islands ultimately rest, is the collective unconscious.

Jung emphasized the powerful forces preserved in the collective unconscious because he believed that they contributed the most to psychic development. The inherited tendencies in the collective unconscious he termed *archetypes*, preexisting determinants of mental experience that dispose an individual to behave in a manner similar to that manifested by racial ancestors who confronted analogous situations.

Archetypes are experienced as emotions and other mental events and are typically associated with such significant human experiences as birth and death, with particular stages of life such as adolescence, and with reactions to extreme dangers. Jung's intensive investigation of the mythical and artistic products of various civilizations resulted in the discovery of symbols common to all, even in cultures so widely separated in time and place that there was no possibility of direct influence. In his patients' dreams Jung found what he considered to be definite traces of these same symbols.

Four of the many archetypes Jung described seemed to occur more often than others, to be laden with emotional significance, and to be traceable to ancient myths of diverse origins. These principal archetypes, which Jung viewed as separate personality systems, are the persona, the anima and animus, the shadow, and the self.

The *persona,* or outermost aspect of personality, conceals the true self. It is the mask we don when we come into contact with others, and it presents us as we want to appear to society. Thus, the persona may not correspond to our true personality. The notion of persona appears to be similar to the sociological concept of role playing, in which persons act as they think others expect them to act.

The archetypes *anima* and *animus* reflect the notion that each sex exhibits both masculine and feminine tendencies. The anima refers to feminine characteristics in man; the animus denotes masculine characteristics in woman. As with the other archetypes, these arise from the primitive past of the species, in which men and women took on some of the behavioral and emotional tendencies of the other sex.

The *shadow* archetype (the darker self) is the inferior, animal-like part of the personality, our racial heritage from the lower forms of life. It contains all immoral, passionate, and objectionable desires and activities. Jung wrote that the shadow urges us to do those things that we ordinarily would not allow ourselves to do. Having performed such actions, we usually insist that something came over us. Jung claimed that the "something" is the primitive part of our nature. However, the shadow also has a positive side. It is the source of spontaneity, creativity, insight, and deep emotion, all necessary for full human development.

Jung considered the *self* to be the most important archetype in his system. Composed of all aspects of the unconscious, the self provides unity and stability to the entire structure of personality. As a representation of the whole person, the self attempts to achieve complete integration, and can be likened to a drive or urge toward self-realization or self-actualization. By *self-actualization,* Jung meant a harmony and fullness or completeness of every aspect of the personality, the fullest development of the self. He believed that this state could not occur until middle age. Jung suggested that the total unity and wholeness toward which we all strive was represented by the *mandala* or magic circle, a symbol that he found repeatedly in various cultures.

Jung perhaps is best known for his discussion of *introversion* and *extraversion,* which are defined in terms of the direction of libidinal energy. He regarded them as two attitudes or modes of reacting to specific situations, and viewed them as part of consciousness.

The extravert directs the libido outside the self to external events, people, and situations. A person of this type is strongly influenced by forces in the environment and is sociable and self-confident in a wide range of situations. The libido of the introvert is directed inward. This individual is more contemplative, introspective, and resistant to external influence, less confident in relations with other people and with the external world, and relatively unsociable and shy.

Jung believed that these opposing attitudes exist in every person to varying degrees, but that one is usually more pronounced than the other. He suggested that no one is a total extravert or introvert; rather, the dominant attitude at a given moment can be influenced by the situation. A normally introverted person may become sociable and outgoing in a situation in which he or she is vitally interested.

According to Jung, personality differences are also manifested through the *functions,* which we use to orient ourselves to both the external objective world and the internal subjective world. Functions include thinking, feeling, sensation, and intuition. *Thinking* is a conceptual process that provides meaning and understanding; *feeling* is a subjective process of weighing and valuing. *Sensation* is the conscious perception of physical objects; *intuition* involves perceiving in an unconscious manner.

Thinking and feeling are rational modes of responding because they involve reason and judgment. Sensation and intuition are considered non-rational because they depend on the concrete and specific stimulus world and do not involve the use of reason. Within each pair only one mode can be dominant at a given time. This dominance of function can be combined with the dominance of extraversion or introversion to produce eight psychological types.

Early in his career Jung developed the *word association* test as a therapeutic and diagnostic tool that he used to uncover personality complexes in his patients. In this procedure a list of words is read to a patient who responds to each word with the first word that comes to mind. Jung measured the time taken to respond to each word, as well as changes in breathing and in the electrical conductivity of the skin. The two physiological measures provided additional evidence of emotional reactions to specific words. If a particular word produced a long response time, irregularity in breathing, and a change in skin conductivity, Jung deduced the existence of an unconscious emotional problem connected with the stimulus word or the reply.

Comment

Jung has had some influence in psychology and psychiatry, but much more in such fields as religion, history, art, and literature. Many historians, theologians, and writers have acknowledged him as a source of inspiration. For the most part, however, scientific psychology has ignored Jung's analytical psychology. Many of his books were not translated into English until 1966, and his less than lucid writing style impedes understanding. His disdain for traditional scientific methods repels experimentally oriented psychologists, for whom Jung's writings, because of their mysticism and religiosity, hold even less appeal than Freud's.

The criticisms noted in Chapter 13 about Freud's supporting evidence are applicable to Jung's work. He, too, relied on clinical observation and interpretation rather than controlled laboratory investigation. Analytical psychology has received less searching criticism than Freudian psychoanalysis, probably because Freud's stature in the field has relegated Jung and others to second place in terms of professional attention.

This is not to deny Jung's importance. His ideas are thought-provoking and novel, and he offers an optimistic conception of human nature that many find a welcome change from Freud. Jung was a scholarly, vital person who inspired loyalty in his adherents. Recently there have been signs of a growing Jungian influence. Jung's attention to such areas as occultism, mysticism, expansion of consciousness, and self-fulfillment appears compatible with the interests of many people in today's Western world.

SOCIAL-PSYCHOLOGICAL THEORIES IN PSYCHOANALYSIS: THE *ZEITGEIST* STRIKES AGAIN

Freud was influenced by the mechanistic and positivist outlook that pervaded nineteenth-century science. Around the end of the nineteenth century new disciplines suggested ways of viewing human nature in other than a biological and physical frame of reference. Anthropology, sociology, and social psychology were finding evidence to support the proposition that we are the product of the various social forces and institutions that compose our environment. These new ideas suggested that humans be studied as social rather than strictly biological beings.

As different cultures came under study by anthropologists, it became clear that some of the neurotic symptoms and taboos hypothesized by Freud were not universal, as he had believed. For example, taboos against incest did not exist in all societies. Further, sociologists and social psychologists had found that much human behavior is a result of social conditioning rather than instinctive biological factors.

Thus, the intellectual spirit of the times revised our conception of ourselves, but Freud, to the dismay of some of his followers, continued to stress instinctual, biological determinants of personality. As a result, some of the younger theorists, less constrained by tradition, began to move away from orthodox Freudian psychoanalysis and to reshape psychoanalytic theory along lines congruent with the orientation of the social sciences. We shall discuss three of these socially oriented dissenters: Adler, Horney, and Fromm.

ALFRED ADLER
(1870–1937)

Adler is usually considered to be the first figure in the social–psychological brand of psychoanalysis because he broke with Freud in 1911. He developed a theory in which social interest plays a major role.

The Life of Adler

Adler was born to wealthy parents in a suburb of Vienna. His unhappy childhood was marked by sickness, jealousy of an older brother, and feelings of being small, unattractive, and rejected by his mother. Despite this unpromising beginning, he worked with great intensity as he grew older to become popular with his peers. As a result, he achieved a sense of acceptance and self-esteem with others that he had not found with his family.

Initially, Adler was a poor student, so poor that a teacher told his father that he was unfit for any job except a shoemaker's apprentice. But through persistence and dedication, Adler rose from the bottom to the top of his class. Both socially and academically, he worked hard to overcome his handicaps and inferiorities, thus becoming an example of his later theory of the necessity of compensating for one's weaknesses. The notion of feelings of inferiority, which was to form a central part of his system, is a direct reflection of his own early experiences.

At the age of 4, while recovering from a near-fatal illness, Adler decided to become a physician. He received his medical degree from the University of Vienna in 1895. After specializing in ophthalmology and then practicing general medicine, he went into psychiatry. In 1902 he began meeting with Freud's weekly discussion group as one of its four charter members.

Over the next several years Adler developed a theory of personality that was different from Freud's in major ways. By 1911 he had become openly critical of Freud's emphasis on sexual factors. A year earlier Freud had named Adler president of the Viennese Analytic Society, apparently in an effort to reconcile the growing differences between them. The inevitable split was complete in 1911, when Adler resigned his presidency and officially broke with the Freudian position.

Adler served as a physician in the Austrian Army during World War I, and later organized child guidance clinics in the Vienna school system. During the 1920s his individual psychology attracted favorable attention throughout the world, and many followers came to study with him in Vienna. He lectured in several countries, and in 1926 came to the United States, where he received a warm welcome. He made several visits and in 1934 became professor of medical psychology at the Long Island College of Medicine in New York. In 1937, while on a strenuous lecture tour, he died in Aberdeen, Scotland.

Freud, replying to a friend who was greatly saddened by Adler's death, wrote: "I don't understand your sympathy for Adler. For a Jewish boy out of a Viennese suburb a death in Aberdeen is an unheard-of career in itself and a proof of how far he had got on. The world really rewarded him richly for his service in having contradicted psychoanalysis" (Scarf, 1971, p. 47).

Adler wrote numerous books and articles, many of them addressed to the lay public. Adlerian theories continue to be propounded in the *American Journal of Individual Psychology* and by the American Society of Individual Psychology.

Alfred Adler (1870–1937), who broke with Freud in 1911, viewed human motivation as the drive for superiority and stressed the unity of personality and social factors in his individual psychology. *(Archives of the History of American Psychology)*

Adler's System:
Individual Psychology

The theoretical positions of Adler and Freud differed sharply. Whereas Freud's theories emphasized the role of the past in influencing behavior, Adler's orientation was toward the future. The division of personality into separate parts or aspects is an essential part of Freudian theory; the Adlerian approach emphasizes the unity of personality.

In another departure from Freud, Adler developed his system of individual psychology along social lines. He believed that human behavior is determined not by biological forces, or instincts, but by social forces: We can understand an individual's personality only through an investigation of his or her social relationships and attitudes toward others. Adler held that social interest develops in infancy:

> The first social situation that confronts a child is its relation to its mother, from the very first day. By her educational skill the child's interest in another person is first awakened. If she understands how to train this interest in the direction of cooperation, all the congenital and acquired capacities of the child will converge in the direction of social sense. (Adler, 1930, p. 403)

Thus, social attitude and interest are developed through learning experiences. Like Freud, Adler recognized the importance of the early formative years of childhood, but his focus was on social rather than biological, forces. As well, he minimized the role of sex in shaping personality.

Another point of difference between the theories of Freud and those of Adler concerns the importance of consciousness. Freud stressed unconscious determinants of behavior, but Adler emphasized the conscious. He considered humans to be conscious beings, aware of their motivations. To Freud, human behavior was determined by past experiences. In contrast, Adler believed that we are more strongly influenced by what we think the future holds. Strivings for future goals or anticipations of future events can modify and influence our present behavior. For example, a person living in fear of eternal damnation after death will behave in accordance with this expectation.

Adler emphasized the essential unity and consistency of personality. He posited a dynamic driving force that channels the various resources of personality toward one overriding goal. This final goal, toward which we all strive, is *superiority* or perfection, which includes more complete and perfect development, accomplishment, fulfillment, and realization of the self. In this view, sex is not the dominant drive, but is one of a number of means to the end of superiority.

Adler saw this striving in every aspect of personality:

> It runs parallel to physical growth. It is an intrinsic necessity of life itself. . . . All our functions follow its direction; rightly or wrongly they

strive for conquest, surety, increase. The impetus from minus to plus is never-ending. The urge from "below" to "above" never ceases. Whatever premises all our philosophers and psychologists dream of—self-preservation, pleasure principle, equalization—all these are but vague representations, attempts to express the great upward drive. . . . a fundamental category of thought, the structure of our reason, . . . the fundamental fact of our life. (Adler, 1930, pp. 398–399)

This striving for superiority is innate, according to Adler, and is responsible for all progress, not only at the level of the individual, but throughout the history of civilization. It carries person and society ever upward from one stage of progress to the next.

We have noted that Adler did not agree with Freud that the primary basis of motivation centers on sexual factors. He believed instead that a general feeling of *inferiority* is the determining force in behavior, as it apparently was in his own life. At first, Adler related this feeling of inferiority to defective parts of the body. The child with a hereditary organic weakness will direct its efforts at *compensating* for the defect, overemphasizing the deficient function. For example, Demosthenes forcefully overcame his stuttering to become a great speaker; likewise, a child with a weak body may, through intensive exercise, come to excel as an athlete or dancer.

Adler later broadened the scope of this concept to include any physical, mental, or social handicap, real or imagined. He also believed that the helplessness and smallness of the infant produce a general feeling of inferiority that is experienced by everyone because all children are totally dependent on their environment. The child, consciously aware of his or her inferiority, is at the same time driven by the innate striving for superiority. The child is goaded by the need to overcome inferiority and insecurity. Adler believed that this "pushing and pulling" process continues throughout life, impelling an individual toward greater accomplishments.

Feelings of inferiority function to the advantage of both individual and society because they lead to continuous improvement. However, in childhood feelings of inferiority that are met with excessive pampering or rejection by the parents can bring about abnormally expressed compensatory behaviors. In addition, failure to compensate for feelings of inferiority leads to the development of an inferiority complex, rendering the person incapable of dealing with the problems of life.

According to Adler, our overriding goal—superiority—is universal, but he recognized the existence of a wide variety of behaviors that could be used to reach this goal. Different people manifest their strivings for superiority in different ways, and each develops a characteristic mode of responding, a *style of life*.

It appears that after the fourth or fifth year of life the style of life has been fashioned as a prototype, with its particular way of seizing upon life, its strategy for conquering it, its degree of ability to cooperate. (Adler, 1930, p. 403)

The style of life involves the set of behaviors by means of which we compensate for a real or imagined inferiority. In our example of the child with a weak body, its style of life involves all those activities, such as exercise or practice at sports, that will result in increased physical strength and stamina. This life style, formed in childhood, becomes fixed and difficult to change, and provides the framework within which all later experiences are handled.

Thus, we can see that Adler emphasized the importance of the early years of life in forming the personality, much as Freud did. However, he differed from Freud in his belief that the individual consciously creates his or her own life style or self.

He also stressed the family as a factor in personality development. A child with a handicap may consider itself a failure, but through compensation and with the help of understanding parents it can transform inferiorities into strengths. On the other hand, a child who is overly indulged by his or her parents may become self-centered, have no social interests, and expect others always to accede to his or her wishes. A neglected child may develop a style of life that involves seeking revenge against society. Both pampering and neglect undermine our confidence in our ability to cope with the demands of life.

Adler's concept of the *creative power of the self* is considered the pinnacle of his theory. He suggested that we have the capacity to determine our personality in accordance with our unique style of life. The creative power represents an active principle of human existence that may be likened to the older concept of soul. Certain abilities and experiences, Adler maintained, are available to an individual from heredity and environment, but these are only

> the bricks which he uses in his own "creative" way in building up his attitude toward life. It is his individual way of using these bricks—or in other words, it is his attitude toward life—which determines his relationship to the outside world. (1935, p. 5)

The concept of the creative power of the self stresses the idea that we are consciously active in shaping our own personalities and destinies. Adler believed that people are capable of participating directly in their own fates, rather than having them passively determined by past experiences, as Freud had claimed.

In examining the childhood backgrounds of his patients, Adler became interested in the relationship between personality and *order of birth*. He believed that the oldest, middle, and youngest child have different social experiences that result in the formation of different personalities. Adler noted that the oldest child, for example, receives a great deal of attention until dethroned by the birth of a second child. As a result, the first-born may feel insecure and hostile toward people and become authoritarian and conservative, with a strong interest in maintaining order and authority.

Adler suggested that criminals, neurotics, and alcoholics are often first-born children.

Adler found the second child to be intensely ambitious, rebellious, and jealous, constantly trying to surpass the first-born. (Adler, a second-born child, had a competitive relationship with his older brother all his life.) Nevertheless, Adler considered the second-born to be better adjusted than either a first-born or a youngest child. The latter was seen as spoiled and the most likely to have behavior problems as a child and as an adult.

Comment

Adler's theories were warmly received by many people who were dissatisfied, and often repelled, by Freud's picture of human nature as dominated by sexual forces and determined by childhood experiences. It is more pleasant to consider ourselves as consciously directing our own development and destiny. Adler presented a more satisfying and optimistic image of human nature. His belief in the importance of social factors, to the relative exclusion of biological determinants, is usually considered a positive contribution. This attitude reinforced an already growing interest in the social sciences and the beginnings of a reorientation by traditional psychoanalysis to render its principles more applicable to the diverse behaviors found in various cultures.

Adler's system does not lack critics. Many claim that his theories are superficial because they rely on a large number of commonsense observations from everyday life. Whether this criticism is valid, however, is debatable; many of his observations, regardless of origin, are considered to be shrewd and insightful.

It is also argued that Adler was not a consistent, systematic theorist because his position leaves too many questions unanswered. What, precisely, is this creative force by which we direct our behavior? Why do people not become reconciled to their inferiority? What are the relative roles of heredity and environment in this process? (Of course, Adler's is not the only system with unanswered questions.) In addition, the criticisms that more experimentally oriented psychologists directed at Freud and Jung apply to Adler.

Finally, it has been said that Adler's influence is greater than is generally recognized because other theorists (Horney and Fromm, for example) have been influenced by his work. Their theories are often considered to be more neo-Adlerian than neo-Freudian. The influence of Adler can also be seen in certain post-Freudian developments in psychoanalysis. As discussed later in this chapter, psychoanalysis has come to emphasize the role of consciousness and to deemphasize the role of sex, in line with Adler's views. Adler also had considerable influence on the development of humanistic psychology and the work of Abraham Maslow (see Chapter 15).

KAREN HORNEY
(1885–1952)

Horney, an early feminist, was trained as a Freudian psychoanalyst in Berlin. She considered her work to involve modifying and extending Freud's system rather than being distinctly non-Freudian.

She was born in Hamburg, Germany. Her father was a devout, morose ship captain many years older than her mother, a liberal and vivacious woman. Horney's childhood was far from idyllic. Her mother rejected her in favor of an older brother, and her father constantly belittled her appearance and intelligence, leaving her with strong feelings of worthlessness. This childhood lack of love fostered what she later called basic anxiety; it is another example of the influence of personal factors on a theorist's view of personality.

In spite of opposition from her father, Horney entered medical school at the University of Berlin and received her M.D. in 1913. From 1914 to 1918 she undertook psychoanalytic training at the Berlin Psychoanalytic Institute. She began private practice in 1919 and became a faculty member at the institute.

Over the next 15 years Horney wrote many journal articles, most of them concerned with problems of the feminine personality and demonstrating her disagreement with certain of Freud's concepts. In 1932 she came to the United States as associate director of the Chicago Institute for Psychoanalysis. In 1934 she established a private practice and taught at the New York Psychoanalytic Institute, but a growing disaffection for orthodox Freudian theories led her to break with this group and found the American Institute of Psychoanalysis. She remained head of this organization until her death.

Before discussing Horney's system, let us consider her points of disagreement with Freud. First, she considered herself a disciple of Freud and accepted several of his basic principles. "Though retaining what I considered the fundamentals of Freud's teaching, I realized . . . that my search for a better understanding has led me in directions that were at variance with Freud" (1945, p. 13). However, parts of her system are so greatly at variance with Freud's that it occasionally becomes difficult to recognize her ideas as falling within the Freudian framework.

Horney believed that some of Freud's basic assumptions were influenced by the spirit of the times in which he worked, and that times had changed drastically by the 1930s and 1940s when she set about formulating her system. The intellectual and cultural mores had changed, and attitudes about sexual conduct and the roles of the sexes had shifted, so that many of Freud's theories were no longer in line with the *Zeitgeist*.

Not only were the times in which Horney worked different from Freud's, but so was the place. Horney developed her theories in the United States, where popular attitudes about sex had changed even more radically than in Europe. As well, her American patients were unlike her previous European

Although Karen Horney (1885–1952) shared Freud's emphasis on early childhood, she viewed basic anxiety arising from environment and culture as the major force motivating people to seek safety and security. (*National Library of Medicine*)

patients, and the differences could only be accounted for in terms of social influence and not universal biological factors, as Freud had claimed.

Horney, therefore, did not agree with Freud that personality development depends on unchangeable, instinctive forces. She denied the preeminent position of sexual factors, challenged the validity of the Oedipus theory, and discarded the libido concept and the Freudian structure of personality.

Opposed to Freud's belief that women are motivated by penis envy, Horney argued that men are motivated by "womb envy," that they envy women for their ability to give birth.

Freud and Horney also differed in their fundamental conceptions of human nature:

> Freud's pessimism as regards neuroses and their treatment arose from the depths of his disbelief in human goodness and human growth. Man, he postulated, is doomed to suffer or to destroy. . . . My own belief is that man has the capacity as well as the desire to develop his potentialities and become a decent human being . . . I believe that man can change and go on changing as long as he lives. (Horney, 1945, p. 19)

There are additional differences, but the important point is that Horney rejected much of Freud's system. She did accept, however, certain tenets, including the notion of unconscious motivation and the existence of emotional, nonrational motives.

Horney's System

The underlying concept in Horney's theory is *basic anxiety,* defined as "the feeling a child has of being isolated and helpless in a potentially hostile world" (Horney, 1945, p. 41). This basic anxiety can result from various expressions of parental attitudes and behavior toward the child, including dominance, lack of protection, lack of love, and erratic behavior. Anything that disturbs the secure relations between the child and its parents is capable of producing anxiety. Thus, basic anxiety is not innate, but rather results from environmental factors; it has social causes.

In place of Freud's life and death instincts as major motivating forces, Horney considered the helpless infant to be seeking security in a hostile and threatening world. She claimed that the decisive driving power for human behavior is the need for safety, security, and freedom from fear and threat.

Horney shared with Freud the belief that personality develops in early childhood, but she believed it could change throughout life. Also, whereas Freud detailed psychosexual stages of development, Horney focused on the way the growing child is treated by its parents. She denied any such universal developmental phases as an oral stage or an Oedipus complex. She believed that a child's possible development of anal or oral or phallic tendencies results from parental behaviors, and that nothing in a child's development is universal. Everything depends on culture and social–environmental factors. Horney attempted to show how the developmental conflicts Freud ascribed to instinctual sources could be attributed instead to social forces.

Thus, Horney emphasized the importance of early childhood experiences and parental relations with the child, because parents can either satisfy or frustrate the child's need for safety and security. The environment provided for the child and the way the child reacts to it form the structure of personality.

As noted, Horney's main concept is the basic anxiety developing out of a child's relations with its parents. When this socially or environmentally produced anxiety arises, a child develops a number of behavioral strategies to deal with the resulting feelings of insecurity and helplessness. The child thus structures its personality in response to the demands of its environment.

When one of these behavioral strategies becomes a fixed part of the personality, it is a *neurotic need* (or a mode of defense against anxiety). Horney postulated ten neurotic needs, including the needs for affection and approval, prestige, personal achievement, perfection, and independence. The neurotic needs can be reduced to one of three directional categories: (1) movement toward people, as in the need for love; (2) movement away from people, as in the need for independence; and (3) movement against people, as in the need for power.

Movement toward people involves acceptance of helplessness and an attempt to win the affection of others and be dependent on them; this is the only way in which the individual can feel secure with others. Movement away from people involves staying apart from others to avoid any situation of dependence. Movement against people involves hostility, rebellion, and aggression against others.

Horney believed that none of these needs is a realistic way of dealing with anxiety. The needs themselves can give rise to basic conflicts because of their incompatibility. Once a person firmly establishes a method of coping with anxiety, his or her behavior ceases to be flexible enough to permit alternative modes of expression. When a fixed behavior is inappropriate in a particular situation, the person is unable to change it to meet that situation's demands. This entrenched behavior intensifies the individual's difficulties because

> the attitudes do not remain restricted to the area of human relationships but gradually pervade the entire personality, as a malignant tumor pervades the whole organic tissue. They end by encompassing not only the person's relation to others but also his relation to himself and to life in general. (Horney, 1945, p. 46)

Horney also invoked the concept of the neurotic's *idealized self-image*, which provides a false picture of the personality. This self-image is an imperfect and misleading mask that prevents the neurotic person from understanding and accepting his or her true self. In donning the mask, the neurotic denies the existence of inner conflicts. The self-image, which to the neurotic is genuine, enables the person to believe that he or she is far superior to the person he or she actually is.

Horney believed that the neurotic's basic conflicts are neither innate nor inevitable, but arise out of undesirable social situations in childhood and can be prevented if the child's home life is characterized by understanding, security, love, and warmth.

Comment

Horney's optimism about the possibility of avoiding neurotic conflicts was welcomed by many people as a relief from the pessimism of Freudian theory. Wolman (1960) suggested that Horney's contribution to psychological theory is considerable because she introduced a model of personality that stressed social factors, attributing little, if anything, to innate factors.

Horney's theory of personality may be weaker than Freud's in clarity, internal consistency, and level of formal development. But many believe that it is easier simply to accept or reject Freud's theory than to attempt to reshape it, as Horney did. So radical is her departure from basic Freudian concepts that her system is frowned on by more orthodox psychoanalysts. Also, her evidence, like that of Jung, Adler, and Freud, is taken from clinical observations and thus is subject to the questions regarding its scientific legitimacy noted earlier.

Although Horney never had a loyal band of disciples or a journal in which to develop and disseminate her ideas, her work nevertheless has exerted considerable influence. Her ideas have drawn a large public following, increased in recent years by the change in the role of women in our society.

ERICH FROMM
(1900–1980)

Fromm studied sociology and psychology rather than medicine before training in psychoanalysis and becoming a therapist. Because of these early interests, his theories have been described as social philosophy rather than psychology.

Fromm was born in Frankfurt, Germany, an only child of neurotic parents. His father was moody and anxious and his mother suffered periods of depression. At the age of 12, Fromm became extremely upset over the seemingly inexplicable suicide of a friend of the family, and a few years later he was shocked by the hatred, hysteria, and carnage of World War I. In an effort to understand such irrational behavior, Fromm studied philosophy, psychology, and sociology at Heidelberg, where he received his Ph.D. in 1922. He took psychoanalytic training in Munich and at the Berlin Psychoanalytic Institute and came to the United States in 1934. He lectured at the Chicago Psychoanalytic Institute before moving to New York, where he worked in private practice. He taught at a number of universities and institutes in the United States, and then at the National University of Mexico, where he established a psychiatry department at the university's medical school. After his retirement in 1965 Fromm maintained his teaching and consulting activities, commuting between Mexico and the United States until 1974, when he moved to Switzerland. He continued to work at his home in Muralto until his death.

Fromm's System

One of Fromm's basic interests was the effect on the individual of large aspects of society. He believed, for instance, that political organizations no longer provide the guidance and security they once did. He suggested that we have succeeded in freeing ourselves from dependence on nature only to find ourselves isolated from other human beings.

Consider the feelings of belonging, dependence, and security that as children we experience in our relations with our parents. When we reach adulthood, we achieve independence, but at the expense of our earlier security. Similarly, as society has evolved toward greater mobility, complexity, and impersonality, we have lost our once secure relationship with smaller, more primary groups, such as the tribe or village, as well as with nature itself. As a result, we feel lonely and insignificant.

Fromm suggested that we are motivated to escape our ever-growing freedom and return to a more secure existence. In Fromm's system the major motivating force in human existence is not the satisfaction of instinctual drives, but the desire to revert to a condition of dependence. In *Escape from Freedom* (1941), written during the Nazi regime, Fromm suggested that Nazism attracted people because it offered an escape from intolerable freedom and a return to security and dependency. In short, Fromm viewed human nature as culturally or socially—not biologically—determined.

The social systems through which we can regain security, according to Fromm, are authoritarianism and humanism. Authoritarianism involves the external imposition on a society of a set of rigid guiding principles that produce a state of bondage or slavery. Fromm rejected this solution to the problem of human isolation because he believed that a society that prevents the individual from realizing his or her full potential must generate hostility against itself. A far more effective solution is humanism, in which we unite in the spirit of love and shared work or mutual cooperation. Fromm envisioned a social system called "humanistic communitarian socialism," in which each person feels a kinship with every other and hence does not feel alone.

Five specific needs arise from the conditions of our lonely existence: the need for a sense of individual identity, the need to feel that we belong to society (rootedness), the need to transcend our base animal nature and become creative human beings, the need to relate satisfactorily to others, and the need for a stable and consistent orientation or frame of reference.

Fromm noted that society does not provide adequate means for satisfying these needs. Further, social and political institutions often produce conflicts by satisfying certain needs at the expense of others. A strong identification with an industrial or national symbol, for example, frustrates the need for personal identity.

Fromm's system offers several ways to escape the isolation and insecurity he believed predominate in modern society. In *Man for Himself* (1947) and *The Heart of Man* (1964) he identified these strategies as dynamic orientations of character: receptive, exploitative, hoarding, marketing, and productive.[1] Although no one exhibits only one orientation, Fromm believed that one may be dominant in a given person. He further suggested that the productive orientation is the only rational and healthy way of behaving.

In the *receptive* orientation, persons believe that the only way to get what they want—whether to satisfy material or emotional desires—is to receive it from some outside source. The idea of love in this orientation is that of being loved, not of loving. These persons become submissive and dependent on others, needing someone (or some system) to take care of them. Such individuals go to great lengths to maintain a strong identification with others. (In Horney's terms, this orientation involves a movement toward people.)

The *exploitative* orientation is manifested as aggressive behavior, and corresponds to Horney's movement against people. Persons so oriented do not expect to receive from others; rather, they take from or exploit others by force or cunning, according to the "might makes right" philosophy.

The *hoarding* orientation involves the perception of the outside world as threatening, which leads to distrust of and rigidity toward people. Hoarding persons tend to save and possess, becoming frugal and miserly and letting out as little as possible (material things or emotions). They evaluate their security in terms of tangible possessions and wealth.

The fourth orientation, *marketing,* reflects the advent of capitalism, according to which personal success is judged by our acceptability to those who use our services or employ us. We must, therefore, play a variety of socially approved roles and concentrate on selling ourselves rather than on fulfilling our potential. Our value depends more on our success in the marketplace and less on personal qualities; such a situation does not lead to a feeling of security. In this orientation, we say to others, in essence, "I am as you want me to be."

Fromm considered all four of these orientations to be pathological. Truly healthy persons manifest the *productive* orientation, in which they are able to realize their full potential and achieve their goals without misusing or abusing others. This may be accomplished by making a creative contribution to family, occupation, or society.

---

[1] In later writings Fromm postulated another pair of orientations: necrophilious, describing a person who is attracted to death; and biophilious, a person attracted to life.

Comment

The overall theme in Fromm's writings is our relationship to society. Fromm remained optimistic about our ability to shape a society that will allow us to develop into fully human creatures. This point of view is acceptable to many because it offers the hope that we can introduce constructive forces into society to render the human condition more distinctly human.

Fromm has been criticized for providing little empirical data to support his theory and for ignoring recent developments in psychoanalysis and humanistic psychology. Also, his allegations that people had a higher degree of security and belongingness in earlier times (particularly in the Middle Ages) have been refuted by scientists who charge that Fromm ignored such calamities as plagues, religious persecutions, witch hunts, and wars, events not usually associated with feelings of security.

Nevertheless, Fromm's work has won great popularity and some of his books have been best-sellers. He deliberately wrote for the lay public rather than for colleagues, and his ideas brought together the impact of psychological, social, economic, and political forces on the human personality.

CRITICISMS OF THE SOCIAL-PSYCHOLOGICAL THEORIES

The theorists discussed in this section have an obvious point of similarity in that they all place considerable emphasis on the role of social variables in personality development. Although they acknowledge varying degrees of intellectual debt to the work of Freud, each system constitutes a vigorous protest against the Freudian notion of the primacy of biological forces in the formation of personality. These theorists see human behavior as determined not primarily by instinctual, biological forces, but rather by the types of interpersonal relationships to which the individual is exposed, particularly in childhood.

Just as the role of instinct is minimized, so too is the role of the libido and its manifestations, such as the Oedipus complex and psychosexual stages of development. Anxiety and other expressions of abnormal behavior do not originate in instinct, libido, and sex, but instead develop from early social relationships. We are not irrevocably doomed to anxiety, as in Freud's deterministic theory, because anxiety can be avoided by the proper childhood social experiences.

According to Freud, human behavior is universally static; the social-psychological theorists consider our behavior to be flexible and capable of being consciously and continuously changed by each of us. Our social organizations, too, are flexible and liable to deliberate alteration. Although they recognize that social mores can be modified only gradually and with difficulty, the social-psychological theorists optimistically agree that we are capable of developing the kind of social system most appropriate to our requirements.

Several criticisms have been directed against the social-psychological theorists. It is argued that their image of humans as rational, conscious, and socialized beings is unconvincing in light of our often disappointing and irrational behavior. One can blame displays of violence and injustice on a particular social system, but critics argue that we shape our society to suit our needs. We are left with the paradox of rational, perfectible, socialized beings who nevertheless have developed social systems that are inadequate, indeed often injurious, to our needs.

The social-psychological theorists have also been accused of neglecting the social processes through which we are shaped, leaving unanswered the question of how we learn to be properly functioning members of society. They draw on the general concept of learning to explain personality formation, but neglect the specific mechanisms of the learning process.

SUGGESTED READINGS

JUNG

Brome, V. *Jung.* New York: Atheneum, 1978.

Evans, R. I. *Jung on elementary psychology: A discussion between C. G. Jung and Richard I. Evans.* New York: Dutton, 1976.

Fordham, F. *An introduction to Jung's psychology.* Baltimore: Penguin, 1959.

Hannah, B. *Jung: His life and work.* New York: Putnam, 1976.

Jacobi, J. *The psychology of C. G. Jung* (Rev. ed.). New Haven, CT: Yale University Press, 1951.

Jung, C. G. *The collected works of C. G. Jung.* (Bollingen series, H. Read, M. Fordham, & G. Adler, Eds.). Princeton, NJ: Princeton University Press, 1953 to date. (The definitive reference source for Jung's writings.)

Jung, C. G. *Memories, dreams, reflections.* New York: Vintage Books, 1961. (Jung's autobiography.)

McGuire, W. (Ed.). *The Freud/Jung letters.* Princeton, NJ: Princeton University Press, 1974. (The correspondence between the two men during their years of collaboration.)

McGuire, W., & Hull, R. F. C. (Eds.). *C. G. Jung speaking: Interviews and encounters.* Princeton, NJ: Princeton University Press, 1977.

Stern, P. J. *C. G. Jung: The haunted prophet.* New York: George Braziller, 1976. (An unflattering biography.)

Storr, A. *C. G. Jung.* New York: Viking Press, 1973.

Van der Post, L. *Jung and the story of our time.* New York: Pantheon Books, 1975. (A flattering biography.)

von Franz, M.-L. *C. G. Jung: His myth in our time.* Boston: Little, Brown, 1975.

ADLER

Ansbacher, H. L. *Alfred Adler revisited.* New York: Praeger, 1979. (An appraisal of Adler's life and work.)

Ansbacher, H. L., & Ansbacher, R. R. (Eds.). *The individual psychology of Alfred Adler.* New York: Basic Books, 1956.

Ansbacher, H. L., & Ansbacher, R. R. (Eds.). *Superiority and social interest: A collection of later writings by Alfred Adler.* New York: Viking Press, 1973.

Orgler, H. *Alfred Adler: The man and his work.* New York: Putnam, 1965.

Sperber, M. *Masks of loneliness: Alfred Adler in perspective.* New York: Macmillan, 1974.

HORNEY

Horney, K. *The collected works of Karen Horney.* New York: Norton, 1963.

Rubins, J. L. *Karen Horney: Gentle rebel of psychoanalysis.* New York: Dial Press, 1978.

Wolman, B. Psychoanalysis without libido: An analysis of Karen Horney's contribution to psychoanalytic theory. *American Journal of Psychotherapy,* 1954, *8,* 21–31.

FROMM

Evans, R. I. *Dialogue with Erich Fromm.* New York: Harper, 1966.

Fromm, E. *Escape from freedom.* New York: Holt, 1941.

Fromm, E. *The sane society.* New York: Holt, 1955.

Fromm, E. *The anatomy of human destructiveness.* New York: Holt, 1973.

Fromm, E. *To have or to be?* New York: Harper, 1976.

15
MORE RECENT DEVELOPMENTS

SCHOOLS OF THOUGHT IN PSYCHOLOGY

Throughout this book we have described how the major schools of thought in psychology came into being, prospered for a time, and then (with the exception of psychoanalysis) became part of the mainstream of contemporary American psychology, or at least contributed to it. We have also seen that each movement grew strong and vital through its opposition to another system. When there was no longer any need for protest—when the new school had vanquished its opposition—that school died as a movement and became an established position, at least for a time.

Each of the schools of thought was successful; each made substantial contributions to psychological thought. Each, therefore, was a fruitful protest and accomplished its mission. This is true even for structuralism, although it left little direct imprint on the contemporary psychological scene. There are no longer structuralists of the Wundtian variety in psychology, nor have there been for decades. Yet structuralism was an enormous success. It accomplished exactly what it set out to do: it established an independent science of psychology that was finally free of philosophy. That it failed to remain the dominant position in psychology for more than a short time does not detract from its revolutionary achievement as the founding school of a new science.

Consider the success of functionalism, which also has not lasted as a separate school of thought. As an attitude, a point of view—which was all it hoped to be—functionalism has permeated contemporary American psychological thought. To the extent that American psychology today is as much profession as science, and is applying its findings to virtually every aspect of life, the functional, utilitarian viewpoint has won a great many converts. Whether this applied-professional orientation will be to the ultimate benefit of psychology is being debated. There is no debate, however, about the source of that orientation: it derived from the functional psychologists of the early years of the twentieth century.

What of Gestalt psychology? It, too, on a more modest scale, has accomplished its mission. Its opposition to elementism, support of a molar approach, and continuing interest in consciousness have entered psychological thinking in a number of areas: clinical psychology, learning, perception, social psychology, and thinking. Unlike structuralism and functionalism, Gestalt psychology continues to maintain the character of a separate school of thought. There are psychologists today who define their research and professional identity along Gestalt lines. Although the Gestalt school did not transform psychology the way its founders hoped it would, it still exerts an influence. For this reason, it must be defined as a successful movement.

As noteworthy as the accomplishments of structuralism, functionalism, and Gestalt psychology have been, they take second place to the phenomenal influence of behaviorism and psychoanalysis. Not only have the effects of these two schools of thought been pronounced, but their continuing identities as separate schools of thought are also important. Large numbers of psychologists, particularly in the United States, have no difficulty identifying themselves as belonging to either the behaviorist or psychoanalytic tradition. Although there has been some rapprochement between these two positions in recent years, in general they stand apart as major forces in psychology today.

We discussed how both schools splintered into differing positions since the days of their founders, Watson and Freud. There is today no single form of behaviorism or psychoanalysis that has won allegiance from all members of either school (though Skinner enjoys a prominent position in behaviorism). The emergence of subschools has divided both viewpoints into competing factions, each with its own version of the true path. Despite the internal diversity of the schools, however, behaviorists and psychoanalysts stand firmly against each other in their definitions of and approaches to psychology. A Skinnerian behaviorist still has much more in common with a Hullian behaviorist than with a Jungian or Adlerian psychoanalyst.

The vitality of these two major schools of thought is found in the fact that they are still evolving. Skinnerian psychology is not the last stage in the development of behaviorism any more than Adlerian psychology was the final stage of psychoanalysis.

We shall examine the most recent stage of evolution in behaviorism, the "cognitive revolution," and some latter-day developments in psychoanalysis, the work of Allport, Murray, and Erikson. We shall also consider the newest large-scale movement in psychology: humanistic psychology. Designated the "third force," humanistic psychology is not a branch of either major force but rather an alternative to both. Although it opposes behaviorism and psychoanalysis, it also draws upon them, trying to build on the best of those approaches. Humanistic psychology has today assumed the characteristics that define a movement as a formal school of thought.

BEHAVIORISM: THE COGNITIVE REVOLUTION

"Psychology," John B. Watson wrote in his behaviorist manifesto of 1913, "must discard all reference to consciousness." This was a strong and highly successful appeal. The many psychologists who followed Watson eliminated the mind, conscious processes, and mentalistic terms from psychology. The result, British psychologist Cyril Burt wrote, "is that psychology, having first bargained away its soul and then gone out of its mind, seems now, as it faces an untimely end, to have lost all consciousness" (1962, p. 229).

Words like "will," "feeling," "image," "mind," and "consciousness" were effectively banned in psychology. They became taboo, never to be uttered by behaviorists except in tones of derision. And so Skinner could talk about the empty organism and build an influential system of psychology that never attempted to investigate what might be going on inside the organism. For decades elementary textbooks in psychology did not contain any reference to the mind or to consciousness. Psychology had indeed lost consciousness, forever, it appeared.

Suddenly—or so it seemed, though it had been building gradually for some time—there was ample and visible evidence that psychology was regaining consciousness. The taboo words were being uttered aloud in the forums from which they had been so vehemently excluded for so long.

Consider a few examples. In 1979, in the *American Psychologist*, an influential journal of the American Psychological Association, there appeared an article entitled "Behaviorism and the Mind: A (Limited) Call for a Return to Introspection" (Lieberman, 1979). Not only did the author use the word "mind," but he also mentioned in the title that suspect technique of introspection.

A few months earlier in the same journal an article had been published with a one-word title, blatantly and openly displayed: "Consciousness" (Natsoulas, 1978). "After decades of deliberate neglect," the author wrote, "consciousness is again coming under scientific scrutiny, with discussions of the topic appearing at entirely respectable locations in psychology's literature" (p. 906).

In his presidential address to the American Psychological Association in 1976, Wilbert J. McKeachie told the assembled audience that our conception of what psychology is has been changing, and that the change involves a return to consciousness. As a result, McKeachie said, psychology's image of human nature is becoming *"human* rather than mechanical, ratlike, or even computerlike" (p. 831).

When we find a president of the American Psychological Association and a prestigious journal discussing consciousness so openly and optimistically, we know that a new movement—another revolution in psychology—is well under way. And when elementary textbooks in psychology now define the field as "the science that studies behavior and mental processes" (Hilgard, Atkinson, & Atkinson, 1975, p. 12), and "the science that systematically studies and attempts to explain observable behavior and its relationship to the unseen mental processes that go on inside the organism" (Kagan & Havemann, 1972, p. 9), we realize how far contemporary psychology has moved beyond the dictates of Watson and the more recent rulings of Skinner.

Like all movements in psychology, the cognitive revolution did not spring into existence overnight. Segal and Lachman (1972) suggested that it formally began around 1960, but early, though weak, signs started to appear in the 1930s.

One of the earliest proponents was E. R. Guthrie (see Chapter 11), who for most of his career was an ardent behaviorist. Toward the end of his life he came to deplore the mechanistic model of psychology and argued that stimuli cannot always be reduced to physical terms. Nor, he said, can overt responses always be reduced to physical "movement in space." We must describe the stimuli with which psychology deals in perceptual or cognitive terms. It is necessary that the stimuli "have meaning for the responding organism" (Guthrie, 1959, p. 17). One cannot deal with "meaning" solely in strict behaviorist terms because it is a mentalistic or conscious process.

Koch (1964) discussed a contemporary positivist philosopher, Rudolf Carnap, who in 1956 called for a return to introspection, noting that "a person's awareness of his own state of imagining, feeling, etc., must be recognized as a kind of observation, in principle not different from external observation, and therefore as a legitimate source of knowledge" (p. 22). Even Bridgman (1959), the physicist who gave psychology the notion of operational definitions that is so compatible with behaviorism (see Chapter 11), later renounced behaviorism and insisted that introspective reports from the individual subject be invoked to make meaningful operational analyses.

The Influence of the Zeitgeist on the Cognitive Revolution

When we find such a dramatic change in the evolution of a science, it is instructive to look for antecedent changes in the Zeitgeist in which the science functions. A science, like a living species, changes in response to new demands and conditions in its environment.

What was the Zeitgeist that led to the cognitive revolution, that dictated a tempering of behaviorism by the readmission of consciousness? We may look to the Zeitgeist in physics, which, as we have noted, is a role model for psychology and has influenced the field since its beginnings as a science. Around the beginning of the twentieth century a new viewpoint developed in physics as the result of the work of Albert Einstein, Neils Bohr, Werner Heisenberg, and others. The approach resulted in the rejection of the Galilean–Newtonian mechanistic model of the universe. It was from that earlier model that psychology drew its mechanistic, reductionist, lawful, and predictable view of human nature expounded by psychologists from the time of Wundt to Skinner. Then the classical Galilean world of total objectivity and the complete separation of the external world from the observer was discarded in physics. What was the new model, and what were its implications for psychology?

Physicists came to recognize that we cannot observe the course of nature without disturbing it. Thus, the artificial gap between the observer and the observed, the inner world and the outer world, the world of experience and the world of matter—posited in the work of Descartes and in Locke's primary and secondary qualities—was bridged. The focus of scientific investigation shifted from an independent and objectively knowable universe to our observation of the universe. The modern scientist, no longer a detached observer separate from what is being observed, became instead a participant–observer.

The previously held ideal of a totally objective reality was seen as unattainable. Today, physics is characterized by the belief that what we call objective knowledge is, in the final analysis, subjective; it is dependent on the observer. All knowledge, therefore, is "personal knowledge" (Polanyi, 1958). It is a position that sounds suspiciously like what Berkeley said some 200 years ago: all knowledge is subjective because it is dependent on the person perceiving it (see Chapter 2).

Another writer described the situation in the following terms. Our picture of the world, "far from being a genuine photographic reproduction of an independent reality 'out there,' [is] rather more on the order of a painting: a subjective creation of the mind which can convey a likeness but can never produce a replica" (Matson, 1964, p. 137).

Physicists' rejection of an objective, machinelike subject matter and their recognition of subjectivity restored the vital role of conscious experience in obtaining knowledge of the world. The revolution in physics was an effective argument for the acceptance of consciousness as a legitimate part of the subject matter of psychology.

Behaviorist psychology successfully resisted the model of the new physics for about a half-century, clinging to an outdated model of science by considering itself to be an objective science of behavior. But now it seems that behaviorism is responding to the *Zeitgeist* and modifying its form. (We shall see later in this chapter that another new movement, humanistic psychology, has been developing in response to this emphasis on consciousness derived from physics.) Let us describe one example of how the cognitive revolution is changing the nature of behaviorist psychology: the work of a contemporary neo-neobehaviorist, Albert Bandura.

Socio-Behaviorism:
Albert Bandura
(1925–   )

Beginning in the early 1960s, Bandura developed a version of behaviorism—*social learning theory*—that takes a socio-behaviorist approach (Bandura, 1977). It is a less radical form of behaviorism than Skinner's, and it reflects and reinforces the impact of the cognitive revolution. It must be remembered, however, that Bandura's approach remains behavioristically oriented. Its research focuses on the observation of the behavior of human subjects in interaction, it does not use introspection, and it stresses the role of reinforcement in acquiring and modifying behaviors.

In addition to being a behaviorist approach, Bandura's system is also cognitive; it considers the influence on external reinforcement schedules of such thought processes as beliefs, expectations, and instructions. In Bandura's view, behavioral responses are not automatically triggered by external stimuli in the manner of a robot or a machine. Instead, reactions to stimuli are self-activated. When an external reinforcement changes behavior, it does so because the individual is consciously aware of what is being reinforced and anticipates the same reinforcement for behaving in the same way again.

Although Bandura agrees with Skinner that our behavior can change as a result of reinforcement, he also believes—and has empirically demonstrated—that virtually all kinds of behavior can be learned in the absence of directly experienced reinforcement. Rather than always having to experience reinforcement ourselves, we can learn through vicarious reinforcement, by observing the behavior of other people and the consequences of those behaviors.

The ability to learn by example and by vicarious reinforcement assumes the capacity to anticipate and appreciate consequences that we have only observed in others and not yet experienced ourselves. Thus, we can regulate and guide our behavior by visualizing or imagining as yet unexperienced consequences of that behavior and making a conscious decision to behave or not behave in the same way.

One can see how powerful cognitive processes are in Bandura's approach and how it differs from Skinner's. For example, it is not the actual schedule of reinforcement that is so effective in changing behavior, as Skinner argues, but rather what the person thinks that schedule is.

Rather than learning by experiencing reinforcement directly, we learn, according to Bandura, through *modeling*, observing other people and modeling our behavior after theirs. In Skinner's view, whoever controls the reinforcers controls behavior. In Bandura's view, whoever controls the models in a society controls behavior.

Bandura's cognitive–behavioral approach has become popular and has generated a great deal of supportive research. It has also led to an approach to behavior therapy in which subjects watch models who display desired behaviors. The acceptance of Bandura's views is indicated by his election to the presidency of the American Psychological Association in 1974.

Comment

It is not only in behaviorist psychology that the cognitive revolution has had an impact. Cognitive factors have influenced many other areas of the field that, although not germane to our discussion of the evolution of behaviorism, deserve to be mentioned.

In his presidential address to the American Psychological Association, McKeachie (1976) discussed several areas that have incorporated cognitive factors: attribution theory in social psychology; the information-processing approach to decision making and problem solving, learning, memory, and perception; motivation and emotion; and personality. In these areas, as well as in applied areas such as clinical, community, industrial and organizational, and school psychology, there is, according to McKeachie, an increasing emphasis on cognitive factors. "The various subspecialties of psychology are once again approaching psychology with concepts that offer hope not only of communication and integration of psychology, but also of understanding the whole person as a cognitive, conative, affective, biological, and social individual" (p. 819).

Influential though the cognitive revolution has been in modifying behaviorism, the general behaviorist approach has hardly been vanquished by this new force. Bandura and others who have been affected by the movement are still behaviorists. Behavior remains their theoretical focus and the subject of their research.

Behaviorism still dominates American psychology today, although it is a different form of behaviorism than was promoted during the first half-century of its existence. The species has evolved, but it is still recognizably similar to its earlier form.

It can be suggested that behaviorism has been broadened and strengthened by this infusion of the recognition of consciousness. That behaviorism has been able to adapt to such a dramatic change in its environment attests to its basic vitality and validity. Of course, not all behaviorists have accepted or embraced the cognitive revolution, and it is too early to judge its eventual impact. It is not yet history; it is very much history in the making.

THE PSYCHOANALYTIC TRADITION: RECENT DEVELOPMENTS

We have shown that the approach of Sigmund Freud to the understanding of the human personality no longer enjoys a monopoly in that field. Our discussions of the work of Jung, Adler, Horney, and Fromm highlighted alternative approaches developed during Freud's lifetime. Also, some of those who in recent times considered themselves Freudians have modified and elaborated Freud's original views.

The area of personality theory and research has grown immensely since the time of Freud and has splintered into many conflicting views. Contemporary textbooks dealing with theories of personality typically discuss 15 or more fully developed theories. Although these approaches differ in their specifics and generalities, they have a common heritage. They all owe their origin and form, in some degree, to the founding efforts of Freud.

Thus, Freud served the same purpose on the psychoanalytic side of the history of psychology that Wundt served on the experimental side, as a source of either inspiration or opposition. Every structure, whether actual or theoretical, depends on the soundness of its foundation, and Freud, like Wundt, provided a solid and challenging base on which later theorists could build. As examples of the evolution in personality theory since the time of Freud we shall discuss the works of Allport, Murray, and Erikson.

Gordon Allport
(1897–1967)

Over the course of a long, productive career at Harvard University, Allport, more than any other individual, made the study of personality an academically respectable part of psychology. Never psychoanalyzed or in private practice himself, Allport took the study of personality out of the clinical setting and brought it into the university.

As a boy, Allport felt isolated and rejected by other children, but his home life was happy and filled with trust and affection. Unlike Freud and the immediate post-Freudians, Allport does not seem to have had childhood experiences that led directly to his adult view of personality. Perhaps that is why he approached the field from an intellectual and academic standpoint rather than from a more personal one through training in psychoanalysis.

Before he began his graduate studies, however, Allport met Sigmund Freud in Vienna, an event that may have influenced his approach to personality. Ushered into the great man's office, young Allport could think of nothing to say. Freud sat still, looking at him, and waiting for him to start the conversation. Finally, Allport blurted out an incident that had occurred on the streetcar that morning involving a small boy with an obvious and extreme fear of dirt. When Allport finished the story, Freud stared in silence for a moment and then asked, "Was that little boy you?" Freud was expressing his belief that Allport was revealing his own inner conflicts and fears through his story (Allport, 1968, pp. 383–384). (It has been suggested [Hogan, 1976] that Freud's question was insightful in Allport's case.)

Allport was shaken by the question. He began to suspect that psychoanalysis focused too much on the unconscious to the neglect of conscious motives, and thus he fashioned a view of personality that was different from Freud's. He minimized the role of the unconscious in normal adults, arguing that they function in more rational and conscious terms. Only neurotics, Allport said, are influenced by the unconscious. He also disagreed with Freud over the role of childhood experiences and conflicts in adult life, insisting that we are influenced much more by present experiences and hopes for the future than by the past.

Another major difference is Allport's conviction that the only way to investigate personality is through the study of normal adults, not neurotics. Unlike Freud, he did not believe that there was a continuum between the normal and the neurotic. Instead, he argued that there were no similarities between the two, and thus no basis for comparison. Finally, Allport stressed the uniqueness of the individual personality. He did not believe that there were universal laws or themes that could be applied to everyone, as Freud had suggested.

Allport's System

Allport believed that the crux of any personality theory was its treatment of motivation (Allport, 1937; 1961). To explain motivation in the normal adult, he proposed the notion of *functional autonomy*, which states that a motive is not functionally related to any childhood experience. The motive is independent of the original circumstances in which it appeared. An analogy can be made with a tree, which is no longer functionally related to the seed from which it grew. The tree becomes self-determining just as the adult human being does. For example, when beginning your career, you work very hard, perhaps to attain the goals of money and security. Years later, when you are successful and financially secure, you may still work hard even though the original goals have been reached. Motivation, in Allport's view, cannot be traced to childhood, but can only be understood in terms of present behavior and intentions.

Allport's term for the self is *proprium*, used in the sense of "appropriate." The self is what belongs to or is appropriate to each of us. It includes everything that is unique, that sets us apart from everyone else. Allport called it "the me as felt and known" (1961, p. 127), and it is an important conscious part of the personality.

The proprium develops through seven stages from infancy to adolescence. These developmental stages are not psychosexual in nature, nor do they involve Freudian-like conflicts around erogenous zones. Important in the development of the self are social relationships, particularly those with the mother, and not sexual conflicts.

Allport's study of personality traits, which began with his doctoral dissertation, was the first ever conducted in the United States. He distinguished between *traits*, which are common to a number of people, such as members of a particular culture, and *personal dispositions*, which are the traits unique to each person. Both can be inferred from observation of behavior over a period of time, looking for consistencies and regularities. Allport postulated three kinds of traits: cardinal traits, ruling passions that dominate every aspect of life; central traits, behavioral themes such as aggressiveness or sentimentality; and secondary traits, behavior displayed less frequently and consistently than the other two kinds.

Comment

Allport's theory has been more influential in psychology than the work of more traditional psychoanalysts. However, it has not stimulated a great deal of research because of the difficulty of translating some of the concepts into propositions sufficiently specific to study under laboratory conditions. Critics charge that Allport's exclusive focus on the individual makes it impossible to generalize from one person to another and to formulate general laws of behavior. Despite these criticisms, Allport is considered a major figure in the study of personality. His books are clear and his concepts easily understood. Probably his greatest contributions have been his definition and assessment of traits and his work in developing psychological tests with which to measure the human personality.

Henry Murray
(1893–   )

Whereas Allport's theory of personality was a complete rejection of Freud's, Murray's system of *personology* built on Freud's theory. Like Allport, Murray chose to study personality in a university setting rather than in a clinic. Although he underwent psychoanalysis, he did not practice it, preferring to investigate the human personality through the intensive study of normal individuals.

Murray's childhood was characterized by rejection from his mother, a high level of sensitivity to the sufferings of other people, and some Adlerian compensation for two defects—stuttering and ineptitude at sports. After graduating from Columbia University medical school, he interned in surgery, conducted biochemical research, and took a Ph.D. in biochemistry at Cambridge University, certainly one of the more circuitous routes to a career in psychology. After spending three apparently illuminating weeks with Carl Jung, Murray began his work on personality at the Harvard Psychological Clinic.

Not surprisingly, considering his training in medicine and biochemistry, Murray emphasized physiological functioning as it relates to personality and stressed the concept of tension reduction, which he considered a primary law of human behavior, much as Freud did. Also in the Freudian vein, Murray noted the importance of the unconscious and the effect of childhood experiences on adult behavior. In addition, he incorporated Freud's notions of the id, ego, and superego in his system, albeit with some modifications.

Murray's System

Murray divided the personality into three structures: id, ego, and superego (Murray, 1938). The *id*, as Murray viewed it, contains all the innate, impulsive tendencies and provides the energy for the operation of the personality; this view is virtually identical to Freud's. However, in addition to containing primitive and lustful impulses, the id contains more socially desirable tendencies such as empathy, identification, and forms of love other than lust. Therefore, parts of the id must be suppressed and other parts allowed expression for normal development to occur. One can see here the influence of Jung's concept of the shadow archetype, which also contained both desirable and undesirable qualities.

In Murray's system the *ego* assumes a much more active role in determining behavior than it does in Freud's theory. Murray believed that the ego is not merely the servant of the id, but a consciously choosing organizer of all behavior. While the ego acts to suppress the undesirable id impulses, it also facilitates the expression of the desirable ones.

Murray agreed with Freud that the *superego* represents the internalization of the culture's values and mores, and that individuals evaluate their own behavior in terms of those internalized values. However, he differed from Freud in his view of the forces that shape the superego and the time period over which it is formed. Murray argued that the superego is formed not only by one's parents, but also by one's peer group and by the literature and mythology of the culture. The superego continues to develop throughout life rather than being fixed by the age of 5.

Motivation is at the core of Murray's theory of personality, and his classification of *needs* to explain motivation is his most important contribution to the field. Needs involve a chemical force in the brain that organizes all intellectual and perceptual functioning. Needs arouse tension levels in the organism, which are reduced only by their satisfaction. Needs activate behavior and direct it in whatever ways are necessary to bring about this satisfaction. Murray's research has identified 20 needs including achievement, affiliation, aggression, autonomy, dominance, and harm avoidance.

Like Freud, Murray believed that personality develops through a series of stages in childhood. Each stage is characterized by some condition that gives pleasure, and each leaves its imprint on personality in the form of a *complex*, a normal pattern of behavior that unconsciously directs all of the person's later development. The pleasurable conditions of childhood and their complexes reveal a partial similarity to Freud's stages of psychosexual development.

(1) Secure existence within the womb	Claustral complex
(2) Sensuous enjoyment of sucking	Oral complex
(3) Pleasure from defecation	Anal complex
(4) Pleasure from urination	Urethral complex
(5) Genital pleasures	Castration complex

Comment

Murray's theory has generated a great deal of research, particularly on certain of his proposed needs and the techniques he developed to assess personality. Much of that research has supported his views. However, the theory has a limited appeal because of the technical and difficult way in which it is presented in his writings. His classification of needs has been criticized as overly complex and not related clearly to the rest of personality.

Murray's needs have had considerable impact on the construction of psychological tests, especially the Thematic Apperception Test (TAT) he devised with Christiana Morgan, a projective test widely used to study and assess many aspects of behavior (Morgan & Murray, 1935).

Erik Erikson (1902–)

Erikson was trained in the Freudian tradition by Freud's daughter Anna. He has developed a popular approach to personality that retains much of the core of orthodox psychoanalysis while moving considerably beyond it. He has extended Freud's theory by (1) elaborating on the stages of development and arguing that personality keeps growing throughout life, and (2) recognizing the impact on personality of culture, history, and society.

Erikson is well known for his concept of *identity crisis*, a notion that may have arisen from several personal crises of identity he experienced in his early years. The first such crisis involved his name. For many years he thought his last name was Homburger, the name of his stepfather, whom he thought was his real father. A second crisis of identity occurred at school in Germany. He considered himself a German but his classmates rejected him because he was Jewish; at the same time, his Jewish classmates rejected him because of his blond, Aryan appearance.

The third crisis occurred after graduation from high school. He dropped out of society for several years to find himself, and wandered throughout Europe seeking an identity. Finally, at the age of 25, he reached Vienna and took a job teaching in a small school established for the children of Freud's patients and friends. He received training in psychoanalysis, married, and found both a personal and a professional identity. Erikson never continued his formal education beyond high school. Nevertheless, he went on to teach at Harvard University and to become one of the most influential psychoanalysts of recent times.

Erikson's System

Erikson's theory of personality is a developmental one in that it focuses on personality growth over the life of the individual (Erikson, 1964a). The central theme in the development of personality is the search for an ego or self-identity. Erikson divided the human life span into eight stages of *psychosocial development*, each of which involves a conflict that must be resolved.

The conflicts arise as the environment makes new demands on the individual. Erikson called these confrontations with the environment *crises*. Each confrontation or stage of growth involves a change in the personality in which the person is faced with a choice between two ways of coping, an adaptive or a maladaptive way. Only when each crisis is resolved satisfactorily does the person have sufficient strength to deal with the next stage of development.

Erikson's first four stages of development are similar to Freud's oral, anal, phallic, and latency stages, although Erikson stresses psychosocial rather than biological correlates of these stages. The last four stages are unique to Erikson's system. They take the individual from adolescence through old age, levels of development ignored by Freud. Erikson's eight stages of growth, the approximate years in which each occurs, and the opposing ways of adapting are as follows:

(1) Oral–sensory, birth to 1 year	Trust–Mistrust
(2) Muscular–anal, 1–3 years	Autonomy–Doubt, shame
(3) Locomotor–genital, 3–5 years	Initiative–Guilt
(4) Latency, 6–11 years	Industry–Inferiority
(5) Adolescence, 12–18 years	Identity–Role confusion
(6) Young adulthood, 19–35 years	Intimacy–Isolation
(7) Adulthood, 35–50 years	Generativity–Stagnation
(8) Maturity, 50 + years	Ego integrity–Despair

Comment

Erikson's work has been influential in psychoanalysis and in fields such as education and social work. His books are popular with professionals and the lay public. Like most personality theories, his has stimulated little research primarily because of the difficulty in defining the concepts with the degree of precision needed to submit them to laboratory test. Critics charge that the theory is more applicable to males than to females, and that much more attention is paid to infancy and childhood than to adult life, despite the claim of dealing with the entire life span. However, many psychologists and psychiatrists have found that Erikson's stages of psychosocial development offer a useful way of dealing with the developmental histories of their patients.

Another contribution is Erikson's work in psychohistory. He has applied his theory of the human life cycle to such figures as Mahatma Gandhi, Adolf Hitler, Martin Luther, and George Bernard Shaw.

Comment on Post-Freudian Psychoanalysis

We have described something of the diversity that marks post-Freudian developments in the psychoanalytic tradition. Some of these contemporary positions bear little resemblance to Freud's views, and are labeled "psychoanalytic" perhaps only by default to distinguish them from the behaviorist–experimental tradition in psychology. Although they owe their origin to Freud in the sense that they grew out of opposition to his views, they may share with orthodox psychoanalysis only an interest in understanding the human personality. It has been suggested that a theorist such as Allport, who has diverged so far from Freudian views, should more appropriately be labeled a humanistic psychologist. Other positions, such as those of Murray and Erikson, bear a clearer similarity to the work of Freud. These viewpoints are certainly Freudian in some of their particulars, although they differ from Freudian psychoanalysis on both major and minor points.

There may be considerably more divisiveness and fragmentation within the psychoanalytic tradition than within the behaviorist tradition in psychology. Despite the changes introduced by neobehaviorists and neo-neobehaviorists, all agree with founder John B. Watson that behavior in some form should be the focus of study. In contrast, not all, or even most, of Freud's heirs agree that the focus of their study should be unconscious or biological forces, or that the motivators of human conduct are sex and aggression.

Today there are many more subschools of psychoanalysis than of behaviorism. This greater plurality of views may turn out to be the field's major strength and vitality, or its major weakness and failing. Like the cognitive revolution in behaviorism, these developments are too recent to judge. They too are history in the making.

HUMANISTIC PSYCHOLOGY: THE THIRD FORCE

The most recent large-scale movement in the century-old history of psychology is humanistic psychology. Unlike the positions discussed earlier in this chapter, the third force in psychology is not simply a newer form of an existing school of thought. Rather, as the term implies, it aims to replace the other two major forces, behaviorism and psychoanalysis.

Humanistic psychology is still too new to be considered an integral part of the history of psychology, and it has not yet entered the mainstream of psychological thought. Its presence cannot be ignored, however, in a discussion of the history of modern psychology. Although it is the newest force in psychology, it has been in existence long enough to have its own history. Humanistic psychology is some three decades old, having begun in the early 1950s. Out of a history of little more than 100 years, 30 years represents a considerable period of time.

A second reason why humanistic psychology should be examined here is that its general point of view is attracting growing numbers of admirers and adherents, particularly among younger psychologists. Also, humanistic psychology has taken on some of the characteristics of a formal school of thought, those requisites of respectability that have in the past helped to transform movements into schools. We shall examine the historical antecedents and contemporary nature of humanistic psychology and discuss the work of two major proponents, Maslow and Rogers.

Historical Antecedents of Humanistic Psychology

The basic themes of humanistic psychology had been recognized and called for in earlier times, as with all movements. These essential points—the emphasis on conscious experience, the wholeness of human nature and conduct, the belief in free will and spontaneity, the creative power of the individual, and the study of all that is relevant to the human condition—can be found in the works of older psychologists.

Consider Brentano (see Chapter 4), a contemporary opponent of Wundt and a precursor of Gestalt psychology. Brentano criticized the natural science, mechanistic, reductionist approach to psychology and proposed that psychology study consciousness as an active, molar quality rather than as a passive, molecular content. Külpe demonstrated that not all conscious experience could be reduced to elementary form or be explained in terms of responses to stimuli. William James argued against the mechanistic approach to psychology and urged a focus on consciousness and the whole individual.

The Gestalt psychologists argued that psychology should take a molar approach to consciousness, and in the face of the primacy of behaviorism, they continued to insist that conscious experience was a legitimate and profitable area of study for psychology. Michael Wertheimer (1978) takes the position that there is such a strong similarity between humanistic psychology and Gestalt psychology that there is no reason to give the newer movement a new name; the label "Gestalt" is adequate to describe the themes encompassed by humanistic psychology.

There are several antecedents of the humanistic position on the psychoanalytic side of psychology. Adler, Horney, and Fromm, for example, opposed Freud's deterministic view of personality (that behavior is determined by biological forces and past events). They also disagreed with Freud's notion that we are ruled by unconscious forces. These dissenters from orthodox psychoanalysis believed us to be primarily conscious beings possessing spontaneity and free will, influenced by the present and future at least as much as by the past. They credited personality with the creative power to shape itself.

As with other movements in modern psychology, the *Zeitgeist* seems to be largely responsible for turning antecedents into an actual movement. Two aspects of the *Zeitgeist* have seemed to favor the humanistic psychology movement in the last half of the twentieth century. One comes from the general culture and the other from physics, psychology's omnipresent model.

Humanistic psychology appears to be reflecting the unrest and disaffection recently voiced against the mechanistic aspects of contemporary Western culture. Humanistic psychologists imply that behaviorism is, if not antihuman, then ahuman, and they resist the conception of human beings as animals functioning deterministically in response to the environment or to childhood experiences.

Many social critics suggest that Western and particularly American culture has dehumanized, depersonalized, and deindividualized us to the extent that we are regarded as infinitesimal parts of an immense societal machine. It has been suggested that people are no longer viewed as humans, but as personnel, statistics, and averages. As individuals, we have a diminished sense of personal identity and a lessened ability to shape our own lives. Society, through the giant bureaucracies, molds our destinies to a greater and greater extent.

We are growing increasingly estranged from society and from ourselves, regimented, controlled, computerized, manipulated, alienated, alone, numbered, and helpless—all qualities that seem ideal for a behaviorist view of human beings as smoothly functioning, well-ordered machines.

> That modern psychology has projected an image of man which is as demeaning as it is simplistic, few intelligent and sensitive nonpsychologists would deny. . . . Of all fields in the community of scholarship, it should be psychology which combats this trend. Instead, we have played no small role in augmenting and supporting it. (Koch, 1964, pp. 37–38)

Voices are being raised against the dehumanizing forces of modern society, warning us against the dangers of an overly objective and numbered society. This *Zeitgeist* of social criticism may be reflected in the humanistic psychologists' plea for the study of people as human beings rather than as machines.

The second aspect of the *Zeitgeist* stems from the altered model of the universe accepted by modern physics, described above. The rejection of an objective, machinelike subject matter for physics, and the realization that conscious experience is instrumental in our acquisition of knowledge of the material world, are sufficient reasons for psychology to readmit consciousness as a legitimate subject of study, as the humanistic psychologists want to do.

The Nature of Humanistic Psychology

We know that every new movement has used its older opponent, the establishment, as a base against which to push to gain its own momentum. In practical terms, the new viewpoint needs to state clearly, articulately, and loudly the weaknesses and failings of the current view. Humanistic psychology has two targets: the two established forces of behaviorism and psychoanalysis. Before we discuss what humanistic psychologists stand for, let us see what they are against.

Humanistic psychologists believe that behaviorism is a narrow, artificial, and relatively sterile approach to the understanding of human nature. The sole emphasis on overt behavior tends to dehumanize us and reduce us "to a larger white rat or a slower computer" (Bugental, 1967, p. vii). They argue that the image provided by the stimulus–response orientation presents at best an incomplete picture of human nature, and at worst one that may be totally inaccurate. Behaviorism does not come to grips with our uniquely human characteristics, those subjective qualities and capacities that set us apart from the laboratory animal. A psychology based on discrete conditioned responses makes of the individual a mechanized, computerlike organism responding deterministically to the stimuli presented. The humanists argue that we are much more than robots, and cannot be objectified, quantified, and reduced to stimulus–response units; we are not empty organisms.

The humanistic psychologists also argue that the vast amounts of research on overt behavior have added little to our understanding of human nature. Maslow wrote: "We are offered beautifully executed, precise, elegant experiments which, in at least half the cases, have nothing to do with enduring human problems" (1965, p. 21). Another leading advocate of humanistic psychology, Carl Rogers, argued that behaviorist–experimental psychology is becoming less and less relevant as a significant science because it continues to model itself after the Galilean form of physics, which has long been rendered obsolete (Rogers, 1973). Thus, humanistic psychologists are opposed to the continued reliance on the behaviorist approach, with its mechanistic, reductionist, elementist, and simplistic tendencies.

The proponents of humanistic psychology are also against the Freudian approach to psychology, with its deterministic tendencies and its minimization of the role of consciousness. In addition, Maslow criticized Freud for studying only disturbed individuals—the neurotics and psychotics. With its focus on only mental illness, how can psychology know anything of our positive qualities and characteristics? Maslow argued that psychology has disregarded such attributes as joy, satisfaction, contentment, ecstasy, kindness, and generosity because it tends to concentrate on our dark side, the "sick" side of the human personality, and to ignore our strengths and virtues. "The study of crippled, stunted, immature, and unhealthy specimens can yield only a cripple psychology and a cripple philosophy" (Maslow, 1954, p. 234).

It is against this "cripple philosophy"—the narrow, ahuman, and sterile psychology put forth in both behaviorism and psychoanalysis—that Maslow and others have proposed their alternative, the third force in psychology. Humanistic psychology hopes to be a fresh orientation, a new framework or attitude toward psychology, rather than a new psychology itself. Its protagonists, like the founders of functionalism, state that they do not wish to start a new school of thought or a specific content area, but rather to reshape and supplement the existing forces in psychology and to build upon them. Maslow argued that the study of behavior and the mentally ill is vital to an understanding of human nature, but these topics are insufficient and too narrow to define psychology completely. J. F. T. Bugental, the first president of the American Association for Humanistic Psychology (1962–1963), described the movement in this way:

> Humanistic psychology has as its ultimate goal the preparation of a complete description of what it means to be alive as a human being. . . . Such a complete description would necessarily include an inventory of man's native endowment; his potentialities of feeling, thought, and action; his growth, evolution, and decline; his interaction with various environing conditions . . . the range and variety of experience possible to him; and his meaningful place in the universe. (1967, p. 7)

All aspects of uniquely human experience come under the purview of the humanistic psychologist: love, hate, fear, hope, happiness, humor, affection, responsibility, and the meaning of life. Many of these aspects of human existence are not discussed in current textbooks of psychology because they are not amenable to operational definition, quantification, and laboratory manipulation.

The American Association for Humanistic Psychology published a four-part statement on the theme of humanistic psychology, noting that there was not unanimous agreement on these points:

> 1. A centering of attention on the experiencing person, and thus a focus on experience as the primary phenomenon in the study of man. Both theoretical explanations and overt behavior are considered secondary to experience itself and to its meaning to the person.
>
> 2. An emphasis on such distinctively human qualities as choice, creativity, valuation, and self-realization, as opposed to thinking about human beings in mechanistic and reductionistic terms.
>
> 3. An allegiance to meaningfulness in the selection of problems for study

384
More Recent Developments

and of research procedures, and an opposition to a primary emphasis on objectivity at the expense of significance.

4. An ultimate concern with and valuing of the dignity and worth of man and an interest in the development of the potential inherent in every person. (Bühler & Allen, 1972, pp. 1–2)

In another position paper Bugental (1967) noted six fundamental points that distinguish psychology from behaviorism.

1. Adequate understanding of human nature cannot be based exclusively (or even in large part) on research findings from animal studies. Again, a human being is not "a larger white rat," and a psychology based on animal data obviously excludes distinctly human processes and experiences.

2. The research topics chosen for investigation must be meaningful in terms of human existence and not selected solely on the basis of their suitability for laboratory investigation and quantification. Currently, topics not amenable to experimental treatment tend to be ignored.

3. Primary attention should be focused on our subjective internal experiences, not on elements of overt behavior. This is not to suggest that overt behavior be discarded as a subject of study, but rather that it not be the only subject of investigation.

4. The continuing mutual influence of the so-called pure psychology and applied psychology should be recognized. The attempt to divorce them is detrimental to both.

5. Psychology should be concerned with the unique individual case instead of the average performance of groups. The current group emphasis ignores the atypical, the exception, the person who deviates from the average.

6. Psychology should seek "that which may expand or enrich man's experience . . ." (Bugental, 1967, p. 9).

If these attempts at defining goals and techniques seem vague, then they adequately represent the current status of humanistic psychology. It is easier to describe what humanistic psychologists are against than what they are for or how they hope to achieve their goals. This is a significant criticism of the movement. Michael Wertheimer noted that the term *humanistic psychology* "has been used with so many different, and such vague, meanings that it is highly unlikely that an explicit definition of it could be written that would satisfy even a small fraction of the people who call themselves 'humanistic psychologists' " (1978, p. 743).

In part, this imprecision may mirror the relative youth of the movement and the fact that it lacks a single leader or founder who can speak authoritatively for the position, as Watson and Freud did for their schools of thought. It may also reflect the looser structure forced upon the movement by the elusive subject matter with which it is grappling.

Although they have not defined their goals and techniques with precision, the humanists are not arguing for the rejection of science as the framework within which to study human nature, but rather for an expansion and enlargement of science. By science they do not refer exclusively to laboratory, manipulative research in which the subject (rat or college student) is viewed as a stimulus–response machine that can be programmed. Maslow wrote that "Scientific methods . . . are our only ultimate ways of being sure that we *do* have truth . . . Only science can overcome characterological differences in seeing and believing. Only science can progress" (1968, p. viii).

Humanistic Psychotherapies

Humanistic psychology, unlike the psychoanalytic positions, focuses more on psychologically healthy persons than on those who are neurotic or psychotic. As a result, the approach to therapy is different. This aspect of humanistic psychology, the *growth therapies*, is the "human potential" movement, well known to the lay public. Growth therapies have proliferated in recent years and have been used with millions of people in all walks of life. A significant portion of the American population has been exposed to growth therapies (encounter groups, T-groups, sensitivity sessions, and the like) in schools, businesses, churches, prisons, and private centers throughout the country.

Deriving in part from the work of Lewin (see Chapter 12), growth therapies are used with people of normal or average mental health to help them raise their levels of consciousness, relate better to themselves and to others, and release hidden potentials for creativity and development. They are designed to make people more psychologically healthy, more self-actualizing, and more fully functioning, to enable them to become all they are capable of becoming.

Unfortunately, the human potential movement has attracted more than its share of quacks, well-intentioned but untrained people, and self-styled gurus or messiahs who may be doing more harm than good. Evidence indicates that not only are some people not helped by encounter groups, but they may actually be hurt. Studies of the aftereffects of participation in encounter groups have revealed psychological casualty rates ranging from less than 1 percent to almost 50 percent (Hartley, Robach, & Abramowitz, 1976).

In spite of the lack of data to support the benefits claimed for encounter groups, they remain popular and represent to many people what humanistic psychology is all about. Humanistic psychology is much more than sensitivity sessions, however. It is a serious study of human nature and conduct, perhaps best expressed in the work of Maslow and Rogers.

Abraham Maslow
(1908–1970)

Maslow has been called the spiritual father of humanistic psychology and probably did more than anyone else to spark the movement and confer a degree of academic–intellectual respectability. Wanting to understand the highest potentials human beings are capable of reaching, Maslow studied a small sample of the healthiest people he could find to determine how they differed from those of average or normal mental health. Out of that study he developed a theory of personality that focuses on our motivation to grow, develop, and actualize ourselves, to fulfill all of our potentials and capabilities.

Initially, Maslow was an ardent behaviorist, convinced that the mechanistic, natural science approach provided answers to all the world's problems. A series of personal experiences—ranging from the birth of his first child to the start of World War II—plus an exposure to nonbehaviorist approaches to the understanding of human conduct (philosophy, Freudian psychoanalysis, and Gestalt psychology), persuaded him that behaviorism was too limited to be relevant to enduring human problems. Maslow was also influenced by his contact with some of the European psychologists who had fled Nazi Germany and settled in the United States. He eagerly met and learned from Alfred Adler, Erich Fromm, Karen Horney, and Max Wertheimer. His feelings of awe toward Wertheimer and the American anthropologist Ruth Benedict led to his first study of psychologically healthy, self-actualizing persons; they were his models of the best of human nature.

Working primarily at Brandeis University, Maslow developed and refined his theory in a series of lucid and provocative books. He supported the sensitivity group movement and the Esalen Institute in California and became one of the best known psychologists of the 1960s.

Maslow's System

In Maslow's view, everyone possesses an innate tendency to become *self-actualizing* (Maslow, 1970). This highest level of human existence involves the supreme development and use of all our qualities and capacities, the realizing of all our potentialities. To become self-actualizing, it is necessary to satisfy the four needs that stand lower in the *hierarchy of needs*. These lower-level needs are also innate, and each must be satisfied in turn before the next need in the hierarchy can emerge.

The needs, in the order in which they must be satisfied, are (1) the physiological needs for food, water, air, sleep, and sex; (2) the safety needs for security, stability, order, protection, and freedom from fear and anxiety; (3) the belonging and love needs; (4) the needs for esteem from others and from oneself; and (5) the need for self-actualization.

The bulk of Maslow's research focused on the characteristics of those who have satisfied the need for self-actualization. These are the most psychologically healthy persons. Maslow referred to them as the "growing tip" of humanity, and they compose less than 1 percent of the population, in his view. They are free of neuroses and psychoses, almost always middle-aged or older, and models of maturation.

Maslow found that self-actualizing persons share the following characteristics: an objective perception of reality; a full acceptance of their own natures; a commitment and dedication to work of some kind; simplicity and naturalness in behavior; a need for autonomy, privacy, and independence; mystical or peak experiences (moments of intense ecstasy, wonder, awe, and delight); empathy with and affection for all humanity; a resistance to conformity; a democratic character structure; and an attitude of creativeness.

Comment

Maslow offered an optimistic and flattering image of human nature, a view of psychological health and fulfillment that is seen as a welcome antidote to the sickness, prejudice, and hostility that we may witness or exhibit in our daily lives. Many find it reassuring to believe that at least some people are capable of reaching a state of perfection.

Maslow's research method and data have been criticized on the grounds that his sample of two dozen people was too small for generalization, his subjects were selected according to his own subjective criteria of psychological health, and his terms were defined ambiguously and inconsistently.

The self-actualization theory has limited empirical laboratory support, but its application in industrial and organizational psychology tends to verify some of its aspects. It has also found application in clinical psychology. Reflecting the interest his work has generated among psychologists, and perhaps indicating a trend toward the humanizing of psychology, Maslow was elected to the presidency of the American Psychological Association in 1967.

Carl Rogers (1902–   )

Rogers is an influential psychologist today, famous as the originator of a popular approach to psychotherapy known as nondirective or *client-centered therapy*. On the basis of data derived from his therapy, Rogers developed a theory of personality that holds that people have one overriding motivation: an innate tendency to actualize all of the abilities and potentials of the self. (This is similar to Maslow's concept of self-actualization.)

Rogers's views, however, were developed not from the study of healthy people, but from the treatment of disturbed individuals through client-centered therapy. The name of his therapy suggests something of his view of the human personality. By placing the responsibility for change on the client rather than on the therapist (as is the case in traditional psychoanalysis), Rogers assumes that people can consciously and rationally rule themselves and switch from undesirable to desirable ways of thinking and behaving. He does not believe that people are controlled by unconscious forces or by what happened to them in childhood. Personality is shaped by the present and by how we consciously perceive it.

Rogers's notion that personality can be examined and understood only in terms of our subjective experiences may reflect an incident in his own life. When he was 22 and attending a Christian student conference in China, he began to question his parents' fundamentalist religious beliefs and to develop a more liberal philosophy of life. He became convinced that people must depend on their own experience and that they can consciously change and improve themselves, concepts that were to become cornerstones of his personality theory. Over the course of an active career, Rogers has developed his theory of personality and approach to psychotherapy, expressing them through a number of popular articles, papers, and books.

Rogers's System

Rogers believed that the major motivating force in personality is the actualization of the self (Rogers, 1961). Although this urge toward self-actualization is innate, it can be helped or hindered by experience and learning, particularly in childhood. Rogers stressed the importance of the mother–child relationship as it affects the child's growing sense of self. When the mother satisfies the infant's need for love, which Rogers called *positive regard*, the infant will tend to become a healthy personality.

When the mother makes her love for the child conditional on proper behavior (*conditional* positive regard), then the child will internalize the mother's attitude and develop *conditions of worth*. In this situation, the child feels a sense of self only under certain conditions, and comes to avoid those behaviors that bring disapproval from the mother. As a result, the self is not allowed to develop fully because all of its aspects cannot be expressed.

Thus, the primary requisite for the development of psychological health is the receipt of *unconditional* positive regard in infancy, when the mother demonstrates her full love and acceptance of the child regardless of the child's behavior. In this case, the child does not develop conditions of worth and therefore does not have to repress any aspects of his or her emerging self. Only in this way can a state of self-actualization be reached.

The goal of the actualization of the self is the achievement of the highest level of psychological health, a process Rogers called *fully functioning*. It is a level of supreme development that is equal, in principle but not in content, to Maslow's state of self-actualization. The theories differ on the characteristics of psychologically healthy persons.

Fully functioning persons are characterized by an openness to all experience, a tendency to live fully in every moment of existence, an ability to be guided by trust in their own "feel" of a situation rather than by reason or the opinions of others, a sense of freedom in thought and action, and a high degree of creativity.

Comment

In terms of general popularity and influence in psychology, Rogers's client-centered approach to psychotherapy has had more of an impact than his theory of personality. Nevertheless, the theory has been well received, particularly its emphasis on the importance of the self. Criticism has been directed at the lack of specificity in stating the nature of the innate potentiality to actualization, and at the emphasis on subjective, conscious experiences to the exclusion of possible unconscious influences.

Rogers's theory and therapy have generated an enormous amount of research and have been widely used in the clinical setting. As a method of treatment, client-centered therapy is almost as popular as Freudian psychoanalysis. Rogers has also been influential in the human potential movement, which his views support. His work, like that of Maslow, is a major part of the growing movement to humanize psychology.

The Future of Humanistic Psychology

Although the humanistic movement is gathering strength, it is too early to attempt an evaluation of its impact on modern psychology. It does, however, warrant watchful and critical attention.

It is also too early to know whether the movement can completely resist becoming formalized into a school of thought. Its members are vocal in pointing out the weaknesses of the older positions; behaviorism and psychoanalysis are both well-developed bases against which to push. Many humanistic psychologists are filled with revolutionary zeal and a sense of righteousness as they do battle with the evils of the establishment. The *Journal of Humanistic Psychology* was established in 1961, the American Association for Humanistic Psychology in 1962, and the Division of Humanistic Psychology of the American Psychological Association in 1971.

Thus, the characteristics of an establishment, of a formal school of thought, the traits that distinguish it from competing schools, are in evidence. Humanistic psychologists have their own definition of psychology—however vague it may be, it is distinct from the definitions offered by the two major forces in contemporary psychology—and their own subject matter, methods, journals, associations, meetings, and terminology. Above all, they possess what every other school of thought boasted in its early days: a passionate conviction that their path is the best one for psychology to follow.

If the history of psychology as portrayed in these chapters tells us anything at all, it is that when a movement becomes formalized into a school, it gains a momentum that can be stopped only by its own success in overthrowing the established position. When that happens, as we have seen, the unobstructed arteries of the once vigorous and youthful movement begin to harden. Flexibility turns to rigidity, revolutionary passion to protection of position, and eyes and minds close to new ideas; in short, a new establishment is born. And so it is in the progress of any science, an evolutionary building to ever higher levels of development. There is no culmination but continuing growth, as newer species evolve from older ones in the never-ending process of adapting to a continually changing environment.

SUGGESTED READINGS

ALLPORT

Allport, G. *Becoming: Basic considerations for a psychology of personality.* New Haven, CT: Yale University Press, 1955.

Allport, G. *Pattern and growth in personality.* New York: Holt, 1961.

Allport, G. *The person in psychology.* Boston: Beacon Press, 1968.

Maddi, S. R., & Costa, P. T. *Humanism in personology: Allport, Maslow, and Murray.* Chicago: Aldine-Atherton, 1972.

BANDURA

Bandura, A. *Social learning theory.* Englewood Cliffs, NJ: Prentice-Hall, 1977.

Bandura, A. The self system in reciprocal determinism. *American Psychologist,* 1978, *33,* 344–358.

Evans, R. I. *The making of psychology.* New York: Knopf, 1976. Pp. 242–254.

Rosenthal, T. L., and Bandura, A. Psychological modeling: Theory and practice. In S. L. Garfield & A. E. Bergin (Eds.), *Handbook of psychotherapy and behavior change* (2nd ed.). New York: Wiley, 1978. Pp. 621–658.

COGNITIVE REVOLUTION

Dember, W. N. Motivation and the cognitive revolution. *American Psychologist,* 1974, *29,* 161–168.

Jenkins, J. J. Remember that old theory of memory? Well, forget it! *American Psychologist,* 1974, *29,* 785–795. (The role of cognitive factors in the study of memory.)

Lieberman, D. A. Behaviorism and the mind: A (limited) call for a return to introspection. *American Psychologist,* 1979, *34,* 319–333.

Mahoney, M. J. Reflections on the cognitive-learning trend in psychotherapy. *American Psychologist,* 1977, *32,* 5–13.

McKeachie, W. J. Psychology in America's bicentennial year. *American Psychologist,* 1976, *31,* 819–833. (McKeachie's APA presidential address.)

Natsoulas, T. Consciousness. *American Psychologist*, 1978, *33*, 906–914. (A discussion of seven concepts of consciousness.)

Schultz, D. P. Psychology: A world with man left out. *Journal for the Theory of Social Behaviour*, 1971, *1*, 99–107. (The impact of the new physics on psychology.)

Segal, E. M., & Lachman, R. Complex behavior or higher mental process: Is there a paradigm shift? *American Psychologist*, 1972, *27*, 46–55. (Argues that the domination of psychology by neobehaviorism has been eroded by the cognitive revolution.)

Wolpe, J. Cognition and causation in human behavior and its therapy. *American Psychologist*, 1978, *33*, 437–446. (Presents the view that thought is behavior and obeys the same mechanistic laws as behavior.)

ERIKSON

Erikson, E. H. *Childhood and society*. New York: Norton, 1964.

Erikson, E. H. *Identity: Youth and crisis*. New York: Norton, 1968.

Erikson, E. H. *Dimensions of a new identity*. New York: Norton, 1974.

Erikson, E. H. *Life history and the historical moment*. New York: Norton, 1975.

Evans, R. I. *Dialogue with Erik Erikson*. New York: Harper, 1967.

Roazen, P. *Erik H. Erikson: The power and limits of a vision*. New York: Free Press, 1976.

HUMANISTIC PSYCHOLOGY

Ansbacher, H. Alfred Adler and humanistic psychology. *Journal of Humanistic Psychology*, 1971, *11*, 53–63. (Adler's influence on the development of humanistic psychology.)

Bühler, C., & Allen, M. *Introduction to humanistic psychology*. Monterey, CA: Brooks/Cole, 1972.

Maslow, A. *The farther reaches of human nature*. New York: Viking Press, 1971.

Matson, F. W. Humanistic theory: The third revolution in psychology. *Humanist*, 1971, *31*, 7–11.

McWaters, B. (Ed.). *Humanistic perspectives: Current trends in psychology*. Monterey, CA: Brooks/Cole, 1977.

Rogers, C. Some new challenges. *American Psychologist*, 1973, *28*, 379–387.

Severin, F. T. (Ed.). *Discovering man in psychology: A humanistic approach*. New York: McGraw-Hill, 1973.

Shaffer, J. *Humanistic psychology*. Englewood Cliffs, NJ: Prentice-Hall, 1978.

Smith, M. B. Humanism and behaviorism in psychology: Theory and practice. *Journal of Humanistic Psychology*, 1978, *18*, 27–36.

Wertheimer, M. Humanistic psychology and the humane but tough-minded psychologist. *American Psychologist*, 1978, *33*, 739–745. (A critical look at humanistic psychology.)

MASLOW

Goble, F. G. *The third force: The psychology of Abraham Maslow*. New York: Grossman, 1970.

Hall, M. H. A conversation with Abraham H. Maslow. *Psychology Today*, 1968, *2*, 34–37; 54–57.

Maslow, A. H. *Toward a psychology of being* (2nd ed.). New York: Van Nostrand Reinhold, 1968.

Maslow, A. H. *Motivation and personality* (2nd ed.). New York: Harper, 1970.

MURRAY

Hall, M. H. A conversation with Henry A. Murray. *Psychology Today*, 1968, *4*, 56–63.

Murray, H. A. *Explorations in personality.* London & New York: Oxford University Press, 1938.

Murray, H. A. Preparations for the scaffold of a comprehensive system. In S. Koch (Ed.), *Psychology: A study of a science* (Vol. 3). New York: McGraw-Hill, 1959. Pp. 7–54.

Murray, H. A. *Encounter with psychology.* San Francisco: Jossey-Bass, 1969.

Murray, H. A., & Kluckhohn, C. Outline of a conception of personality. In C. Kluckhohn, H. A. Murray, & D. M. Schneider (Eds.), *Personality in nature, society, and culture* (2nd ed.). New York: Knopf, 1953. Pp. 3–52.

ROGERS

Hall, M. H. A conversation with Carl Rogers. *Psychology Today*, 1967, *1*, 18–21; 62–66.

Kirschenbaum, H. *On becoming Carl Rogers.* New York: Delacorte, 1979. (A biography.)

Rogers, C. R. *On becoming a person: A therapist's view of psychotherapy.* Boston: Houghton Mifflin, 1961.

Rogers, C. R. Toward a science of the person. *Journal of Humanistic Psychology,* 1963, *3*, 72–92.

BIBLIOGRAPHY

Aaron, R. I. *John Locke.* London & New York: Oxford University Press (Clarendon), 1971.

Adler, A. Individual psychology. In C. Murchison (Ed.), *Psychologies of 1930.* Worcester, MA: Clark University Press, 1930. Pp. 395–405.

Adler, A. The fundamental views of Individual Psychology. *International Journal of Individual Psychology,* 1935, *1,* 5–8.

Allen, G. *William James.* New York: Viking Press, 1967.

Allport, G. W. *Personality: A psychological interpretation.* New York: Holt, 1937.

Allport, G. W. The productive paradoxes of William James. *Psychological Review,* 1943, *50,* 95–120.

Allport, G. W. *Becoming: Basic considerations for a psychology of personality.* New Haven, CT: Yale University Press, 1955.

Allport, G. W. *Pattern and growth in personality.* New York: Holt, 1961.

Allport, G. W. William James and the behavioral sciences. *Journal of the History of the Behavioral Sciences,* 1966, *2,* 145–147.

Allport, G. W. *The person in psychology.* Boston: Beacon Press, 1968.

American Psychological Association. Presentation of the first Gold Medal Award. *American Psychologist,* 1956, *11,* 587–589.

American Psychological Association. Distinguished Scientific Contribution Award for 1958. *American Psychologist,* 1958, *13,* 729–738.

Angell, J. R. *Psychology.* New York: Holt, 1904.

Angell, J. R. The province of functional psychology. *Psychological Review,* 1907, *14,* 61–91.

Angell, J. R. The influence of Darwin on psychology. *Psychological Review,* 1909, *16,* 152–169.

Ansbacher, H. L. Alfred Adler and humanistic psychology. *Journal of Humanistic Psychology,* 1971, *11,* 53–63.

Ansbacher, H. L. The development of Adler's concept of social interest. *Journal of Individual Psychology,* 1978, *34,* 118–152.

Ansbacher, H. L. *Alfred Adler revisited.* New York: Praeger, 1979.

Ansbacher, H. L., & Ansbacher, R. R. (Eds.). *The individual psychology of Alfred Adler.* New York: Basic Books, 1956.

Ansbacher, H. L., & Ansbacher, R. R. (Eds.). *Superiority and social interest: A collection of later writings by Alfred Adler.* New York: Viking Press, 1973.

Asch, S. E. Max Wertheimer's contribution to modern psychology. *Social Research,* 1946, *13,* 81–102.

Babkin, B. P. *Pavlov: A biography.* Chicago: University of Chicago Press, 1949.

Bakan, D. A consideration of the problem of introspection. *Psychological Bulletin,* 1954, *51,* 105–118.

Bakan, D. Behaviorism and American urbanization. *Journal of the History of the Behavioral Sciences,* 1966, *2,* 5–28.

Balz, A. G. A. *Descartes and the modern mind.* New Haven, CT: Yale University Press, 1952.

Bandura, A. *Principles of behavior modification.* New York: Holt, 1969.

Bandura, A. *Social learning theory.* Englewood Cliffs, NJ: Prentice-Hall, 1977.

Bandura, A. The self system in reciprocal determinism. *American Psychologist,* 1978, *33,* 344–358.

Barber, B. Resistance by scientists to scientific discovery. *Science,* 1961, *134,* 596–602.

Beach, F. A., et al. (Eds.). *The neuropsychology of Lashley.* New York: McGraw-Hill, 1960.

Bekhterev, V. M. *Objective psychology.* Leipzig: Teubner, 1907. (Published in English as *General principles of human reflexology.* New York: International Publishers, 1932.)

Bentley, M. The psychologies called "Structuralism." In C. Murchison (Ed.), *Psychologies of 1925.* Worcester, MA: Clark University Press, 1926. (a)

Bentley, M. The work of the structuralists. In C. Murchison (Ed.), *Psychologies of 1925.* Worcester, MA: Clark University Press, 1926. (b)

Bergmann, G. Sense and nonsense in operationism. *Scientific Monthly,* 1954, *79,* 210–214.

Bergmann, G. The contribution of John B. Watson. *Psychological Review,* 1956, *63,* 265–276.

Berkeley, G. An essay towards a new theory of vision. In M. W. Calkins (Ed.), *Berkeley: Essay, principles, dialogues.* New York: Scribner's, 1957. Pp. 1–98. (Originally published, 1709.)

Berkeley, G. A treatise concerning the principles of human knowledge. In M. W. Calkins (Ed.), *Berkeley: Essay, principles, dialogues.* New York: Scribner's, 1957. Pp. 99–216. (Originally published, 1710.)

Bixenstine, V. E. Empiricism in latter-day behavioral science. *Science,* 1964, *145,* 464–467.

Blanshard, B. Critical reflections on behaviorism. *Proceedings of the American Philosophical Society,* 1965, *109,* 22–28.

Blumenthal, A. L. A reappraisal of Wilhelm Wundt. *American Psychologist,* 1975, *30,* 1081–1088.

Blumenthal, A. L. Wilhelm Wundt and early American psychology: A clash of two cultures. *Annals of the New York Academy of Sciences,* 1977, *291,* 13–20.

Blumenthal, A. L. Wilhelm Wundt, The founding father we never knew. *Contemporary Psychology,* 1979, *24,* 547–550. (A retrospective review of Wundt's works.)

Boas, M. *The scientific renaissance: 1450–1630.* London: Collins, 1962.

Boring, E. G. The stimulus-error. *American Journal of Psychology,* 1921, *32,* 449–471.

Boring, E. G. Edward Bradford Titchener, 1867–1927. *American Journal of Psychology,* 1927, *38,* 489–506.

Boring, E. G. *A history of experimental psychology.* New York: Appleton, 1929.

Boring, E. G. Georg Elias Müller, 1850–1934. *American Journal of Psychology,* 1935, *47,* 344–348.

Boring, E. G. A psychological function is the relation of successive differentiations of events in the organism. *Psychological Review,* 1937, *44,* 445–461.

Boring, E. G. *A history of experimental psychology* (2nd ed.). New York: Appleton, 1950. (b)

Boring, E. G. The influence of evolutionary theory upon American psychological thought. In S. Persons (Ed.), *Evolutionary thought in America.* New Haven, CT: Yale University Press, 1950. (a) Pp. 267–298.

Boring, E. G. A history of introspection. *Psychological Bulletin,* 1953, *50,* 169–189. (b)

Boring, E. G. John Dewey: 1859–1952. *American Journal of Psychology,* 1953, *66,* 145–147. (a)

Boring, E. G. Fechner: Inadvertent founder of psychophysics. *Psychometrika,* 1961, *26,* 3–8. (a)

Boring, E. G. *Psychologist at large: An autobiography and selected essays.* New York: Basic Books, 1961. (b)

Boring, E. G. *History, psychology, and science: Selected papers.* New York: Wiley, 1963.

Boring, E. G. The trend toward mechanism. *Proceedings of the American Philosophical Society,* 1964, *108,* 451–454.

Boring, E. G. On the subjectivity of important historical dates: Leipzig 1879. *Journal of the History of the Behavioral Sciences,* 1965, *1,* 5–9.

Brandt, L. The physics of the physicist and the physics of the psychologist. *International Journal of Psychology,* 1973, *8,* 61–72.

Brazier, M. The historical development of neurophysiology. In J. Field (Ed.), *Handbook of physiology* (Vol. 1). Baltimore, MD: Williams & Wilkins, 1959. Pp. 1–58.

Brentano, F. *Psychology from an empirical standpoint.* Leipzig: Duncker & Humblot, 1874.

Breuer, J., & Freud, S. *Studies on hysteria.* Leipzig: Franz Deuticke, 1895. (Vol. 2, Standard Edition. See Freud.)

Bridgman, P. W. *The logic of modern physics.* New York: Macmillan, 1927.

Bridgman, P. W. Remarks on the present state of operationism. *Scientific Monthly,* 1954, *79,* 224–226.

Bridgman, P. W. *The ways things are.* Cambridge, MA: Harvard University Press, 1959.

Bringmann, W., Balance, W., & Evans, R. Wilhelm Wundt 1832–1920: A brief biographical sketch. *Journal of the History of the Behavioral Sciences,* 1975, *11,* 287–297.

Brome, V. *Jung: Man and myth.* New York: Atheneum, 1978.

Brown, J. A. C. *Freud and the post-Freudians.* London: Cassell, 1963.

Bugental, J. *Challenges of humanistic psychology.* New York: McGraw-Hill, 1967.

Bühler, C., & Allen, M. *Introduction to humanistic psychology.* Monterey, CA: Brooks/Cole, 1972.

Buranelli, V. *The wizard from Vienna: Franz Anton Mesmer.* New York: Coward, McCann, 1975.

Burnham, J. On the origins of behaviorism. *Journal of the History of the Behavioral Sciences,* 1968, *4,* 143–151.

Burnham, J. Thorndike's puzzle boxes. *Journal of the History of the Behavioral Sciences,* 1972, *8,* 159–167.

Burnham, J. From avant-garde to specialism: Psychoanalysis in America. *Journal of the History of the Behavioral Sciences,* 1979, *15,* 128–134.

Burnham, W. H. The man, G. Stanley Hall. *Psychological Review,* 1925, *32,* 89–102.

Burt, C. The concept of consciousness. *British Journal of Psychology,* 1962, *53,* 229–242.

Buss, A. R. Galton and the birth of differential psychology and eugenics: Social, political, and economic forces. *Journal of the History of the Behavioral Sciences,* 1976, *12,* 47–58.

Buss, A. R. The structure of psychological revolutions. *Journal of the History of the Behavioral Sciences,* 1978, *14,* 57–64.

Butterfield, H. *The origins of modern science: 1300–1800.* New York: Macmillan, 1959.

Camfield, T. M. The professionalization of American psychology: 1870–1917. *Journal of the History of the Behavioral Sciences,* 1973, *9,* 66–75.

Carmichael, L. Karl Spencer Lashley, experimental psychologist. *Science,* 1959, *129,* 1409–1412.

Carr, H. *Psychology.* New York: Longmans, Green, 1925.

Carr, H. Functionalism. In C. Murchison (Ed.), *Psychologies of 1930.* Worcester, MA: Clark University Press, 1930. Pp. 59–78.

Carr, H. Autobiography. In C. Murchison (Ed.), *A history of psychology in autobiography* (Vol. 3). Worcester, MA: Clark University Press, 1936. Pp. 69–82.

Cattell, J. McK. The psychological lab at Leipsic. *Mind,* 1888, *13,* 37–51.

Cattell, J. McK. The conceptions and methods of psychology. *Popular Science Monthly,* 1904, *66,* 176–186.

Cattell, J. McK. Early psychological laboratories. *Science,* June 1, 1928, pp. 543–548.

Chaplin, J., & Krawiec, T. *Systems and theories of psychology* (4th ed.). New York: Holt, 1979.

Choisy, M. *Sigmund Freud: A new appraisal.* New York: Philosophical Library, 1963.

Cofer, C., & Appley, M. *Motivation: Theory and research.* New York: Wiley, 1964.

Colp, R. *To be an invalid: The illness of Charles Darwin.* Chicago: University of Chicago Press, 1977.

Combs, A. W., & Snygg, D. *Individual behavior: A perceptual approach to behavior* (Rev. ed.). New York: Harper, 1959.

Comte, A. *The positive philosophy of Comte.* London: Bell, 1896. (Originally published, 1830–1842.)

Cornwell, D., & Hobbs, S. The strange saga of little Albert. *New Society,* March 18, 1976, pp. 602–604.

Crannell, C. W. Wolfgang Köhler. *Journal of the History of the Behavioral Sciences,* 1970, *6,* 267–268.

Cravens, H. *The triumph of evolution: American scientists and the heredity-environment controversy, 1900–1941.* Philadelphia: University of Pennsylvania Press, 1978.

Creelan, P. G. Watsonian behaviorism and the Calvinist conscience. *Journal of the History of the Behavioral Sciences,* 1974, *10,* 95–118.

Crombie, A. C. Early concepts of the senses and the mind. *Scientific American,* 1964, *210,* 108–116.

Crovitz, H. *Galton's walk.* New York: Harper, 1970.

Cuny, H. *Ivan Pavlov: The man and his theories.* New York: Eriksson, 1965.

Dallenbach, K. Autobiography. In E. G. Boring & G. Lindzey (Eds.), *A history of psychology in autobiography* (Vol. 5). New York: Appleton, 1967. Pp. 57–93.

Danziger, K. The positivist repudiation of Wundt. *Journal of the History of the Behavioral Sciences,* 1979, *15,* 205–230.

Darwin, C. *On the origin of species by means of natural selection.* London: J. Murray, 1859; New York: Appleton, 1860.

Darwin, C. *The descent of man.* New York: Appleton, 1871.

Darwin, C. *The expression of the emotions in man and animals.* London: J. Murray, 1872; New York: Appleton, 1873.

Darwin, C. A biographical sketch of an infant. *Mind,* 1877, *2,* 285–294.

Darwin, F. (Ed.). *The autobiography of Charles Darwin and selected letters.* New York: Dover, 1958. (Originally published, 1892.)

Decker, H. S. *The Interpretation of Dreams:* Early reception by the educated German public. *Journal of the History of the Behavioral Sciences,* 1975, *11,* 129–141.

Decker, H. S. *Freud in Germany: Revolution and reaction in science, 1893–1907.* New York: International Universities Press, 1978.

de la Mettrie, J. *L'homme machine.* (M. Calkins, Trans.). Chicago: Open Court, 1912. (Originally published, 1748.)

Dember, W. Motivation and the cognitive revolution. *American Psychologist,* 1974, *29,* 161–168.

Dennis, W., & Boring, E. G. The founding of APA. *American Psychologist,* 1952, *7,* 95–97.

Dewey, J. *Psychology.* New York: Harper, 1886.

Dewey, J. The reflex arc concept in psychology. *Psychological Review,* 1896, *3,* 357–370.

Dewey, J. Psychology and social practice. *Psychological Review,* 1900, *7,* 105–124.

Dewsbury, D. A. C. Lloyd Morgan, something old that's often new. *Contemporary Psychology,* 1979, *24,* 677–680. (A retrospective review of Morgan's *An introduction to comparative psychology,* 1894.)

Diamond, S. Francis Galton and American psychology. *Annals of the New York Academy of Sciences,* 1977, *291,* 47–55.

Diserens, C. M. Psychological objectivism. *Psychological Review,* 1925, *32,* 121–152.

Drucker, P. *Adventures of a bystander.* New York: Harper, 1978.

Ebbinghaus, H. *On memory.* Leipzig: Duncker & Humblot, 1885.

Ebbinghaus, H. *The principles of psychology.* Leipzig: Veit, 1902.

Ebbinghaus, H. *A summary of psychology.* Leipzig: Veit, 1908.

Eiseley, L. *Darwin and the mysterious Mr. X: New light on the evolutionists.* New York: Dutton, 1979.

Ellenberger, H. F. *The discovery of the unconscious: The history and evolution of dynamic psychiatry.* New York: Basic Books, 1970.

Ellenberger, H. F. The story of "Anna O": A critical review with new data. *Journal of the History of the Behavioral Sciences,* 1972, *8,* 267–279.

Ellis, W. D. (Ed.). *A source book of Gestalt psychology.* New York: Humanities Press, 1967.

Eng, E. Looking back on Kurt Lewin: From field theory to action research. *Journal of the History of the Behavioral Sciences,* 1978, *14,* 228–232.

Erikson, E. H. *Childhood and society.* New York: Norton, 1964. (a)

Erikson, E. H. *Insight and responsibility.* New York: Norton, 1964. (b)

Erikson, E. H. *Identity and the life cycle.* New York: Norton, 1967.

Erikson, E. H. *Identity: Youth and crisis.* New York: Norton, 1968.

Erikson, E. H. *Dimensions of a new identity.* New York: Norton, 1974.

Erikson, E. H. *Life history and the historical moment.* New York: Norton, 1975.

Erikson, E. H. *Toys and reasons: Stages in the ritualization of experience.* New York: Norton, 1977.

Esper, E. *A history of psychology.* Philadelphia: Saunders, 1964.

Estes, W., et al. (Eds.). *Modern learning theory.* New York: Appleton, 1954.

Evans, Rand. E. B. Titchener and his lost system. *Journal of the History of the Behavioral Sciences,* 1972, *8,* 168–180.

Evans, R. I. *Conversations with Carl Gustav Jung.* New York: Van Nostrand, 1964.

Evans, R. I. *Dialogue with Erich Fromm.* New York: Harper, 1966.

Evans, R. I. *Dialogue with Erik Erikson.* New York: Harper, 1967.

Evans, R. I. *B. F. Skinner: The man and his ideas.* New York: Dutton, 1968.

Evans, R. I. *Jung on elementary psychology.* New York: Dutton, 1976.

Evans, R. I. *The making of psychology: Discussions with creative contributors*. New York: Knopf, 1976.

Fancher, R. E. *Pioneers of psychology*. New York: Norton, 1979.

Fearing, F. *Reflex action: A study in the history of physiological psychology*. Baltimore, MD: Williams & Wilkins, 1930.

Fechner, G. *Elements of psychophysics*. (H. Adler, Trans.). New York: Holt, 1966. (Originally published, 1860.)

Fechner, G. A mysterious illness. In G. Fechner, *Religion of a scientist*. (W. Lowrie, Ed. and trans.). New York: Pantheon, 1946. Pp. 36–42.

Feigl, H. Mind-body, *not* a pseudo problem. In S. Hook (Ed.), *Dimensions of mind*. New York: New York University Press, 1960. Pp. 24–36.

Ferster, C. B., & Skinner, B. F. *Schedules of reinforcement*. New York: Appleton, 1957.

Fine, R. *A history of psychoanalysis*. New York: Columbia University Press, 1979.

Fischer, C. T. Historical relations of psychology as an object-science and a subject-science: Toward psychology as a human science. *Journal of the History of the Behavioral Sciences*, 1977, *13*, 369–378.

Fisher, S., & Greenberg, R. P. *The scientific credibility of Freud's theories and therapy*. New York: Basic Books, 1977.

Fisher, S., & Greenberg, R. P. (Eds.). *The scientific evaluation of Freud's theories and therapy: A book of readings*. New York: Basic Books, 1978.

Flugel, J., & West, D. *A hundred years of psychology*. New York: Basic Books, 1964.

Fordham, F. *An introduction to Jung's psychology*. Baltimore, MD: Penguin, 1959.

Forrest, D. W. *Francis Galton: The life and work of a Victorian genius*. New York: Taplinger, 1974.

Frank, J. D. Kurt Lewin in retrospect—a psychiatrist's view. *Journal of the History of the Behavioral Sciences*, 1978, *14*, 223–227.

Freeman, F. S. The beginnings of Gestalt psychology in the United States. *Journal of the History of the Behavioral Sciences*, 1977, *13*, 252–253.

Freeman, L. *The story of Anna O*. New York: Walker, 1972.

Freud, A. (Ed.). *The psychoanalytic study of the child* (Annual Vols.). New York: International Universities Press, 1945—.

Freud, S. *The standard edition of the complete psychological works of Sigmund Freud*. Translated from the German under the general editorship of J. Strachey, in collaboration with Anna Freud. London: Hogarth Press.

On the origins of psycho-analysis. 1895. Vol. 1.
The interpretation of dreams. 1900. Vols. 4–5.
The psychopathology of everyday life. 1901. Vol. 6.
Three essays on the theory of sexuality. 1905 (a). Vol. 7.
Fragment of an analysis of a case of hysteria. 1905 (b). Vol. 7.
Five lectures on psycho-analysis. 1910. Vol. 11.
On the history of the psycho-analytic movement. 1914. Vol. 14.
Beyond the pleasure principle. 1920. Vol. 18.
An autobiographical study. 1925. Vol. 20.
New introductory lectures on psycho-analysis. 1933. Vol. 22.
Outline of psycho-analysis. 1938. Vol. 23.

Fromm, E. *Escape from freedom*. New York: Holt, 1941.

Fromm, E. *Man for himself*. New York: Holt, 1947.

Fromm, E. *The sane society*. New York: Holt, 1955.

Fromm, E. *The heart of man*. New York: Holt, 1964.

Fromm, E. *The anatomy of human destructiveness*. New York: Holt, 1973.

Fromm, E. *To have or to be?* New York: Harper, 1976.

Fromm, E. *Crises of psychoanalysis*. New York: Fawcett, 1977.

Furumoto, L. Mary Whiton Calkins (1863–1930). *Journal of the History of the Behavioral Sciences,* 1979, *15,* 346–356.

Galton, F. *Hereditary genius.* London: Macmillan, 1869; New York: Appleton, 1870.

Galton, F. *English men of science: Their nature and nurture.* London: Macmillan, 1874; New York: Appleton, 1875.

Galton, F. *Natural inheritance.* London & New York: Macmillan, 1889.

Galton, F. *Memories of my life.* London: Methuen, 1908.

Gantt, W. H. Interview with Professor Emeritus W. Horsley Gantt. *Johns Hopkins Magazine,* February 1979, pp. 26–32.

Gates, A. I. James McKeen Cattell. In *International encyclopedia of the social sciences* (Vol. 2). New York: Crowell Collier, 1968. Pp. 344–346.

Gengerelli, J. A. Graduate school reminiscences: Hull and Koffka. *American Psychologist,* 1976, *31,* 685–688.

Goble, F. G. *The third force: The psychology of Abraham Maslow.* New York: Grossman, 1970.

Goodman, E. Margaret Floy Washburn: 'A complete psychologist.' *APA Monitor,* 1979, *10* (12), 3, 16.

Gould, S. J. Darwin and the captain. *Natural History,* 1976, *85*(1), 32–34.

Gruber, C. Academic freedom at Columbia University, 1917–1918: The case of James McKeen Cattell. *American Association of University Professors Bulletin,* 1972, *58*(3), 297–305.

Gruber, H. E. *Darwin on man: A psychological study of scientific creativity.* New York: Dutton, 1974.

Guthrie, E. R. *The psychology of learning.* New York: Harper, 1935; rev. ed., 1952.

Guthrie, E. R. Association by contiguity. In S. Koch (Ed.), *Psychology: A study of a science* (Vol. 2). New York: McGraw-Hill, 1959. Pp. 158–195.

Hale, N. *Freud and the Americans: The beginnings of psychoanalysis in the United States, 1876–1917.* London & New York: Oxford University Press, 1971.

Hale, N. From Berggasse XIX to Central Park West: The Americanization of psychoanalysis, 1919–1940. *Journal of the History of the Behavioral Sciences,* 1978, *14,* 299–315.

Hall, A. R. *The scientific revolution: 1500–1800.* Boston: Beacon Press, 1956.

Hall, A. R. *From Galileo to Newton: 1630–1720.* London: Collins, 1963.

Hall, G. S. *Adolescence.* New York: Appleton, 1904.

Hall, G. S. *Jesus, the Christ, in the light of psychology.* New York: Doubleday, 1917.

Hall, G. S. *Recreations of a psychologist.* New York: Appleton, 1920.

Hall, G. S. *Senescence* (2 vols.). New York: Appleton, 1922.

Hall, G. S. *The life and confessions of a psychologist.* New York: Appleton, 1923.

Hall, M. H. A conversation with Carl Rogers. *Psychology Today,* 1967, *1,* 18–21; 62–66. (a)

Hall, M. H. An interview with "Mr. Behaviorist" B. F. Skinner. *Psychology Today,* 1967, *1*(5), 21–23; 68–71. (b)

Hall, M. H. A conversation with Abraham H. Maslow. *Psychology Today,* 1968, *2,* 34–37. (a)

Hall, M. H. A conversation with Henry A. Murray. *Psychology Today,* 1968, *4,* 56–63. (b)

Hannah, B. *Jung: His life and work.* New York: Putnam, 1976.

Harlow, H. F. William James and instinct theory. In R. B. MacLeod (Ed.), *William James: Unfinished business.* Washington, DC: American Psychological Association, 1969. Pp. 21–30.

Harper, R. S. The first psychological laboratory. *Isis,* 1950, *41,* 158–161.

Harris, B. Whatever happened to little Albert? *American Psychologist,* 1979, *34,* 151–160.

Harrison, R. Functionalism and its historical significance. *Genetic Psychology Monographs,* 1963, *68,* 387–423.

Hartley, D. *Observations on man, his frame, his duty, and his expectations.* London: Leake & Frederick, 1749.

Hartley, D., Robach, H. B., & Abramowitz, S. I. Deterioration effects in encounter groups. *American Psychologist,* 1976, *31,* 247–255.

Hebb, D. O. The American revolution. *American Psychologist,* 1960, *15,* 735–745.

Heidbreder, E. *Seven psychologies.* New York: Appleton, 1933.

Heidbreder, E. Functionalism. In D. L. Krantz (Ed.), *Schools of psychology.* New York: Appleton, 1969. Pp. 35–70.

Heider, F. Gestalt theory: Early history and reminiscences. *Journal of the History of the Behavioral Sciences,* 1970, *6,* 131–139.

Helmholtz, H. *Physiological optics* (3 vols.). Leipzig: Voss, 1856–1866.

Helmholtz, H. *On the sensation of tone.* New York: Dover, 1954. (Originally published, 1863.)

Helson, H. Why did their precursors fail and the Gestalt psychologists succeed? *American Psychologist,* 1969, *24,* 1006–1011.

Henle, M. (Ed.). *Documents of Gestalt psychology.* Berkeley: University of California Press, 1961.

Henle, M. Did Titchener commit the stimulus error? The problem of meaning in structural psychology. *Journal of the History of the Behavioral Sciences,* 1971, *7,* 279–282. (a)

Henle, M. (Ed.). *The selected papers of Wolfgang Köhler.* New York: Liveright, 1971. (b)

Henle, M. E. B. Titchener and the case of the missing element. *Journal of the History of the Behavioral Sciences,* 1974, *10,* 227–237.

Henle, M. Why study the history of psychology? *Annals of the New York Academy of Sciences,* 1976, *270,* 14–20.

Henle, M. The influence of Gestalt psychology in America. *Annals of the New York Academy of Sciences,* 1977, *291,* 3–12.

Henle, M. Gestalt psychology and Gestalt therapy. *Journal of the History of the Behavioral Sciences,* 1978, *14,* 23–32. (a)

Henle, M. Kurt Lewin as metatheorist. *Journal of the History of the Behavioral Sciences,* 1978, *14,* 233–237. (b)

Henle, M. One man against the Nazis—Wolfgang Köhler. *American Psychologist,* 1978, *33,* 939–944. (c)

Henle, M., Jaynes, J., & Sullivan, J. J. (Eds.). *Historical conceptions of psychology.* New York: Springer, 1973.

Herrnstein, R. J. Introduction to John B. Watson's *Comparative Psychology.* In M. Henle, et al. (Eds.), *Historical conceptions of psychology.* New York: Springer, 1973. Pp. 98–115.

Herrnstein, R. J. The evolution of behaviorism. *American Psychologist,* 1977, *32,* 593–603.

Herrnstein, R. J., & Boring, E. G. (Eds.). *A source book in the history of psychology.* Cambridge, MA: Harvard University Press, 1965.

Hilgard, E. (Ed.). *American psychology in historical perspective: Addresses of the presidents of the American Psychological Association, 1892–1977.* Washington, DC: American Psychological Association, 1978.

Hilgard, E., Atkinson, R., & Atkinson, R. *Introduction to psychology* (6th ed.). New York: Harcourt Brace Jovanovich, 1975.

Hilgard, E., & Bower, G. *Theories of learning* (2nd ed.). New York: Appleton, 1956.

Hochberg, J. Effects of the Gestalt revolution. *Psychological Review,* 1957, *64,* 73–84.

Hofstadter, R. *Social Darwinism in American thought* (Rev. ed.). New York: George Braziller, 1955.

Hogan, R. *Personality theory: The personological tradition.* Englewood Cliffs, NJ: Prentice-Hall, 1976.

Holt, E. B. *The Freudian wish and its place in ethics.* New York: Holt, 1915.

Horney, K. *Our inner conflicts.* New York: Norton, 1945.

Horney, K. *The collected works of Karen Horney.* New York: Norton, 1963.

Hull, C. L. *Hypnosis and suggestibility.* New York: Appleton, 1933.

Hull, C. L. Mind, mechanism and adaptive behavior. *Psychological Review,* 1937, *44,* 1–32.

Hull, C. L. *Principles of behavior.* New York: Appleton, 1943.

Hull, C. L. *Essentials of behavior.* New Haven, CT: Yale University Press, 1951.

Hull, C. L. *A behavior system.* New Haven, CT: Yale University Press, 1952.

Hull, C. L., et al. *Mathematico-deductive theory of rote learning: A study in scientific methodology.* New Haven, CT: Yale University Press, 1940.

400

Hulse, S. H., Egeth, H., & Deese, J. E. *The psychology of learning* (5th ed.). New York: McGraw-Hill, 1980.

Hume, D. *A treatise of human nature.* London: Noon, 1739.

Hurvich, L. M., & Jameson, D. Helmholtz's vision: Looking backward. *Contemporary Psychology,* 1979, *24,* 901–904. (A retrospective review of Helmholtz's *Physiological optics,* 1856–1866.)

Irvine, W. *Apes, angels, and Victorians: Darwin, Huxley, and evolution.* New York: Time, 1955.

Jacobi, J. *The psychology of C. G. Jung* (Rev. ed.). New Haven, CT: Yale University Press, 1951.

Jaffé, A. (Ed.). *C. G. Jung: Word and image.* Princeton, NJ: Princeton University Press, 1979.

Jahoda, M. Some notes on the influence of psycho-analytic ideas on American psychology. *Human Relations,* 1963, *16,* 111–129.

Jahoda, M. *Freud and the dilemmas of psychology.* New York: Basic Books, 1977.

James, W. *The principles of psychology.* New York: Holt, 1890.

James, W. *Talks to teachers.* New York: Holt, 1899.

James, W. *The varieties of religious experience.* New York: Longmans, Green, 1901–1902.

James, W. The Chicago school. *Psychological Bulletin,* 1904, *1,* 1–5.

James, W. *Pragmatism.* New York: Longmans, Green, 1907.

Jastrow, J. American psychology in the '80s and '90s. *Psychological Review,* 1943, *50,* 65–67.

Jaynes, J. The problem of animate motion in the seventeenth century. *Journal of the History of Ideas,* 1970, *31,* 219–234.

Jaynes, J. *The origin of consciousness in the breakdown of the bicameral mind.* Boston: Houghton Mifflin, 1977.

Jenkins, J. J. Remember that old theory of memory? Well, forget it! *American Psychologist,* 1974, *29,* 785–795.

Jonçich, G. *The sane positivist: A biography of Edward L. Thorndike.* Middletown, CT: Wesleyan University Press, 1968.

Jones, E. *The life and work of Sigmund Freud, 1856–1900* (3 vols.). New York: Basic Books, 1953, 1955, 1957.

Jones, M. C. A laboratory study of fear: The case of Peter. *Pedagogical Seminary,* 1924, *31,* 308–315.

Jones, M. C. Albert, Peter, and John B. Watson. *American Psychologist,* 1974, *29,* 581–583.

Jung, C. G. *The psychology of the unconscious.* Leipzig: Franz Deuticke, 1912.

Jung, C. G. *The collected works of C. G. Jung* (H. Read, M. Fordham, & G. Adler, Eds.). Princeton, NJ: Princeton University Press, 1953 to date.

Jung, C. G. *Memories, dreams, reflections.* New York: Vintage Books, 1961.

Kagan, J., & Havemann, E. *Psychology: An introduction* (2nd ed.). New York: Harcourt Brace Jovanovich, 1972.

Katz, D. *Gestalt psychology.* New York: Ronald Press, 1950.

Keller, F. S. *Summers and sabbaticals: Selected papers on psychology and education.* Champaign, IL: Research Press, 1977.

Kinkade, K. *A Walden Two experiment: The first five years of Twin Oaks community.* New York: Morrow, 1973.

Kirsch, I. The impetus to scientific psychology: A recurrent pattern. *Journal of the History of the Behavioral Sciences,* 1976, *12,* 120–129.

Kirschenbaum, H. *On becoming Carl Rogers.* New York: Delacorte, 1979.

Kluckhohn, C., Murray, H. A., & Schneider, D. M. (Eds.). *Personality in nature, society, and culture* (2nd ed.). New York: Knopf, 1953.

Koch, S. Psychology and emerging conceptions of knowledge as unitary. In T. Wann (Ed.), *Behaviorism and phenomenology.* Chicago: University of Chicago Press, 1964. Pp. 1–41.

Koenigsburger, L. *Hermann von Helmholtz.* New York: Dover, 1965.

Koestler, A. *The case of the midwife toad.* New York: Random House, 1971.

Koffka, K. *The growth of the mind.* New York: Harcourt, 1921.

Koffka, K. Perception: An introduction to Gestalt-theorie. *Psychological Bulletin*, 1922, *19*, 531–585.

Koffka, K. *Principles of Gestalt psychology.* New York: Harcourt, 1935.

Köhler, W. *The mentality of apes.* Berlin: Royal Academy of Sciences, 1917. (English ed., 1927.)

Köhler, W. *Static and stationary physical Gestalts.* Braunschweig: Vieweg, 1920.

Köhler, W. *Gestalt psychology.* New York: Liveright, 1929.

Köhler, W. *The place of value in a world of facts.* New York: Liveright, 1938.

Köhler, W. *Dynamics in psychology.* New York: Liveright, 1940.

Köhler, W. Kurt Koffka. *Psychological Review*, 1942, *49*, 97–101.

Köhler, W. Max Wertheimer, 1880–1943. *Psychological Review*, 1944, *51*, 143–146.

Köhler, W. *Gestalt psychology: An introduction to new concepts in modern psychology.* New York: Liveright, 1947.

Köhler, W. Gestalt psychology. In D. Krantz (Ed.), *Schools of psychology.* New York: Appleton, 1969. Pp. 69–85.

Köhler, W. Gestalt psychology today. In E. Hilgard (Ed.), *American psychology in historical perspective.* Washington, DC: American Psychological Association, 1978. Pp. 251–263.

Köhler, W., & Wallach, H. Figural after-effects. *Proceedings of the American Philosophical Society*, 1944, *88*, 269–357.

Krantz, D. L. Schools and systems: The mutual isolation of operant and non-operant psychology as a case study. *Journal of the History of the Behavioral Sciences*, 1972, *8*, 86–102.

Kuhn, T. S. *The structure of scientific revolutions* (2nd ed.). Chicago: University of Chicago Press, 1970.

Kuhn, T. S. *The essential tension: Selected studies in scientific tradition and change.* Chicago: University of Chicago Press, 1977.

Külpe, O. *Outline of psychology.* Leipzig: Englemann, 1893.

Kuna, D. P. Early advertising applications of the Gale-Cattell order-of-merit method. *Journal of the History of the Behavioral Sciences*, 1979, *15*, 38–46.

Lachman, S. *History and methods of physiological psychology.* Detroit, MI: Hamilton, 1963.

Ladd, G. T., & Woodworth, R. S. *Physiological psychology* (Rev. ed.). New York: Scribner's, 1911.

Langer, W. C., & Gifford, S. An American analyst in Vienna during the Anschluss, 1936–1938. *Journal of the History of the Behavioral Sciences*, 1978, *14*, 37–54.

Langfeld, H. S. Carl Stumpf: 1848–1936. *American Journal of Psychology*, 1937, *49*, 316–320.

Larson, C. Highlights of Dr. John B. Watson's career in advertising. *The Industrial-Organizational Psychologist*, 1979, *16*(3), 3–5. (a)

Larson, C. The Watson-McDougall debate: "The debate of the century." *APA Monitor*, 1979, *10*(11), 3, 12. (b)

Larson, C., & Sullivan, J. Watson's relation to Titchener. *Journal of the History of the Behavioral Sciences*, 1965, *1*, 338–354.

Lashley, K. *Brain mechanisms and intelligence.* Chicago: University of Chicago Press, 1929.

Leahey, T. H. Something old, something new: Attention in Wundt and modern cognitive psychology. *Journal of the History of the Behavioral Sciences*, 1979, *15*, 242–252.

Lerner, I. M. *Heredity, evolution, and society.* San Francisco: Freeman, 1968.

Lewin, K. *Field theory in social science.* New York: Harper, 1951.

Lewin, K., Lippitt, R., & White, R. Patterns of aggressive behavior in experimentally created social climates. *Journal of Social Psychology*, 1939, *10*, 271–299.

Lieberman, D. A. Behaviorism and the mind. A (limited) call for a return to introspection. *American Psychologist*, 1979, *34*, 319–333.

Lindenfeld, D. Oswald Külpe and the Würzburg school. *Journal of the History of the Behavioral Sciences*, 1978, *14*, 132–141.

Lockard, R. B. Reflections on the fall of comparative psychology. *American Psychologist*, 1971, *26*, 168–179.

Locke, J. *An essay concerning human understanding.* New York: Dover, 1959. (Originally published, 1690.)

Lowry, R. J. *The evolution of psychological theory: 1650 to the present.* Chicago: Aldine-Atherton, 1971.

Lowry, R. J. *A. H. Maslow: An intellectual portrait.* Monterey, CA: Brooks/Cole, 1973. (a)

Lowry, R. J. (Ed.). *Dominance, self-esteem, self-actualization: Germinal papers of A. H. Maslow.* Monterey, CA: Brooks/Cole, 1973. (b)

Luce, A. A. *The life of George Berkeley, Bishop of Cloyne.* London: Nelson, 1949.

Mach, E. *The analysis of sensations.* Chicago: Open Court, 1914. (Originally published, 1885.)

Mackenzie, B. Behaviorism and positivism. *Journal of the History of the Behavioral Sciences,* 1972, *8,* 222–231.

Mackenzie, B. Darwinism and positivism as methodological influences on the development of psychology. *Journal of the History of the Behavioral Sciences,* 1976, *12,* 330–337.

Mackenzie, B. *Behaviourism and the limits of scientific method.* Atlantic Highlands, NJ: Humanities Press, 1977.

MacLeod, R. B. Review of *Cumulative record* by B. F. Skinner. *Science,* 1959, *130,* 34–35.

MacLeod, R. B. *William James: Unfinished business.* Washington, DC: American Psychological Association, 1969.

MacLeod, R. B. *The persistent problems of psychology.* Pittsburgh: Duquesne University Press, 1975.

Maddi, S. R., & Costa, P. T. *Humanism in personology.* Chicago: Aldine-Atherton, 1972.

Mahoney, M. J. Reflections on the cognitive-learning trend in psychotherapy. *American Psychologist,* 1977, *32,* 5–13.

Malthus, T. *Essay on the principle of population.* New York: Dutton, 1914. (Originally published, 1789.)

Mandler, G. A man for all seasons? *Contemporary Psychology,* 1979, *24,* 742–744. (A retrospective review of William James's *The principles of psychology,* Vols. 1 and 2, 1890.)

Mandler, J. M., & Mandler, G. The diaspora of experimental psychology: The Gestaltists and others. In D. Fleming & B. Bailyn (Eds.), *The intellectual migration: Europe and America, 1930–1960.* Cambridge, MA: Harvard University Press, 1969. Pp. 371–419.

Margenau, H. On interpretations and misinterpretations of operationalism. *Scientific Monthly,* 1954, *79,* 209–210.

Marrow, A. *The practical theorist: The life and work of Kurt Lewin.* New York: Basic Books, 1969.

Marshall, M. E. Gustav Fechner, Dr. Mises, and the comparative anatomy of angels. *Journal of the History of the Behavioral Sciences,* 1969, *5,* 39–58.

Marx, M., & Hillix, W. *Systems and theories in psychology* (3rd ed.). New York: McGraw-Hill, 1979.

Maslow, A. *Motivation and personality.* New York: Harper, 1954; second edition, 1970.

Maslow, A. A philosophy of psychology: The need for a mature science of human nature. In F. Severin (Ed.), *Humanistic viewpoints in psychology.* New York: McGraw-Hill, 1965. Pp. 17–33.

Maslow, A. *Toward a psychology of being* (2nd ed.). New York: Van Nostrand, 1968.

Maslow, A. *The farther reaches of human nature.* New York: Viking Press, 1971.

Matson, F. W. *The broken image.* New York: George Braziller, 1964.

Matson, F. W. Humanistic theory: The third revolution in psychology. *The Humanist,* 1971, *31,* 7–11.

Matson, F. W. (Ed.). *Without/within: Behaviorism and humanism.* Monterey, CA: Brooks/Cole, 1973.

May, R. *Psychology and the human dilemma.* New York: Van Nostrand, 1967.

McConnell, J. V. *Understanding human behavior.* New York: Holt, 1974.

McDougall, W. *Introduction to social psychology.* London: Methuen, 1908.

McDougall, W. *Body and mind.* New York: Macmillan, 1911.

McGuire, W. (Ed.). *The Freud/Jung letters.* Princeton, NJ: Princeton University Press, 1974.

McGuire, W., & Hull, R. F. C. (Eds.). *C. G. Jung speaking: Interviews and encounters.* Princeton, NJ: Princeton University Press, 1977.

McKeachie, W. J. Psychology in America's bicentennial year. *American Psychologist,* 1976, *31,* 819–833.

McKellar, P. The method of introspection. In J. Scher (Ed.), *Theories of the mind.* New York: Free Press, 1962. Pp. 619–644.

McKinney, F. Functionalism at Chicago—memories of a graduate student: 1929–1931. *Journal of the History of the Behavioral Sciences,* 1978, *14,* 142–148.

McWaters, B. (Ed.). *Humanistic perspectives: Current trends in psychology.* Monterey, CA: Brooks/Cole, 1977.

Merton, R. Priorities in scientific discovery. *American Sociological Review,* 1957, *22,* 635–659.

Miles, W. James Rowland Angell, 1869–1949, psychologist-educator. *Science,* 1949, *110,* 1–4.

Mill, J. *Analysis of the phenomena of the human mind.* London: Baldwin & Cradock, 1829.

Miller, G. *Psychology: The science of mental life.* New York: Harper, 1962.

Miller, G., & Buckhout, R. *Psychology: The science of mental life* (2nd ed.). New York: Harper, 1973.

Mischel, T. Wundt and the conceptual foundations of psychology. *Philosophical and Phenomenological Research,* 1970, *31,* 1–26.

Moorehead, A. *Darwin and the Beagle.* New York: Harper, 1969.

Morgan, C. D., & Murray, H. A. A method for investigating fantasies. *Archives of Neurology and Psychiatry,* 1935, *34,* 289–306.

Morgan, N. *The California syndrome.* Englewood Cliffs, NJ: Prentice-Hall, 1969.

Moskowitz, M. J. Hugo Münsterberg: A study in the history of applied psychology. *American Psychologist,* 1977, *32,* 824–842.

Mueller, C. G. Some origins of psychology as science. *Annual Review of Psychology,* 1979, *30,* 9–29.

Mueller, C. G., & Schoenfeld, W. N. Edwin R. Guthrie. In W. Estes, et al. (Eds.), *Modern learning theory.* New York: Appleton, 1954. Pp. 345–379.

Müller, J. *Handbook of physiology.* 1833–1840.

Müller-Freienfels, R. *The evolution of modern psychology.* New Haven, CT: Yale University Press, 1935.

Murphy, G. *Historical introduction to modern psychology* (Rev. ed.). New York: Harcourt Brace Jovanovich, 1949.

Murphy, G., & Kovach, J. *Historical introduction to modern psychology* (3rd ed.). New York: Harcourt Brace Jovanovich, 1972.

Murray, F. S., & Rowe, F. B. Psychology laboratories in the United States prior to 1900. *Teaching of Psychology,* 1979, *6,* 19–21.

Murray, H. A. *Explorations in personality.* London & New York: Oxford University Press, 1938.

Murray, H. A. Preparations for the scaffold of a comprehensive system. In S. Koch (Ed.), *Psychology: A study of a science* (Vol. 3). New York: McGraw-Hill, 1959. Pp. 7–54.

Murray, H. A. *Encounter with psychology.* San Francisco: Jossey-Bass, 1969.

Natsoulas, T. Consciousness. *American Psychologist,* 1978, *33,* 904–916.

Nelson, B. (Ed.). *Freud and the twentieth century.* New York: Meridian, 1957.

Ogden, R. M. Oswald Külpe and the Würzburg school. *American Journal of Psychology,* 1951, *64,* 4–19.

Orgler, H. *Alfred Adler: The man and his work.* New York: Putnam, 1965.

Palermo, D. S. Is a scientific revolution taking place in psychology? *Science Studies,* 1971, *1,* 135–155.

Pavlov, I. P. *Conditioned reflexes* (G. Anrep, Trans.). London & New York: Oxford University Press, 1927.

Pavlov, I. P. *Lectures on conditioned reflexes* (W. H. Gantt, Trans.). New York: Liveright, 1928.

Pavlov, I. P. *Selected works* (S. Belsky, Trans.). Moscow: Foreign Languages Publishing House, 1955.

Pearson, K. *The life, letters and labors of Francis Galton.* London & New York: Cambridge University Press, 1914, 1924, 1930.

Perry, R. B. *The thought and character of William James.* Boston: Little, Brown, 1935.

Peters, R. S. (Ed.). *Brett's history of psychology.* Cambridge, MA: MIT Press, 1965.

Pickering, G. *Creative malady.* London & New York: Oxford University Press, 1974.

Pillsbury, W. *Essentials of psychology.* 1911.

Pirenne, M. H. Descartes and the body-mind problem in physiology. *British Journal of the Philosophy of Science,* 1950, *1,* 43–59.

Planck, M. *Scientific autobiography.* New York: Philosophical Library, 1949.

Poffenberger, A. T. (Ed.). *James McKeen Cattell—man of science.* Lancaster, PA: Science Press, 1947.

Poffenberger, A. T. Robert Sessions Woodworth: 1869–1962. *American Journal of Psychology,* 1962, *75,* 677–692.

Polanyi, M. *Personal knowledge.* Chicago: University of Chicago Press, 1958.

Postman, L. The history and present status of the Law of Effect. *Psychological Bulletin,* 1947, *44,* 489–563.

Postman, L. *Psychology in the making.* New York: Knopf, 1962.

Postman, L. Hermann Ebbinghaus. *American Psychologist,* 1968, *23,* 149–157.

Powell, R. C. The "subliminal" versus the "subconscious" in the American acceptance of psychoanalysis, 1906–1910. *Journal of the History of the Behavioral Sciences,* 1979, *15,* 155–165.

Prentice, W. C. H. The systematic psychology of Wolfgang Köhler. In S. Koch (Ed.), *Psychology: A study of a science* (Vol. 1). New York: McGraw-Hill, 1959. Pp. 427–455.

Progoff, I. *Jung's psychology and its social meaning.* New York: Grove Press, 1953.

Puglisi, M. Brentano: A biographical sketch. *American Journal of Psychology,* 1924, *35,* 414–419.

Rachlin, H. *Introduction to modern behaviorism* (2nd ed.) San Francisco: Freeman, 1976.

Rancurello, A. C. *A study of Franz Brentano.* New York: Academic Press, 1968.

Raphelson, A. C. The unique role of the history of psychology in undergraduate education. *Teaching of Psychology,* 1979, *6,* 12–14.

Reeves, W. *Body and mind in Western thought.* Baltimore, MD: Penguin, 1958.

Reik, T. *From thirty years with Freud.* New York: International Universities Press, 1940.

Rice, B. Skinner agrees he is the most important influence in psychology. *New York Times Magazine,* March 17, 1968, pp. 27ff.

Richards, R. J. Lloyd Morgan's theory of instinct: From Darwinism to neo-Darwinism. *Journal of the History of the Behavioral Sciences,* 1977, *13,* 12–32.

Roazen, P. *Freud and his followers.* New York: Knopf, 1975.

Roazen, P. *Erik H. Erikson: The power and limits of a vision.* New York: Free Press, 1976.

Roback, A. A. *History of American psychology.* New York: Library Publishers, 1952.

Rogers, C. R. *On becoming a person.* Boston: Houghton Mifflin, 1961.

Rogers, C. R. Toward a science of the person. *Journal of Humanistic Psychology* 1963, *3,* 72–92.

Rogers, C. R. Some new challenges. *American Psychologist,* 1973, *28,* 379–387.

Romanes, G. J. *Animal intelligence.* London: Routledge & Kegan Paul, 1883.

Rosenthal, T. L., & Bandura, A. Psychological modeling: Theory and practice. In S. L. Garfield & A. E. Bergin (Eds.), *Handbook of psychotherapy and behavior change* (2nd ed.). New York: Wiley, 1978. Pp. 621–658.

Ross, D. *Granville Stanley Hall: The psychologist as prophet.* Chicago: University of Chicago Press, 1972.

Rubins, J. L. *Karen Horney: Gentle rebel of psychoanalysis.* New York: Dial Press, 1978.

Ruckmick, C. A. The use of the term *function* in English textbooks of psychology. *American Journal of Psychology,* 1913, *24,* 99–123.

Ruitenbeek, H. M. *Freud and America*. New York: Macmillan, 1966.

Russett, C. E. *Darwin in America: The intellectual response, 1865–1912*. San Francisco: Freeman, 1976.

Sarton, G. *The study of the history of science*. New York: Dover, 1936.

Sarton, G. *Six wings: Men of science in the Renaissance*. Bloomington: Indiana University Press, 1957.

Sarup, G. Historical antecedents of psychology. *American Psychologist*, 1978, *33*, 478–485.

Scarf, M. The man who gave us "Inferiority Complex," "Compensation," "Aggressive Drive" and "Style of Life." *New York Times Magazine*, February 28, 1971, pp. 10ff.

Scher, J. (Ed.). *Theories of the mind*. New York: Free Press, 1962.

Schultz, D. The human subject in psychological research. *Psychological Bulletin*, 1969, *72*, 214–228.

Schultz, D. (Ed.). *The science of psychology: Critical reflections*. New York: Appleton, 1970.

Schultz, D. Psychology: A world with man left out. *Journal for the Theory of Social Behaviour*, 1971, *1*, 99–107.

Schur, M. *Freud: Living and dying*. New York: International Universities Press, 1972.

Segal, E. M., & Lachman, R. Complex behavior or higher mental process: Is there a paradigm shift? *American Psychologist*, 1972, *27*, 46–55.

Severin, F. T. (Ed.). *Discovering man in psychology: A humanistic approach*. New York: McGraw-Hill, 1973.

Shaffer, J. *Humanistic psychology*. Englewood Cliffs, NJ: Prentice-Hall, 1978.

Shakow, D. Hermann Ebbinghaus. *American Journal of Psychology*, 1930, *42*, 505–518.

Shakow, D. Psychoanalysis. In D. Krantz (Ed.), *Schools of psychology*. New York: Appleton, 1969. Pp. 87–122.

Shakow, D., & Rapaport, D. *The influence of Freud on American psychology*. New York: International Universities Press, 1964.

Shor, R. E., & Orne, M. T. (Eds.). *The nature of hypnosis: Selected basic writings*. New York: Holt, 1965.

Skinner, B. F. *The behavior of organisms*. New York: Appleton, 1938.

Skinner, B. F. *Walden Two*. New York: Macmillan, 1948.

Skinner, B. F. *Science and human behavior*. New York: Macmillan, 1953.

Skinner, B. F. Critique of psychoanalytic concepts and theories. *Scientific Monthly*, 1954, *79*, 300–305.

Skinner, B. F. A case history of scientific method. *American Psychologist*, 1956, *11*, 221–233.

Skinner, B. F. *Verbal behavior*. New York: Appleton, 1957.

Skinner, B. F. John B. Watson, behaviorist. *Science*, 1959, *129*, 197–198.

Skinner, B. F. Behaviorism at fifty. *Science*, 1963, *140*, 951–958.

Skinner, B. F. Autobiography. In E. G. Boring & G. Lindzey (Eds.), *A history of psychology in autobiography* (Vol. 5). New York: Appleton, 1967. Pp. 387–413.

Skinner, B. F. *The technology of teaching*. New York: Appleton, 1968.

Skinner, B. F. *Contingencies of reinforcement*. New York: Appleton, 1969.

Skinner, B. F. *Beyond freedom and dignity*. New York: Knopf, 1971.

Skinner, B. F. *About behaviorism*. New York: Knopf, 1974.

Skinner, B. F. *Particulars of my life*. New York: Knopf, 1976.

Skinner, B. F. *Reflections on behaviorism and society*. Englewood Cliffs, NJ: Prentice-Hall, 1978.

Skinner, B. F. *The shaping of a behaviorist*. New York: Knopf, 1979.

Smith, M. B. Humanism and behaviorism in psychology. *Journal of Humanistic Psychology*, 1978, *18*, 27–36.

Sokal, M. M. The unpublished autobiography of James McKeen Cattell. *American Psychologist*, 1971, *26*, 626–635.

Sokal, M. M. *An education in psychology: James McKeen Cattell's journal and letters from Germany and England, 1880–1888*. Cambridge, MA: MIT Press, 1980.

406

Sokal, M. M., Davis, A. B., & Merzbach, U. C. Laboratory instruments in the history of psychology. *Journal of the History of the Behavioral Sciences*, 1976, *12*, 59–64.

Spencer, H. *The principles of psychology*. London: Longman, 1855; 2nd ed., London: Williams & Norgate, 1870–1872.

Sperber, M. *Masks of loneliness: Alfred Adler in perspective*. New York: Macmillan, 1974.

Stern, P. J. *C. G. Jung: The haunted prophet*. New York: George Braziller, 1976.

Stevens, S. S. The operational bases of psychology. *American Journal of Psychology*, 1935, *47*, 323–330.

Stevens, S. S. To honor Fechner and repeal his law. *Science*, 1961, *133*, 80–86.

Storr, A. *C. G. Jung*. New York: Viking Press, 1973.

Stumpf, C. *Psychology of tone*. Leipzig: Hirzel, 1883, 1890.

Sulloway, F. J. *Freud: Biologist of the mind*. New York: Basic Books, 1979.

Thorndike, E. L. Animal intelligence. *Psychological Review Monograph Supplement*, 1898, *2*.

Thorndike, E. L. *The elements of psychology*. New York: Seiler, 1905.

Thorndike, E. L. *Human learning*. New York: Appleton, 1931.

Thorne, F. C. Reflections on the golden age of Columbia psychology. *Journal of the History of the Behavioral Sciences*, 1976, *12*, 159–165.

Titchener, E. B. *An outline of psychology*. New York: Macmillan, 1896.

Titchener, E. B. The postulates of a structural psychology. *Philosophical Review*, 1898, *7*, 449–465. (a)

Titchener, E. B. *A primer of psychology*. New York: Macmillan, 1898. (b)

Titchener, E. B. *Experimental psychology*. New York: Macmillan, 1901–1905.

Titchener, E. B. *A text-book of psychology*. New York, Macmillan, 1909–1910.

Titchener, E. B. The schema of introspection. *American Journal of Psychology*, 1912, *23*, 485–508. 485–508.

Titchener, E. B. Brentano and Wundt: Empirical and experimental psychology. *American Journal of Psychology*, 1921, *32*, 108–120. (a)

Titchener, E. B. Wilhelm Wundt. *American Journal of Psychology*, 1921, *32*, 161–178, 575–580. (b)

Tolman, E. C. *Purposive behavior in animals and men*. New York: Appleton, 1932.

Tolman, E. C. A stimulus-expectancy need-cathexis psychology. *Science*, 1945, *101*, 160–166.

Tolman, E. C. Autobiography. In E. G. Boring, H. S. Langfeld, H. Werner, & R. Yerkes (Eds.), *A history of psychology in autobiography* (Vol. 4). Worcester, MA: Clark University Press, 1952. Pp. 323–339.

Tolman, E. C. Principles of purposive behavior. In S. Koch (Ed.), *Psychology: A study of a science* (Vol. 2). New York: McGraw-Hill, 1959. Pp. 92–157.

Toulmin, S., & Goodfield, J. *The architecture of matter*. New York: Harper, 1962.

Turner, F. J. *The significance of the frontier in American history*. New York: Holt, 1947.

Turner, M. *Philosophy and the science of behavior*. New York: Appleton, 1967.

Van der Post, L. *Jung and the story of our time*. New York: Pantheon, 1975.

Von Franz, M.-L. *C. G. Jung: His myth in our time*. Boston: Little, Brown, 1975.

Vorzimmer, P. J. *Charles Darwin, the years of controversy*. Philadelphia: Temple University Press, 1970.

Vrooman, J. *René Descartes: A biography*. New York: Putnam, 1970.

Wann, T. (Ed.). *Behaviorism and phenomenology: Contrasting bases for modern psychology*. Chicago: University of Chicago Press, 1964.

Warden, C. J. The historical development of comparative psychology. *Psychological Review*, 1927, *34*, 57–85, 135–168.

Warden, C. J., & Warner, L. H. The development of animal psychology in the U.S. during the past three decades. *Psychological Review*, 1927, *34*, 196–205.

Warren, N. Is a scientific revolution taking place in psychology? Doubts and reservations. *Science Studies*, 1971, *1*, 407–413.

Warren, R. M., & Warren, R. P. *Helmholtz on perception: Its physiology and development*. New York: Wiley, 1968.

Washburn, M. F. *The animal mind: A text-book of comparative psychology*. New York: Macmillan, 1908.

Watson, J. B. Psychology as the behaviorist views it. *Psychological Review*, 1913, *20*, 158–177.

Watson, J. B. *Behavior: An introduction to comparative psychology*. New York: Holt, 1914.

Watson, J. B. *Psychology from the standpoint of a behaviorist*. Philadelphia: Lippincott, 1919.

Watson, J. B. *Behaviorism*. New York: Norton, 1925.

Watson, J. B. *Psychological care of the infant and child*. New York: Norton, 1928.

Watson, J. B. Behaviorism. *Encyclopedia Britannica*, 1929, *3*, 327–329.

Watson, J. B. *Behaviorism* (Rev. ed.). New York: Norton, 1930.

Watson, J. B. Autobiography. In C. Murchison (Ed.), *A history of psychology in autobiography* (Vol. 3). Worcester, MA: Clark University Press, 1936. Pp. 271–281.

Watson, J. B., & McDougall, W. *The battle of behaviorism*. New York: Norton, 1929.

Watson, J. B., & Rayner, R. Conditioned emotional reactions. *Journal of Experimental Psychology*, 1920, *3*, 1–14.

Watson, R. I. Psychology: A prescriptive science. *American Psychologist*, 1967, *22*, 435–443.

Watson, R. I. The history of psychology as a speciality: A personal view of its first 15 years. *Journal of the History of the Behavioral Sciences*, 1975, *11*, 5–14.

Watson, R. I. *The great psychologists* (4th ed.). Philadelphia: Lippincott, 1978.

Weimer, W. B., & Palermo, D. S. Paradigms and normal science in psychology. *Science Studies*, 1973, *3*, 211–244.

Weiss, A. *A theoretical basis of human behavior*. 1925.

Wells, H. K. *Pavlov and Freud*. New York: International Publishers, 1956.

Wertheimer, Max. Experimental studies of the perception of movement. *Zeitschrift fuer Psychologie*, 1912, *61*, 161–265.

Wertheimer, Max. *Productive thinking*. New York: Harper, 1945.

Wertheimer, Max. Gestalt theory. In W. D. Ellis (Ed.), *A source book of Gestalt psychology*. New York: Humanities Press, 1967. Pp. 1–11.

Wertheimer, Michael. Humanistic psychology and the humane but tough-minded psychologist. *American Psychologist*, 1978, *33*, 739–745.

Wertheimer, Michael. *A brief history of psychology* (2nd ed.). New York: Holt, 1979.

Wettersten, J. The historiography of scientific psychology: A critical study. *Journal of the History of the Behavioral Sciences*, 1975, *11*, 157–171.

White, A. D. *A history of the warfare of science with theology in Christendom*. New York: Free Press, 1965.

Whitehead, A. N. *Science and the modern world*. New York: Macmillan, 1925.

Whitely, P. L. A new name for an old idea? A student of Harvey Carr reflects. *Journal of the History of the Behavioral Sciences*, 1976, *12*, 260–274.

Whyte, L. L. *The unconscious before Freud*. New York: St. Martin's Press, 1979.

Wittels, F. *Sigmund Freud*. New York: Dodd, Mead, 1924.

Wollheim, R. *Sigmund Freud*. New York: Viking Press, 1971.

Wolman, B. Psychoanalysis without libido: An analysis of Karen Horney's contribution to psychoanalytic theory. *American Journal of Psychotherapy*, 1954, *8*, 21–31.

Wolman, B. *Contemporary theories and systems in psychology*. New York: Harper, 1960.

Wolpe, J. Cognition and causation in human behavior and its therapy. *American Psychologist*, 1978, *33*, 437–446.

Woodward, W. R. Fechner's panpsychism: A scientific solution to the mind-body problem. *Journal of the History of the Behavioral Sciences*, 1972, *8*, 367–386.

Woodworth, R. S. *Dynamic psychology*. New York: Columbia University Press, 1918.

Woodworth, R. S. *Psychology*. New York: Holt, 1921.

Woodworth, R. S. Dynamic psychology. In C. Murchison (Ed.), *Psychologies of 1930*. Worcester, MA: Clark University Press, 1930. Pp. 327–336.

Woodworth, R. S. *Contemporary schools of psychology.* New York: Ronald Press, 1931.

Woodworth, R. S. *Experimental psychology.* New York: Holt, 1938.

Woodworth, R. S. J. McKeen Cattell, 1860–1944. *Psychological Review,* 1944, *51,* 201–209.

Woodworth, R. S. *Contemporary schools of psychology* (2nd ed.). New York: Ronald Press, 1948.

Woodworth, R. S. *Dynamics of behavior.* New York: Holt, 1958.

Woodworth, R. S. John Broadus Watson: 1878–1958. *American Journal of Psychology,* 1959, *72,* 301–310.

Woodworth, R. S., & Schlosberg, H. *Experimental psychology* (Rev. ed.). New York: Holt, 1954.

Woodworth, R. S., & Sheehan, M. *Contemporary schools of psychology* (3rd ed.). New York: Ronald Press, 1964.

Wundt, W. *Contributions to the theory of sensory perception.* 1858–1862.

Wundt, W. *Lectures on the minds of men and animals.* Leipzig: Voss, 1863.

Wundt, W. *Principles of physiological psychology.* Leipzig: Engelmann, 1873–1874.

Wundt, W. Zur Erinnerung an Gustav Theodor Fechner. *Philosophische Studien,* 1888, *4,* 471–478.

Wundt, W. *Outline of psychology.* Leipzig: Engelmann, 1896.

Wundt, W. *Folk psychology.* Leipzig: Engelmann, 1900–1920.

Yerkes, R., & Morgulis, S. The method of Pavlov in animal psychology. *Psychological Bulletin,* 1909, *6,* 257–273.

Young, R. M. The role of psychology in the nineteenth-century evolutionary debate. In M. Henle, J. Jaynes, & J. J. Sullivan (Eds.), *Historical conceptions of psychology.* New York: Springer, 1973. Pp. 180–204.

INDEX

Marbe, K., 81–82
Marx, M., 65, 256, 303
Maskelyne, N., 38
Maslow, A., 281, 356, 383–388
Materialism, 25, 41, 185
Matson, F., 371
Maudsley, H., 107
May, R., 7
Mazes, 186, 188, 244–245, 297
McConnell, J., 205
McDougall, W., 3, 229–231
McKeachie, W., 369, 373
Measurement, 17, 41, 75, 110,
    124–125, 155, 158, 252, 255
Mechanism, 16–18, 22–25, 29–35,
    41, 92, 184–190, 219, 251, 252,
    260, 266, 314, 333–334, 383
Memory, 72–76, 81, 220
Memory drum, 76
Mental illness
    early treatments for, 309–312
Mental inheritance (Galton),
    121–124
Mental tests, 113, 126, 129, 157,
    158, 188
Mentality of Apes (Köhler), 283,
    295–297
Merton, R., 117
Mesmer, F., 313
Mesmerism, 313
Mill, J., 26, 35, 67
Miller, G., 3, 62, 140, 192, 274
Miller, N., 256
Mind-body interaction, 20–25,
    51–56, 144, 166
Modeling (Bandura), 372
Molar-molecular issue, 242, 297,
    300, 334–335
Monadology (Leibnitz), 310–311
Morgan, Christiana, 378
Morgan, C. Lloyd, 131–132,
    185–190, 199
Morgan, N., 30
Morgulis, S., 187
Motivation, 84, 179, 235, 375, 377
Motivology (Woodworth), 179
Mowrer, H., 256
Mueller, C. G., 12, 248
Müller, G. E., 76, 277
Müller, J., 39, 41, 60, 314
Müller-Freienfels, R., 55
Münsterberg, H., 142, 159
Murphy, G., 3, 70, 299
Murray, H., 376–378

Nativistic theory of perception, 24,
    26
Natsoulas, T., 369
Naturalistic theory of history, 7–11
Natural sciences, influence on
    psychology, 67, 92–94, 235,
    266
    See also Physics
Nazi Germany, 281, 284, 299, 301,
    324, 362, 387
Need-reduction theory of learning
    (Hull), 254
Needs (Murray), 377
Needs-hierarchy theory (Maslow),
    387–388
Neobehaviorists, 239–269
Neo-Freudian psychoanalysis. *See*
    Post-Freudian psychoanalysis
Nervous system
    early work on, 39–45
Neurotic needs (Horney), 360
Neurypnology (Braid), 313
Newton, I., 33, 266
Nonsense syllables (Ebbinghaus),
    73–76
Normal curve of distribution, 125

Objectivity, 75, 92, 132, 168,
    184–195, 198, 200–205,
    216–222, 228–232, 236–243,
    249–252, 256, 269
Observation method, 17, 26, 38–39,
    65, 78, 91–92, 110, 129–131,
    168, 217, 218
    See also Clinical observation;
    Introspection (self-observation)
Observers (introspectors), 90–92,
    108–109
Oedipus complex (Freud), 316, 322,
    332
One-trial learning (Guthrie), 247
On Memory (Ebbinghaus), 74
On the Origin of Species (Darwin),
    113–115, 117, 123, 129, 137
Operant conditioning (Skinner),
    261–262
Operationism, 237–239, 243
Ophthalmoscope, 44
Order of birth (Adler), 355–356
Order of merit method, 155, 158
Orth, J., 83

Paradigmatic approach to
    psychology, 12
Pavlov, I. P., 9, 187, 192–199, 219,
    223, 247, 249, 254, 257, 261, 273
    conditioning experiments,
    194–197
Pearson, K., 125
Peirce, C. S., 146
Perception
    associationist views, 25–36
    Gestalt views, 274–279, 282–286,
    293–295, 298–300, 304–306
    Wundt's views, 67–68
Peripheral theory of thinking
    (Watson), 225–226
Perls, F., 273
Perry, R., 71
Personalistic theory of history,
    7–11
Personality development, 328–333,
    346–350, 353–356, 359–361,
    375–380, 387–390
Personal unconscious (Jung),
    346–347
Peters, R., 3
Petites perceptions (Leibnitz), 311
Phenomenology, 79, 277, 306
Philosophische Studien (Wundt), 3,
    61, 63, 68, 69, 75
Philosophy, influence on
    psychology, 1–2, 16–36, 41
Phi phenomenon, 279
Physics, influence on psychology,
    12, 16–17, 25, 65, 90, 217, 219,
    222, 238, 239, 251, 252,
    277–278, 299, 372, 382
Physiology, influence on
    psychology, 22–25, 36, 38–57,
    59, 61, 120, 143–144
Pickering, G., 115, 116
Pillsbury, W., 201
Planck, M., 13, 278, 283
Plateau, J., 278
Plato, 1, 310
Pleasure principle (Freud), 314, 329
Polanyi, M., 371
Popularization of psychology, 126,
    159, 206, 223, 226–228, 230
Positive reinforcement, 266, 267
    See also Reinforcement
Positivism, 25, 185, 239, 268, 269
Post-Freudian psychoanalysis,
    342–365, 373–380
Postman, L., 9, 73

A 0
B 1
C 2
D 3
E 4
F 5